Buckle at the Ballet

BUCKLE

AT THE BALLET

SELECTED CRITICISM
BY RICHARD BUCKLE

DANCE BOOKS LIMITED
9 CECIL COURT LONDON WC2

First published in 1980
by Dance Books Ltd
9 Cecil Court, London WC2N 4EZ
Printed by Latimer Trend & Company Ltd Plymouth
Designed by Peter L. Moldon

ISBN 0 903102 53 6

TO DEAREST PATRICIA
alias Whistlebreeches
who used to help me analyse musical scores
and who
whenever she hears that of *Petrushka*
will remember the Plumber's Youngest Son

Contents

Illustrations

Introduction

Much of this book was assembled when I was isolated from the world by snow. Serene in the solitude of my Wiltshire cottage, putting in order, choosing, rejecting and cutting, as I reread the critical articles of thirty years I had the sensation, such as a drowning man is said to experience, of reliving my past life.

But I was not a drowning man, for I felt confident that at sixty-two my life as a writer was just beginning. This harvest of the three post-war decades I regarded as part of my Juvenilia. Some of it was rubbish to be discarded: of some, although I recognized my limitations, I was not ashamed. There is a gap between 1955, when I left the *Observer* with the determination to give up writing about ballet 'for ever', and summer 1959 when I was engaged by the *Sunday Times*. Looking back, I was interested to observe the changes in my style over the years. In the 1940s I wrote in a florid manner; in the 1960s I underwent the influence of Cockney slang and my passion for American dance was reflected in my prose, I 'swung'; then my writing grew simpler. The anthology ends in mid-1975, when I gave up journalism.

John O'Brien and David Leonard, my publishers, asked me if I should not arrange the selected material chronologically. I thought this would be fatal. It is foolhardy enough for a critic to reprint his ephemeral pieces, without aspiring to record a period. I thought my book should retain only general observations, the most readable or amusing passages of prose: that it should be more like a keepsake than a chronicle. The main point of any daily or weekly criticism, I suppose, is to tell the readers whether a play, opera or ballet is any good and whether it is well performed. But I was convinced that all sentences such as 'X is a marvellous ballet' or 'Y danced divinely' must go; so the 'main point' of most articles would be scrapped. I wanted to compile a very short book. The publishers, however, felt it would not be worthwhile to print and bind less than 75,000 words. I said I would arrange the chosen articles under headings, such as 'Classics', 'Russia', etc.

To avoid typing I had xerox copies made of the old press-cutting albums into which I had stuck my articles. I cut up the chosen pieces, pasted them together and sent them to London. Because of the unusual nature of this 'manuscript' it had not been easy to guess the approximate number of words, as one can with a typescript. David Leonard, however, made a count. The book as it stood was incredibly long. He asked me to cut a quarter of a million words. This I did.

The titles of the six sections are self-explanatory. That headed 'Classics' comprises not only performances by British companies but also one or two by the National Ballet of Canada and the Australian Ballet. Articles on Russian or Danish performances of *Giselle*, *Swan Lake*, *Coppélia* or *La Sylphide* occur in the sections called 'Russia' or 'Western Europe'. The omission of London Festival Ballet under the heading 'New Trends in Britain' may cause surprise; but they were never an experimental company. There are numerous references to their work under 'Classics'; and their production of *The Sleeping Beauty* by Nureyev was my favourite of many.

After each section there is an interlude or *entr'acte* made up of miscellaneous oddments, which I have called 'The Changing Scene'. Each of these covers two or three years of my time with the *Sunday Times*, 1959–75. (Some of the pieces included in the six main sections, however, go back more than ten years earlier.)

The dates of all extracts are given. They are from the *Sunday Times* unless otherwise stated.

I was particularly asked not to overload the text with apologia, retractions and 'second thoughts', in which I 'took everything back'. I obeyed: and on the rare occasions when I found my judgements had been wrong—such as when I was mad enough to 'agree with Ninette de Valois that the future of ballet lay with the three-acter' (whereas the spirit of the age, inaugurated by Diaghilev, ordains shorter and shorter ballets)—I refrained from inserting a footnote. (The infrequent footnotes in this book are to explain references which might be obscure.)

I must, however, make one apology. When I worked for the *Observer* in the early 1950s I knew less, was less mature, wrote less well and was allowed less space than when I worked for the *Sunday Times* in later years. My pieces on Balanchine and the first visit of New York City Ballet to London, which in fact begin this book, appear to me quite inadequate. (Although, funnily enough, Balanchine to this day quotes the one about his Weber ballet and what I called his 'tea-cup Tosca'.) The brief tributes included here are merely a form of boast that I was almost the only English critic writing in 1950 who acclaimed the genius of Balanchine. Most reviewers thought his ballets 'mechanical', 'acrobatic' or 'soulless', and deplored that he was 'incapable of inventing dances for men'. Balanchine *had* hardly any classically trained men at that stage in American history. Even the Sadler's Wells Ballet (as the Royal Ballet was then called), with several years start on Kirstein and Balanchine, possessed few. We have some more acute critics today, along with the inevitable nonentities—but one or two of the old donkeys are still faintly braying.

New York City Ballet's London season of 1979 has proved the Shakespearean variety of Balanchine. The great man has his faults—no sense of colour in costume (so that it is safest for him to prune design to the minimum) and a too complacent retention of unworthy works in the huge repertory: but these are minor blemishes. One evening's programme alone—I am thinking of 21 September, when Stravinsky's *Symphony in Three Movements*, *Monumentum pro Gesualdo* and *Movements for Piano and Orchestra*, and Ravel's *Sonatine*, were given—would suffice as proof that he was the most inexhaustibly inventive choreographer of all time. Watching these ballets, my longing to do justice to Balanchine's strange fertility of imagination, to the aptness yet unexpectedness of his genius, and to the divine coincidence of his movement with the music of Stravinsky—combining fidelity with freedom, as in the happiest of marriages—made me want to start being a critic of ballet all over again.

R.B.

Acknowledgements

Having decided to illustrate the book by line drawings only, I was amazed to find how few had been made since the closure of *Ballet*, for which I used to commission artists almost monthly. Apart from a few drawings Patrick Procktor had made of the Kirov Ballet in 1965 and some of Nureyev's *Sleeping Beauty* which I had enlisted Sam Abercrombie to make when I was on tour with Festival Ballet in Australia in 1975, there seemed to be nothing. However, some frantic telephoning and letter-writing produced results. I am happy to express my gratitude to the following: Miss Genevieve Oswald, Curator of the Dance Collection, New York Public Library, Lincoln Center, for allowing me to reproduce Charlotte Trowbridge's drawing of Martha Graham; Mr. Fred Fehl for allowing Astrid Zydower to base a drawing on one of his action photographs of Jerome Robbins; Miss Betty Cage for not only producing Cecil Beaton's drawing of Alicia Markova, which Mme. Karinska had given her, but for giving it to me; Don Bachardy for permitting me to reproduce drawings of Maria Tallchief and Edward Villella done in the 1960s; Iannis Tsarouchis for making a line drawing of Greek dancers, based on one of his existing paintings, specially for this book; Emilia Coia for producing a drawing of Balanchine which he had formerly made for the *Scotsman*; and Michael Wishart for looking out and having photographed for me a drawing he made of Rudolf Nureyev shortly after the latter's arrival in England. Several of these drawings are not, in fact, in line, but contain half-tones, so they inevitably lose some of their quality in reproduction. (We did not want to use shiny paper.)

It proved impossible to find drawings I liked of certain all-important or favourite dancers: I hope Margot Fonteyn, Maris Liepa and other divinities will accept my assurance that their portraits were not omitted out of spite.

I am grateful to David Dougill for his careful proof-reading and detailed suggestions.

I am extremely grateful to the editors and proprietors of the *Observer*, the *Sunday Times*, *Dance and Dancers* and *Weekend* magazine, Toronto, for permission to reprint articles, or part of them, which first appeared in their publications. I edited *Ballet* magazine myself until it went into liquidation in 1953, but I thank the friends who subsidized it, particularly Andrew Sykes, who not only backed it, but worked for it for nothing.

AMERICA

Balanchine always pulls something out of the hat, hardly ever a rabbit.

Sunday Times, 18.2.62

Robbins is one of the world's inventors, and it is amazing that two such original geniuses as himself and Martha Graham should have come out of one country in the same half-century. Of course, America is a big place . . .

Sunday Times, 13.9.59

New York City Ballet

At Covent Garden

Most of us, like Mr. E. M. Forster's Helen in *Howard's End*, see 'heroes and shipwrecks' when we listen to music. Sometimes we have vague impressions of gaiety or languor, and sometimes our mental images are more precise—like Helen's, when in the third movement of the Fifth she heard 'a goblin walking quietly over the universe, from end to end'. George Balanchine is the man above all others in the world who can make those impressions and images visible. Like a diver he plunges into the dark depths of music and comes back quietly with a pearl.

The scantiness of scenery used by New York City Ballet is at first disappointing, but so much is expressed in Balanchine's choreography that in the end we feel more richly treated than ever before.

Serenade shows both the variety of Balanchine's talent and the excellence of the company he has trained. In concerted dances the patterns are striking, and striking, too, is the way the groups change from one formation to another: but it is in the passages where only two or three dancers are employed that suggestions of human tragedy emerge. There is a touching duet when Janet Reed circles in *pas de bourrée* and Herbert Bliss waltzes in counterpoint around her: and in Tchaikovsky's typically sweet, despairing slow movement, which Balanchine has chosen to place after the folk-dance finale, there is a moment when the choreographer turns sculptor, and the lovers (Maria Tallchief and Nicholas Magallanes) form a beautiful group with a mysterious third person (Melissa Hayden). In the moment of stillness and parting Hayden moves her arms, and it is as if the Angel of Fate had flapped her wings; and life continues.

In Bizet's *Symphony in C*, which is a more formal and brilliant ballet, Balanchine introduces us to the long, elegant Tanaquil LeClercq, to the noble, expressive Francisco Moncion and other fine dancers. The Chabrier *Bourrée Fantasque* is another work rich in invention, ranging from burlesque to mauve romance. Jerome Robbins danced admirably in this.

Observer, 16.7.50

George Balanchine.
Drawing by Emilio Coia

Some of my virginal colleagues appear to have been shocked by Ashton's *Illuminations*. I cannot praise their fugitive and cloistered virtue. Rimbaud's prose poems are the record of an adolescent's vision of the world, written down in hot haste before it faded. Britten set some of them to music and Frederick Ashton has fitted dances to the songs, and produced them for New York City Ballet.

The boy Rimbaud, movingly interpreted by Nicholas Magallanes, observes the phenomena of everyday life and the weird diversity of men's occupations; he experiences stirrings of lust and idealism, impulses towards beauty, premonitions of the savagery of mankind and of his own lonely destiny. There are wonderful moments, and Ashton has certainly succeeded in a circuitous way in conveying some of the poet's black brilliance, which combines naïveté with a terrible sophistication. Cecil

Beaton's ink-spattered townscapes and skyscapes form an appropriate décor, though his Pierrot costumes are almost too bizarre and pretty—that is to say, one notices them too much.

I was not at all shocked by the exhibition of love-making, and its natural conclusion: but what does surprise me is that the idea of fitting a ballet, with dancing, décor and dresses, to music which is already busy accompanying a poem should have been seriously considered by anyone at all. The cynical view is that anything which *goes* in the theatre is fine. I cannot concur. There is nothing wrong in dance accompanied by song, but these songs are unsuitable. The ballet occupies our attention to the exclusion of Rimbaud's words, even when sung clear and true by Peter Pears. He might as well have sung 'la'. To encumber the poems with a ballet was wasteful and an error of taste, like using a diamond brooch to hold up one's pants.

One thing that is clear about Balanchine's *Firebird*, which some of my matronly colleagues have been deploring, is that it is a great deal better than Fokine's. Fokine's had atmosphere, agreed, but so has Victoria Station. Balanchine's *Firebird* is an exciting ballet with dancing in it; and as the elemental creature Maria Tallchief has the most spectacular part of her career. Pecking, darting, swooping, and poising all aflame in the dark enchanted garden, she was glorious. Francisco Moncion, whom Balanchine has invested with the shy, proud character of a peasant-prince, conducted himself with a gawky dignity that was captivating. The crowd of supers at the wedding was not much missed. (We got a cake instead.) Masked monsters and witches, I admit, bore me on the stage. They never live up to the designer's sketches; and no mask is really as horrible as some human faces. Chagall's settings are as Russian and magic as Gontcharova's, and perfectly in keeping with the rich mysteries of Stravinsky's score.

Observer, 23.7.50

The solo instrument in Weber's little Clarinet Concerto seems to be imitating the flowers of *bel canto*, to be taking all the principal parts in turn of a miniature opera, so it was an ingenious idea of Balanchine's to invent a *Pas de Deux Romantique* to go with it. The antics of passionate operatic lovers may seem tragic and sublime from one point of view, ridiculous from another: having chosen an impartial central position, Balanchine has backed far into the distance so that the lovers' frenzy seems less an expression of personal rapture and despair than the fulfilment of a pre-ordained ritual common to the whole species. This is all a fanciful and roundabout way of saying that the *pas de deux* has a special quality which is easily missed: it is neither a display of spectacular dancing in the grand manner, nor is it a skit. It is a classical duet with suggestions of *demi-caractère*.

Janet Reed, short, red-headed, unusually swift and light, is certainly a soubrette among dancers, even if here she wears the tiara and trappings of a ballet tragedy queen. She radiates gaiety, and of all the female dancers in the New York City Ballet hers is the personality which makes the most immediate appeal. Herbert Bliss is the most classical among the men. In this *pas de deux* he dances with style and grace and with an air of being naïvely dazzled by the feminine *fioriture* of his teacup Tosca.

Observer, 13.8.50

At Covent Garden

Civil war broke out in the bars of Covent Garden after Balanchine's new version of *Swan Lake*, Act II, was shown there on Thursday. This work was both the most disturbingly beautiful of the eight so far presented by New York City Ballet in their second season at the Royal Opera House, and the most controversial since Balanchine's *Firebird* first crossed the Atlantic two summers ago.

Swan Lake, though, is a drama, not a ballad. It is as near to a tragedy as anything in ballet can be; and the tragedy should be in the dancing. It follows that if one can intensify the emotion *and* make the dancing more rich and beautiful, always keeping within the bounds of the grand style, one can only be improving the old ballet: and this is what Balanchine has done. Few scholars, quite rightly, will dare to touch up an old text in an attempt to bring it to life, but Balanchine, of course, is choreographically both a scholar, grounded in the St. Petersburg tradition, and a poet of movement, the greatest of our age.

I agree entirely with Ninette de Valois, who told the American Press recently that the future of ballet lies with the three-acter. *Swan Lake* should be a long ballet, but Balanchine has compressed the tragedy into one act, and as a complete work we must judge it. Musically it is Tchaikovsky's first lake scene, played rather fast, with the introduction to the second lake scene and part of the final coda interpolated. Ivanov's choreography is retained for the *Grand Adage*, which Tallchief dances with superb assurance, control, balance and style, supported by Nicholas Magallanes. Balanchine has invented a wonderful *pas de trois*, in which, utilizing her elevation, he sends Patricia Wilde soaring triumphantly between two more sedentary swans. This is followed by a strange *pas de neuf*, led by Yvonne Mounsey. The *finale*, with the departure of the swans, came as a heart-lifting surprise. Round and round they wheeled, and through and through each other they swooped; and in the midst of these beating wings the Prince was parting with Odette forever. The more they danced the more 'dramatic' the ballet became. Was this not remarkable?

Observer, 13.7.52

It is time somebody said that, despite occasionally unskilful programme-building, the New York City Ballet is a marvellous company with at least six star ballerinas. All those who enjoy beautiful dancing must find enchantment in any programme containing Balanchine's *Caracole*, *Swan Lake*, *Divertimento*, *Symphony in C*, or *Bourrée Fantasque*. After seeing these, only someone who prefers the trimmings of ballet to the dance itself could deny the high quality of the troupe or fail to be astonished at the inventive, poetical—and difficult—choreography they are given to dance.

  Caracole is for lovers of Mozart. If eighteenth-century music can be compared to a town of fine and regular architecture, Mozart's is the boulevard where children play and lovers meet, just inside the walls: as we walk down it, breezes fan us, we come upon all sorts of evocative smells—bread baking, farmyards, lime blossom—and keep catching glimpses of gardens through archways. Mozart is the poet of the happy life, bound by sweet reason. Incapable of immoderation, he suggests whole worlds by the rounding of a phrase, just as the taste of a ripe peach can conjure around us all the panoply of summer. Balanchine has perfectly adorned with dance the Divertimento No. 15 in B flat major. The variations for his five ballerinas and the dream-like 'Andante' are inventions of pure delight. There is as much choreography in *Caracole* as in *The Sleeping Beauty*, and I can think of no short ballet which has given me more pleasure. Those who, because it has no story or scenery, no love-sick Prince or comic Nurse, find it 'mechanical' and 'devoid of emotion', are like boors who doubt whether a man is capable of love because he does not black his wife's eye on Saturday night.

  During the exquisite understatements of Balanchine's ballet to Haieff's *Divertimento*, I was thinking what a wonderful artist Tanaquil Le Clercq is turning out to be. The old accusation that American dancers are cold and inexpressive no longer holds good. Le Clercq, Hayden and Wilde all have personalities which 'project'; and technically they are prodigious.

Symphony in C and the last movement of *Bourrée Fantasque* are master-pieces of formal choreography, deploying the full resources of New York City's ballet and proving it second to none. *Bourrée* must be the most exhilarating 'closing ballet' ever invented, as much fun as *La Boutique Fantasque* or *Le Beau Danube*, but far richer in choreographic invention. In case this article seems too full of superlatives, let me end by owning myself confused by Balanchine's *Card Game*, bored by Robbins's *Age of Anxiety*, and flabbergasted by Tudor's *La Gloire*.

Observer, 21.7.52

At the Champs-Elyseés, Paris

Western Symphony is an extraordinary work. We expect ballets about the Wild West to have a lot of thigh-slapping and characteristic movements, and, of course, a story. This one, apart from some superficial local colour, is a typical Balanchine ballet, built up symphonically. The score, by Hershy Kay, is a web of familiar popular tunes, the set is a gold-rush town of wooden houses, the dancers are dressed as cowboys and spangled bar-room vampires: otherwise *Western Symphony* is as classical as the Bizet *Symphony in C*. Melissa Hayden has a bounding, exulting solo: she is a more wonderful artist than ever, gloriously strong and expressive, with all the verve we associate with Russian dancers. Wearing an etherealized Mae West hat, Tanaquil Le Clercq makes a big entry in the last movement and does an amazing diagonal of turning jumps in her spiky spidery style. She is most effective, and so is her partner Jacques d'Amboise, who swings and bounds about, looking frightfully pleased with life, exuding athletic glamour. He is now a star personality, and I hope he can't sing, otherwise the company will lose him to Broadway. *Western Symphony* has some of Balanchine's favourite cavalry charges and counter-charges, and ends with everyone spinning joyously.

Balanchine's pretty *Sylvia pas de deux* is finely danced by Tallchief and Eglevsky. I still know no male classical dancer with such accuracy and noble, feline ease of movement as Eglevsky. His slow turns and clear, velvety, unhurried *cabrioles* are royal gestures.

Fanfare, to Britten's 'Young People's Guide to the Orchestra,' was done to celebrate the Coronation of our Queen. A herald standing at the side announces the various instruments, whose characters are ingeniously illustrated in Jerome Robbins's choreography.

Robbins's new version of Debussy's *L'Après-midi d'un faune* was the biggest hit of the season. He seemed to have struck on a new and yet right interpretation of the music, which is sultry and sensual, but dreamlike, as if unsatisfied desires fed the summer afternoon with beauty. The scene is a ballet classroom whose white transparent walls let in the blue sky. The audience is a mirror. Jacques d'Amboise lies sleeping on the floor. When he wakes up he does a few exercises and admires himself. Tanaquil Le Clercq comes in, high-stepping and aloof. They practise a *pas de deux*, and then subside, overcome by the heat. You watch a thought coming into the boy's head. He kisses the girl chastely on the cheek. She is as surprised as if the *barre* had broken out in thorns and blossom. Holding her hand to her wound, she steps gingerly out of the room, leaving the boy to go back to sleep. Robbins's idea is poetic and subtle, its realization impeccable. The two performers were as imposing as Babilée and Philippart in *Le Jeune homme et la mort*. I do not agree with French critics who thought the music misinterpreted. There are fauns everywhere, even in the British Museum Reading Room.

26.6.65

At the New York State Theater

'SAMSON IN LONGHAIR TEMPLE' announced *Variety* on December 16, meaning that Mr William Schuman, President of New York's Lincoln Center for the Performing Arts, was pulling the whole huge highbrow edifice down on top of him. The history of the battle that has been raging is too long to be told in detail here, but the main—if hidden—issue was whether the New York *City* Center Group, which, of course, contains New York City Ballet, should have the New York State Theater for as much of the year as they wanted, should have a say in who performed there during the rest of the time and should be allowed to maintain the popular price level which was always one of their ideals.

Last week the City Center Group won the battle. They are to lease Philip Johnson's handsome theatre (designed in consultation with Balanchine and Lincoln Kirstein) for twenty-five years for the presentation of their ballet and opera companies and will book the theatre for other attractions 'selected in consultation with Lincoln Center.' So if they want Martha Graham or Paul Taylor to get a look in for several weeks a year they can probably arrange it. 'To err is Schuman,' people are saying, 'To forgive, Kirstein.'

I thought it entirely right that in the week of their victory New York

City Ballet should be putting on a way-out experiment in Pop Art, which in fact was booed. What's the point in being a great and glorious national company, with one of the grandest theatres in the world and millions from the Ford Foundation, if you daren't try out new ideas?

The creation *Shadow'd Ground* has a score by Aaron Copland written two years ago, but which is in his early 'folk' manner of the 1930s. The choreography of John Taras is mainly classical and straightforward. The story by the young poet Scott Burton is about two lovers reading epitaphs in a graveyard. It is the decor by John Braden that dominates the show.

On to four large panels divided up by a black framework—back wall, two side walls and an oval ceiling—are projected a series of photographs, some coloured, some black-and-white. These are of clouds, a cemetery, old tombs in close-up, a 19th century church framed in honeysuckle, boats on a river, sea and rocks, bare trees, a nice young man c. 1860, a spring garden, an empty stadium, the Trocadéro seen through the legs of the Eiffel Tower, and back to carved death's-heads on tombs again.

The epitaphs evoke pictures of bygone sons and lovers who were drowned or else fell in the first world war. Robert Maiorano and Kay Mazzo are the attractive pair who finally join the Communion of Saints. 'Their winged Souls are in God's sky,' writes Mr. Burton. One value of this interesting work is that it links the conceptions of 'folk art' and 'pop art'. And what could be more Pop than the sentimental side of Victorian Christianity?

An even more extraordinary work, which though not new was new to me, is Balanchine's *Bugaku*—his homage to the ceremonial art of the dancers of the Japanese Imperial household. Homage, of course: but you begin by thinking it's a send-up, because although the traditional square red and green railed platform is there and the fascinating music by Toshiro Mayuzumi (written for Western orchestra) sounds genuine enough, the boys wear tights and the girls wear *tutus*, and all behave with a superficial imitation of Geisha coyness. It is a wedding, however, with formal confrontations, an erotic bridal battle or *pas de deux*, a re-adornment of the pair and a solemn conclusion. In spite of the mixture of styles, the *pirouettes*, *arabesques* and Samurai stances, *Bugaku* develops a sacred atmosphere like *Les Noces* or the end of *Firebird*. The white-clad Prince and Princess in long organdie trains by Karinska were Arthur Mitchell and Mimi Paul; and that the noble Mitchell is a Negro made it no less strange.

My plane was predestined to be late arriving in New York, so that the

Maria Tallchief.
Drawing by Don Bachardy

first ballet I saw performed at the State Theatre should be, symbolically, Balanchine's *Apollo*, the earliest of his classical masterpieces, made for Diaghilev, and a work which heralded the birth of a new classicism in the New World. Stravinsky's whirring holy music, the dedicated conduct of Jacques d'Amboise as Apollo, the crystal-cold choreography struck me afresh. The next evening's programme began with *Serenade*, Balanchine's first American-made masterpiece; and the swoop, suddenness and impetus of the company's dancing in this (even if certain patterns were untidy) is something we just don't see here. The dancers made me think of Hopkins's woodlark lying on the wind.

> *Through the velvety wind V-winged*
> *To the nest's nook I balance and buoy*
> *With a sweet joy of a sweet joy,*
> *Of a sweet—a sweet—sweet joy.*

When I consider what New York City Ballet have gained since they last came to London in 1952—in their theatre, in their security, in their fame, manpower, girlpower, goldpower, artpower, I look forward with exultation to their summer season at Covent Garden.

31.1.65

Pippa Passes

*To Lincoln Kirstein**

> I am the Pooza of Lincoln's Plaza
> Bred in the shade of Philip's casa.
> The longhair temple where Philistines and stars are,
> And Samson Schuman, eyeless in Gaza.
>
> West Side poozas learn their paces
> When George, John or Jerry hold the aces,
> Keeping at bay the Lucia Chases
> Who'll never know what pooza grace is.

* Mr. Kirstein and the author share a joke about cats, which they call 'poozas'. Mr. Kirstein has the greatest collection of cats in pen, pencil, paint, bronze, stone, steel, porcelain, pottery or plastic in Lower East Side Manhattan. In fact it can be said of him, in the immortal words of James Thurber, that he 'has cats the way other people have mice'. The holograph manuscript of this hitherto unpublished poem was illustrated by an original poozagraph signed Picatto.

The poem alludes to the preceding article.

Ballet poozas hold their poses,
Entrechat and point their toesies;
Yiddischer poozas have long noses;
And Oscar poozas love their Bosies.

(On the Plaza Pippa passes,
Picking her way through broken glasses,
Peering at all the upturned arses
Of ballet boys who are late for classes.)

I know a Nip who's a Bugacruiser
And a Limey hack who's a beastly boozer
And a Russky cat who sets dance to Sousa—
But some of my best friends are Jews—ah!
Yours sincerely, Pippa Pooza.

Unpublished, December, 64, January, 65

At Covent Garden

Balanchine has so many styles, and during these two weeks we have had a sample of most of them. In a sense this triumphant season has been a retrospective exhibition of the master's work—not that all his key works have been shown, for that would have been impossible. How I should love to see *Cotillon* again, perhaps with Suzanne Farrell and Mimi Paul. And the Bach *Concerto Barocco*, and *Four Temperaments*. Of course *La Valse*, which has been given here, is in the *Cotillon* style; and several of the late works appear to have evolved from the exploratory choreography of the Hindemith ballet.

One got this view of Balanchine in perspective during such a programme as Wednesday's, when *Raymonda Variations* was followed by *Allegro Brillante* and *Episodes*. *Raymonda* is purest Petipa. Despite the perhaps deliberate alienation effect achieved by the weeping willows and rambler roses of the set and by the pink and blue costumes, it turns out to be a great feast of dancing to Glazounov's pretty tunes, with Patricia Wilde and André Prokovsky in full cry, and variation succeeding variation as if in a 'digest' of *The Sleeping Beauty*.

Then comes *Allegro* in the master's 1930–40 Tchaikovsky style, with

Maria Tallchief—alone or supported by Anthony Blum—sparkling through the piano cadenza, and the *corps* waiting to swoop in with the orchestra, in parallel formations. Then you get the Webern ballet in the newest amazingest style.

It is hard to say which is the most perfect, stunning and glorious of the three recent masterpieces. Stravinsky's *Agon* has the incredible *pas de deux*, danced by Farrell and Arthur Mitchell. Stravinsky's *Monumentum pro Gesualdo*, danced by Farrell, Conrad Ludlow and six couples, with its suggestion of old court dances, contrasts happily with the eccentric *Movements*—Farrell, Jacques d'Amboise and six girls—which is given *en suite*. Webern's *Episodes*, with Mimi Paul, Patricia McBride, Magallanes, Blum, Patricia Neary, Ludlow, and others is perhaps my favourite, because the interplanetary flashes are followed by the serene Ricercata of Bach and we end up safely in heaven.

No more diverse or grander series of masterpieces can ever have been crammed into fourteen performances. The season will continue in our minds.

12.9.65

At Monte Carlo

Outside the door (now barred) through which Diaghilev and his company used to pass to their classroom in the rabbit-warren of the Monte Carlo casino's basement, has been erected a plaque inscribed with the words (I translate):

> *From this rock*
> *By favour of its Princes*
> *Serge de Diaghilev (1872–1929)*
> *Beaconed forth the glory*
> *Of his Russian Ballet.*

You now have to approach the classroom by a labyrinth of stairs and unlit passages. I remarked to Balanchine on the lowness of its ceiling. 'No, no,' he said, 'it's quite high enough. Anyway, dancers were smaller in Diaghilev's day. I was almost the tallest person in the company. Only Doubrovska was tall, of course.' That morning one of his girls—not lifted, just jumping—cracked open her head on a girder. Most of the Americans are giants.

Edward Villella.
Drawing by Don Bachardy

The New York City Ballet had come to dance at Garnier's gorgeous theatre (seating 560) in the casino to commemorate the fortieth anniversary of Diaghilev's death. *Jewels*, which constituted the first programme, revealed what a galaxy of glorious ballerinas the company can boast, even though Farrell has left: Violette Verdy and Allegra Kent, both exquisite creatures, in the Fauré Emeralds, wonderful Patricia McBride, supported by Edward Villella in the Stravinsky Rubies—the most interesting piece— and Kay Mazzo (whom we recall at sixteen in Robbins's *Faun*) shining out as a real star in the rather conventional Tchaikovsky Diamonds.

Nicholas Nabokov (who described to me Diaghilev's annual reaction on passing beneath the naked lady caryatids of the Hôtel de Paris— 'Quelle anomalie! I hope next year they won't have grown hair') had suggested the composition of the second programme, which was ideal and showed Balanchine's Zeus-like versatility. *Le Fils prodigue* (Prokofiev and Rouault), which was rehearsed in this very theatre in 1929, to be danced by Lifar and Doubrovska in Paris and London, is a violently imaginative work, forestalling the eccentricities of Merce Cunningham and Alwin Nikolais and Graham's use of costume as an extension of the dance. It was thrillingly performed by Villella, who in spite of his bravado was clearly a little boy terrified of strangers and sex, with Patricia Neary as the alarming siren.

The great Stravinsky *Agon* was danced by Kent, Anthony Blum, Gloria Govrin and that demi-god Arthur Mitchell; and it was followed by the Bizet *Symphony in C*, apotheosis of the classical style.

In the third programme we had the new ballet of Jerome Robbins.

Dances at a Gathering is the most dreamy and transporting ballet since—well, some might say *Les Sylphides*, but I'll settle for Balanchine's *Liebesliederwalzer*. Like the former, it is set to a series of Chopin pieces —many more—but not orchestrated, played on the piano by the admirable Gordon Boelzner. There is wonderful and inventive choreography, moods are evoked, even little dramas boil up: it is a series of poems about youth, varied, magical and perhaps five minutes too long.

It begins with a number of mazurkas, during which at one point the dancers stop and form funny groups, pretending to pose for photographs. Three girls walk on, alone in their own worlds, a boy joins them briefly and leaves them to become three Graces in a group. Two men do stunts in rivalry; one man does a *perpetuum mobile*; another is danced round by a fairy, whom he disregards; a slow number becomes a whirlpool and something unpleasant is going to happen, but it blows over; the group watches a thunderstorm; they bow to each other and walk off in couples. It is a glorious ballet.

29.6.69

At New York State Theater

New York taxis now have barriers of Plexiglass to protect the driver from the passenger, who may be a mugger. Smoke billows from the manholes in the pavement. What unseen race of slaves are toiling in the boiler-rooms below to keep the party going? As the cab stops at traffic lights a wild-eyed derelict stretches in his hand, demanding money. My driver unhesitantly gives him a dime. Have these urban Abraham-men, who abound in doorways and at street-corners, escaped from the boiler-rooms, and is the penalty for deserting the machine ostracism, alcoholism and despair? A glimpse of hell.

And yet to climb the steps to the golden promenade of the State Theatre at Lincoln Center for the week of Stravinsky ballets is like entering heaven. To see it in an intermission at night, with crowded floor and with scattered groups of silhouetted spectators looking down from the three surrounding galleries, built on Dantesque principles, is *paradiso*.

The people who have created this festival seem cool, as if the difficult part—the decision to present twenty new ballets to Stravinsky's music by seven different choreographers plus ten old ones in a week—lay far behind them. Inside this palace the shining ones are too preoccupied to consider rumbles from outside or from below.

The opening night's programme last Sunday couldn't stop opening. First we had Stravinsky's Fanfare. Then Lincoln Kirstein welcomed us—then Balanchine explained that he was interpolating a little unannounced *pas de deux* to the scherzo of a piano sonata written in 1902 and recently found in a Russian book by Mme André Malraux. She played it, while Sara Leland and John Clifford performed a springlike childish dance. Then Robert Irving's fine orchestra gave us the 'Greeting Prelude' (happy birthday), for Stravinsky would have been ninety that day. Next we had flashing *Fireworks*, not danced—*then* the opening ballet.

The first performance of this music in 1909 was the occasion of Diaghilev's 'discovery' of the young composer. Jerome Robbins's arrangement of the short *Scherzo Fantastique* is magical. In a blue night three bright-coloured boys flutter, admiring their own hands. Are they dragon-flies taking off? The music cues us: they are heralds of the firebird. A fourth boy in yellow leaps on, then a girl: a big Petipa-ish *pas de deux* seems about to develop but the other boys return to throw the girl and bounce her to be held aloft by her partner, and they all whizz off.

The best new works up to Thursday were Balanchine's *Violin Concerto*, *Danses Concertantes*, *Divertimento* from *Le Baiser de la Fée*, and *Duo Concertant*, Clifford's *Symphony in E Flat*, John Taras's *Scènes de Ballet* and *Song of the Nightingale*.

In *Violin Concerto* Irving's marvellously resonant soloist was Joseph Silverstein of the Boston Philharmonic. He leads the two couples, Karin von Aroldingen with Jean-Pierre Bonnefous and Kay Mazzo with Peter Martins, through their two labyrinthine arias—and the final capriccio is a happy get-together.

Danses Concertantes is plain sailing. In the *marche* the brisk passage of four groups—each a boy and two girls—and of the leading couple before Berman's pretty 1944 front-curtain makes it clear that these are strolling entertainers. We can sit back and enjoy their variations on a theme, funny or solemn, and the dazzle of choreography expounded by strutting Lynda Yourth and breeze-borne Clifford.

The storyless, fairyless, kissless 'Divertimento' from *Le Baiser de la Fée* is another triumph of choreography, divinely danced by Patricia McBride and the amazing but modest-mannered Icelander Helgi Tomasson, surrounded by a smart corps of peasant girls. *Duo Concertant* has the piano and violinist on stage, with Mazzo and Martins weaving corresponding garlands in the air.

Who has heard Stravinsky's *Symphony in E Flat* of 1907, and who, not knowing it, could guess it was not by Tchaikovsky? Seizing the rare chance to catch Stravinsky doing his 'big romantic stuff', Clifford deploys his pastel-coloured corps, who bring the lovers together from the ends of the earth in the allegro moderato, react with some mazurka steps when a Slav tune appears, assist at the doom of the lovers' duet in the largo, and circle and charge around the couple's lifts and fish-dives in the allegro molto.

Taras's *Scènes de Ballet*, with one poet and many mauve nymphs in a wood, is the new *Les Sylphides*, and it is wonderful how amenable the music is to his simple treatment, being in fact intended for a grand *pas de deux* with solos, coda and a framing corps de ballet. Lovely groups and ecstatic dances for McBride and Bonnefous.

The Nightingale has fabulous costumes by Rouben Ter-Arutunian, splashes of plain primary colour in a black void. Much of it is processional, but the emperor's duet with death is effectively arranged, and the passing of the fisherman with the nightingale perched on his shoulder is a lyric in itself.

It was during Robbins's *Cage* to the short *Concerto in D for Strings* that doubts rose as to the truth of Balanchine's idea (seed of this festival) that all Stravinsky's music can be danced. Twenty-one years ago Robbins deftly fitted this horrordrama to the score—and Melissa Hayden, as the man-eating predatrix, tellingly crunches and stamps on Nicholas Magallanes. But I could not help worrying about what Robert Craft, who was sitting nearby with Mme Stravinsky (and who had conducted the *Symphony in Three Movements*), thought of the choreographic accretion. With few exceptions the best ballets have been those danced to theatrical music.

Each of the last three nights had its own character. Friday was funny. To *Dumbarton Oaks* Robbins had arranged a 1920s tennis party in which Allegra Kent and Anthony Blum led a company of bandeau-ed flappers and bouncing undergrads.

Pulcinella was the joint production of Balanchine and Robbins, who both appeared in it briefly as two masked, ragged, befeathered rival beggars, duelling with sticks. An unrecognizable Edward Villella, miming as to the manner born, was the violent hero, surrounded by a crowd of minor and minimal Pulcinellas clad alike in white and scarlet. Eugene Berman's stage picture was constantly changing, Piranesi ruins yielding place to trophies of rococo laundry against a turquoise sky. His wildly imaginative costumes derived from Jacques Callot. Violette Verdy, who had a long solo, was the only dancer unmasked.

Saturday was classical, with no new works. *Apollo* was followed by *Orpheus*, which, in Noguchi's set, looked more wonderful than ever. Last came *Agon*, a tournament of dance, in which the duet by Kent and Arthur Mitchell struck me as one of Balanchine's finest inventions.

Sunday was solemn. Stravinsky's last composition, *Variations on Bach's 'Vom Himmel hoch'*, had been arranged by Balanchine for three pairs and a large corps, including children. The soloists followed Stravinsky's wreathing woodwind while a choir sang the slower music of Bach's chorale. For *Requiem Canticles* Robbins had made a strange and daring choreography. The incredible season ended with Robert Craft taking over Robert Irving's indomitable and privileged orchestra to conduct the *Symphony of Psalms*, which was not danced. The whole audience was then given vodka.

There has never been anything like this festival before in the history of ballet. I am sure there will be other Stravinsky seasons, but they should have more choral and orchestral works mixed with the masterpieces of dancing.

For a week the State Theatre has become the temple of Stravinsky, and it will not be that for one week only. The convergence at this time and place of Kirstein, Balanchine, Robbins, Taras, Irving and Craft make it inevitable that the temple will be rededicated season after season, to continue perhaps long after these ministrants are dead, until the over-loaded showboat of Manhattan—which some have mistaken for an island—boarded by pirates and looted by savage mutineers, sinks into the sea.

18.6.72 and 2.7.72

At New York State Theater

I have a small etching by Sickert of a woman's face contorted with terror, on which the artist has written 'Sonia Alomis in The Dybbuk—the greatest actress of the age'. I suppose this was done when the Habima Players came to London in the Twenties; and I imagine that the thrilling moment which Sickert chose to record is when the heroine is possessed by a spirit and speaks with a voice not her own.

Jerome Robbins's 50-minute *Dybbuk*, of which I saw two performances, creates its magical atmosphere by different means from the playwright Ansky or the artist Sickert. There is no expressionist violence—in fact, hardly any facial expression—and not much narrative, but the resulting ballet is a work blazing with imagination and genius.

No, 'blazing' is the wrong word. The Robbins ballet smoulders darkly. It is so odd, so unexpected, so original and so quiet that there is a danger that many people will miss the point altogether: many *have* missed it. There are eight numbers to a fine, simple, thinly orchestrated score by Leonard Bernstein, which employs two cantors and in which the harp plays a dominant role. Only at the big moments of magic-making and exorcism was I conscious of strings and wind playing together.

I recall Katherine Dunham lecturing to an invited audience at London University in 1948. When Arnold Haskell, introducing her, said (something like) 'Miss Dunham is going to talk about the ethnic dance,' the scholarly lady said, 'No, I'm not. I'm going to speak about the prevalence of cults among deprived peoples.' We must bear in mind that the background to *Dybbuk* is the cult of the Kabbalah among the persecuted Jews of Central Europe, whose life centred around their religious studies, but some of whom also sought in the ancient mystical book an explanation of the entire universe.

In a ritualistic dance six holy hatted young men set the scene. Two devoted friends swear that if they have a son and a daughter one shall marry the other. A boy and a girl are born (no time is wasted: this is all part of the same dance, which ends as it began with the friends linked and swinging slowly around each other). The children, the inspired Helgi Tomasson and Patricia McBride, fall in love (*pas de deux*). But (it is implied, not shown), the girl's father has arranged a more ambitious marriage for her. We see her reject a veil: that's all the narrative we are bothered with. (When you think of all those bedroom scenes in *Romeo and Juliet*—what a relief!)

In the Invocation of the Kabbalah, there are mysterious solos for the boy and six men, which are like spells. The boy dies of this most potent magic, and is wrapped up. By a clever trick another body has been substituted and the boy suddenly emerges on the opposite side of the stage, wearing a transparent white gown like the girl, to enter and possess her. He is now a Dybbuk. In the strangest of dances they become one person. There follows the terrible Exorcism. The girl dies, too. In a tender group the lovers are united in death.

I have not mentioned the Angel. He appears twice, and his second entry is a stroke of theatre so simple that only an angel like Robbins or Cocteau could have thought of it. He takes one step out of the wings downstage left, and stands for a couple of seconds looking at the girl's dead body. No expression. Then he courses gently in a horseshoe curve and exits upstage left. Running off to tell God, I suppose.

It is a commonplace that great poets work miracles by combinations of ordinary words; 'With thee conversing I forget all time.' One critic here has inveighed at length against the 'nullity' of Robbins's ballet. 'It's incredible that so sketchy and aimless a work could have resulted . . . from a long-standing project that was first discussed more than 30 years ago.' I expect she would have complained bitterly about the Sermon on the Mount. *Dybbuk* has the simplicity and condensation of genius (I repeat the word). Robbins possesses an original mind, as does Martha Graham, and like her he has forged an individual language to express his ideas. I also bless him for abolishing narrative links. Nobody in *Dybbuk* travels by limousine to church, orders dinner or consults the family doctor.

Balanchine's new offering is a very odd duet to concrete music of Pierre Henry called *Variation pour une Porte et un Soupir*. The magnified creaking of a door is represented by a tall, sadistic vamp, whose draperies fill the stage. Her male victim, an embodiment of bronchitic breathing, rolls in agony at her feet. I thought it clever—there was some booing. I loved the idea of the Gershwin score for *Who Cares?*, but found it obstinate of Balanchine to confine the dances to a purely classical style. John Clifford's *Bartok No. 3* was skilfully worked out, but the lack of *épaulement* in the School-of-Balanchine choreography by Jacques d'Amboise for *Saltarelli* to Vivaldi music reduced the dancers to aimless eels.

9.6.74

American Ballet Theatre

At Covent Garden

In 1930 Colonel de Basil assembled the orphans of Diaghilev and kept the old family together while new families, sprung from them, were growing up in Britain and America. Ten years later, when world war threatened the very existence of ballet and the continuance of its traditions, Lucia Chase fulfilled an historical function hardly less significant; for in founding Ballet Theatre she seemed to combine the best of the Old and New Worlds, recruiting her choreographers and dancers from the young American school, from the Russian guardians of ancient secrets, and from those talented British who sought transatlantic refuge from the thunder of the guns. Before the war ended Fokine, Massine, Balanchine, Nijinska, Tudor, Howard, Dolin, de Mille, Robbins, Loring and not a few others had mounted ballets for her.

Eclecticism has always been the line of Ballet Theatre, or seemed to be. 'Show me the best of its kind, and I'll buy it'—and very nice, too. Their programmes, far more so than those of New York City Ballet, have always been deliciously varied and appetizing. Yet, even in 1946, when they brought us so many exciting new works, I felt there was something missing from the company. Was it an artistic policy? Was it unity? Or was it a true sense of values?

Let us see how things are working out this season at Covent Garden. This first week we have seen eight ballets by—hurrah!—eight different choreographers. How were they? *Les Sylphides*: pretty good in a rough way, rather dragged out, with fine performances by Melissa Hayden and Ruth Ann Koesun. *Aleko*: a glorious muddle by Massine, with Chagall having high old Russian jinks with his scenery, and Youskevitch going the whole Slav hog of nightmare and passion to Tchaikovsky's high old Russian Trio. Robbins's *Fancy Free* still holds some of its charm, though it has worn thin, as even the most brilliant of such farces is apt to do. *Theme and Variations* is not vintage Balanchine, but this company and orchestra do not bring out its values; while its sets and dresses are unbelievably vulgar. Dollar's *Constantia* is a treachery to Chopin, ill orchestrated, played, designed and choreographed. De Mille's *Fall River Legend*, which stirred some of my colleagues to the core in 1951, now seems to me more boring than ever, though Alicia Alonso and Lucia Chase are both good in it. The *Black Swan pas de deux* is splendidly danced by Alonso and Youskevitch. Lichine's charming *Graduation Ball*, unimaginatively redesigned, with an awkward *pas de deux* replacing the pretty Sylphide and Scotsman, is graced by the attractive performances of Koesun and Eric Braun, but disgraced by the incredible clowning of the company's ballet master. There are excellent dancers in Ballet Theatre and for the most part they seem in good form.

There is good and bad in what we have seen: probably, since many people will enjoy much that I do not, the programmes of Ballet Theatre will give pleasure. But there is something lacking, and I think it is the quality a troupe acquires from having a resident choreographer whose creative impulse suffuses dancers, repertoire and performances with a unifying radiance of style. I was thinking that to Melissa Hayden working for Ballet Theatre after leaving Balanchine's company must be like taking a course at the Polytechnic after being apprenticed in Titian's studio.

Observer, 19.7.53

The dancing of Alicia Alonso and Igor Youskevitch in *Giselle* and *Theme and Variations* was the best thing that Ballet Theatre gave us last week at Covent Garden; while Agnes de Mille's ten-year-old *Rodeo* was the happiest production.

Agnes de Mille tells in her memoirs how, after the first performance of *Rodeo* at the Metropolitan, she met Massine in the passage. Staring at her with his 'binocular eyes', he said, 'You have done a characteristic ballet. And in Europe I think it will have success.' He was right. And from *Rodeo* de Mille went on to *Oklahoma!* and in Europe that had success, too. On Monday the gallery enjoyed themselves so much that they began clapping in time to the square dance and threw the dancers off the beat. This tale of how a cowgirl got her man by the simple expedient of discarding breeches for skirt is told in forthright American slang which anyone could dance without fear of being called sissy: the New World princess of the Colorado plain is awoken from her sleep of tomboy adolescence by a slap on the bottom. John Kriza is irresistible as ever as the Champion Roper.

Observer, 26.7.53

At New York State Theater

When we revive an old play or ballet we either change it deliberately or we are the unconscious instruments of its change. Everyone aims at an 'authentic' production of *Les Sylphides*, but who achieves it?—everyone in the Western world, I should say, for Russian producers, bowing perhaps to the Heracleitan Law, seem to have started rearranging classics like *Swan Lake* immediately after their first performance, and never stopped.

I mustn't start writing about Clifford Williams's enthralling production of *The Jew of Malta*, which I saw at Stratford the other day. Marlowe's Barabas became the hero of an adventure story, a comic strip (with a satirical anti-Christian slant), in which our fun consisted in seeing what further enormities he could get away with: he was Punch, Superman. I also realised that Marlowe, poor, queer, bitter and scornful of conventional hypocrisy, had written in this and other plays his wish-fulfilment, as Corvo did in *Hadrian VII*. And four things were certain to me: (a) that the audience were in ecstasies; (b) that Williams had been convinced this was how Marlowe had meant the play; (c) that I agreed with him; and (d) that scholars would say we were wrong.

Then I have been thinking about *Les Sylphides* since seeing it at the opening night of Ballet Theatre's (successful) season in New York a month ago. Is it *still* about what we were told it was originally about —a poet dreaming in a wood haunted by sylphs? Is it about Chopin's music? Is it just girls forming lovely poetic patterns, with a man to hold them up when necessary? Is it a period piece—a bit of *art nouveau*? Is it about a boy who wishes he was a girl like all the others? Should he wear a wig?

The point is, what should they do with their faces, always supposing they've got the steps right and learnt the soft flowing style? And how manly dare the man be? Was Youskevitch too athletic in 1946? Is Nureyev too dreamy today? Of course we should love to have seen Pavlova, Karsavina and Nijinsky in it in 1909, but has it occurred to you, looking at old photographs, how terrible we should think that *corps* of stout little middle-aged Russian ladies in baggy bodices today?

In Ballet Theatre's *Les Sylphides* the dancing was well ordered and gracefully performed. (There were a few presumably authentic alterations in the choreography, no doubt made by Fokine himself. He must have been mad, by the way, to suggest—as the programme said he did—playing the

Polonaise Militaire as an overture.) It was the facial expressions which
threw me—or the lack of them. In the waltz, neat Eleanor D'Antuono was
genteel, a deb, and because of her name I saw her as an Italian or Spanish
heiress on her best behaviour abroad. In the first Mazurka Sallie Wilson
with her big jump and frank open face, was up from the country. In the
Prelude pretty Ruth Ann Koesun, who I know to be of Chinese descent,
seemed a porcelain princess, a rather mannered one, who twice shot a
glance at the audience to make sure they were appreciating her. (To
notice the public in this ballet is like turning on the TV before making
love.) While Royes Fernandez, exercising remarkable restraint and skill
in not seeming either too male or too moist, reduced himself to a noble
abstraction—but because people can't really remain blanks, his clear-cut
face, sideburns and name made me think of him as the very best and safest
type of Latin-American escort.

So how would I produce *Les Sylphides*? I believe that Chopin's pieces
ought never to have been orchestrated; that this is the most beautifully
arranged of ballets; and that the poet-dreaming-in-a-wood business is no
longer tenable today. I should leave the dances unchanged but dress
everyone in asymmetrical greeny-goldy Tiffany-glass-coloured draperies,
with beetlish masks, so that they wouldn't have to act, and have the ballet
done partly in silence, but with Chopin's tunes, played on a piano,
coming and going on the breeze.

Is it baroque to care?

18.4.65

Martha Graham

At the Saville

I have long thought myself the most diehard *abonné* of classical ballet in the town. 'Modern' dancers have always embarrassed and bored me. Now, I conjure every idle habit-formed fellow in need of a third eye to see new beauty that he should visit the Saville Theatre and watch Martha Graham. She is one of the great creators of our time.

Imagine inventing a kind of dancing which owes nothing to ballet! This she has done. But why bother? Well, certain creative artists, like dragons with thrashing tails, must have everything their own way. Martha Graham has sought new simplicities to enable the heart to speak. For her new art she needed a new kind of dancer, and the dancers needed a new system and a new training; she needed a new dance music, new forms in scenery, new lighting, and dresses cut in a new way. Martha Graham's dancers, her music, scenery, lighting and dresses are all wonderful.

Contrary to expectation, only three of the six works given this week have dealt with tragic battles of the mind. *Errand into the Maze*, with music by Menotti and set by Noguchi, uses the symbols of Labyrinth and Minotaur to show how we can get rid of our fears only by facing them. It is beautiful and dramatic as well as a psychological lesson. In *Night Journey*, Graham turns another black and splendid myth to her purpose. We see Jocasta dying, haunted by visions of Oedipus as son and lover. *Deaths and Entrances*, about the Brontë sisters, seemed at first sight to be less successfully conceived. In all these Graham brought a tremendous sweep to large movements and an Oriental delicacy to small ones. Stuart Hodes, a magnificent dancer, showed a menacing intensity as 'Heathcliff', Tiresias and 'Minotaur'. I liked the noble Oedipus of Bertram Ross and the romantic 'Edgar' of Robert Cohan.

Unexpectedly again, I liked Miss Graham's happy dances best of all. In these she shows an inspired invention; and they are perfectly worked out. *Appalachian Spring*, with a fine set by Noguchi and lovely music by Copland, conveys so strong an impression of energy, hope and joy.

Canticle for Innocent Comedians is Whitmanesque, a paean of acceptance. *Diversion of Angels*, to an admirable Dello Joio score, is Wordsworthian. We 'see the children sport upon the shore, and hear the mighty waters rolling evermore'.

Strange that this great American artist, who has inspired de Mille, Robbins and Tudor, should have waited so long to bring her company to London! I hope all thoughtful people will see her, for she has enlarged the language of the soul.

Observer, 7.3.54

I am delighted that a number of discerning people have discovered and warmly appreciated the life-enhancing qualities of Martha Graham, whose season continues at the Saville to small but enthusiastic audiences. Miss Graham interested me by saying that she had always thought of herself as a performer first and foremost, and that English admirers had been more interested in her choreography than the American public had ever been.

As a performer, she is certainly astonishing. She can make gestures tell in a way which is a lesson to ballet dancers; and she can teach her company to do this, too. Everything she does is true and essential. There is something in her of the miraculous originality and intensity of Emily Dickinson, whose life is presented in *Letter to the World*, perhaps Miss Graham's most important work. I shall never forget her performance in this, or the grace of Pearl Lang, who spoke the crystalline words. What a creation!

I prophesy that Martha Graham's first appearance in London will be as historic as Isadora Duncan's in St. Petersburg at the beginning of the century. It is with real distress that I am obliged to miss the end of her season.

What shall I remember most, after *Letter to the World*? I feel I have hardly begun to appreciate *Dark Meadow* and other works seen once only. *Canticle for Innocent Comedians* had the greatest number of extraordinary joys. Yuriko as the Moon, and Bertram Ross lying out of the window to look at her; the capricious pranks of Stuart Hodes as Fire; Helen McGehee and Robert Cohan as two swinging stars; Ross tumbling about the sky: all these were beautiful.

My first sight of Martha Graham revealed her as the woman in the Labyrinth, quivering with fear in silence; my last, more happily significant, showed her seated in the rocking-chair in *Appalachian Spring*, rejoicing at her world and at her part in it, one of the heroic women who made America.

Observer, 14.3.54

At the Empire, Edinburgh

Martha Graham and her Dance Company paid their first visit to Edinburgh last week, and one could feel the impact. Shock, usually followed by a glow of delight and admiration. Some people didn't get it, some didn't get it all, some responded passionately and came back for more. The company open in London for a fortnight's season on Tuesday.

Graham is firstly a poet—a theatrical poet. The technique of dancing she has invented, the company she has built up and trained, the new kind of scenery and lighting she has evolved with Isamu Noguchi and Jean Rosenthal are merely the component parts of her personal language, her means of communication.

Sometimes the ideas she wants to express are visual, sometimes complex and psychological. Sometimes she is clear, sometimes dark. I see Graham as a kind of Sibyl whose temple and holy cave is the theatre. You pay your money and you get your answer, your oracle, or your vision.

I have been wondering, if I wanted to give the maximum of delight to my 400 wisest and loveliest friends, which programmes I should take them to at the Prince of Wales's. It's not easy, because some of the deep, dark works are probably the most rewarding, yet I feel that *Clytemnestra* and *Judith*, for instance, ought to be seen twice. I haven't got them quite straight in my own mind yet.

For sheer physical beauty it would be hard to beat *Secular Games*. The tableau when the curtain rises on seven nakedish men of various shades of brown perched on Noguchi toadstools against a torrid black sky suggests Fire Island, Michelangelo, Bali and Proust's frieze of sporting boys before their sex-change into *les jeunes filles en fleur*.

I do not know whether in view of the programme note about 'a Socratic island' the ball which is gently thrown and deftly caught and which threads them together in a web of perfect parabolas drawn invisibly on the air, is meant as the ball of talk, or some more physical link, or both. Then girls arrive and it becomes a different sort of island—with hats and towels, flirting and wind-milling and Richard Gain going all goosey-goosey-goo.

Embattled Garden is *Private Lives* in the Garden of Eden. Adam, Eve,

Lilith and a predatory stranger change partners, love, brood, gloat, sympathize, feel left out, assert themselves and fight. Peter Phillips and other Pop artists should book balcony seats to get the benefit of the glossy red and green floor of Noguchi's forest—a machine for chasing girls through and having sex in. The music of Carlos Surinach is rather Spanish and so are the men's black trousers and the floor-slapping. Louring, thunderous images remain in the mind—of Bertram Ross and lovely Yuriko making love and hate while Linda Hodes in yellow with a red fan lies aloof, and handsome Robert Cohan hangs and gloats in fascination from a tree. Everyone agreed, by the way, that this was the best-looking company ever.

Seraphic Dialogue must not be missed. Handkerchiefs at the ready for those like myself who are suckers for martyrdom. It is a religious work about Joan of Arc (the luminous Ethel Winter) seeing herself as Maid (Yuriko), Warrior (Helen McGehee) and Martyr (Linda Hodes) and being taken into Heaven by St. Michael (Bertram Ross) and two female saints. I marvel at the way the gleaming skeletal scenery takes apart to be used as a sword or a cross, at the leaping exultation of Michael, at his crowning of the martyred Joan—his fingers suggesting the spikes of a tall Gothic crown, which is also of thorns—and at Joan's admittance to the hierarchy of Heaven, the golden gates shutting her in with God for good.

Martha Graham usually dances one work per performance, the last. She is older than the (Noguchi) rocks among which she sits. (By the way, that paragraph of Pater's is a great scenario for her.) And she has evolved a technique of flashbacks for works in which she herself appears which allows younger versions of the heroine to do the tougher dancing—though when there is an orgy going, as in *Judith*, Graham is in the thick of it. In the long *Clytemnestra* she is on stage all evening.

Phaedra is the easiest of the dark works to take in, because there is only one flashback—to Pasiphaë and the bull-dancers. Mischievous Aphrodite, bright with evil glee (Ethel Winter, *toute entière à sa proie attachée*), blinds and maddens the scarlet-clad queen with lust for her stepson Hippolytus—certain aspects of him in particular. But he is dedicated to the chaste goddess: such a waste. Phaedra looks at him through holes in the wall and *imagines* him melting in her arms. Death, Death. Graham and Ross are thrilling.

Legend of Judith is a more elaborate and profounder work which, with *Night Journey* and *Clytemnestra*, deserves extended study. What makes the last confusing is that not only does one person play several parts in it, but that several people play one part. The *ménage à trois* in *Judith*, Graham's

Martha Graham. Drawing by Charlotte Trowbridge

caressing Ross's neck where the knife will go, and the rolling off of his head in her silver cloak are memorable.

Apropos the use of draperies in choreography, it is ingenious how the magenta and vermilion carpet spread for Agamemnon becomes a robe for Clytemnestra and, at last, the curtains of the fatal bath house. But then there are enough ideas in these programmes to keep us going for years.

1.9.63

At the Prince of Wales's

When Martha Graham came to the Saville in 1954 there were twelve Christians in the house at one matinée, but the company say they didn't notice this because there was always such a warm reception. Most of the dreary ballet critics were against her, but I had the impression that theatre people—as opposed to ballet people—were fascinated, because I got fan letters from actors and directors for what I had written. Anyway, look what happened in the British theatre two years later: the New Wave.

Now flags are flying, and every newspaper is a trumpet and the tiny conquering woman comes in glory and angels are laughing on the roof-tops. Packed houses at the Prince of Wales's.

Anyway, I think it is time for me to say what I don't like in the repertory. Dello Joio's music for *Dialogue* is pretty functional, though it works. With a greater score the piece could be greater—*could. Embattled Garden* which has marvellous flamenco music by Surinach is *really* perfect and great. El Dabh's music for *Clytemnestra* is a war of nerves, which you may say is just right for the tale of a murderess in hell. Those glissandos, that squeaking and twittering, that playing the piano without striking the notes, those falsetto shrieks of the male singer! O.K., well, O.K. Still, I should hide the singers. And I believe the prologue could be cut.

I don't like the women's red wreaths in *Dialogue*. I don't get that pro-gramme note for *Judith* about 'a teller of the tale and a poet-fool who listens'—I can never *find* them, though I look everywhere. I think some of *Judith* is turgid and confusing. The set, not being by Noguchi, is much less well-designed than the others.

Clytemnestra is a gigantic endeavour with noble and awe-inspiring moments. Think of taking the whole of the *Oresteia* and then remaking it so that it seems to be thrashing about in the mind of the tormented heroine, whose punishment and salvation is that she has to come to terms with her own past!

The scene when Graham flirts with Robert Cohan as Aegisthus is wonderful. Graham wiggles, looks coy, trails her mauve veil. She shudders when he puts the idea of murdering Agamemnon into her head; then rehearses the crime as a dance. Cohan acts realistically, he is extraordinary —he is *sick*. He relaxes on the throne, fiddling unconsciously with her veil, twisting it, watching, smiling, basking.

And wonderful is the scene of Agamemnon's triumphant entry, reception, disarming and murder. Ross makes the King a conceited fool. He is boorish to Clytemnestra, kicks her hand away, finds the bath-water too hot. Graham abases herself, salaams to him, crawls. The murder is cleverly arranged. We just get glimpses through curtains. And all the time the King's soul (i.e., the head and extended arms of Ross) is visible above them, appealing to the gods. You have to admit this is tremendous, but I wouldn't blame you if you had got muddled and given up after the prologue.

Graham is such an artist that to watch her sit or even to watch her back view veiled from crown to toe is a joy. A queen of style: but also a kingmaker. Ross is great but also subtle in everything he does, soul utterly invested in body. Cohan is a committed artist. Ethel Winter beacons. Helen McGehee's sharp face travels like a spear of passion. Compare sultry Linda Hodes and impulsive Yuriko in *Garden*: incomparable!

In *Circe*, world-premièred on Friday (a triumph), beautiful Mary Hinkson was fantastically squirmed around by Robert Powell, Richard Gain, Gene McDonald and Peter Randazzo. I never knew I never knew the facts of life before. If sex hadn't been here already Graham would have invented it. But staunch Clive Thompson saved the heroic and yearning Ross for tea and sympathy in a tub for two. '*Heureux qui comme Ulysse a fait un beau voyage.*'

8.9.63

If to Joachim du Bellay Ulysses was primarily someone who came home, and to Tennyson he was the dissatisfied romantic, driven 'to sail beyond the sunset and the baths of all the western stars,' while Shakespeare gave him—somewhat arbitrarily, one dares to suppose—the famous speech on degree, Martha Graham in her new work *Circe* presents him as the modern man who has to decide whether to shoulder the responsibility of his human calling or to revel in a sensual stye.

'What it costs to choose to be human,' says the programme note, and we may wonder what this means. I think Graham's *Circe* will have different meanings for different people, and is intended to have. You could read the rout as beatniks, I presume.

Brecht won't let us use vague words like 'beautiful', but it must, somehow, be said that, its moral theme aside, *Circe* is almost painfully a seduction to the eye. Such movements, poses and groups, electrically charged with passion, have never been seen even on the Graham stage before; and part of the pain is in the newness. Martha Graham seems to have arrived at such a pitch of incandescent creativity that she has a new or partly new language for every new idea.

It is very hard to describe *Circe*, though it is short and wonderfully complete: this is chiefly because there is no symmetry, none of the seven characters does anything twice and no two do anything together. Bertram Ross as Ulysses and Clive Thompson as his Helmsman (an echo of the apprehensive Eurylochus) are first seen on a simple Noguchi boat to the right. In the left background there is an arch-like form through which the animals will twist and which conceals a platform for the beckoning enchantress. The perfect lighting is by Jean Rosenthal.

The action is of course a battle between the Circe gang and the Helmsman for the body and soul of Ulysses: glittering glamour and fabulous caresses against the stern reminders of conscience.

Graham has seized a superb cast. Richard Gain, the Lion, looks like a lion anyway. Gene McDonald is tall with a startled air, and makes a fine Deer. Handsome Peter Randazzo is certainly not like a Goat in real life, but he is faunlike. As the Snake, Robert Powell, blue-faced, is infinitely undulant.

I doubt if anyone could replace Mary Hinkson in the role of Circe: no one could replace her in my memory. Praxitelean Clive Thompson is as grand a symbol of man's higher instincts as, say, Epstein's *St. Michael* at Coventry. Of Bertram Ross it could be said that if Shakespeare had written *Hamlet* as a ballet, he would have cast Ross in the title role. It is rare to see nobility of movement informed by such intelligence.

The moment of decision comes. The music of Alan Hovhaness, which has been remarkably helpful, mysterious and magical throughout, draws itself out to an unbearable tension of wailing woodwind. Ulysses decides; boards ship; and not without a farewell salute to his angel of sensuality, sets out to sea. The animals vanish one by one from sight. Circe's tower sinks below the horizon. The lights fade on the two firm, aspiring male figures, and the hero sails with his soul away.

15.9.63

At the Saville

Martha Graham's ballets—or plays, as Leroy Leatherman calls them in his extremely interesting and original book—are easily divisible into dark and bright. Two new dark ones and three new bright ones have been brought into the repertory this week and there are signs that the young London audience prefers the bright ones—although that epic marathon *Clytemnestra* was acclaimed.

The bright ballets are about young people being young and making love and dancing and being beautiful. *Secular Games* is the most shining example. *Part real—Part dream* is a rather mysterious one, with more depths and allusions. I think it is about Hyde Park (or Wimbledon Common). Mary Hinkson goes by, jingling—playing her transistor, as it were. Ethel Winter comes out of a fountain, Bertram Ross out of a bush and Robert Cohan out of a public convenience. Love is made by some, others fall back on fetishism. As four men bestride four girls something comes from the sky which must be rain, and I think this is about fertilization, spring. At the end the four principals are adorned by the others with gorgeous cloaks, and this is either marriage, or a salute to youth for being beautiful. Like dear Tchelitchev used to say, pointing at a stranger, 'Give that boy some money, he's so pretty.' Glittering sound-track by Mordecai Seter.

Dancing Ground, to Ned Rorem's *Eleven Pieces,* in a fine Jean Rosenthal set, is about a nymph who haunts that stretch of waste ground where lovers go outside the city wall. She loses one man but gets another at the end, and in between there has been some marvellous dancing by a party of twelve.

Of the dark works, *Night Journey* is about Jocasta finding out Oedipus is her son; *Clytemnestra* is about the murdered murderess in purgatory, learning to face her guilt in order to atone for it. Graham's extraordinary version of the latter story, wide as Homer, deep as Freud, backed up by Halim El-Dabh's haunting music (in the first and third scene there are two singers), with Noguchi's heroic stage furniture, constitutes one of the pyramids of our tormented age. You have to work at it. But there are a hundred unforgettable images and Graham herself is great.

But the bright ballets with their naked men and the dark ballets with their tormented queens are really about the same thing seen from different viewpoints. Or rather, in the dark ones we are looking at the bright ones through a hole in a wall—the hole in the lavatory wall of age. Clytemnestra has to admit she killed her husband not because he sacrificed Iphigenia but because she desired young Aegisthus. Jocasta must pay for having sex with a twenty-year-old by discovering he is her son. Phaedra yearned to be one of the boys horsing around in the showers with Hippolytus. Judith would have liked to play secular games with Holofernes.

Oscar Wilde said: 'The tragedy of old age is, not that one is old, but that one is young.'

9.4.67

Ballets U.S.A.

At the Empire, Edinburgh

Nothing like Jerome Robbins has happened to us in the ballet world for a long, long time—I say 'in the ballet world' because it is true we have had *West Side Story*, whatever world that belongs to. Nothing *quite* like Robbins's *Ballets U.S.A.* has *ever* happened to us, because now, in his maturity, the dazzling choreographer of *Fancy Free* and *Interplay*, who later became the (to me rather tiresome) intellectual choreographer of *Age of Anxiety* and *The Guests*, has found or forged for himself a language as new and personal as those of Gerard Manley Hopkins or Van Gogh.

Robbins, in fact, is one of the world's inventors, and it is amazing that two such original geniuses as himself and Martha Graham should have come out of one country in the same half-century. Of course, America is a big place and we know nothing is impossible there.

In Edinburgh last week the company performed against curtains, the plane with all their scenery having gone to the bottom of the Mediterranean (no lives lost): by the time they open in London tomorrow at the Piccadilly (for one brief week) the scenery will have been rebuilt and repainted, heaven knows how. I cannot imagine the four ballets any better than they were, though two are designed by Ben Shahn and Steinberg, artists I greatly admire: besides, their lighting by Jean Rosenthal and Nananne Porcher is gloriously imaginative, a joy and an atmosphere in itself. If it had been the plane with Robbins and the company that had gone down, 'then you would have left unseen a wonderful piece of work'. You would have missed what I consider one of the most exciting shows I have ever seen on a stage.

It is hard to describe why *Moves*, the ballet without music (which I rather dreaded), should seize and fascinate us as it does. The absence of music and the odd mixture of movements, classical, modern and natural-istic, combine to bounce us *out* of the theatre into a fresh awareness far removed from our usual level mood of evening apathy.

How often we obtain tickets for the ballet, invite a friend, rush home after work, change, arrive breathless, settle in our seat, listen to the orchestra tuning up—and suddenly wish we were on Hampstead Heath. The familiarity of the theatre-going process nauseates us. In *Moves*, somehow, we *are* on Hampstead Heath. We are lying on our stomachs on the ground doing 'nature study' between blades of grass. We are scientists glued to a microscope, or astronomers with glass turned to the stars.

As we watch the dancers, now two, now four, now twelve, advance, group, break away, dissolve in darkness and reassemble in a changed light —as we observe their precise, elastic bounds, their asymmetrical patterns, the way one of them lifts a limb, looks at it, then thinks of something to do with it, the way they extend like signals or curl up like grubs—we feel almost like a Thing from Outer Space discovering the myriad potentialities of human motion—a happy, enraptured Thing, be it said, who exclaims with Miranda: 'Oh brave new world that hath such people in't!'

I have not the slightest doubt that Diaghilev would have approved strongly of Robbins's new version of *The Afternoon of a Faun*, for he was continually trying to pep up his old ballets if he liked their music—or else to bury them for good. After all, a summer afternoon is a summer afternoon is a summer afternoon, whether in Manhattan or on Mount Hymettus, and there are fauns at every street-corner. Instead of a sunbaked hillside the scene is a breathless New York dance studio, and in this a young man awakes from siesta to practise his steps, looking, as dancers do, in the mirror. The mirror is the eyes of the audience. A girl arrives, and they work together until, suddenly seeing her as a woman, he kisses her tentatively on the cheek. As if stung, she darts from the room, leaving the faun to dream.

The sensation I received from this modern interpretation of Debussy's silvery steamy score was like nothing I can remember except the shock of immediacy I once had in Jerusalem, when I read the story of the Passion in the all-too-familiar Gospel according to St. John *in French*. Wilma Curley and John Jones were stunning.

N.Y. Export, Opus Jazz, is the main meal of the Robbins beano, and apart from stating it is the hottest, coolest orgy I have experienced, and wondering whether the London management will have to restrain their customers from dancing in the aisles, as in the days when rock 'n' roll first burst upon this sleepy old cathedral town, I shall put off writing about it until I have lived through it again. *The Concert*, which concludes the programme, is the only ballet I have ever seen which had the audience laughing aloud throughout.

13.9.59

At the Piccadilly

Don't say I got it in first! Last week Russia hit the moon, Khrushchev hit Washington and Robbins hit London. London and the British theatre—not only ballet, I think—will never, like the lady in Betjeman's poem about the Regent Palace, 'be quite the same again'.

Had we but world enough and time, I could write you a short essay on each one of Jerome Robbins's nineteen star dancers, whose personalities are now very distinct to me in spite of all that teamwork and their unison in different styles. They are *very* good dancers, and marvellous to look at, with their pan-American faces—Italian, Jewish, Negro, Slav, Korean, Red Indian, Irish and Scotch. (Hitler would have gone out of his mind.) And they are so funny.

Why is *The Concert* such a funny ballet? It is a 'New Yorker'-ish joke (with pretty drops by Steinberg) about what goes on in people's minds at a Chopin recital. Much of the joke is in the dancers' deadpan reaction to the farcical situations they get into.

The company's pianist, imperturbable Betty Walberg, who first takes the stage, flicks a little dust off the piano, and proceeds to play very well a series of favourite pieces, cocking a polite and patient eye over her shoulder at conductor Torkanowsky when necessary, is as hilarious as anybody, with her two vast mad black ospreys.

Enter (to put it mildly) a soulful student, two sweet-eating stenographers, a tall girl who thinks she is Markova, a Lesbian who thinks she is Toscanini, a culture-prone wife with a mutinous mate, and a mouse-boy. Joke about everyone in wrong seats. Mutineer gets a lech on Markova. Suddenly everyone sees him—and herself—as ballet-dancers.

There's a joke about the different ways of carrying women, an all-in *pas de deux* during which the mouse-boy tries vainly to cope with Markova—who becomes Toumanova (Tommy Abbott and Barbara Milberg are beyond everything in this), a spot of wife-murder by Michael Maule to the sacred Prelude from *Les Sylphides*, a charge of exulting, mazurka-ing hussars, in the course of which mutinous Maule nearly makes Markova, and a *ballet blanc* in which one or other girl is always out of step—an old joke, but turned to pure gold by the faces of Beryl Towbin, Patricia Dunn, Wilma Curley, Erin Martin, and the others.

That crazy Assyrian princess Muriel Bentley buys a hat; the Raindrop Prelude induces an epidemic of umbrellas in a scene which is not only funny but beautiful and sad: and then when everyone has turned into rather 1905 butterflies, Maule really does seem as if he'll make Markova in mid-air, when—

The thing about Robbins is that he has a mind and he has a touch. He dreams up something titanic, but he dishes it out to you with a light hand, real cool. To have ideas, to invent; to have theatre sense, the know-how; and to be reticent withal, seeing when to stop: surely this is greatness.

20.9.59

Sure, J. Robbins's *Op. Jazz* belongs to what an Italian critic described—in the *démodé* slang common to us layabouts and camp-followers—as '*il mondo hot*', but it also belongs to '*l'epoca atomica*' and is an epic of our time. To what can we compare it? *Le Sacre du Printemps* was an epic all right, but its scene was laid in prehistoric Russia not in the Europe of 1912. I agree that to ante-date the setting of your work need not necessarily make it less contemporary—did not Verdi pour into certain of his 'period' operas all the white-hot aspirations of the Risorgimento? And it could be argued that the great ballets of the Romantic era, such as *Giselle* or *La Sylphide*, even if 'epic' is the wrong word for them, were entirely representative of the modernity of Romantic youth, with its passionate excesses played out in fancy dress. But *Op. Jazz* is about the young of today, and addresses those mistrustful creatures in their own language.

On the first drum roll of Robert Prince's score, Ben Shahn's curtain, a crisp cubist design in rainbow colours, pronounces the ballet's title *N.Y. Export: Op. Jazz*. Curtain up on a world of television aerials; then in come running, to the summons of a klaxon trumpet call, one by one, the kids.

All wear different coloured wind-cheaters, black tights, white socks, track shoes. The tights no doubt are stylized jeans—if anything could be more stylized than jeans. At least tights are easier to dance in. *They* stare resentfully at *us*. We are the elders, the insiders, the establishment: we gave birth to *them* and the H-bomb, and they hate us because we are square. They form a group, circle with a low judo crouch and line up to forget us and dance. The tide of jazz rises; they click their fingers, let their heads loll, stick out their backsides and hang their hands like rabbits. Grouped together again, swaying and snapping, their eyes are drawn to a portent in the sky; they reach up in horror—fall flat. They know.

Next a roof-top. Phallic chimneys against a city's red night sky. Three—later five—boys, to whom there comes one girl, who takes charge. The sexual pounding of the drum solo dictates their contortions: the trumpet leads them to orgasm. Ten upstretched arms sustain the rigid girl, and pitch her out. This was a gang-bang.

Three. Improvisations in a playground, which might as well have been a club where dancers vie in daring, clowning and cool ease. Solos, duos, scrums, mockery, shimmies, hand-shakes, somersaults, belly-slides, noise. The way the dance keeps picking up with new fever just as you think it is over is half the fun.

Four. Almost dark. Blues. Boy meets girl. He moves her head with his head, her arm with his elbow, her foot with his foot. He twines her up on to his shoulder, and she becomes a crest on his helmet, a weather-cock on his roof. Sliding down the bannisters of his back, she returns to earth and him. Kneeling, they clinch; but before the music ends they walk unsatisfied away from each other into the dark. This 'Passage for Two' seems to be about modern love. Gone are the serenades and the bouquets of Parma violets. Just a one-night affair, and you don't even give your telephone number.

For the final Theme, Variations and Fugue, the rainbow colours are gathered into the backdrop, a luminous screen, abstract Chartres; the dancers are in black and white; and the music is jazz in terms of Bach. The formal opening, with its dreamy variations, quicker, syncopated, grotesquely orchestrated, deliriously elaborated, leads eventually to an ordered riot which includes a Cha-cha; and at last the fugue booms drunkenly home, while the kids present themselves defiantly to us, crying 'This was us. We did it. Take us or leave us or drop dead.'

27.9.59

At the Saville

Jerome Robbins's *Moves* was not the result of a gimmicky yearning to surprise: for Robbins knows as well as the hairiest critic that ballets without music have been done before. He was working on a new score of Copland's when the non-arrival of some music for rehearsal sent him off at this tangent, into this groove of silence, which he began, like an incredulous Aladdin, thrillingly and profitably to explore.

A painter of today, besides whatever he has which is individual and his own, carries all the experience of the centuries poised on the tip of his brush. What I like about *Moves* is that, new as it is, the past shines through it. It is as if Robbins had sat at a window across whose square of changing blue a perpetual procession would pass throughout the centuries, from which at last a recurrent pattern of life could be deduced; for, year after year, the same though different babies would learn the wonder of walking, the same courtesans comb their hair, the same fishermen put out to sea.

I must not be too pretentious. *Moves* is an essay in different kinds of movement, but to these movements, tentative, assured, humdrum or majestic, the pointing finger of Robbins has electrically conveyed a knowledge of past civilization.

Out of the darkness the line of kids advance. Those about to live salute us. Stillness. Movements are made. Legs flex, an arm is raised. They run, they jump, they discover possibilities.

1. In this *pas de deux* a man, bending a woman into different shapes like a sculptor, seems to learn from her limbs about the conjunctions of love. 2. A world of women who patiently adorn themselves for performance or for seduction. A Balinese arm movement reminds us that religion, drama, dance, and sex are sometimes combined in one profession. Finally the four women take up a striding posture on their toes, forward knee bent, a hand on shoulder; and one raises her arm, exhorting 'Women of Athens!' I recall *Lysistrata*. 3. The Stadium. A man's world. Sporting and martial exercise, fatigue. Brotherly, dedicated, they school each other. They salute epically on parting. 4. Artists and models. The men admire and arrange the women. I think of that series of drawings Picasso did in '54, two hundred in three months, all about the old painter and his goddess-model —so many, many variations on the theme. Then the stage empties but for six people: man and woman in the foreground, in the dusky rear a man with a man, a woman with a woman. The motives of love, physical culture and dedication are simultaneously reiterated. Again a solemnity of parting. 5. Gentle ballet exercises, working up to jumps and soaring lifts. A whirring, thudding crowd of bird-dancers. Then a summons. The kids line up; salute us; pause; turn about; and walk away into the embracing darkness.

Noble! And by surrounding this work in silence, Robbins creates a climate in which we are suddenly able to see ourselves in a perspective of history.

30.8.61

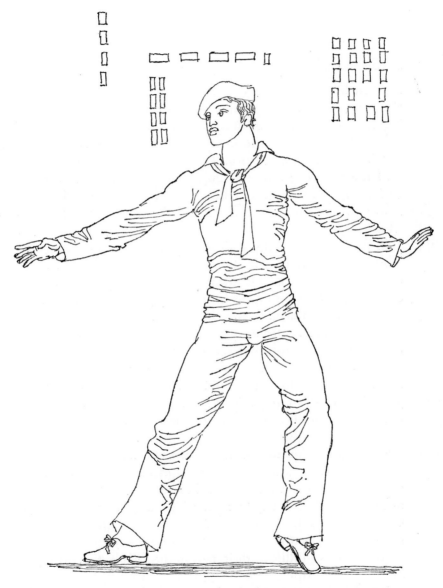

Fancy Free. Drawing by Astrid Zydower based on a photograph of Jerome Robbins by Fred Fehl

Merce Cunningham

At Sadler's Wells

So what like is the work of Merce Cunningham who, with his Dance Company, has been giving us a much-needed shot in the backside this last week at Sadler's Wells? Well, we knew his work fell into the category of so-called Modern Dance and that he is one of the two or three most famous American exponents of it.

So it comes as a surprise to find how classical his choreography is. He owes far more, I should say, to Balanchine than to Graham. But, of course, he is very modern in spirit and has affiliations with the Theatre of the Absurd.

In brief, Cunningham is an inventive and witty choreographer and an expressive dancer. His small troupe is admirable. His music by John Cage and others is always a surprise and often a delight. His simple costumes by Robert Rauschenberg are designed with the dance in mind and never seek to distract attention from it.

Cunningham has a tendency to make his dancers execute a more or less classical step, then sort of scrub it out by doing something fidgety or taken from everyday life. In *Rune* at one moment three girls take up varying attitudes in the foreground and hold them, while a fourth in the background stands awkwardly leaning sideways with legs apart. The three leap up and down in the second position then pose and do *port de bras* in an open fourth while the fourth girl just wiggles.

Cunningham likes to turn his dancers into flowers unfolding on their stalks, which means he uses balance to an exceptional extent. A typical step is an arabesque with unpointed toe. The dancers are often expected to hold these poses a long time, which they do immaculately. Since Cunningham and his composers also make an exceptionally large use of silence, I was often lost in admiration for the way the dancers managed to time and co-ordinate their movements. Were the darlings counting?

A typical floor pattern is the diagonal. An idiosyncrasy which happens in at least two works is to bring down the curtain at an inconclusive moment when things still seem to be going on. But this is an old and effective theatrical device.

According to the programme Cunningham and his collaborators like Chance to play a part. Christian Wolff's music for *Rune* is for six *or* seven instruments and '*sometimes* restricts the performers to particular notes'. In *Story* 'the dancers are involved with objects that change from evening to evening . . . found by Rauschenberg in or outside the theatre'. (The management can accept *no* responsibility for *anything* when he's around.) The sounds in Cage's *Suite for Five* 'correspond to imperfections in the paper upon which the music was written'. This is all fine and in the good old Happening tradition, but when applied to choreography (as it only occasionally is) one tends to suspect that the dancers' improvisations are really rehearsed and to think it a very good thing that they should be.

Suite for Five has some lyrical compositions and encounters. The very intermittent music—one chord, twang or bang, about every ten seconds —is like two lost and toothless pianos calling to each other through a dark night. Perhaps it is better than complete silence and perhaps the dancers have learnt to disregard it. In *Crises*, to the tape of a pianola roll by Conlon Nancarrow which incorporates jazz, isolated noises, a fugue and silence, the hero is sometimes attached to one of four girls and they to each other by elastic bands. Back to back, wrist to wrist or hand to ankle, they strive. Cunningham made an interesting final entry, sliding recumbent; and a reaction was produced by the dirty look a girl in red shot at the audience.

In *Untitled Solo*, a twitching neurotic dance, Cunningham showed fine control and balance. Jerking, circling with twisting hands, nodding, falling, casting dice, playing out rope. *Story* is a funny work about dancers improvising in *costumes trouvés* and exchanging character. In the score of Toshi Ichiyanagi, easily my favourite composer, there are marvellous bangs, squeaks, cracks, rattles, whistles, clangs, railway noises, unloadings of coal, Morse, whines and wa-wa-ings. *Objets trouvés* by Rauschenberg on Wednesday included a length of hose, a scaffold tower and an enormous property bird. Everyone had a ball.

Septet danced to Satie's *Trois morceaux en forme de poire* was entirely delightful. There are funny bits when people shake hands or make bicycling movements, there are lovely poses, a distorted variation on Balanchine's harnessed Muses in *Apollo*, a bit when Cunningham becomes Pygmalion, and a skit on Martha Graham's typical *arabesque penchée*, wrist to forehead. *Night Wandering* is a cold, menacing *pas de deux*—the courting of the Macbeths. At the end Cunningham becomes an Egyptian couch and

Carolyn Brown does a Pauline Borghese on top of him: thus imparting a curious feeling of impersonal ecstasy.

Antic Meet, a comic closing ballet, went down like iced Coke in a heat-wave. John Cage's music is amplified piano and noise-makers, all electrified. It is hard to make dancing really funny, but this ballet was. 'Door comes on by itself, M.C. with chair on back, opens door, girl comes through . . . . Girls in smocks bob to each other, one picks flowers, throws them, other jerks head, first reciprocates, ballet steps, pulling at tights, collisions . . . 2 men cartwheel, machine-gun, wriggle on floor, competition of jumps and handstands, mad death agonies . . . re-enter in fur coat, all girls suddenly in spectacles, four-armed sweater . . . soft toe number. . . .' My notes don't make it sound much, but of course in this sort of ballet it's not what you do but the way you do it.

I'm delighted to hear that the company is transferring tomorrow for a two-week season at the Phoenix, partly because I have been thinking that this chance business need not just be confined to the performers; and I'm working on a little plan for joining in.

2.8.64

Alvin Ailey

At the Shaftesbury

On Tuesday I got to see Alvin Ailey's American Dance Theater at the Shaftesbury, and I highly recommend this delightful company. But don't go expecting anything slick. There is a vague and cosy feeling about the troupe, as if they were treating the audience as friends to surprise rather than strangers to win over. I think they put their heads together and say, 'Well, what shall we give 'em tonight?' 'Oh, not *that* old thing!'

The silly, giddy programme seems madly subject to alteration, and guess-work is rife. Brother John Sellers, in a pretty, checked cap, sings his splendid folk songs into a mike in the pit, and I think controls a four-man combo who plod homeward after the interval, and leave the world to Tannoy and to me.

Ves Harper's simple costumes and staging are admirable and so are the lighting effects. There are twelve remarkable dancers, and not the least charming and unusual thing about the company is the modest part Alvin Ailey, its director, chooses to play in it. He gives the centre of the stage to Joyce Trisler (the only white dancer), to James Truitte, who seems an older man, or to Dudley Williams, whom we knew with Martha Graham.

Reflections in D, a solo to Duke Ellington choreographed by Ailey and danced by Williams, is the most stunning single item on the programme. Not only is this an enthralling display of modern dance technique, it is a moving combination of plastic beauty and passionate expression. I was hypnotized by Williams's lithe body yearning beneath two spotlights. The dance was like a cry.

Gillespiana, a group dance, is rather nondescript. But to the changing rhythms of *Been here and gone* (folk songs), *Roots of the Blues* and *Revelations* (spirituals), in the first two of which most numbers were galvanized into being by the powerful voice of Sellers, I abandoned myself uncritically and with a kind of voluptuous delight. The dancers were so attractive and so well trained, the numbers they were given to do were so well calculated to bring out their good qualities and had so direct a message, and the

E

lighting was so helpful, that I could not imagine a more agreeable combination of art and entertainment. It was like basking in the sun.

18.10.64

At the Church Hill, Edinburgh

We who come to Edinburgh every August as regularly as Edwardians went to take the cure at Baden-Baden get a kick from finding it always the same only different.

What varied associations we had with the old Empire Theatre! Now the smaller but cleverly converted Church Hill Theatre looks like becoming part of our annual treat. Two years ago we had Paul Taylor there: this year it is Alvin Ailey's American Dance Theater.

They have been absolutely sold out and I was quite unhappy to see for three nights running the queues of patient people desperately hoping for returned tickets.

The company is remarkable for the number of choreographers whose work it presents, as well as for the outstanding personalities of three or four talented artists. Most successful of the big works have been Ailey's *Revelations*, Talley Beatty's *Black District* and Geoffrey Holder's *Prodigal Prince*. *Revelations* is a kind of symphony of spirituals with epic choreography and lighting, a sure-fire success.

Black District is a protest piece, starting with a picture of the cheerful everyday life in a Negro quarter, developing through 'an incident of violence' into an intolerable (i.e. effective) assault on the audience's nerves and consciences. In its Blues duet the mocking and imperious Judith Jamison and the tall, gentle and bemused Kelvin Rotardier impress us with their very different characters. In a tortured solo of dedication, dynamic Dudley Williams wears his soul outside his body.

Prodigal Prince has music, choreography, decor and costumes by the Trinidadian Geoffrey Holder and it is very fine and original and provides a stunning role for Miguel Godreau. The latter is short, nervous and fiery, with a mop of curls, and I am not sure if he is a Negro or not.

The theme is Hippolite the primitive painter of Haiti, who was a Voodoo priest and made a possibly imaginary pilgrimage to Africa. There are amazing apparitions of Rotardier as St. John the Baptist and of Jamison as Erzulie, the Voodoo goddess, looking like the Queen of Heaven. Godreau is superb.

Ailey's *Knoxville: Summer 1915* to Samuel Barber's music (canned like all the rest) is in an entirely different mood—a dream of childhood, with Godreau snatching a different opportunity.

1.9.68

Paul Taylor

At the Shaftesbury

I am full of goodwill for Paul Taylor and his Dance Company, who opened at the Shaftesbury on Thursday, and delighted to see yet another exponent of the modern dance arrive from America: but his first programme, though interesting, was not a 100 per cent success. Perhaps this bill was not typical. I liked very much the first work, *Aureole*, which I suppose is the company's *Sylphides*; the second, *Scudorama*, is murky in theme and at first sight baffling; the third, *Piece Period*, is a funny which I didn't think came off.

In *Aureole* Paul Taylor presents his credentials and gives us a sample of the style of dancing he has evolved to express his ideas. He and his delightful barefoot troupe of two men and five girls have all clearly profited from classical training—they have *ballon* and control: but Taylor has undergone the tensions and relaxations of Martha Graham. Soaring in the air of classical ballet these dancers seem always on the point of descending to grovel on the earth, which is the arena of Graham's soul-battling, but they stop before they get there. Like Merce Cunningham, Taylor makes a great use of *plié*.

Taylor has evolved a personal style. The peculiarity of *Aureole* is that it imposes on the courtly music of Handel a frank, buoyant, teenage behaviour, devoid of any courtly gesture. Girls glide in and out in line sideways; there are *port de bras* as in a Scottish reel; hands scoop and carve the air or pat imaginary balls; there is much bouncing with deep *plié*; Dan Wagoner, jumping *sur place*, puts in extra beats with one foot, and later produces a telling effect by simply advancing in jumps with legs alternately together and apart; at the end of Taylor's *pas de deux* with Elizabeth Walton he is crouched with her cradled across him, then he very slowly stands up straight.

Scudorama—enigmatic title!—is hard to connect with its programme note by Dante. To the accompaniment of eerie, orgy and railway music by C. Jackson, the dancers crawl about like slugs, sometimes covered in patterned bedspreads, then, rising to their feet, seem to regret having done this. It is rather horrible and rather effective and I thought it was about the bestial side of man, and man trying to rise above it. I liked the bit when Wagoner ate Bettie de Jong while the other girls looked through their legs, holding their ankles.

22.11.64

I guessed as much. Either out of contempt for or fear of the brutish public, directors and choreographers unerringly fail to give their best programme on the opening night. If Paul Taylor, whose Dance Company continues at the Shaftesbury, had put on *Junction* and *3 Epitaphs* with *Aureole* the Thursday before last he would have had a rave notice from me, and, like Robbins and Graham, sold out his season. Uniformly favourable criticisms in the daily papers have failed to fill the house.

Taylor is an *echt, véritable*, genuine, *original* choreographer (like the two mentioned above), and you know how scarce they come. In fact, during *Junction*, automatic-writing my notes in the dark, which I always do, words failed. I fell back on pictograms and invented dicnotation—named after me.

As usual Taylor's programme note is no help at all. The Bach cello solo is just for alienation effect. The costumes by Alex Katz give the clue. They are tights but they break up the body—back blue, front red, stripes and extra colours twisted round the pelvis. And the movements are an utter abolition of all previous dance behaviour. What is the marvellous meaning of these squirmy confrontations, these girls crouched on men's backs or passed like imperial embryos from hand to hand? Who ever saw such curling, tumbling, knitting and interlocking, such a rolling-on of men like coloured balls or such an odd exit for a girl as to be *pushed* off stage?

Junction is men becoming cheese. It also shows men standing erect and being men: there are straight lines sometimes and noble poses. Avoiding talk of imagery and meaning, you could say that Taylor, having conceived these dehumanised gyrations, had to set beside them a standard of normality, a vertical principle, to show how odd they were. In contrast with the writhing uncertainties of Hamlet's mind, good plain Horatio. However you analyse it, *Junction* is new, thrilling, breath-taking and an experience.

3 Epitaphs is an experience, too, both strange and funny. Like certain wines or poems it has two tastes. The music—American folk tunes played off-key by the village band—accompanies odd glimpses of Negro life and skits on loose-limbed Negro movement and dancing. But Thomas

Skelton's lighting (indispensably admirable in all these 'ballets') adds a sad, dreamlike element to the comedy. When the curtain rises two black figures (all five dancers wear black tights and featureless stocking-caps over their heads) stand in a pool of pinky-mauve light against a misty blue sky; and it is like one of Sidney Nolan's mirage pictures of Africa, in which the hallucinatory atmosphere on plain and desert turns trees into men and men into monkeys. We laugh at and are touched by this world of sagging knees, limp wrists and dangling ape-like arms, in which courtship is in the style of the Moor in *Petrushka*.

29.11.64

At the Church Hill, Edinburgh

The most fantastic example of grouping, movement and dramatically focused emotion to be seen in Edinburgh is Elsheimer's *Martyrdom of St. Stephen*, newly acquired by the National Gallery of Scotland. Though only about a foot high this jewel is so organized that in a black-and-white postcard you'd think it a *pendant* to El Greco's vast *St. Maurice and the Theban Legion* in the Escorial—I counted 65 heads. By a curious chance the nude on the right standing on tip-toe and holding above his head the first stone to be thrown at the first martyr looks very like Paul Taylor, and his pose could be Taylor choreography too.

And, my dear, talking of Christianity, the latest thing is you close down churches, turn them into theatres and put on ballets about God in them. The Paul Taylor Dance Company, nine strong, appeared last week with an orchestra, 25 strong, under John Perras, at the newly perverted Church Hill Theatre, which holds 379, though the proscenium opening is too low for a good Martyrdom and impossible for Ascensions, Assumptions and Last Judgments.

Taylor's latest work, *Orbs*, was the main feature of the first programme, and when I say it's about God I mean it is about the sun imparting life and light to other planets; about the Primal Force teaching men and women to generate; about a wedding and banquet at which the clergyman gets drunk; and, since it is divided into four seasons I suppose it is about the life and death of Man, and, perhaps, about the extinction of life on this planet.

Not the least extraordinary element of the ballet, which is lit by flashes of genius, is its music—taken from Beethoven's late Quartets. The introduction and the Venusian Spring are danced to the middle movement of

Opus 127; Martian summer to Opus 133, the Grosse Fuge; Terrestrial Autumn (the comic bit in modern dress) and Plutonian Winter to Opus 130.

If Taylor's grammar of movement is classically based, the classicism is bent and blunted and unsweetened in the interest of communication. Toes are not pointed; hands are carefree; nobody smirks. Then, there are all sort of pats, pokes, sexy quivers, tumbles, tangles, crawls, convulsions, with girls lifted (only apparently) by the head and movements naturalistic and unnatural. For Taylor is that rarest of birds, that Albatross, an original choreographer. He is also the only one of all those innumerable post-Graham, post-Cunningham American choreographers with something to say. He says profound things in a witty, compressed, magical, throw-away and sometimes quite nasty manner, like Auden.

Taylor's sun God is not only Ra: he can be mischievous as Krishna, he is a bit of a voyeur, and like Shiva Nataraja he's a destroyer as well as creator. His cymballing together of the wrists, in fact, comes from Hindu dance. This seeming con-man or professional charmer, with sanctimonious downcast gaze, can thunder, can send his copulating nymphs and satyrs hurtling to hell. Taylor marvellously brings out the mean side of God.

28.8.66

Alwin Nikolais

At Sadler's Wells

If I say that the Dance Theatre of Alwin Nikolais is wonderful I mean that it is full of wonders. Mr. Nikolais writes his own electronic music, designs his costumes and sets, devises his own lighting and, of course, creates his own choreography. He is a very inventive man.

His first programme at Sadler's Wells was one long work called *Imago* with two intervals. In this Mr. Nikolais has imagined the society of another planet whose inhabitants are very different from us, but bear certain resemblances to us all the same. The comedy sometimes comes from their human side.

This society has dignitaries who have no arms because, presumably, they are waited on hand and foot and have the ability to lean on the air at an angle of forty-five degrees. It has amusing little girls who mock their elders. It has men-mantises with an extra joint on their arms ending in a plunger, so that they can walk on all fours without bending double. It has men attached to kites: when the men dance the kites make patterns in the air. It has gliding lamp-shade-ladies and ladies who have an insect stateliness and ladies over whose heads are ceremoniously borne sprigs of giant luminous cape-gooseberries and ladies who can cast shadows a mile high. We are not sure if we are watching germs under a microscope or being initiated into the harmony of the spheres. But we marvel and that is very good for us.

22.6.69

At Sadler's Wells

This year the return of Nikolais to Sadler's Wells, where he will remain for another fortnight, has caused some disappointment. I think I know why.

The first work *Divertissement I* is four glimpses of a new world such as we saw in *Imago*. Five men are encased in tall rectangular 'boxes', whose outlines are suggested by elastic tapes. These rise, fall and slant marvellously. Then three women in wired lampshade dresses glide as if on castors, recline and tilt prettily. Then some stripy people do something. Then the company (which is only fifteen strong but seems like thirty) play games and make patterns with elastic stretching from ceiling to floor: they become incredibly wound up, yet there is method in their madness, for the unwinding is ceremonious and without a hitch.

Echo is notable for its projections. With the dancers on stage, with their shadows or the shadows of other dancers moving on the back screen— which simulates the angle of two walls—and with the static larger projections of motionless figures, we are lost between reality and illusion. It is the acme of surrealism.

In *Tent* we have the David Storey–Lindsay Anderson act,* with such a succession of spotted and stripy projections on tent and people that it is like choosing materials at Liberty's.

Nikolais gluts us with the fantasy of his Frankenstein creatures, gives us too much electronic music and far too many projections: profusion debases his currency. How wonderful if his new worlds could be bent to the service of the fairylands which our choreographers have such trouble in rethinking when they mount new productions of *Nutcracker* and *The Sleeping Beauty*!

4.7.71

If I draw attention to the parts of Alwin Nikolais' programmes which appear to me less good than others it is not through a spirit of perversity born from annoyance that so many people have been enchanted by the American inventor, or through a blind lust to attack, but because I admire so much the fantasy of Nikolais that I want to see his works in as perfect a condition as possible.

Divertissement II, which opened the third programme at Sadler's Wells, illustrates all his strengths and weaknesses, but emphasises the former, as all four numbers are short: the newcomer is amazed by a profusion of novel ideas and nothing goes on for too long.

In *Group Dance* the performers wear cocoons of elastic crêpe material, open down the front and back: their hands are kept inside, so that if they make a gesture they carry the sheath with them. They begin lying down and the first flicker of life is like a stirring of insects or the involuntary signals of an erotic dreamer beneath a sheet. Mood and lighting change as

---

* Reference to Storey's play *The Contractor*, directed by Anderson, in which a tent was erected and struck on stage.

they leap to their feet, face us and become Alexandrian mummies against a bright striped tent. After we have had a glimpse of 'the terrific immobility of Egyptian things', which so enchanted Firbank's Mrs Shamefoot ('particularly in the train'), we are amazed and delighted to see them hopping lightly, sideways, in and out. But then alas, they bow, breaking into a third dimension, and this is wrong. I cannot tell why it is charming for mummies to hop sideways, and wrong for them to bow, but so it is. Finally they expand into rocking lozenges and squares, which is an effective and logical climax.

Trio is for three chessmen-lampshade ladies whose *gamelan* music prepares us for their Siamese gestures and quaint reclinings. The thought here dawns that the Nikolais company, attractive as they are, do not need the high skill of dancers: to be obedient and agile pawns is enough.

I found *Noumenon* quite awe-inspiring. Faced with the three red faceless Judges of Hell, rocking like mindless tetrahedrons on their plinths, we know we are doomed. Except for a momentary tendency near the end for the three figures to conspire with the electronic music and do something out of keeping in order to get a laugh, this was a tremendous invention.

In *Tensile Involvement*, the veering arrow-head, zig-zag, herringbone, chevron patterns woven by the dancers from floor-to-ceiling elastic seem to be pointing the way to an imminent climax of virtuosity or, perhaps, to the birth of some triangular Apollo: but when at last a tall solo dancer takes the centre of the stage he does nothing of interest and soon runs off again.

Total Theatre—OK. But rather less than seldom, I maintain, is Man the Dancer given his chance to shine amid the other halcyon elements which hurtle from the brain of Zeus-Nikolais. So I propose, in the interests of the new Super-Art, a collaboration between Zeus and Dionysian Paul Taylor or Apollonian Robbins. Less profusion of projections I have previously urged. One more constructive plea—a bid for silence. The magic would be enhanced by a respite from Vulcanic sound. And so I back away, finger to lips.

18.7.71

Louis Falco

At Sadler's Wells

Louis Falco is the young American who made *Journal* and *Huescape* for Nederlands Dans Theater and *tutti-frutti* for Rambert. Now it turns out that he has a company all of his own—he must be very rich—and on Tuesday they began a two-week season at Sadler's Wells. Falco has six dancers plus his dynamic self, a group of four musicians headed by Burt Alcantara called Vertical Burn, a groovy artistic adviser called William Katz, a lot of crazy ideas and an expectant audience. What more can a guy want?

When you are trying to do something new (for which you get the Buckle gold medal, anyway) you can't expect to bring it off every time. I will start with the work I liked best, Falco's *The Sleepers*. Mr. Katz's whimsical way of suggesting that the stage is a bed, is to sprinkle it vaguely with crumbs of white polystyrene, I suppose to represent feathers. Very good. Two couples lie sprawled hugger-mugger. Apart from an occasional drift of 'Rock-a-bye, Baby' the only sound is words, and the rather funny words spoken by the dancers promote the action. 'Come over to my side,' says Georgiana Holmes to Matthew Diamond, and in the middle of their strange carnal tangles, she goes on about her childhood in that psycho-American way. As he ties Jennifer Muller in knots, Louis Falco exclaims 'If you did what I told you, I wouldn't need to give you so many orders.'

I am all for doing it with words, but I'm not so keen on doing it with water. Try anything once, I suppose. The apparently ritual immersions in a bath-tub which take place at the beginning of Jennifer Muller's *Tub* are turned to comedy by the stately entry of Matthew Diamond in diving flippers. I felt uncomfortable to see those girls moving and balancing so elegantly in wet dresses and I have a thing about people using other people's towels. I am also against serious works which suddenly decide to send themselves up.

In Falco's *Caviar*, the musicians, playing Robert Cole's rock music, were visible behind a pink-lit gauze and formed a pretty background, but

I couldn't see much point in carrying about a lot of foam-rubber sturgeon, and the pop-style solos and duets did not hold my attention. I haven't yet said what a fine dancer the rich Mr. Falco is.

18.11.73

Everybody seemed to enjoy the second programme of Louis Falco's Dance Company, which was perhaps more light-hearted than the first. It began, though, with a serious piece, *Huescape*, a triangular dance of passion and conflict, splendidly performed by Falco, Jennifer Muller and Juan Antonio. Here Falco demonstrates his unmistakable gifts as a choreographer in a free style of his own.

Twopenny Portrait is a sad-funny duet for two melancholy urban lovers, danced by Georgiana Holmes and the tireless Falco. What struck me chiefly about it was the setting by William Katz. Who would have thought that six or eight ribbed metal dustbins on an empty stage could be transformed by gentle coloured lighting into magic and monumental objects—a kind of slummy Stonehenge for lost souls to wander in?

Jennifer Muller's *Nostalgia* panders to our passion for the Golden Voices of the Thirties. Three girls in modern rags and clogs react ecstatically to the songs of Mae West, Bessie Smith and Billie Holliday, and the audience reacts with them. I thought, however, that the sentimental end was out of key. I do see it was a problem how to terminate these improvisations other than for all three girls to exit kicking, but when Jennifer Muller tore off her flowered chiffon and gazed at it tragically—as much as to say 'All our dreams are but dust and ashes'—it did strike me as all wrong.

Falco's *Soap Opera* is funny and original. Burt Alcantara and his Vertical Burn are ticking over in the background, there is a subdued tape of the dancers' voices, and against this the dancers all speak out loud. The six are dressed alike in flame-coloured pyjamas and each impersonates a character—Mum, Dad, Young Man, Girl, Doggie and Pussy. Their banal exchanges—text by Gary Lasdun—are uproarious, but with Falco surrealism is always round the corner, as well as wit: and when, towards the end, some of the dancers rebel and try to change their roles it gives the game a new twist. I don't know why it should be so funny for Matthew Diamond to say sullenly, staring at the audience, 'I'm Louis', when we see Louis quite plainly carrying on at the other side of the stage, but it is.

Now we want to see how Falco can combine words and dancing in a dramatic—as opposed to a comic—way. On this first visit he has made friends and influenced people.

24.11.73

Twyla Tharp

At the Roundhouse

Absurdly heralded by the critic of the *New Yorker* as 'the Nijinska of our time,' Twyla Tharp has brought her company of five girls and two boys to the Roundhouse for a fortnight. One of the boys, Kenneth Rinker, has personality and talent. The three principal girls, whom I think of as the Typist, the Wardress and the Show-off, make up in persistence for what they lack in charm.

In certain numbers such as *The Fugue* in the first programme, and *The One Hundreds* in the second, I had the feeling that the girls were actually trying to be repulsive—or by taxing our nerves and patience to the utmost to batter us into submission. Neither piece has music. The former is an endless exercise in stamping for three. In the latter two girls perform in unison a series of quite difficult stunts, pausing to sweat and stare antagonistically at us in between, and a crowd of strangers are brought on, I cannot think why, to take a curtain-call at the end.

The jazz-type dancing of *Eight Jelly Rolls* is far preferable, but no commercial management would allow artists the self-indulgence of going on and on with this limited form of movement as these dancers do.

Talking of self-indulgence, a string quartet is hired solely to play a Haydn slow movement for Part Two of *Bix Dances*, while a woman reads extracts from Miss Tharp's autobiography into a mike; Parts One and Three being danced to old popular songs and 'Abide with me' on tape.

I think that Twyla Tharp's originality consists in making her troupe repeat nightly movements which appear to be improvised.

19.5.74

Dance Theatre of Harlem

At Sadler's Wells

It is common knowledge that, of God's four archangels, Michael, Gabriel, Raphael and Arthurmitchell, one at least is black. But Arthur has said in an interview that he does not wish his company to be judged as black dancers. O.K., O.K.

On Monday the all-white Dance Theatre of Harlem opened at Sadler's Wells to resounding applause; and after their second programme on Thursday the applause was even resoundinger. As if to insist that they are primarily a classical company, the first ballet they gave was the celebrated arrangement to Bach's Concerto in D minor for two violins, called *Concerto Barocco*, by the Black Russian, George Balanchine. This was followed by that miracle of our time, the Stravinsky-Balanchine *Agon*, in which, in 1957, Arthurmitchell himself created so unforgettably the principal role. How do these dancers perform these classics, which we have been used to seeing performed—Arthur excepted—by dancers of another colour? It is extremely interesting to observe. They dance well; they are applauded; and they smile with pleasure.

Now this may be splendid in the interests of general happiness and international goodwill, but it throws the classical works of Balanchine off-balance. If *Agon* is about anything it is about being cool: it is a contest in skill, based on ancient court dances, the most aristocratic ballet ever made by the coolest of all choreographers. If the performers give so much as a sign that they know they are being watched it is wrong.

The company's lack of cool is a temporary state of affairs—just as this is a temporary criticism, like all criticisms: for we are all going to get blacker, whiter, browner, yellower in the years to come. And Arthur's dancers are going to become more finished and perfect, his 'ethnic' ballets like Geoffrey Holder's *Dougla* less Broadwayish, his ovations more merited.

15.8.74

The Changing Scene
(1959–1960)

F

Jean Babilée in *Le Jeune Homme et la Mort*. Drawing by Leonard Rosoman

Babilée

I well remember the spring evening in 1946 when the Ballets des Champs-Elysées first came to the Adelphi, and when Babilée, dressed as a joker, first rocketed into our ken, sneering and looking down his nose. Stultified by war and stuck on Sadler's Wells, most critics then looked askance at the halcyon Parisian décors, at the novel choreography of Petit and at the moody, modern twist which Jean Babilée gave to classical dancing. Most critics, but not Cyril Beaumont, whose jealous guardianship of ballet's traditions never prevented him from keeping open a calm, honest and appraising eye for all that was good and new. He was a supporter of the young French dancers from the word go.

Long before the beatniks and angries it was from Paris and the left-bank troglodytes whom we called 'existentialists'—without knowing what it meant—that the first sign came to warn us of an anarchistic young generation which had taken over the world. Looking back I now realize that Babilée's was the first of these new faces we ever saw.

His magic rodent mug is unchanged, he still does the same tricks, and still looks down his nose; but he now has his own company, Les Ballets Babilée, who were dancing last week at the Empire Theatre, Edinburgh.

30.8.59

Chita Rivera

A week ago Chita Rivera came out of the cast of *West Side Story* after giving for nine months in her 'America' number the most electric performance in London.

I cannot tell whether she made the role of Anita the vivid thing it was, or whether the role made her: one can only aver that 'America', with its words by Stephen Sondheim, its music by Leonard Bernstein, its dance by Jerome Robbins and Peter Gennaro—and with Chita Rivera—was fast, funny and furious, and that the way she put over her lines of repartee between the convolutions of the dance was nothing short of breathtaking.

We have seen high-speed sambas, mambos and cha-chas before, and a number of attractive dark beauties have shaken their bodies and skirts at us; but no one has ever had the pace of Chita or her puma spine of flexible steel to write swift S's in the air. Odd to think that this spinning, incandescent creature, with her flashing cyclamen skirt, was evolved in the brain of Robbins from that most lumbering of *confidantes*, Juliet's nurse.

11.10.59

Gala

Tuesday, March 1. Day of the Gala performance at Covent Garden. Read in the paper that Tony Armstrong-Jones is to make his first public appearance at the Gala,* and that thousands of pounds have been turned away at the box-office. On these occasions critics only get one seat each, so one can't plan an evening out.

Sudden awful thought—I suppose we wear white ties. Ring Bill Beresford at the Opera House, who says yes we do—*and* decorations. Clean my paltry war medals. Try on coat. Mrs. T. (my cleaner) says 'What a difference! You look quite a gentleman in tails.'

Letter from my mother, saying 'I expect you will be at the Gala—what fun,' but I don't really see where the fun is—in fact I think I look a fool dressing up to walk across the market and go to the theatre by myself, then walk back, cook sausages and eat alone in the kitchen.

Go out to buy sausages. See interesting pictures through the window of Zwemmer's Gallery. Find it is a show of George Chapman, just hung: get very excited and buy a picture. Buy sausages. Dress. Have a drink.

* On his engagement to H.R.H. Princess Margaret.

Walk across Covent Garden to the Opera House. Crowds waiting all up Bow Street. Feel rather an ass running the gauntlet. Frightfully impressed by the appearance of Serjeant Martin in sky blue and gold livery, knee breeches and white silk stockings. Meet Bill Beresford in the foyer, who says it isn't decorations after all. Put medals in pocket. Find I am sitting next to Cyril Beaumont.

Very well placed for seeing the Queen Mother, Princess Margaret and T.A.-J. Wonder if tiaras give one a headache. Decide that if I were as good a photographer as T.A.-J. [who had been told he had to give up working as a photographer] I should go on publishing books of pictures under a different name.

Folk dances by nice-looking students of the Royal Ballet School. Cyril Beaumont says folk dances should be done for enjoyment of participants not spectators. Can't help enjoying them all the same.

Merle Park quite at ease doing *La Fille mal gardée* for the first time. Blair is as stunning as usual, and Holden's clog dance goes over big.

Meet Nina and Gordon L. in the bar, who ask me out to supper with them and Sol Hurok. Accept with alacrity.

Programme concludes with *divertissements* ... Linden and Blair in the showy Minkus *Don Quixote pas de deux* a great success—Linden obviously

Nathalie Philippart in *Le Jeune Homme et la Mort.*
Drawing by Leonard Rosoman

able to out-Toumanova Toumanova. Fonteyn and Somes in Ashton's effective *Raymonda* scene to Glazounov's ultra-Palm-Court music, with the solo violin making swoony *vox humana* noises, and Margot melting about the stage in a marvellous *art nouveau* way.

Supper at the Caprice—I say! Dame Ninette looking regal at the next table. Reflect that if I married her I should presumably have to give up being a ballet critic.

Wednesday, March 2. Sausages for breakfast.

6.3.60

Ramayana

Usually, when we go to watch Indian dancing, we expect to see men impersonating gods and heroes, but with *Ramayana*, which the Little Ballet Troupe, Bombay, brought to the Empire, Edinburgh, we were surprised to see men impersonating *puppets* impersonating gods and heroes.

This seems quite mad. Even if we subscribe to the curious theory put forward by Kleist that puppets are capable of feats of agility and expression out of range to mere humans—which could equally be argued about the nimble homunculi of the film cartoon—there seems no point in a mere human imitating a creature whose range of movement and breadth of mime he cannot excel. In imitating the superficial awkwardness of puppets, their stiff, jerky gestures, men are obliged to resign their natural grace without gaining any of the puppet's inhuman resilience. What is the point?

In *Ramayana* the Indian dancers hide their handsome features behind masks. Their legs and feet are encased in soft, shapeless boots and the superb stance of Kathakali, with its deep *plié* and the body supported on the outer edges of the feet, is abandoned for a wooden strut half-way between that of the Blackamoor in *Petrushka* and the Castles in *Checkmate*. Their hands, being encased in fingerless mittens, are incapable of the divine language of *mudras*. But *Ramayana* is an enormous success.

The whole thing comes off. We are absorbed by the story of Sita's abduction and rescue. Though we begin by laughing at these funny dead-pan mannikins, by the time Sita has been reunited with Rama we have experienced wonder at man's heroic endeavour and respect for the solemnity of love. I cannot tell why the late Shanti Bardhan's ballet is so moving, any more than I can guess what inspired him to turn his dancers into puppets.

Perhaps *Petrushka* prompted Mr. Bardhan to give an extra dimension to his work by making it a play within a play. We have a fairground, a crowd and a puppet theatre. The two comic puppet-masters act as barkers, as prologue, scene-shifters, and commentators on the epic drama which the puppets perform. Their subdued clowning is delightful. After some *contretemps* they will come in, hand laid to cheek, with a woebegone expression which seems to say 'This is a nice carry-on! What have we started?'

So with their aid the story is acted out. Rama battles and is made love to by a wicked queen, whose nose his brother cuts off. A vendetta ensues; Sita is abducted by Ravana from her sylvan hideout; she drops a jewel which leads to her tracing by Hanuman the monkey king and her rescue by the splendid blue-faced Rama.

The music of Bahadur Hussain Khan is not the least delightful part of this extraordinary entertainment.

11.9.60

Musicals

I used to think the musical—or the musical comedy, as we called it between the wars—was the lowest form of theatrical art: now I am coming round. Something, it seems, can really be done with the medium. There are signs.

Less than a decade ago we watched with the utmost complacency on the stage of Drury Lane a King of Siam singing 'This'll make you whistle', or some such rubbish, on his death-bed. That couldn't happen any more. The musical of today has got to connect with real life.

The two best musicals running in New York are based on the lives of famous contemporaries. *Fiorello* is about Mayor LaGuardia, and *Gypsy* is about Gypsy Rose Lee.

Besides having an arresting, credible story and a heart-warming gnome-like hero in the little man who fought Tammany and cleaned up New York (perfectly portrayed by Tom Bosley), *Fiorello* has a high percentage of hit numbers. In *Politics and Poker* Howard Da Silva and his group of opposition 'politicians' lament their fate of perpetually having to put up a candidate to be defeated by Tammany; in *The Bum Won* they comment incredulously on LaGuardia's victory; and in *Little Tin Box* they parody the trial of the corrupt State officials.

Composer Jerry Bock, who shares the honours with lyric-writer

Sheldon Harnick for these very funny numbers, has written a pastiche hesitation waltz of the First World War period called *Till Tomorrow*, which is the prettiest tune since *My Fair Lady*. The drifting high-waisted dresses of 1917 are pretty, too, and nothing could be prettier than Peter Gennaro's gentle arrangement of the dance. What makes all this prettiness acceptable is that the farewell party for Fiorello going off to war takes place in a dingy back yard.

> *You can pull all the stops out*
> *Till they call the cops out,*
> *Grind your behind till you're banned,*
> *But you've gotta getta gimmick*
> *If you wanna getta hand.*

So sings one of the strippers in *Gypsy*, who does it playing a trumpet. And you must either be very clever, or fall back on the old dream-sequence, or else have a good gimmick, to work some dancing into a realistic musical.

The scene I liked best in *Gypsy* (a show which contains Ethel Merman, some imaginative effects by Jo Mielziner and some inspired direction by Jerome Robbins) is one in which a young man demonstrates to an enraptured small girl in a stage alley the tap routine and night club act with which he hopes to conquer the town.

Impossible to describe why Paul Wallace is so touching in this number invented by Robbins, 'All I Need is the Girl'. 'I start easy—now I'm more debonair—ssh!—*Break!*—Then I sell it. *She* appears all in white. I take her hand, kiss it and lead her on the floor. This step is good for the costume. Now we waltz—strings come in—and I lift her—again—*once more*. And now the tempo changes—now the lights come up—give me your hand—again—again——'

I don't know if it's the idea, or Jule Styne's tune, or the dance, or the fellow, or the breathless, excited whisper in which he says the words '*Once more*' . . . .

24.1.60

Edinburgh

I was nearly burnt as a witch a few years ago when I suggested that tax should be levied on profits made during the Festival by Edinburgh traders and lodging-house keepers, and a new Opera House built with the proceeds. Now that it looks as if Edinburgh really is, somehow or other, to have a new theatre for opera and ballet,* the dance enthusiasts can regard the obsolescent Empire, with its shallow stage and inadequate lighting, almost in a mood of Betjemanic nostalgia.

The Proustian sensation of going back, or re-living the past, which assails us, year by year, as we emerge from Waverley station into Britain's most beautiful city, was intensified for me last week by the accident that a programme of dance films began with an all too short one of the last movement of Jerome Robbins's *U.S. Export; Op. Jazz*, the thrilling ballet we saw at the Empire only last year.

28.8.60

India

One need not have made in the flesh a passage to India to be aware that a certain mystery—not to say muddle—surrounds performances of dancing in that land. Nurtured on the travellers' tales of Mr. J. Ackerley, Mr. E. M. Forster and Miss Beryl de Zoete, one knows that festivals long awaited may take place unexpectedly, or may be postponed indefinitely for obscure reasons, or, just when one has given up hope of seeing them, may be rumoured to be starting in the next village but two. Then, the dancing may go on for days and nights without anything much seeming to happen, till suddenly—Flash! God is present. In fact, one is prepared for all contingencies.

When, therefore, a runner brought word that Markova was about to appear with Ram Gopal I showed no surprise. Had not Pavlova been instrumental in furthering the renascence of Indian dancing in this century? 'We were fortunate enough to find in London a young and educated Hindu who had studied dancing in his own land,' wrote Dandré in his fatuous life of the Russian ballerina, not naming Uday Shankar, who danced with her in *Oriental Impressions*.

It was next reported to me that Markova had appeared at a Press conference seated in the lotus posture, and that Ram Gopal had said she was the greatest living *female* exponent of the Indian dance. This may not have been true, but what is truth? as Dr. Godbole probably said just before the court assembled in Mr. Forster's Chandrapore. The Press party, according to the invitation, was held, or was to be held, or may be said to have been held, at the *Princess* Theatre, *Shartesbury* Avenue. I began to

* It was never built.

get into the mood (or *rasa*) of *adbhuta* (or wonderment), and left for Wiltshire.

On the road from Wilton to Salisbury on Monday morning I saw a blackbird with a white head; then, soon after my return to London, I saw Cliff Richard outside a shoe-shop in Wardour Street—and fainted dead away. So naturally, on discovering my stalls at the Prince's were B1 and B2, notoriously bad for visibility and exposed to draughts, particularly during the monsoon, I veered off in a southerly direction to observe the black arts of Marie Bell. Arriving at the Prince's twenty-four hours later, I found the performance was still going on, and settled down to study my programme notes.

Now, programme notes can serve at least three purposes: to impart information, to list one's achievements, and to let off fiendish cracks against one's rivals. When I found Ram Gopal writing with reference to the 'all-male Kathakali dance-drama of Malabar' that 'some females have even gone so far as to become male impersonators of this most masculine and virile of Indian dances,' meaning Shanta Rao, I remembered Shanta complaining that Ram danced Bharata Natya, which she thought should be an all-female affair. But although the Bharata Natya dance of dedicated temple servants (or divine prostitutes) degenerated into sexy numbers by Nautch girls, it seems that at times the performers have been men—dressed, if necessary, as women. 'Lovely India!', as Queen Mary used to say.

The performance, though it had rather an air of improvization, contained moments of delight; but I must put off discussing it till next Sunday, leaving you, I fear, in a mood (or *rasa*) of *vibhasa* (or disgust).

13.3.60

RUSSIA

Leonardo wrote in his notebook that it is the extremities which lend grace to the body; and invented the early English school of ballet. Michelangelo, who had seen the newly unearthed Belvedere Torso, went one further, twisted the whole body into a shape more expressive of the soul; and invented the Russian school.

Sunday Times, 28.5.72

The Bolshoi Ballet

At Covent Garden

After the first act we were all very excited and went around saying: 'Well, wasn't that something?' or 'This is the genuine thing,' or just 'I say!' Only English Opera Groupers assembled at the smart end of the bar (the end nearest to Aldeburgh) sounded a discordant note—excuse my metaphor—in reminding us how commonplace the music of Asafiev was. It was, too—it sounded as if it were written in the 1880s by someone who got around very little even then. But the action and dancing had been so surging that I had hardly noticed this.

The scene of the first act of *The Fountain of Bakhchisarai* is laid in the garden of a Polish country house, at night. A party is in progress and the illuminated lattice windows of the house shine through the trees. Maria and Waclaw make love in the garden. Candelabra are carried out, and the guests, in national costume, dance the Polonaise, Mazurka and Cracovienne. The lovers do a romantic *pas de deux*. Then a wounded nobleman staggers in. The castle is surrounded by the Tartar hordes of Khan Girei. These soon invade the stage, and a scene of slaughter takes place. The house is burnt. Waclaw is slain and Maria becomes the Khan's prisoner.

This act gave the Russians a chance to show some of their best qualities. The Polish character dances were done with a dignity and attack which were invigorating. Struchkova was much better as Maria than she had been as Juliet. She looked lovely and danced like a dream. Her partner, Yuri Kondratov, a strong little man, was a fine dancer too. Their *pas de deux* had some exciting moments and culminated in his holding her with one arm fully outstretched above his head. The infiltration of lithe and evil Tartars was most alarming. The battle raged magnificently. The house burned well. Alexander Lapauri, as the Khan, appearing just before the curtain fell to claim the captive Maria, made a powerful impression of virility and barbaric might. We did not realize the ballet was over.

I happened to be sitting next to Danilova and Frederic Franklin. The ballerina agreed with me that Struchkova was a lovely dancer, but said that, in common with others of the Bolshoi company, she lacked that distinction of style which came from giving every movement its full value. I said I thought the modern Russians, fearful of formalism, which they called decadent, had perhaps deliberately evolved this new 'natural' style which blurred the choreographic outline, and made for a greater emotional impact. Danilova said she thought they had simply lost the true style of classical ballet. She added that these were, of course, Moscow dancers; she herself had come from Leningrad.

Pushkin's poem about *The Fountain of Bakhchisarai* may be perfect, but as a subject for ballet it presents difficulties. Waclaw can no longer go on being the hero after his death in Act I, so Khan Girei becomes the hero. (Actually he is the main point of the poem—an animal being regenerated by love.) Maria goes on being the heroine, but she will have nothing to do with Girei, and dies unkissed. The two threads of the story, therefore, are never knotted. Maria mourns her way to a virgin grave. Girei, unrequited, lives on and mourns by the fountain, which is Maria's monument. The libretto is unsatisfactory; the music is insipid; the dancing is incidental.

Act II is a milk-and-water *Scheherazade* number. Quite a cheerful set, as harems go, with the usual lazy good-for-nothing women, a dangerous-looking favourite wife and some waddling eunuchs. Girei returns with his trophies, including Maria. But she, clasping her lute, scorns the murderer of Waclaw. He is in despair: love has got him badly. Zarema, the former favourite, tries to divert his attention with an erotic dance. This is a psychological mistake. The Khan is suddenly overwhelmed with boredom at his genteelly shimmying women and the music of B. Asafiev. And so are we.

At this point the intervals grow longer than the acts.

The scene of Act III is Maria's bedroom: it is blue tiled, and the walls are decorated with texts from the Koran, which Maria cannot read. Maria plays her lute, the Khan comes in and makes love to her; she rejects him. A maid comes in and goes to sleep on the floor. Zarema comes in and makes a scene: she murders Maria. The Khan, who has come back in time to witness this, desists from knifing Zarema, as he thinks she will like it, coming from him. All that can be said about this act is that Struchkova died beautifully, clinging and falling round a column. Lapauri's miming as Girei is powerful enough almost to make one forget the unsatisfactory nature of the scenario.

Nothing really happens in Act IV in the way of action, except for Zarema being pushed over the battlements. Nobody misses her. Khan Girei sits on his throne, bored and miserable, and that is all. The act

contains, however, some warrior dances, which the choreographer
Zakharov has arranged after the style of Fokine's *Prince Igor*, though they
are not nearly so varied and thrilling. These are done with frenzy by
I. Peregudov and the wonderful Russian *corps de ballet*, who would undoubtedly have been even more wonderful on a bigger stage, such as
they are used to at home. Alas! these dances seem irrelevant dramatically
—their only point being that the Khan should look bored through them.
And the fact that he looked bored had a depressing effect on us.

There is a simple epilogue in which Girei leans mourning beside the
Fountain of Bakhchisarai, and the spirit of Maria appears to him. This is
somewhat of an anti-climax.

I do not think Diaghilev would ever have countenanced so ineffectual
a collaboration between librettist, composer and choreographer as resulted
in *The Fountain of Bakhchisarai*. The company still seems glorious, but one
would like to give their artistic directors a shake.

Giselle was the first ballet I ever saw, and I have always had a passion
for it. And since that fateful matinée at Sadler's Wells in 1936 (near a
century after the ballet's original production in Paris), when I fell victim
to the elfin Markova—how many dancers have I seen in the great role!
Danilova, Toumanova, Slavenska, Darsonval, Chauviré, Kaye, High-
tower, Schanne, Fonteyn, Grey, Shearer, Gilmour, Goldwyn! I was born
too late to have been taken to see Pavlova and Spessivtzeva, who were
probably supreme, but for me Alicia Markova has always had a special
quality which sets her apart. Now I have seen Galina Ulanova I can say
that she, too, in quite a different way, is amazing and wonderful.

From the very beginning we saw that the Bolshoi Ballet's was going to
be a superb production of *Giselle*; at the end I for one was sure it was the
finest, taken as a whole, that I had seen.

The brisk beat of the admirable Yuri Faier (who I see has become a
great favourite with Covent Garden audiences), the sunny autumn
scenery of B. Volkov—surely better lit than that for our own *Giselle*—the
entry of the elegant and admirable Fadeyechev, holding his cloak over his
face, the natural acting of Erik Volodin as his Esquire, the handsome
Hilarion of Lapauri—no longer a stagey villain, but a rough and sympathetic young forester who would clearly make Giselle an excellent
husband—these had all impressed us favourably within a minute of the
curtain's rising.

But everything about this first act was enchanting. . . .

One of Ulanova's most extraordinary gifts is her faculty for showing
on her face the play of different emotions. Her features like a landscape

are shadowed by the passing clouds of thought. Sometimes her acting is so subtle, so cinematic, one might say, that I wondered if the finer shades of expression were legible in the gallery. Because of this faculty of hers, Ulanova's Giselle is more a portrait in the round than any other interpretation by any other ballerina I have seen.

I have never, I think, seen another dancer dare to risk giving at certain moments, a peasant gawkiness to Giselle's behaviour. I forget just when, but twice I saw Ulanova tuck in her chin and wag her head, grinning with the uneasy heartiness of a land-girl laughing off a compliment. As in Juliet, though, she paints all the shyness, doubts and delicate hesitations of first love. At times she conveys rapture. Her dancing is exquisite: her feet are as precise as pens, yet as light as feathers. There is a delicious exhilaration in her *petits battements*, and her *pas ballonnés* are like a draft of mountain air. Is it her lightness that has made people put her in a special class with Pavlova and Spessivtzeva?

In the 'mad scene' the sensitive sweep and lulls of the orchestra, the frantic rushes and sudden silences with which Ulanova suggests the breaking heart of Giselle, the active sympathy of the crowd and the noble desperation of Fadeyechev's transports as Albrecht combine to make a great work of theatrical art. If I have one criticism of Lavrovsky's loving revival it is that I should like Giselle's final fall to the ground to be more sensational.

In the second act Rimma Karelskaya made a fine Queen of the Wilis, but somewhat underplayed the sinister, cruel aspect of the character. The *corps de ballet* were impeccable, and once received a spontaneous round of applause in the *middle* of a movement—something I never remember happening before. This was when the lines of white-clad Wilis cross in and out of each other, hopping in *arabesque*. Their extended back legs, never wavering, remained marvellously extended throughout.

In his dance of exhaustion Nicolai Fadeyechev showed himself more than ever to be an artist of the first class. His carriage, his line, his perfect double turns in the air, his slow *pirouettes* and his proud, unhurried back *cabrioles* were a joy to see.

Ulanova, dancing divinely, enacted the spirit of Giselle, for the most part with downcast eyes, allowing eventually no other expression than one of godlike compassion to shine from her pale, sculptured face.

The Russian version has a few extra bars of music at the end to give Albrecht more time to register despair at losing his beloved once more. Fadeyechev, standing alone in the middle of the stage, facing the audience, made the most of this moment of tragic realization.

I returned two days later to see Struchkova as Giselle. I thought she was very fine indeed. Her lovely heart-shaped Russian face, with dome-like eyelids reminiscent of Danilova, is beautifully expressive. She dances with the big, free movements, the amazing extensions and the carefree splendour of movement which we have come to love in the Russians. Her 'mad scene' was most moving. . . .

It is time, however, that a breath of fresh air was let into the Soviet hot-house. The artistic direction of the company seems to live in ignorance of all the revolutions in art which have taken place in our century, many of which were initiated or publicised by Diaghilev. The directors, choreographers and *régisseurs* of the Bolshoi Theatre should take a sabbatical year off and see the world.

Dance and Dancers, December, 1956

At Covent Garden

I thought Diaghilev had proved a false prophet when I read in his memoirs the pronouncement that 'Tchaikovsky would never be understood in Europe' (his habitual way of describing Western Europe), but I now see he may have been righter than I believed possible. For although in the last twenty years Tchaikovsky has been more plugged in this country than any other composer, it does strike us when we hear the Covent Garden Orchestra playing *Swan Lake* under Algis Zhuraytis that we are hearing the music for the first time.

It was *Swan Lake* with which the Bolshoi Ballet opened their welcome second season at the Royal Opera House on Monday; and their conductor's changes of speed and sonority took us by surprise, brought the score to shimmering life and were largely responsible for the extraordinarily subtle impression made by Act I.

This of course was Gorsky's version (one of them)—or most of it was. His rebellion against the Petipa tradition is mainly evident in the abolition of symmetry, in the close interweaving of dance and story (as in modern musicals) and in the rejection of the old sign language in favour of a more realistic behaviour.

We lose Benno, the Prince's friend, and gain a jester. Rothbart has much more dancing to do in Acts II and IV and we consequently accept him as being younger and perhaps even the lover of Odette (as it were the Baron in *La Dame aux Camélias*). These changes are one reason for the

G

diminution of the Prince's importance—it is as if in *Romeo and Juliet* Shakespeare had cut Mercutio, Romeo's friend, and built up the character of Paris, his rival. Another reason, of course, is that Plisetskaya is dancing Odette.

I think it a pity that the Prince should no longer be the protagonist of his own fairy tale, and the device of his final vanquishing of Rothbart by tearing off a wing is rather childish. But there can be no doubt that Act I is now full of interest and atmosphere, a kind of autumn dream behind a veil.

There was a ravishing *pas de trois* in Act I danced by Samokhvalova, Karelskaya and Nikonov. I was at once struck by the girls' glorious arched backs and feet. The man rose in the air like a lark, performing feathery *entrechats*, the smoothest turns, the gentlest *cabrioles*. The fair girl had a lovely ease and speed in her darting *bourrée*.

In Act II I noticed, as I did in 1956, how the fine *corps de ballet*, picked artists, seemed to be allowed more individuality of timing and expression and were less regimented than ours. But Act II is Maya Plisetskaya.

She is one of the most astounding dancers I have seen, and perhaps the strongest. Firmly based on steely perfect legs and feet, her body arches into incredible *arabesques*. She does everything more than other ballerinas: jumps higher, opens her legs wider, kicks higher, turns quicker, bends more double and flings her arms into more exaggerated gestures. She has not Fonteyn's poetry or Ulanova's warmth: her long handsome face burns with a cold fire.

Nothing is more wonderful in classical dancing than the line which can result from sensitive, controlled, relaxed yet correctly placed arms, coming from a strong but flexible body established on strong and elegant legs. But the gods have been so prodigal in their gifts to this dancer that she seems drunk with power and too ready to abuse it.

Having discovered she has the Oriental knack of undulating her arms like serpents, Plisetskaya does this to excess. When this snake-charming act, which has nothing to do with classical ballet or with being like a swan—for swans don't ripple either with their necks, wings or feet—is carried on to such an extent that she can't even stop doing it during curtain calls, it becomes ludicrous and I begin to giggle.

Ivanov is not credited with the Act II *pas de deux*, which is mostly his, though Act IV is given to Messerer. I think Plisetskaya deserves some mention, too, for the serpentine innovations. Our old friend Nicolai Fadeyechev, grown heavier and somehow humbler, fades into his ballerina's background.

In Act III Plisetskaya as Odile showed furious precision, aplomb and bravura, broke speed records in her *diagonale* and made the stage seem too small for her *manège*. There were enchanting character dances, of which the Spanish was particularly applauded. And I liked the way Elena Vanka, the Princess Mother, knew at once there was something fishy about the unexpected guests, recognizing them as only minor Royalty, probably Balkan.

I am sure the designers of *Swan Lake* and *The Little Hump-backed Horse*, which followed it on Thursday, had no trouble at all with Mr. Khrushchev: to us their sets and dresses seem extremely provincial.

The Little Hump-backed Horse is a version made by Alexander Radunsky in 1960 of the old ballet based on an older folk tale; and it has functional music by Rodion Shchedrin with echoes of Prokofiev, and a few pretty tunes, one of which I thought, when I heard it at the Albert Hall three summers ago, sounded American folk (early Copland) style, and still do.

The story of a magic pony making everything possible for a hero who is browbeaten by two bullying brothers, of a fat, foolish King and a beautiful Tsarevna, reminds us of *The Firebird, Cinderella* and *Coq d'or*, but the hero being a simple peasant, who mocks the King and makes the Tsarevna, is a modern touch. Besides supernatural elements the ballet has a lot of comedy, that is to say that the characters never stop falling down, which I never think funny. Even the delightful hero in his shabby smock, Vladimir Vasiliev, has to try to win our additional sympathy by finishing one of his capering, exultant Russian dances on his backside.

But the classical dancers don't fall down, of course, and that means Plisetskaya as the Tsarevna, and Ekaterina Maximova, Mikhail Lavrovsky and Shamil Yagudin as denizens of the underwater kingdom. The last three perform a thrilling adagio act; the boys leap and corkscrew and fall like magic missiles and support the exquisite Maximova in some fantastic lifts.

Her role itself, or her casting for it, is perhaps to blame for an un- attractive coyness sometimes shown by Plisetskaya; but she executed superb *fouettés*, both on one spot and turning round the stage (these gave the King hiccups), displayed her line in noble *promenades en attitude*, and did a charming little Russian character dance at the end, just before Vasiliev's final soaring solo.

First impressions are of an incomparable company which I long to see in handsomer productions, of an incomparable ballerina whose manner and mannerisms tend to tarnish her greatness.

7.7.63

At Covent Garden

I suppose Shakespeare, Cervantes and Ibsen might be rather surprised to know that their *Romeo and Juliet*, *Don Quixote* and *Peer Gynt* were running concurrently in London as wordless ballets.

Romeo and Juliet is the high-spot of the Bolshoi season so far. Leonid Lavrovsky and Sergei Prokofiev were clearly fired with a single flame when they worked the ballet out: it was conceived with passion and grew up to embody many of the noble qualities of its famous ancestor. The ballet has something of the meteoric quality of the play. As Caroline Spurgeon pointed out in her great book *Shakespeare's Imagery*, 'The lovers meet on Sunday, are wedded on Monday, part at dawn on Tuesday and are reunited in death on the night of Thursday.' Their brief love flashes like a comet across the dark sky of a wicked world. (Indeed Renaissance Italy must have been bloody in both senses: reading its history, I hate those warring, pride-drunk princes and honour Lorenzo dei Medici above all for his determination to be reasonable, pacific and middle-class.)

This page would be too small a space to list all the virtues of the production and all the individual triumphs of the performers. It is extraordinary how the whole big company lives the drama and makes it live for us.

The opening brawl builds up excitingly and is impressively stilled by the almost sacred authority of Igor Seleznev's Prince. Then we meet the adorable Raissa Struchkova as Juliet, throwing cushions at her jolly nurse, Valentina Peshcherikova, in the bedroom. The invention of two characters called Juliet's Friend and Troubadour allow Maya Samokhvalova and the gloriously leaping Vladimir Nikonov to open the ball. But the most fascinating part of the ball is the cushion dance for the older guests, the men in heavy gowns, the women in trailing skirts. They slowly advance, pause to execute a simple heel-toe step, kneel, kiss— nothing much, but it is all done to Prokofiev's majestic tune with such an immensity of stately reticence. Juliet is hopping about merrily, listening to the lute players when Romeo sees her.

Maris Liepa is the tall, romantic Romeo, and in the garden scene (no balcony) he performs turns in the air ending in a fall on one knee with the head and arms flung backwards in such a glory of abandonment that we think: This is Romeo. Struchkova, lifted high in the air, swung round, fearfully approaching her lover, caressing his face, sighing, stretching out her arms in ecstasy, is the embodiment of young love, absolute Juliet.

The marriage in the cell is very simply and movingly arranged. Mercutio's fight with taunting Tybalt is vividly done by Yaroslav Sekh and Vladimir Levashev: Romeo's with Tybalt is dazzling and quite different. In this big crowd scene, rippling with life and movement, every performer seemed to be an artist and to contribute blood and breath. The mourning of the Capulets over Tybalt is epic, monumental. Capulet's oath of revenge, as sworn by Alexander Lapauri, strikes terror; and Elena Vanke's Lady Capulet, borne aloft on the bier, is a fury—Siddons and Bernhardt. Brass; breast-beating; slow marching; and a waving of huge swords. Curtain.

Struchkova-Juliet's lonely decision to dare to take the potion and Liepa-Romeo's tragic solo in Mantua, rolling on the ground and embracing the air, were two more superb moments of a great production. If I have any complaint—apart from Williams's old-fashioned décor, which is anyway more genuinely gorgeous than that for *Cinderella*, and the inclusion of *five* jesters (who capered admirably)—it is of the absence of the peacemaking Prince from the tombside tableau. Prokofiev's magnificent score, so much superior to his *Cinderella*, was splendidly played by the Covent Garden Orchestra under Gennadi Rozhdestvensky.

21.7.63

At Covent Garden

Paganini and *Lieutenant Kije* are two new short Soviet ballets, which makes it possible for us to discuss them just as if they were two new ballets by Ashton or Morrice. Making, meanwhile, a mental note that the 'one-act' ballet of atmosphere, local colour, drama, satire, etc., which Diaghilev, Fokine and Benois invented between 1905 and 1909 and brought out of Russia in 1909 has taken over fifty years to get back there. (Those who are prepared to mock the Soviet authorities for being slow to see the possibilities of three short ballets in an evening should remember that the Imperial regime was just as suspicious of new ideas. Diaghilev could never get one penny of subsidy out of the Russian Emperor, though Grand-Duke Vladimir, the Tsar's uncle, did his best to help: his patrons were enlightened Westerners such as Gabriel Astruc, Sir Joseph Beecham, Sir Oswald Stoll, C. B. Cochran, Prince Pierre of Monaco, Lord Rothermere and Lady Juliet Duff.)

I remember reviewing the London première of Fokine's version of *Paganini* in 1939. Lavrovsky's *Paganini* also sets out to illustrate the trials and tribulations which beset a creative or interpretive genius. A bit dodgy, really: for whereas Cyril Connolly would list the hardships of an artist as underpayment, under-appreciation and not enough holidays in the south of France, Paganini made a fortune, was a legend and travelled extensively. His chief trouble, I believe, was (like that of many less romantically successful men) digestive and his later diaries alternated between '*vomitivo*' and '*purgativo*'. But then one cannot make a ballet with the hero alternately taking medicine and rushing to the Gents.

Fokine fell back on various impersonifications of envy, slander, gossip, etc. I recall crowds of dwarfish imitators, malicious audiences and a couple of lovers who ran away scared at the sight of the long-haired genius playing a guitar in the grounds of the Villa Doria-Pamphili. Then there was the Muse who inspired, consoled and led the musician to heaven. All this was corny and cumbersome, but I thought Fokine brought it off at the time.

Lavrovsky has the muse and four minor musettas, who balance and drift so exquisitely amid wafting chiffon veils that they make one see the point of the Pavlova style. He also has little mocking violinists in pink, threatening monks, a funeral and stained-glass windows.

Vladimir Vasiliev dances superbly and gives everything emotionally at the same time; but when he is not executing *grandes pirouettes à la seconde*, playing an imaginary violin or supporting the lovely Maximova, he is expected feverishly to conduct an imaginary orchestra, and this is embarrassing.

Whatever the *artist's* problems are (cf. Kipling's *If*), one problem facing the *choreographer* of *Paganini* is that Rachmaninov's lush, tear-jerking music with its celestial apotheosis does not represent any kind of struggle in any kind of soul. Another problem for a musical beginner like myself, who is only just getting, with Ben Britten's aid, to find his way round the orchestra, is that after the opening section the hero's violin is represented in the pit by a piano.

Lapauri's *Lieutenant Kije* is an anti-Tsarist satire. The Imperial pen makes a blob which creates a non-existent officer. This chap has consequently to mount guard, to be flirted with by a Countess, to be exiled, promoted and killed off, then given a State funeral.

A good idea, and helped by Prokofiev's strident *faux-naïf* music, which I believe was written for a film. I think the reason the comedy doesn't quite come off is to do with scale. This sort of satire is delightful on the small stage of intimate revue: in fact the work is reminiscent of Balieff's *Chauve-souris*, and so are its gay, childish sets by Boris Messerer. On a huge opera house stage it seems wrong.

But Struchkova as the Countess bends her romantic personality to the artificialities of rococo comedy and Nina Sorokina is a pert and stylish stilus. Watching the female *corps de ballet* wheeling into formation as the Imperial Guard it struck me how much better women are at drill than men, and that the Changing of the Guard would be even more popular and effective a spectacle if it could be done by pretty girls.

4.8.63

At the Festival Hall

Renouncing almost all numbers which aim at dramatic expression, Mr. Hochhauser gave as his last week's programme of the Bolshoi Ballet at the Festival Hall Messerer's *School of Ballet* and no less than thirteen *divertissements*. It was an orgy of virtuosity during which there were moments when superb dancers showed that they could also be moving interpreters of the soul's language.

As the Bolshoi are now going on a provincial tour I thought a guide to these *divertissements* with my rating of them might be useful for those who have not yet booked.

★★★*Spartacus*. A dramatic extract from Yacobson's ballet about the revolt of the Roman slaves, with music by Khatchaturian. Probably an absurd ballet, and a rather absurd number, in which Maya Plisetskaya pleads with Dmitri Begak either to go or not to go to war—over-emotional when taken out of context and very old-fashioned, but illuminated by the noble lines and impassioned performance of beautiful Plisetskaya, who just arrived for the last week in London.

★★★*Don Quixote*. Excerpts from that famous old firework with cheerful tunes by Minkus. Little, pretty Milika Sabirova is thrilling in her speed, neatness, finish and bravura, spinning away like mad and caught and raised in breathtaking leaps and lifts by the tall cavalier, Vladimir Tikhonov.

★★★*Flames of Paris*. Extract from Vainonen's ballet about the French Revolution. In this number it is incongruous to see the revolutionary hero, with his splendid, savage motions, partnering an elegant attractive ballerina on point, who clearly qualifies for the guillotine. But Nina Sorokina is delightful and Yuri Vladimirov is not only a dancer but a personality. He has a modern face, odd, thoughtful, wild, moody, unconventional; long hair; that fantastic jump; a coltish awkwardness; fire. A great choreographer, inspired by Vladimirov's original character and

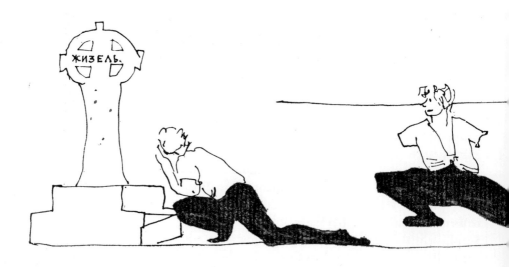

ЖИЗЕЛЬ.

Yuri Soloviev with Natalia Makarova rehearsing *Giselle*.
Drawings by Patrick Procktor

style, could make him a great dancer by creating great roles for him in great ballets.

***_Spring Waters_. Messerer's famous duet which combines acrobacy and ecstasy, now danced by Nina Fedorova with Maris Liepa. Liepa gives it an extra glory: performing tremendous physical feats, he seems to exult, godlike. I have said before, perhaps in other words, that for noble, romantic roles I think Liepa's artistry, style and looks make him the completest male dancer and partner in the world today.

**_Romance_. A lyrical duet admirably danced by Elena Cherkasskaya and Mikhail Tikhomirov. **_Gopak_. Exciting character-dance by the ebullient Shamil Yagudin.

**_The Doves_. The only-one-hand number, heroically dared and done by Ludmila and Stanislav Vlasov, this would win three stars for its feats of skill if it were not really a bit ridiculous. **_Polonaise and Krakowiak_. Aristocratic group dance to Glinka music, which, by the way, should begin and not end a programme.

*_Waltz_. A bit of Fokine's _Sylphides_ danced with poetry by Bernara Karieva, supported by Boris Kokhlov. *_The Dying Swan_, Fokine's solo for Pavlova, danced by Plisetskaya. It seems insulting to vote only one star to anything rendered by the august Plisetskaya, but this is an awful, vulgar, sickly number, done to death thirty years ago. And even if Pavlova undulated her arms, she didn't make a feature of these oriental snake movements. Coming after _Spring Waters_, which was encored, this had to be encored. It should _never_ be danced twice. It shouldn't be danced once.

Not recommended: _Narcissus_. Solo by Goleizovsky performed by Vladimir Vasiliev. Not to be believed! I vastly admire Vasiliev's fabulous technique and like his looks. The _Evening Standard_ votes him the Greatest Dancer in the World. O.K. He's young, fair and handsome. He does a number about a dishy Greek falling in love with his own face in a pool. So he chooses to wear a shaggy grey wig! The choreography is ludicrous. Glamorous Vasiliev appeared like a mad old queen trying on some sexy bathing trunks thirty years too young for him. No stars either for _Russian Dance_, a flirting-peasants numero; or for _Gypsy Dance_, which is the number I used to do when I was a plaything of Colonel Redl, at drag balls in Old Vienna.*

22.8.65

---

* Reference to John Osborne's play _A Patriot for Me_.

At Covent Garden

The theme is liberty. And it has inspired the Bolshoi Ballet to give us in *Spartacus* the most powerful of their productions. There are absurdities and *longueurs*, but it is a whale of a show. Can you accept Roman courtesans and slave girls *sur les pointes* in a pre-Fokine way? And love or lust expressed in acrobatic lifts, flings and contortions—what used to be called an adagio act?

Anyway, the choreography and production of Yuri Grigorovich, the settings of Simon Virsaladze and the dancing of the company add up to something tremendous, and they were uproariously acclaimed on Thursday. The music of Khatchaturian, nearly all in an Eastern European idiom, sometimes reminiscent of *Scheherazade* and *Prince Igor*, is dull, but it serves its purpose.

There are four characters. Crassus, the tyrant, embodiment of Rome's imperial power; Spartacus, a Thracian captive, who leads the revolt of the slaves; Aegina, the evil mistress of Crassus, who by introducing booze and whores into the rebel camp helps to crush the insurrection; and Phrygia, the wife of Spartacus, separated from him in slavery, but reunited during the rebellion, and who makes the final gesture of appeal to us over his corpse.

Maris Liepa was dancing Crassus with a bad leg, thus showing not only physical courage in this exacting role but also moral courage, as he knew he was not being judged by his best. Yet what an incredible performance he gave! What a characterization! Handsome and cruel as Nero, threatening the whole world with his will, he looms above the eagles. Exultant in battle, at the orgy cold; his only pleasures power and the sight of pain. When two blindfolded gladiators fight to the death, he watches with sick intensity the death-throes of the one and the remorse of the other, who is Spartacus. He has a terrifying way of putting his head down and advancing with a dragging step. His gesture—used only twice, I think—of clapping his left hand to his right biceps, with a triumphant, decisive glare, sums up the whole character. When he leaps through the air, curved backwards, he is an iron boomerang. His goose-step is a page of history. When he runs we know he is mad. Liepa is the Laurence Olivier of the dance: a genius, certainly.

The role of Aegina suits Timofeyeva perfectly. What fabulous, steely extensions! What carnivorous *écarté*! And how balefully she glitters! As Phrygia the long-limbed Natalia Bessmertnova pleads and yearns and mourns with plaintive arms.

Mikhail Lavrovsky has the burning eyes of a fanatic, a social worker, a righter of wrongs. Just the sort of slave one would avoid getting landed with. He is wonderful both in his loving *pas de deux*, when he executes phenomenal lifts, bearing Besmertnova with one hand horizontal in the air, and on his heroic occasions, dedicating himself to the cause and swearing in the troops. His jump is glorious.

Some of the ensemble dances for soldiers, slaves, herdsmen, senators or courtesans are impressive, others rather ridiculous—any dance with spears and shields is bound to be awful. Some advance the action, others hold it up. The device of having successive tableaux of dinner-parties, imprisoned gladiators, or unindoctrinated yokels grouped at the back, leaving the whole stage free for dancing, is excellent. The all-grey monumental stony sets speak 'Rome!'

Liberty! Fretting under the petty tyrannies of the restored Bourbons and the Austrians in Lombardy, Stendhal said the obvious thing to do was to go to America—only there was no opera there. Now they have opera, but also a lot of fat, rude, bullying police. We are fundamentally awful and shall soon be re-building Hitler's camps and Russian prisons on the moon, policed by pigsticking Anglo-lunatics.

But Rome brought us civilization, after all. What would have happened if Caesar had subdued and civilized Russia seventeen hundred years before Peter the Great?

20.7.69

At Covent Garden

Expectations were high at Covent Garden on Wednesday. The great Plisetskaya had arrived to grace the Bolshoi Ballet's triple bill; we were to have Maximova and Vasiliev in *Don Quixote*, and the glorious corps would be deployed in *Chopiniana*, Fokine's early Petersburg version of *Les Sylphides*. Alas!

We are familiar with the jolly fourth act of the old-fashioned *Don Quixote* ballet, with its merry-making peasants, and its brilliant *divertissement* watched by the Don, seated outside the inn. But the Russians had left the set behind, they had left the peasants behind, and they had left Don Quixote behind. What we had was the *divertissement* against black curtains—just dancing in cold blood to the tunes of Minkus.

Let it be said that in their extended *pas de deux*, which was the *raison d'être* of the show, Maximova and Vasiliev danced like a dream. He did superb corkscrew turns in the air and she flung herself at him, was caught, lifted high and suddenly plunged diving to brush the floor with her pretty upturned face. No dancing could be more spectacular. Yet alas! that is all it was. When a dance has no feeling and nothing to express, vulgarity is bound to creep in—yes, and even lovely Maximova was smirking.

Chopiniana was not, as the programme says it was, inspired by Taglioni. Only the long dresses were, and its second title, chosen by Diaghilev for his first Paris season. It originally had Mazurkas danced by dashing couples in Polish costume, ghostly monks and Chopin seated at a piano. When it was reduced to nineteen sylphs and a dreaming poet, Diaghilev realized that Chopin's Polonaise Militaire was no longer a possible overture and he replaced it with the Prelude (Op. 28, no. 7). The Bolshoi have retained or restored the former rousing tune, during the last bars of which the curtain rises on the tableau of sylphs, so we start off with a good laugh. The delicate ballet is performed against black curtains—not a tree in sight. Pity.

If Fokine could have been told that one day a Russian company would take calls after the individual solos in this work—would recross the stage, bowing—he would not have believed it. Not even in his most sprightly ballets, such as *Carnaval*—and of course not in his dramas like *Sheherazade* —would he allow the mood to be broken or the action interrupted. But in *Les Sylphides*! The Bolshoi dancers are always asking to be introduced to Mme. Karsavina. If she knew what was going on she would murder them. At the end of Karsavina's Valse, when the dancer's back is turned, Vasilieva's arms were much too symmetrical. Golikova (a good Queen of the Wilis) was miscast in the Prelude. Akimov is a fine, long-limbed dancer, but he should not have been allowed to lift his girl above his head. Horrid orchestration and some funereal *tempi*.

Carmen Suite by Alberto Alonso shows a worthy intention on the management's part to do something a little daring and up-to-date. But alas! In the dances for Plisetskaya and her three rival lovers the mixture of sex, comedy and drama has gone wrong. She is wasted on this absurd work. An appalling arrangement of Bizet. The set is a bull-ring, around the top of which twelve masked Fates or Executioners sit on high-backed Charles II chairs. No.

27.7.69

At Covent Garden

Ballet lives permanently on a tight-rope between the sublime and the ridiculous, and the greatest choreographers have produced bad ballets. Yuri Grigorovich, whose imagination pervaded the whole production of *Spartacus*, made something quite stupid out of *Legend of Love*. It may be unfair to judge a full-length ballet by one of its acts, but companies must be judged by the programmes they put on.

Impossible to lay down rules about how not to make a stupid ballet—especially as what goes in Moscow may be unacceptable in London. However, an awareness of the *Zeitgeist* enables one to venture a few hints. Avoid subjects 'based on an ancient Eastern legend'. Eschew all pseudo-Oriental music. Jealous tragedy queens are out. Tremendous scissory *arabesques* and *développés* in Oriental ballets are out. Turbans are out. Jesters—aaahhh! If I were a Persian queen 'heartbroken because of [my] unhappy love for Ferkhad', my sister's lover, and 'the Jester and dancers [tried] to cheer [me] up', they would pay for it with their lives.

Timofeyeva, admittedly, is admirable as the queen, Lavrovsky dances Ferkhad with powerful conviction and the exquisite Bessmertnova, like a spider who has seen visions, extends her infinite limbs: but the old-fashioned absurdity of the ballet spoils my pleasure in watching them.

But let us praise the Bolshoi Ballet for their great qualities. They opened with the wrong ballet, having apparently no one to advise them about what the London public would like best; their *Swan Lake* and *Nutcracker* are not as interesting as their *Giselle*, although Maximova and Bessmertnova have been triumphantly acclaimed in some or all of these; and Plisetskaya must have been bitterly disappointed that *Carmen Suite*, her favourite ballet, was not liked here: but it has been a marvellous season all the same because of the dancing and because of *Spartacus*.

It was harder to get in to *Spartacus* on Wednesday than into any performance in living memory. The wonderfully patient Press Officer had been battling all week to enable several critics to buy one seat each. Some stood. This was partly because of the sudden fame of Grigorovich's production (so superior to the other choreographic version I saw in Leningrad), partly because of Liepa's already legendary Crassus and partly because Vasiliev was to dance Spartacus. Let me say at once that the leader of the rebel slaves was Vasiliev's greatest role.

Wearing a moustache and a slight beard like the Dying Gaul, Vasiliev looked a bit like Lenin, a bit like Delacroix's self-portrait and a bit like

Terry Stamp, only blond. I knew he was a superb, incomparable dancer, but I did not know he could act like this. I think the moustache helped, and he had something to express (not like in the mindless *Don Quixote pas de deux*) and perhaps the theme of freedom set him on fire. Well, it did me and *he* did me. His performance was a heroic blaze.

Timofeyeva conveyed well the fanatic devotion of Aegina to her Führer and in her sexual dances she was as cold as a snake. As the pathetic Phrygia, Maximova would melt any tyrant's heart. Any tyrant except the sadistic, power-drunk Crassus of Liepa. His performance is overwhelming. The contrast between Vasiliev's slave and Liepa's general, though they are both fair-haired and exactly the same height, is a dramatic miracle. Vasiliev could play Othello. Liepa should play Iago. The audience stood to applaud for twenty minutes, during which time the rain of flowers never ceased.

3.8.69

The Kirov Ballet

At Covent Garden

One of the dangers of going out of doors, for a ballet critic, is that of meeting old friends in the street who force upon him ballet scenarios by their bedridden mothers or grandmothers—scenariitis tends to be hereditary—which he is supposed not only to read, report on and find a composer for, but also to get staged at Covent Garden. These libretti are usually inspired by horticulture, entomology or mineralogy: that is to say, the dancers represent flowers, insects or semi-precious stones. (A welcome exception, I remember, was a scenario by Violet Trefusis, partly autobiographical, about the Loch Ness Monster; and this I passed to Frederick Ashton.)

Poor Prokofiev married into a scenariitic family. ('My wife writes ballet scenarios, you know. . . .') The story of *The Stone Flower*, with which the Kirov Ballet opened their season at the Royal Opera House on Monday, is by her, M. Prokofiev, and by L. Lavrovsky. It is one of those mineralogical stories, and very boring indeed.

'Danila, a stone carver in the Urals, is trying to accomplish his dream of creating a vase perfect and simple as a living flower.' Now, Richard, a prose writer in W.C.2, is always trying to write English which will endure for ever: but in order to impart imperishability to it he doesn't stare fixedly at St. Paul's Cathedral. Danila hacks away at the vase—a very ordinary garden urn except for being made of malachite—with one hand, while holding up some gladioli in the other: and we turn against this carry-on from the start. Or rather, we very much like Yuri Soloviev, who impersonates Danila, for he is a fine looking fellow with a strong jaw and highly developed thighs, and with a splendid sweep and conviction in his dancing; but we pity him for the foolish things he has to do.

To continue the story: Danila has a girl-friend Katerina, modestly and prettily played by Alla Sizova, who tactlessly keeps bringing him more and more flowers. His views on the relationship of art to life being what they are, this only increases his dissatisfaction. They have a slap-up engagement party, with vigorous character dances by the male guests, but this is spoilt by the overseer Severian (the admirable mime and dancer Anatoli Gridin), who tries to get a free vase out of Danila, then makes passes at the girl.

By the way, we know Severian is the villain because he makes the sign of the *cross* on entering the house: he is a dirty Christian. I suppose this, and the fact that Danila wields a *hammer*, while Katerina in Act II finally chases Severian off with a *sickle*, are intentional allusions.

The Mistress of the Copper Mountain appears to Danila, shows him a vision of the Stone Flower, and, now in the guise of a lizard, now as the Malachite Maiden, leads him underground, where the precious stones come to life and perform a mineralogical ballabile in the Palladium style. The versatile immortal, alternately slinky and dazzling, is well danced by Alla Osipenko.

The second act has a vivid gypsy scene—I liked all the gypsies being dressed differently. Katerina resists rape by the overseer and finds her lover under the hill; while Severian, after being turned to stone, is swallowed up, gesticulating madly, by the earth. The Mistress of the Copper Mountain, having taught Danila the secret of art (*not* to sculpt gladioli), is reluctant to release the gorgeous creature, but suddenly decides to be her age—*Honi soit qui* malachite—and lets the better woman win.

So the Russians have these sort of ballets, just like we do. Prokofiev's serviceable music is the mixture as before; much of it just like *Cinderella*. The choreography by Yuri Grigorovich (1957), his first, is more exciting in *ensembles* than in *pas de deux*. The décor by Simon Virsaladze is un-interesting. The dancers are excellent.

25.6.61

At Covent Garden

When in 1600 Boris Godunov sent an ambassador to Queen Elizabeth I, this big fellow Ivan Mikulin was lodged with his retinue of sixteen at the house of Sir Cuthbert Buckle in St Mary-at-Hill near Billingsgate; and I am all for carrying on the family tradition of giving Russian visitors a warm welcome. But on this their second visit to Covent Garden the Kirov seem almost to have gone out of their way to make a bad impression on the opening night, thus putting their hosts—if such we can be called—in a proper quandary.

First, we never want to see *Swan Lake* again; second, the sets and dresses

H

for the new production are the dreariest imaginable; thirdly, Kaleriya Fedicheva, a big jolly girl, is utterly miscast in the role of Odette. Of course it was thrilling to see Yuri Soloviev again, but even so, his first appearance was marred by an absurd hair style and poor make-up. We must face the fact that in matters of design, lighting and make-up the Kirov Ballet are terrible—then try to concentrate on their dancing.

Soloviev's ease, accuracy, elevation and *ballon* were a joy to watch; as the Princess-Mother Angelina Kabarova was warm and friendly; and the Mazurka and Czardas were danced with style. The happy ending was a bit tame, but I imagine they have some going-up-to-heaven machinery at the Kirov, which we lack.

Friday's *Cinderella* with new choreography by Sergeyev will always be remembered for the triumph of glorious Irina Kolpakova, supported by Soloviev, in the most hideous and vulgar décor ever seen at the Royal Opera House. Poor dancers! What they have to rise above.

In this *Cinderella* the spiteful step-sisters are not ugly; they are young and handsome, they are danced by Natalia Makarova and Fedicheva, they are given brilliant variations to do and they don't fall over. They have a clownish mother. The Fairy Godmother remains a doddering, sentimental old lady throughout: she summons up not only the seasons but some ghastly green grasshoppers and twelve bearded redcapped dwarfs (like Snow White's) who have a very tedious way of crossing the stage. The courtiers are mincing caricatures. After the ball the Prince visits Spain, Ethiopia and Persia, which gives rise to some quite nasty cabaret numbers, interspersed with soaring solos by Soloviev.

Judged as a way of displaying all Soloviev's repertory of amazing feats —his various jumps, scissors and changes of position in mid-air, his *manèges* and spins—the ballet is wholly successful.

Irina Kopakova is not only pretty (she is blonde but I count this a slight disadvantage in a ballerina) with a sweet, expressive face, she has the most perfect legs, a powerful technique and queenly relaxed arms. It is breathtaking to watch her flying angelically through the air and marvellous, at the end of the *pas de deux*, to see her come to rest in a perfect open *attitude*, right hand so exactly raised, left hand so classically hanging. She is a wonder. But I shall venture one suggestion. She has a small head, and the close-fitting white cap she wears in the kitchen scene makes her feet look big. I had better not start on about the costumes.

11.9.66

At Covent Garden

If Soloviev is the greatest male dancer in the world, where does Nureyev
—who is the most publicised dancer in the world—come in? Let's get
that over first. Soloviev has not got Nureyev's photogenic and fascinating
face, nor has he his interpretive power. From the beginning I said
Nureyev was more amazing for his expressive qualities than for his
dancing: he excels in certain steps, but Soloviev excels in all. Nureyev has
not Soloviev's supreme flow or lightness, nor has he been subjected to so
steady a course of discipline. Soloviev, slightly the younger of the two,
is now better than in 1961: purely as a dancer he is incomparable and
unsurpassed.

The Kirov's first *Sleeping Beauty* had the same Aurora and Prince as the
performance I was invited to in 1961. Vladilen Semenov is a hero in the
grand tradition, the heir of Guerdt and Pierre Vladimirov. Irina Kolpakova, who was still tentative in 1961, now beams out with the splendour of
a great ballerina.

The conductor Victor Fedotov gave us some sharp contrasts of tempo,
always desirable in Tchaikovsky. Certain high-speed entries were exhilarating, but I thought Aurora's Vision solo was taken so slowly it lost
the magic of the tune. The fairies (handicapped only by their wigs) covered
the stage with splendour; Fedicheva was a glorious, swooping Lilac
Fairy; Vsevolod Uchov's King was a real and royal tyrant; crowds of
children heaped their offerings of blossom; and Kolpakova balanced,
extended, span and soared like an angel.

It seemed almost unfair, when the ballerina's triumph had nearly unfolded to the full, that the Blue Bird and Florine should appear and share
(or steal) our passionate admiration. Makarova (whose Giselle we shall
consider next week) was exquisitely elegant. As for Soloviev—we had
never seen such dancing, such curves in the air. If anybody ever jumped
higher, no one ever landed so lightly. There never were such *brisés volés*.

18.9.66

At Covent Garden

A word should perhaps be spoken in honour of Agrippina Vaganova, that
great teacher who made a system out of the several dance traditions inherited by the Leningrad school, and whose work is carried on by

Natalia Dudinskaya, principal ballet mistress of the Kirov company, and her colleagues. For we have never seen such visions of grace, symmetry and dreamlike co-ordination as the *corps de ballet* conjured up for us in *Giselle* and *Chopiniana*.

In the latter, which is Fokine's early version of *Les Sylphides*, it was wonderful to see how the *avant garde* poetry of Fokine had retained its 1908 freshness in Russia, for, after all, Fokine only paid two visits to Russia after its production and left it for ever in 1918. The dancers seemed less to move into their varied formations than to drift on a breeze of music, becoming festoons, wreaths, tufts and aerial trophies of the night.

When Mme. Karsavina, at the party on Wednesday to celebrate Dolin's new book, said of Spessivtseva that she had an ethereal quality combined with strength of technique, I thought of the Kirov's Natalia Makarova, who is no doubt a very different dancer—and a blonde. She has amazing strength in steps of elevation and amazing balance, and she appears inexhaustible, yet nothing could seem more frail and delicate than her slender legs and fragile arms and she looks like a fairy blown in Venetian glass. She had a new and telling way of acting Giselle's Mad scene—when she came forward to the footlights and held her head it was alarming—and her dancing with Soloviev in Act II sets a standard for the world. Soloviev revealed his handicap, however, in the role of Albrecht: although his physical acting is thoroughly able his charming face appears childish in romantic-dramatic passages (like Gilpin's).

There was a new solo to show off the great man's paces in Act I, and we had hardly caught our breath when the peasant *pas de deux* was upon us, with Vadim Budarin doing *cabrioles* further from the ground than seemed possible, and partnering the spinning delightful Natalia Bolshakova. Of Hilarion (called *Hans* by the Kirov) Anatoli Gridin (who had been a terrific Carabosse in *The Beauty*) made the most effective character, taking no more lording from the Count than a Scots ghillie from his laird. When Albrecht said '*See* what you've done!' he countered '*No*, it was *you*', with a threatening finger. I still think it a great mistake for the Count to be hustled off before the Act I curtain: after all, this is his ballet, not Mum's.

Now to consider briefly some of the short works and *divertissements*. It seems unfair to judge the Belsky-Shostakovich *Leningrad Symphony*, inspired by the heroic defenders of Leningrad in 1942, by the two and a half movements shown us. The incomplete music is dull and the Nazi stamping too continuous: but at least we saw Fedicheva and Soloviev in an epic light, patriotism incarnate. The familiar act of *La Bayadère* was superbly danced and Sergei Vikulov, whom some extol above Soloviev, leapt spinning through the air into falls on the knee, and did a *manège* of double turns with arms rising *en couronne* which was incredible, but he sometimes shows a certain jerkiness between movements which may be due to a sudden tensing of the arms. *Gayaneh* gave opportunity for some hearty character numbers. Budarin astounded us in a Turkish dance from that ballet; Soloviev, looking much better in an exotic make-up, flew beyond praise in *Le Corsaire*; Alexander Pavlovsky did crazy character steps in *Taras Bulba*.

I have kept till last the Rose Waltz and *pas de deux* from *Casse Noisette*, which had a pretty set and dresses, because it is a pleasure to write that Irina Kolpakova is the most adorable, sparkling, shining, shooting and God-sent Sugar Plum Fairy who ever cometed through space into a Prince's arms to the sound of Tchaikovsky's crashing chandeliers, and that I want her for Christmas.

25.9.66

At the Festival Hall

At a time when thinking people are asking themselves whether the old classical ballets—even if they are by Tchaikovsky and Petipa—are anything more than diversions for idiots; when, even with the full resources of a great opera house like the Kirov or Covent Garden, with all the glamour of décor and the refinement of lighting, such productions as the Kirov's *Cinderella* or the Royal Ballet's *Swan Lake* can seem to hold nothing for us; when the expressive simplicities of the modern dance have made all technical display repellent—at such a time, i.e., now, it is rash even for the Kirov Ballet, whom we all look to for an example, to present at the Festival Hall a programme devoted solely to virtuoso dancing. The fact that we were given the third acts of *Bayadère* and *Nutcracker* before the *divertissement* did not prevent the evening being one long *divertissement*, from which all art was banished.

It is wonderful of Victor Hochhauser to bring these lovely dancers here, and it is wonderful of Natalia Dudinskaya to train them so well. But as *pas de deux* succeeded *pas de deux*, applauded (not only after but during) in proportion to the difficulty of its technical feats—which it used to be the proud Petersburg fashion to make light of—I looked across the theatre at the company's artistic director, Konstantin Sergeyev, guardian of the traditions of Fokine, Pavlova, Karsavina and Nijinsky, and wondered if, behind his complacent exterior, he was dying of a broken heart. It was the nature of the show which brought out the worst in this kind of audience, and denied ballet as an art.

The dances had a common denominator of leaps, spins, turns, lifts and falls. All looked alike, so that one is tempted merely to award marks, as in a school report or exam. Kolpakova—8 for technique, 9 for charm—smiles too much. Osipenko and Makarova—8, 9 or 10 for practically everything—('That boy Vikulov, keep your mouth shut'). Soloviev—everything comes easy to him. Markovsky—10 for partnering and good manners. Welcome to the new boy, brilliant Baryshnikov, due to be Master's favourite—'Jump this way, dear.'*

26.7.70

At the Festival Hall

Within the Olympian symmetry of the Kirov *corps de ballet*, if I am not mistaken, a tiny freedom is permitted and the evidence of a girl's individuality goes unchecked. (I am reminded of Gerard Manley Hopkins's dialogue about the chestnut leaf in New College Gardens.) Not a leg is out of line in the military formations of *Swan Lake*, but here and there an arm extends with a special languor or a hand is slightly more or less clenched. Thus one remarks the beauty of a limb or a girl—and what girls with what limbs the Russians have brought us!—and the superb machine is seen to be composed not only of bodies but of souls: the harvest of Natalia Dudinskaya's classes.

Elegant and mournful Osipenko was Odette at the Festival Hall on Friday, supported by the tall, boyish and eager Markovsky. And we had good old *Spring Waters* with the Desnitzkys; and Evteyeva and Budarin in a spectacular *Coppelia* duet; and fascinating Sizova with soaring Soloviev in a bit of Bournonville; and exquisite Kolpakova supported by Semenov in a dance to music of Vivaldi.

Then as a surprise or as a gesture the Russians gave Anton Dolin's celebrated *Pas de Quatre*, his evocation of the number performed by Taglioni, Grisi, Grahn and Cerrito at Her Majesty's Theatre in 1845, and in thirty years I have never seen it better danced. So often the touches of comedy—consisting in the ballerinas' faintly bitchy good manners towards each other—can outbalance the subtle period tang of the choreography. This time the dances seemed the very essence of all the old romantic

* He did.

prints and music covers, and it was wonderful to see the Russians making their points with such sophistication and wit. Shining Makarova was Taglioni, and Komleva, Bolshakova and Kovaleva were the other flowers in the Victorian posy.

London has taken Mikhail Baryshnikov to its heart, but on Friday, when he danced the *Don Quixote pas de deux* with Komleva, there was a particular feeling of coronation in the air, as if he were being formally acclaimed as the great dancer of our day, which indeed he is; and Dolin was seen to be standing to applaud—some accolade! It is not just the height or perfection of Baryshnikov's *cabrioles* that delights so much as his flow of line and the timing and ease with which he comes to rest. He is also a prince of partners. Here is the ultimate glory of the classical Leningrad school.

16.8.70

The Changing Scene
(1961–1962)

Patronage

If I were Mrs. Harkness (and some people think I am), whose Rebekah W. Harkness Foundation subsidizes Ballets U.S.A., I should be a proud woman; for it isn't everyone who gets the chance to help a genius and enable him to develop his ideas at leisure. What Ludwig did for Wagner, what Mme. von Meck did for Tchaikovsky and what Lincoln Kirstein did for Balanchine, she does for Robbins.

Leisure for rehearsals is all-important to Robbins, who is a slow worker, or rather one not easily satisfied, and who likes to try out a number of variations, even publicly, before he calls a ballet finished. The single programme we saw two summers ago was a freak of perfection, because not only was each of the four ballets almost perfect, but the order they were danced in and the contrast between them was perfect programme-planning. These perfections were the result of endless trial and error.

6.8.61

Madam (on T.V.)

In last Sunday's *Monitor* Huw Weldon's approach to Dame Ninette de Valois was that of a housemaster taking on the headmaster's wife. A certain deference was due, but he knew he'd lose face with the boys if he didn't venture an occasional question which implied a criticism of the well-loved lady's supposed shortcomings.

He asked whether she had had a 'ruthless determination' to have a great company like the Royal Ballet ever since 1930. Dame Ninette wasn't going to let him get away with a single adjective. 'Why do you call it ruthless?' she asked sharply. We knew at once, if we hadn't known all along, that the poor man didn't stand a chance.

'Madam' would reveal nothing more than she wished to reveal; there were certain questions she would answer and certain she would only appear to answer, like a Conservative Minister;* she knew quite well how to put him firmly in his place without making too much of a fool of him in front of the boys; and if he thought he could get her to criticize adversely any of the Royal Ballet's 'rivals' he was in for a nasty disappointment.

* When I wrote this Sir Harold Wilson had not yet established his world record for evasiveness.

But 'oh yes', she admitted easily, the great plan had always been there. Although, of course, 'you must be elastic and prepared to contradict yourself.' Had she always seen herself as a choreographer or producer more than a dancer? Yes, even when, as kids, she and her family and friends had acted plays, she had tended to leave herself out of the distribution of roles, for she felt 'someone must take control,' and she had 'an ambition to be responsible for the whole.' She was just going on to say something fascinating when Weldon interrupted her, changing the subject, and I could have killed him.

To an implied criticism of the academic and un-revolutionary nature of the Royal Ballet, Dame Ninette said, 'We can't take half a dozen risks in six months ... We must become a habit in the end ... There's always a contemporary form of dance ... and I should be proud if the Royal Ballet produced its own offspring ...' (as the Russian Imperial Ballet had produced the rebel Diaghilev, she meant).

Asked about national styles of dancing, Dame Ninette said the Russians thought there was definitely an English style. But 'the English school must go on developing.' The Russians said our backs were weak. Posture and poise were better in Eastern Europe, where they had more plastic quality and danced with their whole bodies. But our footwork was neater than theirs. She was all for English dancers getting backs like the Russians.

What would happen to the Royal Ballet if she retired? 'It would make no difference', replied Ninette de Valois, Dame of the British Empire, Empress of the Land of Sylphs and Swans, Maker and Unmaker of Princes, founder of a dynasty, Red Dragon of the Tong. 'The scale of the Royal Ballet is far too big. It no longer rests on the shoulders of one person.'

And the Cherubim beat their scarlet wings in exultation.

29.10.61

Japan

Odd things happen in the world of musical and revue, and so they should: one of the oddest was to hear the dance of the captive women in Borodin's *Prince Igor* turned into 'Take my hand, I'm a stranger in Paradise'. But nothing quite as odd as the Japanese show, *Tokyo 1961*, at the Coliseum, has happened to me for a long time.

Yet what the little darlings do—apart from two remarkable numbers—

is quite ordinary: it is only that it's ordinary in such an extraordinary way. *Tokyo 1961* is an imitation of a Radio City Music Hall programme, complete with Rockettes, popularised classical ballet, crooning, scat singing, tap, adagio-act and big production numbers—a programme, naturally, with a Japanese slant to it.

But is it an admiring imitation or a parody? When attractive Miss Mitsuko Sawamura sings in English her songs 'My funny Valentine' and 'Funky Cats', it is really the works. At other moments I wonder if Western entertainment is not being laughed at up those snazzy sleeves. I *thought* I heard the smooth Mr. Yoshiaki Takei ('Tokyo's peak vocal heart-throb') putting over a silken Neapolitan ditty in the Hawaiian scene, but then I always think a lot of Indian folk songs sound Scotch. Having lulled you into acceptance of his American style of delivery Mr. Takei sometimes disconcerts you by covering his face with a fan and running off stage.

For ballet-lovers there is part of the second act of *Swan Lake* in modern dress. The evil magician as Odette's ponce is rather a good idea, and it makes a change to have Tchaikovsky syncopated, with the solo violin replaced by tenor sax. In this and in the *Don Quixote pas de deux*, which was danced by about twenty people, the Japanese display a curiously soft imitation ballet style which is quite up to cabaret standards.

5.2.61

The Seasons

The huntsmen are up in America, and they are already past their first sleep in Persia. Yet rolled in its diurnal course, relentlessly, inexorably, the Royal Ballet revolves its great repertory of royal (i.e. kingsize) ballets. *Cinderella* at Christmas, and then, if winter comes can *Coppélia* be far behind? Nerina for *Coppélia* and *La Fille mal Gardée*, Beriosova for *Swan Lake*, *Les deux Pigeons* for Seymour. Oh to be at *Ondine* now that April's here!

Soon will the high midsummer pomps come on, soon shall we have gold-dusted snapdragon and Fonteyn in *The Sleeping Beauty*. The long, long Sundays after Trinity are with us at last, and *Giselle* is back in the repertoire. (August for the people and their favourite festivals.) But who is *Sylvia* demand the horns of elfland? The sedge is withered from *Swan Lake* and the first sneeze of Advent heralds Prokofiev.

19.3.61

Telegram

To The Poet and Critic
Edwin Denby
on his sixtieth birthday

(Sent during the New York newspaper strike of 1962)

Outrageous DENBY, scandal of our age!
Does Death still hesitate to blot your page?
Asleep all day, only by night you're seen,
Gloating on sarabandes by Balanchine.
When clocks on Eighth Street sound the witching hour
Then to the full we feel your evil power.
Then hoodlums by the pricking of their thumbs
(And vice-versa) know that DENBY comes.
Compact of vice, you lord it in your den,
Spreading your poison amid younger men.
Poets from pubs you tear, dancers from school,
And every night's a season of misrule.
Enough! Begone! Prepare to meet your fate.
A younger generation's at the gate.
From whiter houses whiter men must rise
Whom DENBY's paradoxes won't surprise.
With DENBY gone the country stands a chance,
Papers will publish, knowledge will advance—
Though, rendered radio-active by his glance,
Dancers may versify and poets start to dance.

Read aloud by Virgil Thompson at Denby's birthday-party

Karsavina

I went the other day to a gymnasium in Drury Lane to watch Mme. Karsavina rehearsing Western Theatre Ballet in *Carnaval*. Though she wore an anonymous working costume, black jersey, full black cotton skirt and heel-less slippers, she seemed nevertheless what she was—an exotic visitor from another world, travelling incognita, the Queen of Sheba and of Shemakhan.

She showed Estrella the exact degree of surprise to put on in greeting Florestan, insisted that Eusebius kiss his caught rose with keener rapture, and told him not to do *emboité* in his running exit after Chiarina.

The dancers were not to wag their heads from side to side in the waltz, and the girls were to remember they would be wearing crinolines and that they would kick them if they raised their legs too high. Mme. Karsavina demonstrated passages from the roles of the dapper, silly and self-deluded old Pantalon, of the moon-drenched Eusebius and the butterfly-besotted Pierrot. (Everyone in this ballet is in love.) When she mimed you could see her eyes believed in what her hands were doing.

Papillon was shown how in her running entrance she must alternate between point and half-point, that her arms would be fluttering above her head when she was on point and down behind her back when she was on half-point.

Mme. Karsavina made Harlequin insert *glissades* between his *cabrioles* and showed him the angle at which to hold his extended leg in *grandes pirouettes à la seconde*, as Fokine must have shown Nijinsky. Of the passage of mime when Columbine hears Pantalon coming, she said 'I have that in my bones'. Suddenly Columbine was among us in person. Flutter of the hands before the face for laughter, a pointing finger, ssh!, and an effacing gesture of the upraised palms which means 'Let's hide'.

She mimed Pantalon's jaunty strut, his business with the watch and letter, and timed his arrival on the sofa at the exact moment when Columbine was there to put her hands over his eyes. The charm of her face when she showed how Columbine chucks Pantalon under the chin was irresistible. Introducing the rival lovers she folded her arms prettily and looked pert. The reactions of Pantalon when Harlequin produces his letter were pruned of farce.

In the finale Mme. Karsavina abolished the wobbling of Pantalon's leg, which is meant to convey his reluctance to be reconciled to Harlequin and is a foolish interpolation. She showed a couple how to look ironically over their shoulders at Eusebius and Chiarina. In the polonaise she made the girls raise their right elbows as they held up imaginary skirts.

I never realised before that when Pierrot lies on the ground, with Harlequin and Columbine at the extremities of the stage on either side of him, he is not stretching his long-sleeved arms in vague yearning for nothing in particular, he is intercepting kisses the two lovers blow each other.

7.5.61

Publicity

The 'feverish interest' which, according to her Press agent, swept London after Inesita's recent recital of flamenco dancing at Morley College did not bring many people to see her at St. Pancras Town Hall on Tuesday.

Less stalwart birdwatchers than myself may have been put off by such pronouncements as the following: 'Inesita was born in New York's Manhattan, but her heart, body and soul belong to Spain.' 'Eventually a legend spread, saying that the spirit of a great Spanish flamenco dancer had been flown on an angel's wings to the New World to be reincarnated in this young girl's body.' 'When she returned to Los Angeles in 1953, Inesita gave her debut dance at the Kauffman Auditorium. The impact was so terrific that [wait for it] she was immediately asked to repeat her programme six weeks later in the same hall.' 'Ever since she remembers, she wanted to dance . . . and she did!'

Yes, she did.

28.5.61

Fonteyn

Looking back over Fonteyn's life as a prima ballerina, I see it divided into four periods.

The first or Pearl Period of comparative immaturity ended when she danced *The Sleeping Beauty* on 20 February, 1946. Then there followed a time when people went around saying 'Of course she's wonderful, but she's so withdrawn, so restrained, so cold. Can so private a performer be called great?' That was her Moonstone Period.

The Diamond Period can, for the sake of convenience, be said to date from 9 October 1949, when Fonteyn danced Aurora at the Met. The acclamations of America, her crescent fame and her marriage in 1955, no doubt all contributed to her triumphs in the fifties.

Now she really 'gave'. She knew all the tricks and brought off dashingly everything she attempted. She had always had correct line, a sense of music and a lyrical quality. Now her extra radiance made her more wonderful than ever. We thought of her then as the ideal classical ballerina, and knew her *Swan Lake* was the best in the world.

Fonteyn possessed a reliable technique, but she was not built to dazzle by feats of virtuosity; and it is possible that the emergence of the more technically brilliant Nadia Nerina (not to mention the appearance here of Ulanova, who gave her roles an unprecedented psychological depth) might have put her in the shade. But Fonteyn—and Ashton—had a surprise in store for us: her Opal Period.

The first sign of this, come to think of it, was as early as 1948, when, dancing a *pas de deux* with a broomstick in Ashton's *Cinderella*, she suddenly shrugged her shoulders and gave a little giggle. Ashton recognised and brought out in Fonteyn a girlish, capricious, fun-loving character which, combined with the qualities of wistfulness and soulfulness she had shown all along, proved irresistible. So Ashton made the roles of Chloë and Ondine for her: and those who had always thought of Fonteyn as a princess or a swan realised to their amazement that she could be a girl, an elf, a silly giddy thing. Fonteyn at forty was younger and more fascinating than at twenty (but aren't we all?).

Today Fonteyn's opalescent roles seem to me her most special achievement. Flirting in front of Pan's altar, pleading with pirates in her underclothes, limp with love for a layabout, doing the Madison with a lot of pretty shepherds under the fig trees, slipping out of a fountain for a crazy number with her own shadow, snatching childishly at a necklace, then pressing it impulsively on her rival, ruling the waves like an irresponsible teenage Britannia and sporting sadly on their surface like a boy-struck dolphin, she is the youngest and up-to-datest of our ballerinas.

Can we now expect a Black Jet Period, with our girl as a ton-up kid on a Triumph Roadstar? Or a Ruby one, with Margot stalking about in crimson velvet, waving a scimitar, as Lady Macbeth?

14.11.62

Bucchlismo

I returned from a flying visit to Menotti's Festival of Two Worlds at Spoleto—a place one can well understand Shelley describing as 'I think the most romantic city I ever saw'—nursing a new ambition in my breast:

I

that is, to have my name turned into an Italian adjective. In an intelligent appraisal of Jerome Robbins's new ballet *Events*, Gino Tani, the critic of *Il Messagero*, hailed it as one of the greatest triumphs of the 'spoletine season, that menottian institution', and saw the varied programme— *Interplay*, *Moves*, *The Cage* ('il piú dramatico balletto del coreografo neviorchese') and *Events*—as a sort of retrospective exhibition of 'robbinsian' art.

23.7.61

THE ROYAL BALLET

BUCKLE: Have you done what you set out to do in life?
FONTEYN: I didn't set out to do anything.

Sunday Times, 17.5.64

Ashton, by the way, was always modest about his genius and never 'went mad'.

Sunday Times, 30.7.72

MacMillan's first season as Artistic Director has shown him [to be] one who sticks his neck out.

Sunday Times, 8.8.71

Ashton

Les Patineurs

(First performed 1937)

Watching *Les Patineurs* at the Royal Ballet School matinée last Saturday,
I realized it was just on thirty years since I had seen its first performance
at Sadler's Wells. In those days the Sadler's Wells Ballet, as it then was,
performed only on Tuesday evenings, Saturday afternoons and every
other Friday evening, and they found it hard to fill the house. A month
earlier the seventeen-year-old Margot Fonteyn had danced her first
Giselle. We have come a long way since then.

And Nadia Nerina can write quite naturally in *The Queen* magazine:
'There are few ballerinas of world class today—Fonteyn, Struchkova,
Plisetskaya, Chauviré, Beriosova and me,' and no one thinks it odd that
three of these should have grown up and made their names in what is no
longer called the Sadler's Wells Ballet. Nerina has a few complaints against
the state of affairs prevailing in the Royal Ballet today: and yet it seems to
me almost a sign of strength that Dame Ninette should have felt free to
retire from administration to occupy herself with the school; that Sir
Fred, our pride and leading choreographer, should lay off inventing
dances for a while in order to administer the company; that Kenneth
MacMillan, our second genius, should be allowed to go to Berlin; that
Nerina herself, fed up with getting no new roles, should be released to
become a mere guest artist . . . .

At the Royal Ballet School matinée we had the experience of Wayne
Sleep as the Blue Boy in *Les Patineurs*. Never have we seen that series of
big *pirouettes* embarked on with such Dionysian frenzy or carried out
with such intoxicating speed. With this dynamo inside him, Mr. Sleep
need not worry about his lack of inches. Sir Fred must get cracking and
provide special roles for him, as Diaghilev did for Idzikovsky. I see
Wayne and Nerina in fabulous juxtaposition—two turning twins—'The
Whizz Kids'.

17.7.66

Symphonic Variations

(First performed 1946)

Custom has not staled the noble simplicity of *Symphonic Variations*, which is obviously built to endure. It was carefully danced by Antoinette Sibley, Ann Jenner, Jennifer Penney, Anthony Dowell, Robert Mead and Michael Coleman.

Some ballets are born with programmes, some achieve programmes and some have programmes thrust upon them. The other day I was re-reading an interview I did with Ashton about *Symphonic Variations* over twenty years ago. He put an awful lot of thought and philosophy and 'meaning' —even story—into the ballet, and although in the course of choreographic composition nearly all of this was eliminated the work was undoubtedly richer for the process.

Where, for instance, can we look in this limpid choreography for Frazer's *Golden Bough*, St. Teresa of Avila and St. John of the Cross? Of Ashton's idea of making the four sections represent the four seasons there is still a trace, but one realizes that if he had gone through with this autumn would precede summer.

While César Franck's music is human—reflective, mournful, doubting, searching, exultant—Ashton's choreography is celestial and aloof. The six dancers do not express the score: they merely dance to it: it is as if 'the still sad music of humanity' was necessary for these angels to perform their function. Or, to put it in another way, perhaps these purified beings have transformed into a blessed rite the patterns of their former life on earth.

26.10.69

Cinderella

(First performed in 1948)

'The big hit of Ashton's *Cinderella* is its pair of Ugly Sisters, Helpmann and Ashton himself, and it is the one Ashton plays, the Second Ugly Sister, who becomes the charmer of the evening. She is the shyest, the happiest, most innocent of Monsters.'

Edwin Denby wrote that in 1948 and it is still true. In the new production only these Ugly Sisters and the Jester of Alexander Grant survive from then. And on the night before Christmas Eve Margot Fonteyn, who

Frederick Ashton
in *Cinderella*.
Drawing by
George George

should have created the role of Cinderella in 1948 but was prevented by an accident and danced it two months after Moira Shearer, spellbound us with her undimmed youthful magic. Nerina and Beriosova followed her last week.

The trouble with *Cinderella*, Denby found, and most of us agreed, was that in spite of the comedy and the glittering ball and the cosily familiar story—nothing happened. The Prince was nobody, his relationship with Cinderella never had a chance to develop into anything, nothing worked up to a climax—not even to an orgy of spectacular dancing in Act III. If the Act II ball had amounted to more we might not have minded the quiet ending. The fault perhaps lay in Prokofiev's score. But Ashton, for brevity's sake or shunning national character dances, cut a long series of numbers at the beginning of Act III in which the Prince was meant to go round the world, from country to country, presumably trying the slipper on whinnying English debs and lugubrious Hottentots. Dramatically, I now see, this would have been useful.

To summarize the new production: the first Act is much improved; the second is still meandering and the intrusive Jester is more annoying than before; the third still gets nowhere.

A word about the Jester, around whom, in an odd way, the Ball seems to revolve—much more so than round the Prince. I must make allowances for Alexander Grant, who has risen from a bed of hepatitis. But if he was *just* strong enough to dance he must have been strong enough to put on the red and white clown make-up. Without it, in that sparkling skull-cap, one has the impression that he is trying to look romantic; and his leering at us across his bauble, coming after the rather heavy capers, has something provocative and obscene about it.

'The Seasons' were ravishing (and their evocative music—indeed, the whole score—sounded better under Sergiu Commissiona than we have ever heard it). Antoinette Sibley as darting Spring, Vyvyan Lorrayne as leisurely Summer, Merle Park as frantically spinning Autumn were all a joy and David Walker had given them perfect Vigano-style dresses— drifting wisps from high Empire no-waists, dotted with poppies or leaves; only Deanne Bergsma seemed not quite as serene as she can be in a slightly altered Winter dance, wearing a too tinselly costume. 'The Seasons' are preceded now by a fine introductory variation to extraneous music for the Fairy Godmother.

David Blair brings a hail-Cinderella-well-met breeziness to the non-existent role of Prince; while Donald MacLeary, oozing svelte allure (try it!), even at moments of most strain—while impeccably supporting

Beriosova—parts his lips in ecstasy, makes his eyes beacon, looks radiant.

Svetlana Beriosova is a touching and soulful—in the Russian way—Cinderella, and on the first night Fonteyn really shone. Such a tiny waist, such perfect judgment of poses, such starry dazzle! This, combined with the two clowns of genius, was quite overpowering in Act I. Only later we began to quibble at the ballet's weaknesses.

David Walker's bracken and pale gold court dresses are 1804, Napoleon's coronation, the style Lila de Nobili revived for *Ondine*. This style, by the way, in Empire days was a nostalgic harking back to Henri IV. Henry Bardon, designer of the sets, has gotten himself a new nostalgia, perhaps for the Empire music-hall *c.* 1900. His rococo woods, clouds and terraces are Fragonard seen through Edwardian eyes. Do you know those machine-made 'tapestries' of pastoral subjects from which all colour has been drained? Or the faded decorations of provincial music-halls? Well, that's it. Fancy in 1965 having a yearning for the way 1900 yearned for 1760! Then, I suppose, even Fragonard and Hubert Robert were yearning for an imaginary classical Arcadia. It is all too grey for me.

2.1.66

Cruelty is not funny, but it has to be made so in ballet and panto. I was thinking how odd it was that the Ugly Sisters, who were so beastly to Cendrillon in Perrault's tale, are now the darlings of children and gods at the season of goodwill. It is odd, too, that Ashton's Second Ugly Sister, that extraordinary creation, is not only funny but pathetic, so that she almost steals our sympathy from Cinderella.

In the panto of *Cinderella* at the Golders Green Hippodrome the ugly sisters are delightful. Alan Haynes corresponds to Helpmann, the uglier, knockabout one: but to say that Danny La Rue is sympathetic like Ashton is an understatement. First he is pretty and secondly his face positively exudes goodwill. I have never seen him off stage, but he looks a dear: and the act is subtle and hilarious.

Watching Ashton and Helpmann one day from the unusual viewpoint of a stage box, I decided that the secret of their achievement even in broad passages is understatement. This may seem surprising of the violent Helpmann, but I think it's true. And, of course, economy. Sometimes, from close to, Ashton seemed to be just walking through his movements as if his thoughts were elsewhere, but I knew how everything 'told' from a few yards farther off, and caught a glimpse of the secret of this art, which underlines its points, its jokes, and sketches lightly the bits between.

Ronald Emblen and Stanley Holden, both excellent comedians whom I have adored in *La Fille*, seemed busy by comparison. Because they did not relax between the points, these were not made with such effect. Understatement plus Economy equals Simplicity, and I suppose that is almost always an attribute of the highest art.

Why does the Prince lack character, even when jovial Blair, glamorous MacLeary, or Gable, with shining morning face, play him? Because we meet him cold, knowing nothing of his background. The princes in *Swan Lake* and *Sleeping Beauty* are not attracted by Court ladies and prone to melancholy. The former has a friend, a tutor, and an overwhelming mother, and he drinks. The Prince in *Giselle* is a randy double-crosser. Cinderella's Prince merely has a jester to whom he allows outrageous liberties. A passage of mime in Act I telling how he is dying of boredom, or won't inherit Rembrandt's 'Night Watch' unless he marries before he is twenty-one, might help.

Brian Shaw's Jester in chalky make-up has an element of quizzical mystery to balance his cocky intrusions, which is good.

I should think Nadia Nerina, small, cheerful, eager, neat and given to bursts of happiness, is Everychild's idea of Cinders, and it was fun to watch her thrilling the kids at a Saturday matinée.

23.1.66

Sylvia
(First performed in 1952)

Nobody has read Tasso's *Aminta*; nobody, perhaps, gives a damn about the story of Frederick Ashton's long spectacular ballet *Sylvia*, which is based on it; and nobody, possibly (though this I can't quite believe), bothers to read Arnold Haskell's programme note when attending the seventy-eighth performance of the work at Covent Garden in June, 1963.

Yet the old tale holds a message for us all.* In Act III Diana, Goddess of Chastity and Prime Ministress of this legendary Westminster, is aroused by a rude knocking to the knowledge that one of her trusty virginal hench-women is illegally involved with a mere mortal. What is more, the militant Sylvia has been drinking with the thirsty representative of a foreign Power, 'Orion, the robber Khan and terror of the peasants'.

---

* The following two paragraphs refer satirically to the 'Profumo affair' which had startled the British press and public into one of their recurrent fits of hypocrisy. The 'neo-classical residence on the river' refers to Lord Astor's Cliveden.

Diana is on the point of getting rather bloody about the whole thing when Eros, the Leader of the Opposition, points out (producing, as it were, an old newspaper cutting in the clouds) that she, Diana, too, once had her fling (with Endymion); upon which the virtuous Goddess comes over quite human and attends a party for the erring parties in the grounds of a neoclassical residence on the river (at which the Ministers of Agriculture and Fuel and Power, and representatives of the Arts Council, are also present).

Although I quarrel with Ashton's (1952) treatment of *Sylvia* (which has been continuously performed in another version at the Paris Opéra since 1876) I must admit his hands were, to a certain extent, tied. Delibes's very pretty score was one of the earliest written for ballet to use leading motifs, and the recurrence of these conditions the story line. For instance, unless you cut the magical horn call which announces the approach of the nymphs through the woods, and the music for Eros shooting Sylvia, and the getting-drunk music, and the apparition of Diana music, you must stick, more or less, to the old story.

The story (which I think could have been treated as a nineteenth-century comedy) is a very silly one, even for ballet. Briefly: Sylvia, having shot Aminta, is shot in turn by Eros and falls in love with the unconscious Aminta before being carried off by Orion. Act I ends with Eros (like Pan in *Daphnis*) showing Aminta the way to go to rescue Sylvia. But Act II, during which Aminta *doesn't* rescue Sylvia, is entirely devoted to Sylvia saving her virtue by plying Orion with vodka; and it ends with Eros showing *Sylvia* the way to go to find *Aminta*, who clearly has no sense of direction. Act III, apart from the Diana episode, is a divertissement.

The revival is almost justified as a vehicle for Melissa Hayden, who flings herself into the dull choreography with a Balanchinean incisiveness. Her relaxed hands, which seem to drip off the ends of her arms, like rain from swaying tendrils, look very exotic to us.

Flemming Flindt dances in the grand style. He has splendid turns and jumps, including backward jumps *en attitude*; and in Act I his swinging looped *port de bras* were beautiful.

23.6.63

Ondine

(First performed in 1958)

Frederick Ashton is a great heroine-worshipper, as anyone who has heard him on Pavlova or Karsavina or Isadora will confirm—in old days he would surely have sighed the night through on Lily Langtry's doorstep: he also has a knack for poetic conceits. So I should not be surprised to learn that in planning a role of roles for the divine Margot, and in building the three-act ballet of *Ondine* around it, he consciously delighted to make Fonteyn first appear from a fountain.

I don't know what the title of the film means—*The Singer not the Song*: but it is the Ballerina not the Ball that makes *Ondine* go over big. That is to say that the choreography Ashton has made for Fonteyn and the way she interprets it are the whole of *Ondine*. The rest, Henze's music apart, is not very interesting.

There are annoying things about the story. The return from hunting and the hoydenish hunting-crop Countess strike a reminiscent note from the start. So does the Prince who wants to be alone and is clearly waiting for a girl from outer space. That the Prince, having followed Ondine into the forest and got married to her by a hermit, should be so inefficient as to sail on the same ship as the fiancée he is escaping from is like one of those plays in which Mr. Cecil King, the Prime Minister, Lord Shawcross and Mr. Bernard Levin all get snowed up in the same inn on Exmoor—or stranded together in the V.I.P. lounge at London Airport. And the final divertissement with two thrones on one side of the stage is, well, traditional.

The designer, Lila de Nobili, like Ashton, is a creature of poetic ideas (I remember the fairies in full Elizabethan court dress, but with bare feet, at Stratford), and her last act costumes particularly, with their autumnal burnish and glitter, are superb. But her architectural sets are too shapeless and seem to be painted by a near-sighted fly.

Fonteyn's role, though, and Fonteyn herself are beyond criticism. The airborne style of movement which Ashton invented for her in the 1953 *Spirits of the Air pas de deux* is here varied and perfected. The playful dance with her own shadow is incomparably pretty; and the pseudo-solo, in which, invisibly manoeuvred by a strong arm, she appears to be sporting sadly in the waves like a lonely dolphin, is an invention and a delight. Never have her limbs seemed more expressive or her line more heartfelt.

The character she projects, alternately fond and soulless, is that of an incorporeal kitten playing with water and air.

5.3.61

La Fille mal gardée

Fifteen years ago M. Alexandre Benois, the great-uncle of modern ballet, said to me 'La Fille mal gardée must be revived', and I couldn't see why. A rustic, comic ballet first given at Bordeaux in 1789 with music by no one in particular—it sounded like a dead loss, and anyway I loathe peasants. Then Mme. Karsavina told me that, along with Giselle, it was the only old ballet worth reviving, and, although I knew her judgment was pretty well infallible, I thought she was getting carried away by nostalgia for a favourite role.

So, when Fred Ashton announced that he was going to do La Fille mal gardée, I said 'Oh Lord! Can't you do something new?'

But we have to face the fact that Ashton lives in a sort of nineteenth-century dream world, just as a lot of talented writers and whatnot today get their kick from playing cops and robbers in cellars or guys and dolls in jeans; so who am I, the oldest living teenager, to blame him?

A fragmentary story and the music of Hérold are what Ashton thought it worthwhile to take over, for the original choreography has not survived (except perhaps parts of it in the memory of Mme. Karsavina); but the main thing was that these, and perhaps the sense of adding to a long tradition, inspired him to invent some glorious choreography, and La Fille mal gardée is a tremendous success.

The success is due to the dazzling inventiveness of the several pas de deux and solos danced by Nadia Nerina and David Blair like gods from Olympus; to the attractive music of Hérold, gaily edited by John Lanchbery, with traditional interpolations from Rossini and Donizetti; and to a cosy, pastoral atmosphere which is also particularly Ashtonesque, like his romanticism, reminding me of picnics and of the painted pottery in his kitchen.

Osbert Lancaster's scenery can only aspire to limited praise: for though he has gone so far in a sentimental direction as to introduce shading, and his clouds are less flat-bottomed and McKnight-Kaufferish than usual, and his farmyard architecture is evocative in the light of dawn, to him trees will always be symbolic, corn will always be chrome yellow and a landscape, however full of witty allusions and cows like Church of England archdeacons, will never be much more than a coloured illustration from *Punch*. Mr. Lancaster's dresses are delightful.

Another reservation I must make in praising the production is with regard to the comic characters, particularly the heroine's mother, confidently played in the British style of pantomime dame by Stanley Holden. Old Cecchetti used to take this part in Russia, and Tamara Karsavina has said that not only was he funny, but he was so *real* that the shame on his face when the lovers were publicly discovered, thus ruining Widow Simone's plan for her daughter's ambitious marriage, used to make her cry. A (spoken) comedy can have touches of farce only—the line must be drawn; and the same should apply in ballet. But it seems that in England boys will be dames; and this is an artistic loss.

Nevertheless, Holden does a funny clog dance, cloppity-clop, which varies the texture of the harvest celebrations. In the other comic role of Alain, the half-witted potential bridegroom who is more attached to his red umbrella than to any girl, Alexander Grant has some good grotesque dances, and times them brilliantly.

Nerina and Blair as Lise and Colas have never been so good before, or had such wonderful steps to do. Victor Hugo wrote: '*Quand on est jeune on a des matins triomphants*'; and dancing of this kind, which is *perhaps* the highest kind, imparts the pang of wonder we had on summer mornings when we were young, and ran to bathe with bare feet on the dew.

His amazing corkscrew turns, her joyous *écarté*, their *pas de ruban* in which they wind each other spinning in and out before knotting themselves into a cat's cradle, his lifting her at one arm's length above him like a shining prize, her tripping runs, his great spins, their tenderness and gaiety together—these are a few memories from a triumphant evening.

31.1.60

I was thinking how well Frederick Ashton had worked out the action of *La Fille mal gardée*, so that the set pieces of dancing seem to emerge quite naturally from the story, and I began to wonder how much John Lanchbery had actually done to Hérold's old score and whether, apart from re-orchestrating most of it, he had revised the whole thing for Ashton's dramatic purposes. A telephone call brought the interesting answer to my question.

'Hérold's score,' said Ashton, 'was a series of quick monotonous numbers, mostly in six/eight time, which on first hearing all sounded alike. It was only when we started analysing the music, playing some pieces slower than others, and identifying, for instance, what must have been the churning dance, that we began to see its possibilities. The only indications on the score were *"Lever du rideau"* and *"Orage".'*

I asked whether Mme. Karsavina could not have helped in describing what action or dance had been fitted to which music; and was told, 'In Russia they used quite different music by Hertel, though they kept to Dauberval's story.'

'Did you say to Lanchbery, "Let's bring in that romantic theme before we start the *pas de deux*", and so on?' 'Oh, yes, we reshaped and rewrote the whole score according to what I needed. It's practically a new composition.'

I was fascinated, though not altogether surprised, to hear Ashton and Lanchbery had worked together much as Fokine had worked with Stravinsky on the creation of *The Firebird*—with the difference that, musically speaking, the Englishmen were building a new house with old bricks. Lanchbery's score, apart from contributing enormously to the success of the ballet, contains much music which would give pleasure on its own, and a selection from it should certainly be recorded.

It was a poetic and wayward idea of Ashton's to introduce the theme of 'ribbons' throughout the ballet, as if he were exploring every possible use a ribbon could be put to in choreography before he finally tied his hero and heroine together with a true lovers' knot.

Lise, rising at dawn, ties a rose ribbon as a signal to her lover on an iron ring let into the stable wall: when Colas finds it he knots it to his pitchfork. The lovers' first dance, the traditional *pas de ruban* which gave Ashton his hint, begins with the unfurling of a pink parabola of ribbon through the air. This shining band of satin is used by Lise and Colas to spin each other like tops, to tie each other into a cat's cradle, as a skipping-rope and as bit, bridle and reins in a game of horse and rider.

Alain, the comic rival, is next to be harnessed with ribbon; but the real orgy of ribbon development takes place at the picnic in the cornfield. During the lovers' *pas de deux* eight girls make geometrical patterns in ribbon, spelling out some virginal code of their own—there are Xs for kisses, and something which would be described in heraldry as 'fusils conjoined in fesse' and might mean either diamonds or mountains.

A pretty effect is produced at the end of this dance, which Lise finishes sitting on her boy-friend's knee; the girls in V-formation, who have been making (warning?) triangles, one foot holding down the end of their ribbon, in a pose familiar from an old print, suddenly let go with one hand, so that the ribbons flutter loose like harpstrings melted by love. Lise next becomes the hub of a girlish wheel, the spokes of which are ribbons pulled taut to hold her in position as she revolves *en attitude*. Finally there is the maypole with everybody circling and folk-weaving in and out.

I have still only touched on two aspects of this ballet, which is such a finely wrought artifact. It amazes me how the choreographer could have divined the gleaming frieze he would raise from the unpromising quarry of Dauberval's rustic anecdote and Hérold's six/eight tunes. Karsavina, who never knew the original French score but who could recount the magic of the Russian production, must have inspired Ashton as once she inspired Fokine.

7.2.60

It is always a mixed pleasure to agree with your boss, but when J. W. Lambert wrote in a theatre review a few months ago that comedy was the highest art, he was stating something I have felt for at least a quarter of a century, even before the days when I tried to write comedies myself (I wrote ten).

Comedy should aspire to the condition of Mozart, in whose music there is so often a feeling of sadness behind the gaiety, with good (musical) manners keeping the *lacrimae rerum* at bay—so as not to embarrass the aristocracy. (I stole this last idea from a radio talk by Antony Hopkins.)

There are several fine comedies running in London at the moment, supreme among those I have seen being Clifford Williams's impeccable production of Barrie's *What Every Woman Knows*, which made me laugh and cry more than any play for years and which I am just going to see for the third time; John Copley's *Rosenkavalier* at the Coliseum, so divinely sung; and Ashton's *Fille mal gardée* at Covent Garden.

Park and Nureyev were dancing this last Wednesday, and although I know some people think Park too 'urban' and Nureyev too princely for the pastoral, for me it was a magical occasion. Park is so finely formed and has an aurora borealis of happiness which lights up the theatre. Nureyev, hobbledehoying away, is not so much being a yokel as making yokel jokes. I loved his teasing, and the way, when Widow Simone finally accepted him as a son-in-law, he did a stiff comic swoon forward into her arms.

Ronald Emblen's Widow reminded me of Mme. Karsavina describing how, when Cecchetti, playing her mother, came to the scene of disgrace and disappointment, the mingled expressions on his face made her cry. In Emblen's wildly funny performance, in Grant's inspired clowning, in

Edwards's ineffective bluster there is always a hint of latent sorrow. Just as the Marschallin grows old and Barrie's Maggie has a humourless husband, Simone's daughter fails to marry the landowner's son. In my exalted state I imagined that even the freakish little Notary's Clerk of Wayne Sleep was dreaming of impossible promotions.

16.2.75

The Two Pigeons

One of the pampered horde of spies I am obliged to maintain (eating their heads off in the servants' wing) reported by microdot that Frederick Ashton's sister Edith was heard to say she knew exactly what Buckle would write about the new ballet—he'd complain that nobody was wearing blue jeans in it. Well, of course I am all for everyone wearing blue jeans all the time, particularly at court, but I don't see why they should worry what I think, as *Les deux Pigeons* is obviously destined to be a mad, popular hit with the so-called ballet public for years to come.

Ashton's *Les deux Pigeons* is another work of his Ivor Guest period. Guest is a nice lawyer who, because he once lived at Chislehurst, got keen on Napoleon III, and this led to a mania for the Paris Opéra, on which he has now written innumerable books. Ashton is mad about the nineteenth century anyway, and, incited by Guest, he has done *Sylvia*, *La Fille mal gardée*, and now *Les deux Pigeons*, all of which are the stock classics of you've guessed which theatre.

The point is do you realize the danger? Do you realize that the male leads in these ballets were always danced by *women* (I've *seen* it)? And the next step might be to introduce *that* at Covent Garden? You didn't, but then you probably didn't know that at the Paris Opéra all the stage-hands have to wear white ties and walk backwards carrying silver candelabra.

Ivor Guest tells us in an Historical Note on the programme that the ballet was first performed at the Paris Opéra in 1886, that André Messager, its composer, revived it at Covent Garden in 1906, when he was artistic director there, and that 'the discovery at the Royal Opera House of the score for the 1906 production prompted Frederick Ashton to stage a new version for the Royal Ballet', which seems as bad a reason as any.

The music is ghastly—that is to say, you may love it. And I think I once ate Dundee cake to one of the tunes at Bournemouth. As a matter of fact, it is skilfully put together and must have had some deft arranging by John Lanchbery—though I see one critic, who must be a frightful swot to

K

have mugged up the original version, comments that 'the boy is thrown out of the gypsy camp to music that literally illustrates the destruction by lightning of a huge oak tree.'

Ashton's version of the story concerns two lovers who live with two doves in an attic, which, though it is at the top of a high house with a marvellous view of Paris, you have to come down a flight of stairs to get into. *He* is a painter and sulks because *she* won't sit properly. Their solitude is interrupted by a band of gypsies who happen to drop up. The boy flings them some money which he can ill afford, and they dance. Beglamoured by a dusky enchantress, the boy leaves his girl and goes to the gypsy camp. Act II, Scene I, is a big gypsy ball, which ends with the volatile vagrants turning on the boy and throwing him out. One of his doves comes to fetch him home, and his girl friend forgives everything. This is a truly Christian ballet.

The choreography is always effective, though never surprising; Lynn Seymour and Christopher Gable are delightful; and the doves are impeccable performers—at least, they were at the Gala on Tuesday.

19.2.61

It's something to do with how sophisticated you can get. We all know there are things you can do one year straight which a year later can only be put over with the tongue in the cheek. You not only have to be quite clear what you want to do, you have to know what you can get away with. Like the divine Beatrice von und zu Lillie should never sing sentimental songs because you are always waiting for her to be funny.

I can imagine Frederick Ashton mounting a Victorian ballet with corny story, palmcourt music and conventional choreography, and doing it absolutely straight and deadpan, and it might be funny and charming in turns and we might love it. But *Les deux Pigeons* is not quite like that.

Starting by liking the score, which certainly has one or two good tunes in it, Ashton must have decided the story with its Greek setting was a bit much. To give his love-birds a Paris studio for their dovecote was a pretty parallel; and he devised some nice action and movements for them, half comic, half lyrical, with suggestions of preening, billing and cooing.

But how was he to bring in the gypsies? After all, there was a *czardas* in Act II. Despairing of making them plausible, I suppose he decided just to let them occur. And this was the lapse in style or sophistication which (apart from the banal music) let down the ballet. The first scene with the lovers, which makes jokes about love, is good and new and true; then the gypsies burst in and we are in the world of that operetta in which they sang 'Only a rose' and 'To hell with Burgundee!'

In the gypsy camp, which designer Jacques Dupont, who seems to compromise between the attic and the operatic, has disappointingly made as grey as his first scene, teeth flash, cloaks swirl, crinolined ladies teeter in to cross palms with silver, top-hatted gents lose their watches, charms are flaunted and bangles jangled, and the only sign that anyone is sending the whole thing up is when Johaar Mosaval begins trucking madly at the back in earrings.

I like very much what Ashton has given Lynn Seymour to do—awkward, touching little flutters of the hands and feet—and the modern way he sometimes makes her flop about. She strikes the exact note: she is a sort of strip-cartoon heroine. Christopher Gable is less remarkable for his actual dancing than for his impetuous naturalism. The way he grins and lets his arms swing loose at the end of a solo, his boyish 'Anyone for tennis?' manner is something quite new in ballet. (I wonder if he can sing.) From now on, one feels, male dancers will never be able to stand with both hands on one hip again, like after seeing *The Connection* we realized with a blush that to be 'daytime' was as square as you could get.

26.2.61

We have remarked before, and we intend to remark again annually around Trinity Sunday, that nowhere but in ballet does anyone use the expression 'The Young Girl'. Parents don't say 'Has my Young Girl returned from her lesson in taxidermy?' Lovers don't say 'Allow me to introduce the Young Girl to whom I am affianced'. Even journalists don't write 'Young Girl, held on arson charge, slays nine'. But if all the Young Girls who had been the heroines of ballets from the first performance of *Le Spectre de la Rose* in London till the present day could be laid side by side my bed wouldn't be big enough.

The Young Girl in the revival of Ashton's *The Two Pigeons* at the Royal Opera House is Doreen Wells and the Young Man is David Wall, and they are delightful. We find it much easier to take the *pot-pourri* prettiness of *The Two Pigeons* now that it is an old ballet (thirty-fourth performance at the Royal Opera House). When it was born piping hot from the forehead of Sir Fred, we were put off by the sweetness of the tunes and story, by the nostalgia for the nineteenth century, by the insipidity of the sets and by those glittering brown gypsies with their strong white teeth. Now we accept the work as part of the repertory, part of our French inheritance like *Giselle* and *La Fille mal gardée* and *Coppélia*. Have you noticed, by the way, that the heroine or Young Girl in French ballets always has eight Friends? This in itself is not so remarkable as the fact of their all being in town on the same day.

We wouldn't swear to it, but we think Elizabeth Anderton has danced the gypsy girl—or rather, A Gypsy Girl—in every one of the thirty-four performances we have been following with mounting passion. And Johaar Mosaval's peculiar electric impersonation of A Gypsy Boy is so striking that we are thinking of making a ballet for him around the character of Larry Zed, a Mad Boy, from J. C. Powys's novel *Weymouth Sands*.

Doreen Wells we have seen in this ballet before: she is pretty, touching, funny and perfect. David Wall has not appeared until now in London in the role Gable created, and it is a pleasure to see that in addition to being a fine dancer with the ability to carry off a classical role like Albrecht, he can switch easily to *demi-caractère*, playing romantic comedy with humour, timing, zest, charm and lightness of touch. They made an irresistible pair in the tender little *pas de deux*. Ashley Lawrence wrung every drop of languid sugar from Messager's Parma-violet-coloured score. We have to admit that, once we can bring ourselves to accept the premise of Ashton's ballet, it can't be denied that he made an absolutely craftsmanlike, telling and effective job of it. Every tiny punch goes home.

But we think it was going a bit far to put on Cranko's *The Lady and the Fool* before *The Two Pigeons*. After all, what may the tourists think?

We are not going to use that four-letter word denoting excessive mannerism of a sometimes hysterical type, much used in the theatrical profession, because we thought there had been a tacit agreement this year not to use it (or 'kinky' or 'with it') any more—an agreement being regularly infringed, we observe, by critics who shall be nameless, nay, who have long cringed under assumed names—*but* . . . we must break off here as some gypsies are passing in the street below, and we are going to ask them up chiefly to see whether, as at Covent Garden, they manage to climb *down*stairs into our fourth-floor studio.

19.6.66

Marguerite and Armand

Of course, Ashton, Beaton and Liszt have collaborated before: and looking back to *Apparitions* in 1936 we can see it as the beginning of a success-

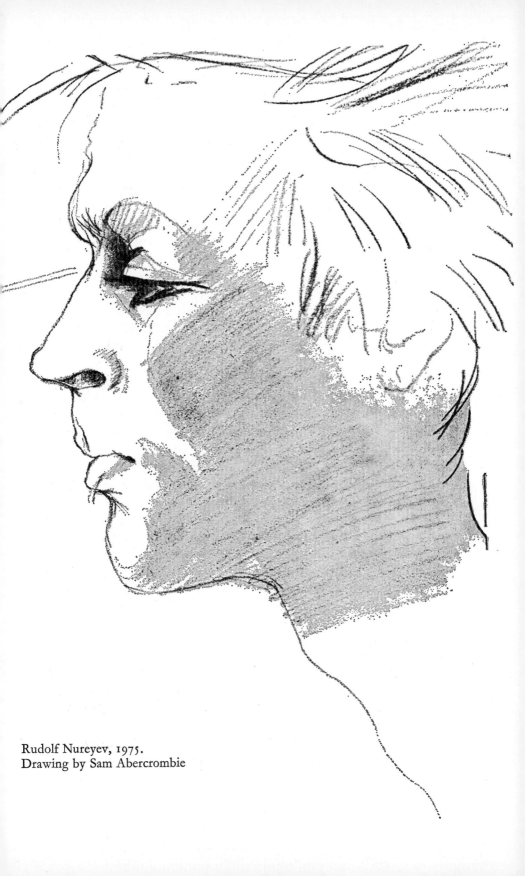

Rudolf Nureyev, 1975.
Drawing by Sam Abercrombie

ful partnership. In those days Ashton was not yet a Knight nor Beaton a Commander of the British Empire, but Liszt, I think, was already in Holy Orders. In those days, thanks to Sacheverell Sitwell, Liszt was just beginning to be taken seriously, and Constant Lambert chose the *Liebestraum* and other pieces for Gordon Jacob to orchestrate, and lured us to Sadler's Wells.

In those days, thanks to Kenneth Clark and John Betjeman, but to the consternation of our aunts, we were beginning to be mad about the Gothic Revival; and Cecil Beaton gave us a vision of Fonthill Abbey. In those days Margot Fonteyn was the Romantick heroine in a huge 1830s skirt, and Robert Helpmann the haunted hero.

Now, thanks to Lord Harewood's homage at the 1961 Festival, Liszt has come in on a new wave and Humphrey Searle, his staunchest apostle, has lovingly orchestrated the B minor sonata. Now, thanks to Brecht, Noguchi, and the former ballet critic Peter Brook, painted sets are out, whereas projections and sculpture—preferably in welded metal—are in; so Cecil Beaton to create his Paris *salon*, on the walls of which huge visions of Nureyev come and go, has had to invoke the spiritual aid of a Japanese blacksmith. The huge skirts of 1830 are still the same; and still the same, only better, is Dame Margot Fonteyn, *das ewig Weibliche*, the elusive dream-girl whom Ashton, Beaton and Liszt have always been after, and who comes to earth to do a ballet with them every thirty years. Now her partner is not Helpmann but Rudolf Nureyev.

But enough of musings on the history of taste! *Marguerite and Armand*, which was given at the Gala on Tuesday, has stolen upon us so secretly, heralded by such mouselike publicity, that you will be bursting for the first news of it.* The story, which concerns a good-natured but consumptive call-girl who gives up her sugar daddy for love of a dishy young man, is persuaded by his father to leave him, returns to her gilded cage, is publicly insulted by the dish, but makes it up with him in time to die in his arms, has been used before.† Ashton tells it in a series of flashbacks from the death-bed.

Marguerite and Armand is a tremendous vehicle for the special gifts of Fonteyn and Nureyev. I cannot imagine anyone else doing it, and, as it is less a ballet than a series of psychological close-ups, its choregraphy is not important enough to make it worthwhile giving without these two power-ful personalities. But this is O.K. by me. I am all for *pièces d'occasion* which exist only for the artists who inspired them.

By 'special gifts' I mean this. Fonteyn's genius is for the expression of

* This is a joke.   † So is this.

emotion, chiefly with her face and arms. And Nureyev, though a dancer of splendid nerve and dash, has much greater potentialities—as I wrote on first sight of him—as an expressive artist. His characterization of Armand, in turn gay, impassioned, cruel and heart-broken, is much the best thing he has done.

The moments that stand out in memory are not particularly dancing ones, which is unusual in an Ashton ballet. *Margot and Rudolf* should be a godsend for television. The falling-in-love is wonderful. Nureyev, with yearning arms, is seen from behind, and as Fonteyn stands motion-less everything happens on her face. In three-quarter view she looks pleased but shy. They have a laughing *pas de deux* on the floor. I recall her *bourrée*-ing off, broken by duty and coughing; Nureyev's snakelike rage, his pointing at her in jeering love-hatred; her climbing into the air over his head to clutch at happiness, life and the sun before falling dead.

17.3.63

I don't know how much of a ballet *Marguerite and Armand* would be with-out Fonteyn and Nureyev, and don't much care. What is *Le Spectre de la Rose* without Karsavina and Nijinsky? And without Pavlova *The Dying Swan* is absolutely disgusting. Fonteyn and Nureyev were wonderful in Ashton's ballet when they first danced it eight months ago; now they have improved their interpretations and are altogether beyond praise.

From the wild opening wood notes of Humphrey Searle's subtle arrangement of the Liszt sonata we recognize that we are due for a bout of all-in romanticism; and fine frenzy is what we get from Fonteyn and Nureyev.

In the prologue Nureyev does perfect yearning attitudes round the death-bed of the girl we are supposed to think is Fonteyn. For the lovers' meeting Cecil Beaton dresses them, with one of his curious and daring felicities, in red and blue. The man has a rather obvious royal blue coat over white tights, the girl an indescribably subtle red ball gown. Total success.

Watch Fonteyn's face when the love-at-first-sight takes place. She is such a cool pussy-cat at first, almost sucking in her cheeks and primly pursing her pretty mouth, perhaps to stop herself smiling with too broad a joy. Then his uninhibited monkey yearning. She looks slowly and bashfully down, recognising the *coup de foudre*. And, after all, they are at a party and she is the cynosure of neighbouring eyes. But in the ensuing *pas de deux* he becomes cat-like in his different way and possesses her utterly, a cheetah gorging.

In the country scene Fonteyn's white dress with its fluttering satin ribbons reminded me of Herrick's 'When as in silks my Julia goes, Then, then (me-thinks) how sweetly flowes That liquefaction of her clothes.' A subtle Japanese green lighting effect. Somes as Armand's father, the god of Duty, comes and strikes his tragic gong and goes. Marguerite loving Armand before renouncing him—a white battle.

Next the party: Fonteyn coughing in black with camellias in her hair and a new diamond necklace. Nureyev comes in and yearns. He twirls her round, then madlier; flings her to the ground; lifts her with one finger under her chin; stares; suddenly pulls off and rejects her necklace; does low pirouettes in arabesque on a bent knee. With a change of mood he seems to try to sweep her off. But no, he flings banknotes at her and wipes his hands down his sides with a grimace of repellence. But when his back is turned his right arm is drawn back miserably towards her and his face is piteous. 'Oh now, for ever Farewell the tranquil mind; farewell content.' Turning again to the sobbing Fonteyn, he seems to relent, then points at her with dagger derision and backs out, fiendish, laughing.

To her death-bed, cloak swooping, a desperate nightrider, he soars. Whisks her up, whirls her round, cuddles her on the floor, smothers her with smiling, mocking sympathy. Mad embraces. She is lifted, diving to the sky; then falls. She raises a hand, touches his brow, gazes wildly. Her hand drops. Death. Sour chords.

24.11.63

Monotones

Frederick Ashton's *pas de trois*, *Monotones*, seen once before at a Gala a year ago, glowed like a pricey pearl.

Monotones is danced to the *Gymnopédies* of Erik Satie, piano pieces orchestrated—why?—by Debussy and Roland Manuel—perhaps in a friendly effort to drag the eccentric of Arcueil out of his suburban obscurity and to get him concert performances. It is odd to hear the terse composer of *Mercure* sounding Debussian in this arrangement, as the voluptuous impressionistic colour of Debussy was a quality against which Cocteau and Satie later led their young Six in revolt.

Clad only in white light, Ashton's girl and two boys, shining against the darkness, seem knotted together in some mysterious battle for humanity up on the high wire. At first it is a very tight knot: the balancing girl contracts, revolves and extends, motivated by two pairs of hands which continually take over from each other. Then the movement gets freer, opener, grander; and the men parade the girl at arm's length. As the music expands they dare to hold the extremities of the stage, guiding, as it were, her magic movements by remote control.

In this very difficult piece Ashton displays three wonderful gifts to an extreme degree: the linking of poses by movement, the relating of dancers to the framing rectangle of the stage so that they trace clear though invisible patterns in the air, and the rendering of the sense of a piece of music rather than the notes.

6.3.66

Trois Gnossiennes, orchestrated by John Lanchbery, is now danced before the *Trois Gymnopédies*, the whole to be called *Monotones*. I'm not sure what Gnossiennes are, but I guess them to be ritual dances performed privately by captive Greek slaves in the houses of Smyrna merchants during the rainy season. Anyway, Antoinette Sibley, Georgina Parkinson and Brian Shaw, as one would expect, are very good at them. They involve feats of balance, hopping in unison backwards and forwards in *arabesque*; and if their charm is a little unvaried I don't blame Sir Fred so much as the Smyrna merchants, who can't take in anything very complex after those enormous dinners.

They make an agreeable introduction to the serene *Gymnopédies* (danced by Vyvyan Lorrayne, Robert Mead and the hard-worked Anthony Dowell), which I think is such a lovely realization by Ashton of such a lovely piece of music, and which develops with the irrefutable simplicity of a flower or a Petrarchan sonnet.

1.5.66

These Satie *pas de trois* are not storyless to me, though they plunge me into uncritical dreams of '*luxe, calme et volupté*'. In *Gnossiennes* watchers on a roof-top await the arrival of their prince from another island. In *Gymnopédies* a doll-girl is rehearsed in love-knots for her lord. The bustle of the fish market is miles below.

5.1.75

Enigma Variations

India wants us back, Enoch Powell for Viceroy! Touching their forelocks, the lower classes beg to be underpaid and undernourished again. *Enigma Variations!*

Elgar wrote 'I've written the variations each one to represent the mood of the "party".' ('Party' means 'person'.) 'The result is amusing to those behind the scenes and won't affect the hearer who "nose nuffin".'

Frederick Ashton's ballet is nostalgically designed by Julia Trevelyan Oman, great-grandmother of two famous historians. Mellow is the word for this country house and garden with its staircase for children to wave goodnight from, its hammock for the cream of British womanhood to be swung in by the best type of Englishman. One autumn leaf simply, touchingly and inevitably falls. We get the picture. The days are drawing in.

The costumes are realistic, so dancing is not what we are going to see. A mood, however, will be evoked; and the movement will perhaps resemble Tudor's for *Lilac Garden*.

It doesn't. Tudor's nervous spurts and hesitations added up to a choreography into which 'the soul with all its maladies had passed'. Ashton's is altogether simpler.

The wife, Beriosova, loves and worries about her composer husband, Derek Rencher. There are visits from eccentric neighbours. A dear friend, A. J. Jaeger of Novello's, the music publishers, is welcomed—Desmond Doyle at his most Dr. Watson-ish.

But Ashton, master of theatrical know-how, has realised that to embody the anecdotic character sketches explained by Elgar in his notes is not enough.

After the moody No. 8, a twisting, turning, looping solo for Parkinson, and No. 9, Nimrod, with its Beethoven bit, which is where Jaeger comes to stay, and the No. 10 Scherzo flitted through by Sibley, and the jokey No. 11 in which Wayne Sleep in a moustache romps with children, and No. 12 in which Leslie Edwards plays the cello to Rencher, and No. 13 in which Deanne Bergsma's ocean crossing is represented by clouds of dry ice, a telegram arrives! Mr. A. J. Jaeger opens it, not forgetting to tip the messenger boy (a likely lad from Ludlow town). The telegram is to say that Richter agrees to conduct Elgar's *Enigma Variations*. Masterstroke by Ashton. Down in the pit John Lanchbery looks disappointed. *He* thought *he* was going to conduct it. Collapse of stout party. General rejoicing, in which we all join. To use the composer's Edwardian expression, Sir Fred is 'a trump'. And I have joined the Scouts.

27.10.68

There was all too little space a fortnight ago to mention all the artists whose subtle and finished performances contributed to the success of Ashton's *Enigma Variations*. Everybody was remarkable in this *tour de force*, which was such an odd ballet to want to do and such an amazing feat to bring off successfully.

It was awkward that Elgar placed three comic characters one after the other; that the penultimate variation danced by Deanne Bergsma should be about a lady who was absent at sea; and of course there was the risk that a man wearing tweeds and a genuine watch-chain would look ridiculous expressing feeling by a *rond de jambe*.

Besides Derek Rencher and Beriosova who beautifully portray the central characters, and Desmond Doyle as the true-hearted but buttoned-up family friend, there are fine comic cameos by Stanley Holden, Brian Shaw and Alexander Grant, a bounding dance for impetuous Dowell and a twirling one for ecstatic Sibley.

10.11.68

It is curious that Elgar should have envisaged the possibility of his *Enigma Variations* being danced as a ballet, as John Lanchbery tells us he did in the programme, and even curiouser that he should have 'visualised the setting as a banqueting hall with a veiled dancer as the Enigma'. What could all those old friends of his 'pictured within', the country neighbours, music publishers and amateur musicians, be doing in a banqueting hall?

Ashton's evocation—with the impassioned aid of Julia Trevelyan Oman—of an exact moment of time in Worcestershire at the end of the last century seems much more to the point; and the scene is conjured up with an accuracy which is almost psychic. I guess than in ten years' time this mixture of ballet steps and realistic acting will appear as absurd as Fokine's *Scheherazade*.

26.10.69

Lament of the Waves

What anonymous demi-god despatched and what insouciant Mercury—
what whistling postman—delivered the small parcel which was to seal the
fate of Marilyn Trounson and Carl Myers? What seraph parted the curtains
of cloud and let the sun's ray fall upon it, what guardian angel whispered
in Ashton's ear, 'Open it!', and when he unwrapped this score on tape,
which had come to him out of the blue, what inner angel prompted, 'Play
it!'?

And when the choreographer's Muse nodded, 'This is for you', what
spirit of youth guided him to devise such free forms and Tetleyan tumbles
as he had never invented before, and what elf urged, 'Let it be danced by
these two kids whom no one has ever heard of'?

The music of *Lament of the Waves*, which became a ballet at Covent
Garden on Thursday, is by Gérard Masson (b. Paris, 1936), who has
experienced Varèse and Stockhausen. It is an impressionist Debussyish
piece, but with newer noises. For instance, there are two bursts of
strange muttering, which are the orchestra saying their names and the
instruments they play. It is water music and the ballet is about two lovers
drowning.

The only décor is a billowing mottled velarium, suspended aloft to
represent the surface of the sea. In blackness the boy and girl drift down-
ward to the sea-floor. (Actually, they are descending on a lift.) Changing
shafts of light fall upon their last convulsions. The moment of drowning
in which they recall their brief lives and loves is represented by a seventeen-
minute *pas de deux*. This is very long for a dance, longer than *Le Spectre
de la Rose*, five minutes longer than *L'Après-midi d'un faune*. How many
choreographers could successfully hold our interest in a duet of this sort?

Ashton has hit upon a most varied and composite kind of movement,
in which classical steps merge into somersaults and undulations, just as
the loving merges into drifting and drowning. The tall, handsome Myers
and Trounson with her long fair hair are given the most fantastic chance,
which they seize triumphantly. Before the end a dark sphere appears with
orange Argus eyes of light, which may be God come to greet or a fish
come to eat them. Ashton's genius has most often been evident in images
of water and air.

15.2.70

MacMillan

Le Baiser de la fée

Ida Rubinstein commissioned it from Stravinsky in 1927, Benois suggested the story, Nijinska did the choreography—and Diaghilev was derisive, for he hated his old collaborators ganging up on him, particularly Stravinsky. He had cause for jealousy, because *Le Baiser de la fée* was a beautiful score. It has since tempted Ashton and Balanchine, and now Kenneth MacMillan has choreographed it for the Royal Ballet—with tremendous success.

The more I see of it the more sure I am that ballet is the hardest art in the world to bring off. It is not just a question of good dancing to good music in a good décor. If dancing, music, décor, production, interpretation, timing, lighting do not jell like *mayonnaise* the labour has been in vain. Diaghilev had a genius for mixing, and I do not think he would have laughed at *this* production.

Stravinsky intended his score as a homage to Tchaikovsky, and privately interpreted the story in a way personal to his great forbear: the fairy's kiss bestowed on the exposed baby brought with it the divine discontent of a romantic artist, whom no mortal love would ever console. In fact the words of Goethe's song, Tchaikovsky's setting for which is one of the numbers Stravinsky worked into his score, might well be the motto of the earlier composer: *Nur wer die Sehnsucht kennt, weiss was ich leide*! If any artist was inspired by self-pity and a sense of isolation, *allein und abgetrännt von aller Freude*, it was the homosexual composer of the *Pathétique*, so perhaps the allusion is deliberate.

Stravinsky's instrumentation, with which he clothes and glorifies this and other songs and a few piano pieces by the older master, is magical, and MacMillan, with his ear to the ground, has perfectly translated into movement the filigree of shimmering insect splendour which is a special characteristic of this score.

Not that all the ballet is like that—there is a resounding variation for the hero when he thinks he is going to marry a mortal bride, and some hearty boomps-a-daisy for the villagers. Colin Davis conducts with understanding.

Donald MacLeary as the young man has a slightly incredulous and boyish appeal: he dances with strength and smoothness, bringing a skilled assurance to the support of his two partners. As his village bride the irresistible Lynn Seymour skims and flits like a happy gnat through her lovely *allegretto* variation: she has the priceless gift of lending to art an air of spontaneity, and without question makes a triumph of her first created role.

I do not think I have ever seen Svetlana Beriosova better in a modern ballet. As the Fairy, her swooping boreal gestures and Alpine style point the difference between god and human. Hölderlin might well have addressed to such a being as her the lines:

Ihr wandeldt droben im Licht
Auf weichem Boden, selige Genien!

In his décor Kenneth Rowell has invented a new kind of fairyland, and I applaud him. We have had enough Gothic, baroque and rococo. His abstract sets have sometimes the holy glow of Samuel Palmer's Shoreham, sometimes the cataclysmic gloom of a mountainscape by John Martin: they owe a debt to Tchelitchev's transparencies and perhaps a nod to de Staël. But they are quite original in their geological, intestinal way. After all, to discover a land of miracles we only need a spade, a scalpel or a microscope.

17.4.60

The Invitation

Kenneth MacMillan's new ballet, *The Invitation*, is an extraordinary mixture of experiment and cliché, beauty and absurdity. He has at least had a bash at something other than a fairy tale.

His subject is the loss of innocence: but whereas the authors of *Giselle* and *La Fête étrange* dealt cloudily with a girl's betrayal and a boy's disillusion over his first love, MacMillan is specifically concerned with his heroine's loss of virginity and his hero's sexual initiation by an older woman. We witness both these occurrences, and they are imaginatively done.

It seems a pity that someone should have got cold feet and ordered a covering-up programme note from A.L.H. (my old friend Haskell?) which turns the subject to favour and to prettiness. For 'the boy and girl . . . look out upon a strangely disturbing world' read 'They learn the facts of life from observing the private parts of statues.' For 'the boy is flattered by the older woman's interest' read 'he finds it easier, as many do, to make love for the first time with an older woman.' The note concludes 'For [the girl] nothing can ever be the same again.' I should think not, indeed.

But why set the action in 1905? This, combined with the stilted unre-thought-out mime of the mother and the governess, takes us back to the conventions of *Lilac Garden* or *Fall River Legend*.

Nicholas Georgiadis has painted some lovely *tachiste* scenes on gauze, among which four hideous academic statues, even if necessary props, seem an unforgivable intrusion. The composer's contribution to a ballet with so intricate a plot is reduced to providing atmospheric accompaniment. When Matyas Seiber gets going in the children's dancing class, his music sounds like Walton's *Façade*.

1.1.61

For years we have longed for a new wave in British ballet, comparable to that which has reanimated the spoken drama. Well, MacMillan *has* done something new: he has dealt directly with a real and tragic event. For this he deserves credit.

Choreographically this is MacMillan's best work, and I no longer doubt his quality. His children's dancing class with its little mishaps and inter-ruptions is well arranged. The *pas de deux* in which the boy, Christopher Gable, has sex for the first time, initiated by the older woman, could have been embarrassing but is moving and true—while Anne Heaton's warmth and Edwardian grace as the mother-mistress are quite perfect.

The sexual consummation in the rape *pas de deux* is achieved with the girl, Lynn Seymour, being flung, spread-eagled, around the older man in a dramatic adagio act: the final movement, when, knotted into a symbolic hoop round Desmond Doyle's body, she slips slowly to the ground, is inspired by a similar one in the orgy scene of Balanchine's *Fils prodigue*.

But. . . . The acrobats and cockfight in the middle, intended to in-augurate the night of misrule, don't come off at all. And though I know Picasso's Blue Period coincided with *la belle époque*, acrobats seem a very un-Edwardian house-party diversion. Then, the ballet is overweighted with parents, governesses and garden-party guests in huge, smart hats. And if I couldn't eliminate the statues from the story altogether I'd have them painted larger than life on the scenery, like those on Georgiadis' handsome drop.

15.1.61

The Rite of Spring

The Rite of Spring is about attracting the attention of God. In a time before history no tribe can be sure of daily sunrise or the return of spring. They only know that unless the crops ripen they will starve, so they stamp around to catch God's eye and send him what they guess he would like best—a girl.

By 1912, when Stravinsky wrote the score of this 'primitive' work, Gauguin had died in the South Seas, and Picasso and Epstein had for several years been collecting African sculpture. Trying to make something very old, the composer invented a music which was incredibly new, and his orchestra was called on to make noises never heard before. A work of visionary genius made history.

But *The Rite of Spring* was also a ballet, and written as such for Diaghilev. Stravinsky says Nijinsky's choreography was inadequate; Rambert says it was inspired. Stravinsky says that Massine's version of 1920 was 'incomparably clearer'; others say it lacked mystery. Maurice Béjart showed us an unworthy version two years ago. I suspect that Stravinsky thinks no choreographer can match the epic greatness of his score; and I suspect that MacMillan said, 'Whatever steps I arrange people will say they are inadequate'.

It might indeed seem almost miraculous to find a choreographer who could equal the poetry and terror of the music—though without question Martha Graham would be my bet. MacMillan has poetic invention but it is not the right kind for *Le Sacre*. His ballet begins and ends well, he never goes against the music and there are imaginative passages, such as when the prostrate crowd become the furrows of a ploughed field and the newly chosen Maiden skims like a rook over its surface.

However, this *Rite* does not come off. Fashionable Sidney Nolan, the folk-lore-conscious Australian painter, was perhaps wise to discard the would-be ancient-Russian style of Roerich; but all-over tights are *not* an equivalent to the daubed nude bodies of aborigines. They turn this tribe into nothing more than ballet-dancers with zips up their backs, which kills the work stone dead from the start.

Any suggestion of ballet is fatal and a sudden *grand jeté en tournant* from the Maiden, after all the jigging and waggling, is a shock. Equally, any suggestion of revue is fatal, such as certain dives by the girls, and that spiral of subsiding bodies *à la Rose Marie*.

Partly because much of the old scenario was scrapped, partly because

MacMillan runs out of ideas, a lot of the choreography seems like padding. The dance of the Chosen Maiden does not look exhausting enough and does not build up to a climax. Certain screams and explosions in the music, which MacMillan ignores, always make me think the work should have another dimension besides the human.

13.5.62

Sidney Nolan's setting for the first scene of MacMillan's *Rite of Spring* at Covent Garden is a simple all-over pattern of diagonal brownish streaks on a sandy background. The ballet is about fertilizing the earth, and Nolan was presumably thinking of those central deserts of Australia where they have seven-year droughts: but his skyless earthscape, which would make a good linoleum for the bathroom floor, seems to me a feeble way of representing what I am told is one of the most colourful and extraordinary landscapes in the world.

But of course MacMillan may have asked for something non-representational. Nolan's set is quite inoffensive—a painted backcloth and four painted wing-flats on each side—the same all over.

What I cannot comprehend is why anyone thought it would be all right to leave over the eight brown flats to frame the more exciting backcloth of the second scene.

This is a streaky blue night sky against which a giant disc on a stalk—moon, stylized tree, mushroom, mirage, totem or phallic symbol—looms hugely. The disc has, or cleverly appears to have, a surface of flaking gold-leaf, and when the drama mounts to a climax it glowers, bloodshot. A striking image: but could it not shine forth in a great emptiness of crepuscular sky, instead of being hemmed in by the brown streaky screens left over from Scene I? If any episode in the repertoire of ballet calls for a setting of infinite space it is this one.

Only parts of Stravinsky's music, I think (the majority, admittedly), can be rendered in terms of dancing and ritual: some of it represents the earth bursting into life. So I see the dancers as beings in the foreground—and not necessarily always in the foreground—of a landscape which is coming alive. In fact, the choreographer should only be one of a team—director, designer, stage mechanic and electrician—essential for harnessing Stravinsky's cataract for the purpose of the theatre.

So, if I were staging the ballet, either by using cinematic projections or by constructing a primeval vegetation, I should place the dancers in their context amid the terrors of nature. Sometimes they would be thudding

L

away in darkness when a cloud covered the moon; sometimes lightning would reveal distant valleys.

The introduction to Scene I is a dark landscape populated by small creatures, with brooks. The introduction to Scene II might be either trees or people swaying in the wind. During the Dance of Adolescents and in the Sacred Dance of the Virgin we hear the squawking of pterodactyls. There would be a holy tree with vast red sticky buds; and at the moment of the virgin's death, when a glutinous rising arpeggio in the music just before the final chord represents both her giving up the ghost and the consummation of her union with the god, I should have a bud burst open to let fall a shining sap.

27.5.62

La Création du monde

If Pop Art is an art which draws images from the commonplaces of every-day life—such as newspapers, advertising, cigarette packets or detergent packets—to use them in a decorative and/or evocative way, I suppose the Cubist painters' sticking of fragments of newspapers on to their pictures had something Pop about it, though Braque and Picasso would have used different words for what they were trying to do from Rauschenberg or Peter Phillips.

The huge Victorian watercolour of a fence covered with posters which hangs over the fireplace in the Circle bar at the Vaudeville is as Pop as you can get. Then Léger with his industrial subject matter, his ladies with hair like corrugated iron, his posterish colours and metallic surface of paint, was another precursor.

It was Léger who designed the original production of Darius Milhaud's *La Création du monde*, in 1923; and Kenneth MacMillan's arrangement for the touring section of the Royal Ballet, which we went down to Stratford-upon-Avon to see on Wednesday, is designed in the Pop manner. It is high time Pop art reached ballet, but James Goddard is rather a confused and wishy-washy kind of Pop artist to represent it.

Milhaud's music, with jazz dances given the French—Les Six—1920s treatment, originally accompanied a primitive African vision of the world's beginning. The score was too much of the moment not to date, but like Satie's *Parade* (which Massine is reviving with its original Picasso décor in Brussels next week) and Poulenc's *Les Biches*, it has a pungent period charm.

What interests me about MacMillan's version (if I read it right) is that using a childish language, he has tried to illustrate the concept of infinity. In a Pop setting kids appear to be dressing up and trying on disguises. A surpliced Clergyman stands stage centre concentrated on his holy book. A bicycling Butcher Boy delivers a Little Man in a Top Hat, who becomes a Union-Jack-clad Master of Ceremonies. The M.C. beckons on Adam and Eve, but in Adam we recognize the Clergyman—Richard Farley. He and Doreen Wells wear white tights with words for 'man' and 'woman' printed in black all over them—Bloke, Jo, Fella; Bird, Chick, Bint. That's all right.

While the story of Eden is enacted the M.C. conjures up some very funny captions by Mike Hodges on a film screen: 'Instant people: aroma rich'; 'I was a teenage snake'; apropos of the apple 'I was seduced by Granny Smith'; then 'Meanwhile, back at the Garden. . . .' Very much all right.

The choreography for Adam and Eve, Snake, fat Apple and *corps* did not *appear* to amount to much in all the confusion, but it may be better than I think, besides serving its purpose.

Then the M.C. resumes his top hat and is wheeled off by the Butcher Boy, and the Clergyman who has been Adam is back praying, and kids pass making derisive gestures. It is box within box within box. God creates man in his own image, then man creates God in *his* own image. Man mocks God and sends him packing; and God starts all over again. But who created God in the first place? I see no reason why these sublime considerations should not be treated in a Pop and jazzy way.

16.2.64

Romeo and Juliet

Very few people know that the row between the Capulets and the Montagus started when they opened their houses to the public, and the Montagus stole a march by showing veteran cars as well. The Montagus had a fancy dress dance at Beaulieu last Saturday and the Capulets had one at Covent Garden on Tuesday. There were more monks at the Hampshire do, but both parties went with a swing.

It was jolly brave of Kenneth MacMillan to tackle Prokofiev's *Romeo and Juliet* after the overwhelming Lavrovsky version—but then I think it's brave of anyone to make a ballet out of a Shakespeare play. MacMillan has tried to forget Lavrovsky and he has juggled with Shakespeare's story —why not? The ballet begins with Romeo serenading Rosaline. (Paris loses his wedding-day *aubade*.) Lord Capulet insists on the Montagus being treated politely at the party and eventually sees them off civilly at the gate (along with some veteran sedan chairs). There is no scene with the Apothecary in Mantua. The ballet ends with Juliet's death, and there is no ducal peacemaking over the grave. I don't say this is a better end than Shakespeare's or Lavrovsky's but it does give Margot Fonteyn the last word—or gesture.

MacMillan is a lyric poet: he is at his best when he focuses your attention on a solo or *pas de deux*, on the predicament of one person or of two. I don't think he is temperamentally equipped to organize large canvases, crowded with character and incident. This is not a criticism—after all, we don't complain that Chekhov, that divine artist, didn't tackle an epic like *War and Peace* or that Chopin wrote no opera. But choreographers attached to State theatres have to take on these big assignments. MacMillan's intimate scenes are lovely: the crowd scenes are tame and conventional, the fighting dull.

Then the physical organization of the stage is awkward. MacMillan and Nicholas Georgiadis have devised a semi-permanent set with movable units. It is on two levels, a double arcade with rather ready-made-looking columns, the upper floor connected with the lower by two high steep flights of steps. This serves, with variations, for the street scenes and the ballroom, and part of it for the balcony scene. Juliet's bedroom is different: so is the cell and the crypt.

The two-level arrangement for the 'big' scenes restricts the possibility of vertical composition. Lavrovsky's asymmetrical street scene had a gentle slope of steps to the right as well as a higher level at the back, and these steps were fine for fighting up and down. His ballroom on the flat somehow showed to perfect advantage the stately simplicity of the formal dances. MacMillan's steps are too steep for duelling; and the upper arcade appears to cramp the ballroom floor space.

These are basic faults. But Georgiadis is a wonderful designer. There are marvellous effects of luminous marble and all the costumes are perfect. None of these Renaissance dresses is literal in a theatrical costumier's way, but each is subtly worked out, and the total effect of the crowd at the ball is of browny-pinky-greeny-gold gorgeousness. There is a delightfully painted marble nursery for Juliet's first presentation to Paris and a handsome act drop of Gothic tombs based on a design Georgiadis made for the Shakespeare Exhibition. Friar Laurence's cell is splendidly adorned with religious frescoes, but it is in Byzantium. (I know there were painters before Cimabue in Italy, but this set is very Greek indeed.) The final crypt, a composition of delicate greys, is infinitely imaginative, subtle and mysterious, with perfect lighting by William Bundy.

MacMillan's Romeo is full of mischief, the leader of a gang which rules the market place. Nureyev bring the character to life. He specializes in a kind of mocking approach. This Romeo's courting of Rosaline is catlike, satirical. But love pricks him into spurts of ecstasy, expressed by wheeling suddenly round the stage. We know how well he can convey tenderness and tragedy. I liked him for appearing sincere and religious in Friar Laurence's cell. Nureyev's was a portrait in depth. I look forward to seeing him dance it when his foot is better.

His mates, Mercutio and Benvolio, were David Blair and Anthony Dowell, both excellent. There is a lively bit when they mock the Capulets' guests, Blair being funny and supercilious, Dowell breaking up couples. Mercutio's death dance was bound to echo Lavrovsky as its hesitations and defiant spurts are dictated by the same music. It was very striking. Our old friends Michael Somes and Julia Farron were the haughty Capulets, the latter with a disapproving air like Ninette de Valois. Gerd Larsen was a hearty, credible Nurse.

As Juliet, Fonteyn looked radiantly beautiful. There is an extraordinary moment at the end of the garden scene when she and Nureyev suddenly gaze horror-struck at each other, thinking 'God! What agony love is!' How terrified she is of taking the drug! How physically averse to the handsome Paris! (Derek Rencher was excellent, and I should have agreed with Henri IV, not Juliet: this Paris was worth a Mass.) How frantic her despair in the crypt! And how elegiacally she falls over the tomb, not quite reaching Romeo, but getting her hand to his lips and dying with head hanging and arms framing her face!

14.2.65

This week let us concentrate briefly on a few highspots in MacMillan's *Romeo and Juliet*. At the big moments of the story, expressed in ballet by a solo or duet, MacMillan never lets us down; and he has found in Lynn Seymour an ideal Juliet and in Christopher Gable a delightful Romeo. Next week, besides discussing the third pair of lovers, Sibley and Dowell, we might observe the minor characters and comment on some effective and less effective incidents in the production.

We first see Romeo serenading Rosaline, flirting with tarts, taunting Capulets. On our first glimpse of Juliet she is introduced to Count Paris, made to throw away her doll and accept from the evidence of her swelling breasts that she is a woman. (How much more advanced her upbringing is than that of the heroine of MacMillan's *Invitation*, from whom statues had to be veiled!) It is when Juliet is dancing with Paris at the ball that the lovers first set eyes on each other. Romeo backs away spellbound; she looks up slowly. In this, as throughout, the babyish Seymour is odd, modern, original, touching and perfect. Juliet sits to play a lute for six girls to dance. Romeo keeps butting in and taking over the floor. The girls are embarrassed. Juliet does a little solo and Paris watches aghast as the lovers come together. The gate-crashing Montagus then break up the ball. Alone on stage Romeo and Juliet dance—a gentle slide back, lift, swimming through the air, yearning arms, turn in *attitude*, low swings into *arabesque*.

The balcony scene is expressed in another *pas de deux* (preceded by organ music which was in the original score but omitted by the Bolshoi). She coyly retreats and advances and spins into his arms. Then an ecstacy of lifting, rocking, sliding, turning, gazing, dipping, drifting, kneeling, clasping and kissing. He kneels in profile and she kneels on his upraised hands. She circles alone as he reclines; backs with eyes closed, and is drawn again to him as if by an inhalation of his breath. A sad gaze, clasp, kiss, and she runs up the steps.

The bedroom scene of the lovers parting, in which the rival claims of lark and nightingale are represented by two windows to right and left, passes with a sweep of despairing strings, of twisting supported turns in the air becoming swallow-dive *arabesques* of frenzied embraces.

Thereafter Juliet is alone. Seated on the bed's edge, gazing ahead, wondering what to do, Seymour presents us with the girl's predicament. Her wedding-eve dance with Paris is a clever invention; she twisting away from him as he lifts her. Seymour does a bit of the mad scene from *Giselle*, contemplating the fearful potion; she drinks, hiccups, climbs on the bed, yearns toward the window of the lark, sleeps curled up on one side. Another successful invention is Romeo's dance in the tomb with Juliet's lifeless body.

MacMillan rises to all these tragic occasions. Seymour and Gable, as in previous works, seem not only to have been inspired by his expressive choreography but themselves to have inspired it.

21.2.65

It could reasonably be held that Antoinette Sibley and Anthony Dowell danced MacMillan's *Romeo and Juliet* better than either of the couples who preceded them. Fonteyn and Nureyev are incomparable for the luminosity of their personalities, but of course Nureyev had a bad foot on the first night. Seymour, without Fonteyn's glamour, but half her age and almost abreast of her as an actress, is the most acceptable as the heroine-victim of square unsympathetic parents in a modern love story; and Gable matches her in charm and modernity, but his dancing has more zest than accuracy.

Sibley, we have said before, is the perfect Royal Ballet product, musical, with good line, feet and arms, sweet and pretty (as opposed to Seymour, who is clearly a rebel); and her body is expressive *while* it is being beautiful. In her early scenes her facial acting had a Royal Ballet characteristic which I find rather annoying—a kind of smiling, self-satisfied ballerina look (no doubt very important to learn early on in your career as a professional way of making light of technical exertions)—you might call it the 'Look, Ma, I'm dancing' look. As the ballet gained in tragic impetus Sibley increased in emotional conviction, and in the end I liked her very much.

Anthony Dowell, whose first long role this is, was playing Romeo dead-pan. This may have been because he was shy or because he was feeling his way or because he was sensibly afraid of over-acting. The result was quite acceptable—some young people are very poker-faced—and I thought that, like a painter, he was blocking in the main composition before working on details. His dancing was extremely distinguished.

The dance of the lovers' parting at dawn seemed much more remarkable to me than on previous nights, either because I am getting to know the ballet or because Sibley and Dowell were so splendid in it. Each Juliet has died differently: Fonteyn on her side, Seymour on her back with arms hanging; and the dying Sibley manages to lift Dowell up to her to be kissed, which seemed incredible.

I have heard that MacMillan wanted Nureyev to dance Mercutio. That would certainly have been a role for him. But David Blair is first-rate as the mocking charmer, and one can well imagine, as Walter de la Mare did, the girls falling silent and spellbound as he went by, 'leaving the spring faint with Mercutio'. Yes, it is his most telling interpretation to date. His backward tripping with palm extended in teasing politeness at the ball is vivid. His stabbing in the back by Tybalt is a shock—people gasp. His defiant death dance enthrals.

Desmond Doyle, tough, taciturn and formidable, is a very real Tybalt too: he could not be bettered. I wonder if MacMillan might not re-edit his death convulsions without betraying Prokofiev's drumbeats—they verge on the comic.

It occurs to me that if Shakespeare had known what a frantic scene of grief Prokofiev, Lavrovsky and MacMillan would build up for Lady Capulet he would have made Tybalt her son rather than her nephew. As MacMillan's Capulet is a potential peacemaker it would have been a change if Michael Somes played him slightly less like God the Father. In the Royal Ballet tradition, all noble fathers are haughty, all ladies are gracious and all court officials are Leslie Edwards.

The spectacle devised by Georgiadis continues to delight. The weakest design is the bedroom with its blue drapes high up over the balcony windows. We have a bit too much of Verona's three early-rising prostitutes. The fencing is too clickety-click and should be worked on. I am shocked by the lack of medical attention for street casualties. And those stiff carcasses of oxen dragged to and from the butcher's shop must be the earliest victims of deep freeze in history.

28.3.65

Song of the Earth

Clapping and crying a little we were, in our tipsy elderly way, for it was with mixed feelings (and I suppose all the best feelings in life are mixed) that we watched Kenneth MacMillan take his calls after *The Song of the Earth* on Thursday. His hair was grey like ours, but he was grinning in his nice childish way; and we remembered him in younger and perhaps unhappier days, soaring across the stage in Florestan's pink jacket with feet wonderfully arched (and we must have been rather mad about him, for we put him on the cover of *Ballet* magazine).

That was a thought from the past; and MacMillan's future lay in Berlin and in battling to create a great company there and a glorious repertory for them, so he was lost to us; and at present he was grinning rather collusively, we thought, sharing a joke with us two thousand lovers out here, but a bit pleased no doubt, though not entirely, for there is even something sad about having created a masterpiece.

Das Lied von der Erde is Mahler's symphony, for tenor and alto voices and orchestra, about looking at the beauty of the world and accepting death; and we see clearly how the songs sung by the man and woman happen to be German translations of Chinese poems, for in our limited knowledge of Chinese poetry we know that a Chinese poet only has to see a spray of plum blossom to be pierced by the thought of all the best friends he will never see again or will shortly have to part with for ever.

Mahler inset six songs into the six movements of his composition—that is, the singing is intermittent, and clear and heartfelt it came from the

mouths of Yvonne Minton and Vilem Pribyl. Under the guest conductor
Hans Swarowsky our orchestra really sounded like one, which it hadn't
in the preceding Tchaikovsky Piano Concerto. This was music. The
symphony is wonderful. MacMillan has clearly been living with it—been
married to it—for years. He has had time to work out what movements
can be put with it; and he has made no mistakes.

Drinking song of Earth's Misery. Men are tumbling about the world. The
music expresses the profusion of nature. The Man, MacLeary, has an
alter ego, a shadow of the Death he carries inside him, Dowell, who will
one day separate him from the Girl, Marcia Haydée. *Dunkel ist das Leben,
ist der Tod.* MacMillan composes a final group to demonstrate neatly—
almost epigrammatically—the drop into the coffin which is Everyman's
last move.

Autumn Solitude. MacMillan gives this number about melancholy, loneliness and the lack of a loving companion to the Girl. Three other girls
and three men are incidental: the Messenger of Death chases them away.
Mein Herz ist müde: here the choreographer first uses a Grahamish movement, a deep *plié à la seconde* with knees pressing ever further open, to
evoke lonely yearning. The moan of the unfertilized womb, as it were.
Death stalks her like a shadow and watches her touching her wet cheeks or
marking her wrinkles—the Marschallin.

Of Youth. The song is about a porcelain pavilion in the middle of a pool
where young people fleet the time carelessly as they did in the golden
world, and, like the arched tiger's spine of a bridge which leads to it, are
reflected upside down in the water. Four men coquette with four girls.
There are slightly Oriental movements. A fifth girl, Jennifer Penney, is
spun by her seated friends, their hands holding her leg only, swung as on a
swing, passed to and fro, then while the *Freunde, schön gekleidet, trinken,
plaudern* leaps off into Death's arms.

Of Beauty. This is an idyll. Girls pick flowers in sunshine. Boys on
horseback thunder by. My girlfriend saw Matisse's *La Danse*: I saw
Nausicaa, and Wordsworth's 'And see the children sport upon the shore'.
A solo for Georgina Parkinson of swift turns and gentle poses. Exultant,
athletic, the *Schöne Knaben* advance. Kenneth Mason, smiling irresistibly,
shows his strength. At first the girls are aloof, then they pair off. Against
the fading light, Lovers' Lane—with Chinese *attitudes*.

Spring boozing. 'If life is nothing but a dream/Why all the carry-on?/I
drink as much as I can hold/And another day has gone' (my translation).
Four men reeling—then we notice that one of them is Death, Dowell. The
others are MacLeary, Mason, Mead. Some triumphant jumps, but it all

ends with Death astraddle the stiff slanted body of a man, cocking a transcendental snook.

Leave-taking. This is by far the longest and most complex movement, as well as the sublimest. Much of it is an elaborate *pas de trois* and/or *pas de deux* of the Man, the Girl and Death. Now MacMillan has always been a master at the invention of *pas de deux*: for the personal, the intimate, the lyrical, are what he is angelically gifted to express in terms of classical dance—we recall *Le Baiser de la fée, The Invitation, Romeo and Juliet.* This is his most amazing creation, for it is an intimate poem, but one in which the *corps* is also used, and it is on the scale of a complete ballet. Although I find I filled five pages with notes I rather funk writing about it until I have seen it again. The first part is about beauty, the second about saying goodbye. There is a lovely passage to that sweet pulsing tune: first Haydée alone, then watching a ritual dance of three girls; then as the girls are lifted and the music swells to an ecstatic dream fulfilment, Haydée yearns, treads a subtle measure, spins and is confronted by Death.

After the last embrace, with the Man wearing Death's mask, the Girl is left alone: but there is a dawn of consolation, and the marvellous Haydée advances undulating, with her two companions, a goddess in slow motion swimming through the eternal spring.

Goodbye, Kenneth MacMillan, and thanks a million. Parting is such sweet sorrow.

22.5.66

In MacMillan's *Song of the Earth,* revived last Saturday evening, Monica Mason was superb, better than I have ever seen her in anything, which is saying a good deal. The work has sublime moments: but, paradoxically, it is when it most reaches out to match the grandeur of the music that we feel most strongly the superfluity of the dance. In the Chinese tea-garden scene and in the scene of boys and girls making love on the beach choreography can perhaps add a little to Mahler's songs. In the noble last sunset and farewell nothing can be added. And, as Desmond Shawe-Taylor pointed out, the masterpiece when used for ballet will inevitably be less well played and sung than in the concert hall.

But, as Peter Darrell says, if you don't set ballets to the music you most admire, you're left with—etc., etc. It's the old problem.

2.4.67

Anastasia

If I were God—which we all are, more or less—zooming about Space, juggling with stellar systems, doing anything that came into my head to get through the long afternoon of Eternity; and if I had the crazy idea of breeding a race of thinking creatures on some minor planet, I can imagine that my main interest in watching them would be to see how they made use of the horrors of history, the consolations and disappointments of religion and the problem of good and evil—cruel by-products of my careless creativity—by turning them into works of art. Thus the long ignorance of Russia, absurd emperors, unhappy Tchaikovsky, inexplicable Rasputin, and the suffering of uprisen workers might all be justified if an imaginative choreographer could make a ballet out of them to show off the gifts of a dancer of genius.

If I were Kenneth MacMillan and had the notion of adding to a one-act ballet I had made, with Martinu's music, about the woman who thought herself (or had been persuaded to claim to be) the heir of the Romanovs— of taking the story further back, and utilising two whole symphonies of Tchaikovsky, the first and third, I should well foresee the dangers ahead. What a perilous path should I face, fitting known facts to two famous compositions, complete in themselves! And how to make a Tsar dance, or a cold Tsarina and her dull daughters, a limping Tsarevitch, a frozen court? Better perhaps to commission a new score? Or scrap the whole thing and think again?

And yet. And yet. Britten and Berkeley and Maxwell Davies are not Tchaikovsky. Here was an idea, a big one; and ideas are hard to come by. In his symphonies Tchaikovsky wrote the history of Russia—at least the history of the Russian soul. What a challenge! I should have a go.

If I were a ballet critic—which God forbid—I could complain of a bit of cheating (Tchaikovsky's omissions); of so many stars lost behind moustaches; of noble choreography camouflaged by skirts and trousers; and so on. I don't. I acclaim Barry Kay's clever sets in which a ship is a birch forest, a ballroom the hustings of Revolution, a sickroom the archives of the past. I acclaim the choreographer as dramatist, story-teller and poet. I acclaim the art of Rencher as Nicholas, Beriosova as Alexandra, Sibley as Kchessinskaya, Dowell as her partner, and above all the funny, tragic, miraculous Lynn Seymour. There will be time on more spacious Sundays to go into detail. It was an epic, golden endeavour.

I refer, of course, to MacMillan's *Anastasia*, first performed by the Royal Ballet at the Royal Opera House on July 22nd at 7.30 p.m.

25.7.71

Derek Rencher's hesitant Tsar, totally dependent on his wife's willpower, is a very subtle creation. No praise could be too high for Svetlana Beriosova's Tsarina, beautiful, graciously aloof with courtiers, affectionate with her children, a driving force behind the Tsar: this seems a portrait from life and is one of the glories of our stage. Georgina Parkinson is good, but has not yet found a way of living the role: she seems slightly self-conscious like the Queen-Mothers in classical ballets. Susan Lockwood is extraordinarily real and charming as the Tsarevitch: no boy could be more boyish. Adrian Grater's Rasputin has a touch of Rothbart, but he makes us believe in his sinister power. The sycophantic gush of Anna Vyroubova, the Tsarina's middle-class *confidante*, is perfectly sketched by Gerd Larsen (though I do not think she would have taken part in a court ball). Leslie Edwards' aide-de-camp, with his soldierly bearing and well-bred reticence, is a small masterpiece.

The above-named characterizations shine out most clearly in the first act, which is a wintry idyll—one might say a Chekhov play—complete in itself. Tchaikovsky's First Symphony serves its purpose well, providing MacMillan with some pretty Russian dances for the Tsarina and Anastasia, a patriotic slow march for the little Prince to practise walking to, under hypnosis after his fall, and some martial music for the stirring finale on the outbreak of war.

17.10.71

The court ball of Act II, danced to Tchaikovsky's Third Symphony, is also subtly imagined, but suffers from a surfeit of polonaises and mazurkas, and Tchaikovsky provides no music for the revolutionary outburst at the end. (I think that instead of the brawling and flagwagging we should merely see the workers looming motionless and larger than life on a projection at the back, while the ball sweeps on to its formal conclusion.) After the tremendous *pas de deux* for Kchessinskaya and partner, Merle Park with Anthony Dowell or Desmond Kelly, in glittering form, the choreographer makes imaginative use of the mysterious *andante* to convey the heroine's misgivings as she observes unexplained intimacies between the Tsar and Kchessinskaya, the Tsarina and Rasputin.

The tomboy Anastasia of Act I becomes the well-mannered deb of Act II, then the tormented exile of Act III, on the brink of madness. This last, to the music of Bohuslav Martinu, is the climax of Lynn Seymour's varied and wonderful performance. She is truly tragic, bringing a new dimension to ballet, as Garbo did to the screen. Lesley Collier, who replaced her, has the advantage of youth to compensate for lacking the dark initiations of experience, but she, too, is remarkable and was granted hardly less of an ovation.

24.10.71

As Anastasia, last Friday, Lynn Seymour looked remarkably slim, young and pretty in the first two acts. In the third, haunted by nightmares in hospital, she comes into her own as an actress. How cleverly conveyed are the flash-backs of flight from Russia! With what urgent desperation David Adams, as Anastasia's peasant husband, and his accomplices, push the Mother-Courage cart with its precious burden, the repository of so much royal and imperial blood! Then, at last, rising like a figure-head to circle the stage on her hospital bed, Seymour-Anastasia, in her own mind at least, is the heir of Peter and Catherine, ruler of half the world.

Of course there are imperfections in this epic, and of course the Martinu music and the electronic music in Act III do not match the Tchaikovsky, but the wonder is that MacMillan, in depicting a personal tragedy against the downfall of a civilization and doing it in terms of ballet, came so near to total success.

26.1.75

Triad

If the reaction of the first night audience is anything to go by, *Triad* is destined to be a popular success. To what extent the warm applause was due to the presence in the cast of Antoinette Sibley and even more so of Anthony Dowell—for, don't ask me why, male dancers evoke more ecstasy than female today—it is hard to determine. These two were certainly superb, and the third of the 'triad', euphemistically described as Dowell's *Brother*, was the admirable Wayne Eagling.

Three other men completed the cast, Ashmole, O'Brien and Sherwood: these were needed for lifting etc., for the choreography made use of the air, Ashton's element, as well as the earth, Martha Graham's. Not that there was anything particularly Grahamish about this classical choreography, arranged to Prokofiev's first Violin Concerto. MacMillan has always had a lyrical gift for the invention of *pas de deux*, and this extended *pas de trois*, with Cain and Abel overtones, showed him at the height of his powers.

The painted shapes on the backcloth by Peter Unsworth suggested a subaqueous world, while the veined tights were Tchelitchevian.

23.1.72

Second sight of *Triad* leaves me in no doubt that it is MacMillan's best ballet. The slides, the curious standing-sitting *manège*, the tangled knots of choreography resolved in extensions, the parting of the lovers' bodies by the probing brother—so many inventive passages of dance, together with the drama caused by Dowell's alternate tenderness for his brother Eagling and rejection of him in favour of the vampire Sibley—all seem to spring so naturally from the contorted hysteria of Prokofiev's violin concerto.

13.2.72

Manon

One advantage of the three-act ballet is that it makes possible the creation of roles which artists can really get their teeth into. In his *Manon*, presented for the first time at Covent Garden on Thursday, Kenneth MacMillan has provided wonderful parts for Antoinette Sibley, Anthony Dowell and David Wall, and the two men have never done anything better.

The Massenet music (from everything but the opera *Manon*) is a hotch-potch of bits and pieces, conventionally orchestrated, which nevertheless rises to its dramatic occasions. There is some original and striking choreography, particularly in the several *pas de deux*. In his designs Nicholas Georgiadis shows not only the imagination and sure colour sense we expect of him, but considerable ingenuity. Act II Scene I in the brothel is superb. The last scenes in New Orleans, except for the death of Manon, are a let-down, and make us think the ballet too long.

Sibley is admirable as the wanton with a heart of silver-gilt, conveys exactly the battle raging inside her between love and money, looks marvellous both in rags and diamonds and throws herself passionately into the difficult dances. But it is destined that our sympathies must go to des Grieux: and Dowell, in a fair untidy wig which hides much of his high papal forehead and makes him look fifteen, is extraordinarily touching and credible as the shy theological student, who has never said boo to a mouse, who does not know how to push himself forward, yet who is turned by the surge of first love into a cheat and murderer. It is a beautiful performance.

What a contrast is the Lescaut (Manon's brother) of David Wall! Where has he learnt the ways of this charming, funny con-man? His gradually increasing drunkenness in the brothel, his dance with Monica Mason, and all the good-humoured, bad-mannered business that goes on at the side are amazingly subtle. Drunken reeling can be such an obvious joke, but what Wall does is a masterpiece of art.

MacMillan has introduced odd bits of *verismo* into his spectacular classical duets—awkward clinches and sudden clumsy sitting-downs—which add a drop of bitters and are telling in their unexpectedness. One reason that New Orleans is a bore, coming after the whorehouses of Paris, is that there are *more* whores there. I thought we might have had male ones for a change. Those nice half-naked hippy convicts who hang around the waterfront would qualify.

10.3.74

Nobody could say that the flamboyant Nureyev was cut out for the part of des Grieux in *Manon*, which MacMillan created for the quiet, serious Anthony Dowell, so we were agog to see him in the role, with Merle Park.

I should guess that Dowell is the kind of artist who has to be carefully directed, while Nureyev by instinct hits on a way of interpretation. Nureyev did one tiny thing which struck me as so marvellous that I shall always have it in my Golden Treasury of Theatrical Thrills.

He was excellent as the country bumpkin in Scene I; and his surge of love in the bedroom *pas de deux* was wonderful. In the brothel scene he has the hard job of standing doing nothing while everyone else dances, flirts and drinks. Whereas Dowell looked pathetic, Nureyev smouldered. During the drunken dance of Lescaut and his mistress, one of the best numbers a British choreographer ever invented, Nureyev, a mere spectator, stole the show. Desmond Kelly may not have Wall's magic wit in this duet, but he was very good indeed. Yet one's eyes were drawn to Nureyev, who did nothing but stand stiffly in his new suit, while a group of tarts prodded him and made remarks about the promising bulge in his pants. Yet that was not *the* marvellous thing that he did, which came later.

A different hair-do might prevent Park from looking like Cleopatra from the word go. In her death agony she was much less mad than Sibley, more beautiful and holy and going to Heaven on a wave of Wurlitzer music. Something had happened to the last act—Nureyev?—which no longer drags.

I think, after all, I will put off describing Nureyev's Golden Moment until I see if he can do it twice, which is the proof of greatness.

21.7.74

As the timid divinity student demoralized by love, Nureyev was shown how to cheat at cards. He turned up an ace the second time running. His expression was such a mixture of shyness and amusement as he looked across the table at his sophisticated rivals, like a schoolboy wondering if he would be caught out, that the gesture became a moment of genius.

Weekend Magazine, Toronto, 1.10.77

Elite Syncopations

The thought struck me at Covent Garden on Tuesday that while the Dance Theatre of Harlem, with their *Agon* and *Concerto Barocco*, are trying to be white, the Royal Ballet, with their *Elite Syncopations*, are trying to be black. Neither quite succeeds.

MacMillan's *Elite Syncopations* was first given when I was away, and I read several notices besides David Dougill's,* none of which appeared to be very enthusiastic. Yet I had the impression on Tuesday that the ballet was popular with the public.

I know exactly what is wrong with *Elite Syncopations*. It is overdressed. Clever Ian Spurling's clever costumes literally prevent you from seeing the dancing. He must have had a whale of a time designing them, but they are so full of ingenious stylizations and learned, witty allusions that it is like singing 'The Waste Land' in a pub. Take one example: in his hat I did not know who Wayne Eagling was. Surely half the fun in this kind of crazy diversion is to see familiar dancers doing their eccentric thing but being themselves at the same time. Graham Fletcher scored, in his dance with the tall girl, Judith Howe, because his friendly face was not disguised, and the comedy got through.

If *Elite Syncopations* had no costumes at all—well, white T-shirts and black tights, with, at the most, the dancers helping themselves to a few old rags from a basket, it would be acclaimed as the smash-hit comedy

* He had replaced me when I was recovering from a broken leg.

ballet we have all been waiting for, the *Façade* of our day. It is crammed with grotesque inventions and the ragtime music of Scott Joplin and others, played by Philip Gammon's onstage band, is so divine that it makes me quite nervous not to have a record of it.

12.1.75

M

Tudor

Shadowplay

At last Antony Tudor has been invited to create a ballet for the Royal Ballet at the Royal Opera House, and has taken a marvellous, unfamiliar score of Charles Koechlin, and wrestled with his angel, and made a work prickly with poetry, and had a triumph and been acclaimed.

Why! Before *Shadowplay* the last ballet he had made in England was in 1938. Anyway, Lucia Chase, for whom he did *Pillar of Fire, Dim Lustre* and *Undertow* during the war, and Marie Rambert, for whom he did *Jardin aux Lilas* and *Dark Elegies* before the Flood, were both there on Wednesday to bear witness to the fact—which some, including, it appears, Tudor himself, have doubted—that he still has it in him.

Koechlin (1867–1950), a neglected genius, still largely unpublished, was inspired by Kipling's *Jungle Book* to compose a series of symphonic poems, of which *Les Bandar-Log*, used by Tudor with two interpolations from another work, is one.

When to the golden gloom of Michael Annals's stage, empty, but for a huge twisted banyan tree and some hanging trapeze-like creepers, there enters young Anthony Dowell, we realize this will be a ballet of adolescent experience, like Howard's *Fête étrange: Alice in Wonderland*; Mowgli in the jungle. But Tudor classifies all the other characters under the heading 'Penumbra'; they will therefore be the invisible angels and demons who hover round the hero's head, and his adventures will be those of the mind.

What happens to a youth who seats himself beneath a tree at dusk in an attitude of princely contemplation? He may have a vision; he may attain divine serenity; he may be distracted by the twitch of sexual desire; he may be disturbed by birds or monkeys; he may be bitten by mosquitoes. In the branches above his head are hanging all the thoughts of the day, memories, hopes, promises and prayers.

The costumes for monkeys and birds are mercifully very un-animal—Balinese rather. Then Derek Rencher appears, as if the spirit of some passionate dead king to possess the boy—or was he the father who must be ritually killed when the boy becomes a man? Then, borne aloft, comes Merle Park, the woman in his dream, at first a goddess then a kicking fiend. The choreography, except for some *singeries*, is simple, classical, clear. The dancers form a tunnel, which suggests the architectural avenue at Angkor, and a plunge the boy takes into it must be sexual. At the end he resumes his Indian posture of meditation, while the subdued monkeys mimic him mindlessly: but as the music shimmers into silence the itch of a flea and the bite of a mosquito remind him and us that no matter *what* a piece of work is man, how noble in reason, how infinite in faculty, in form and moving how express and admirable, the animal kingdom is with us, in us and on us for keeps.

More than in any other art form, I believe, the success of a ballet balances on a razor's edge. As it is, there are some people who thought *Shadowplay* was nonsense. Had Tudor left it even a shade obscurer than it is, had the set been ugly, had Dowell not been cast, had it not been for Koechlin's score, it might have been a failure: but Tudor's poetic imagination carried it through. Merle Park seems infallible; Rencher looked superb and his strange duet with the boy was perhaps the best part.

29.1.67

Tudor's *Shadowplay* still has its peculiar fascination but seems to contain some padding.

The bit which doesn't strike me as having much significance is the entry of the girls called 'Aerials', whom I take to be birds. We know that the Arboreals or monkeys who came before to disturb the meditative boy and reduce him to their kicking, scratching, bickering level represent the trivial side of life and the problems a Beatle has to overcome (Press photographers, fans, pot, too much money) before he attains Nirvana; but what exactly are these helmeted girls for except to fill in the music until something exciting happens?

The exciting thing that happens is the apparition of Derek Rencher with a gleaming torso; he is a sort of angel to Anthony Dowell's Jacob, an ancestor to be lived up to or the hero he wishes to become or his Platonic other half or a demon of desire or ambition who possesses him or just a symbol of his arrival at manhood. . . .

Then who should swoop in but wonderful Merle Park, first to seduce our hero in a love duet, and later, after a ring has formed, to disenchant him in the *Karate* of marriage. . . .

29.10.67

Knight Errant

It is very hard to make an original ballet within the classical tradition, but this is what Antony Tudor has done with his *Knight Errant*, which the Royal Ballet's touring company gave at the Opera House, Manchester, on Tuesday. The work is extremely original and totally unexpected.

Why unexpected? If a choreographer can evoke as Tudor did so successfully in *Lilac Garden* a picture of late nineteenth-century Proustian yearning and disappointed love, why should he not be able to take an episode out of Laclos' *Liaisons Dangereuses* and evoke a picture of eighteenth-century lust? It *is* odd because the resulting ballet is not only a comedy, but a black comedy: it is not only conceived in formal terms but also crammed with subtle characterization.

It would seem that Tudor had had in mind for some years the idea of using Richard Strauss's music for *Le Bourgeois Gentilhomme*, and that the special gifts of David Wall drew this ballet out of him. This is the way I like ballets to be made. It is therefore sad that Wall hurt himself last Friday and could not dance at the first performance.

The essential scenic ingredients for one of those amorous anecdotal French engravings so popular under Louis XV were a bed, a door and a window. A bed for the adultery to be interrupted on, a door for the husband to burst in at, and a window for the unbuttoned lover to escape from.

But Stefanos Lazaridis, whose simple silvery abstract décor is a cross between Juan Gris and Metro-Goldwyn, obviously did not want to litter his stage with furniture; and Tudor has ingeniously provided six lackeys or postillions with tall wooden L's which can become bedroom doors, bedroom windows and beds, but also coaches and church doors which a girl enters as a virgin and from which, after one simple revolution by the postillion-caryatids, she comes out on her husband's arm, ready for anything.

The L's literally form an architectual framework for the story, which is told in a series of classical but sexual solos and *pas de deux*, sometimes with two things going on at the same time. The comedy lies in the contrasting characters of the three Ladies of Position, who, coy at first, become available to the Gentleman of Parts after he has married them off to his friends, three Gentlemen of Means.

Alfreda Thorogood remains a lady even when granting the ultimate favours, Margaret Barbieri can protest her passion in any position and Elizabeth Anderton is hell-bent on fellatio.

Having had his way with all three, the cocky Don Juan mischievously sends their own husbands to fulfil his next rendezvous with them; but he is humiliated in the end. Hendrik Davel puts up a brave show, but there are undoubtedly a lot of subtleties still to be brought out.

Knight Errant is both simple and complicated like all the best comedies; and there is something sad behind the gaiety, like in Mozart.

1.2.68

In a gallery in San Francisco there is a still-life by Oudry with colours so subdued and subtle—cream, ivory, pale ochre, silver grey, two shades of mole and a faint suggestion of aquamarine—that it seemed to me last year the quintessence of late eighteenth-century French style.

We think of that time as tinted by an even tone of elegance: clothes, panelled rooms, painting, letters, manners, cooking, all contributory to an infinite *douceur de vivre*. Antony Tudor's *Knight Errant*, which David Wall danced at last at Eastbourne on Friday, is an essay in the style of this period when manners were so much more important than morals. Subtlety is the keynote of the ballet: the scandalous situations, the erotic poses are delicately sketched, and lovers learn, yearn, perform, are jealous and suffer with a smile. That the music—Richard Strauss's *Bourgeois Gentilhomme* with a bit of *Ariadne*—should not be genuine eighteenth-century and that the décor of Stefanos Lazaridis should be a 1920-ish abstraction in silvery tones contribute to the unobviousness of this classical ballet which was built round the personality and talents of David Wall; and I should not be surprised if the girls' grey, blue and green dresses were planned to show off his red hair. 'Built round' is a bad phrase because Wall is obviously such a nice kid and so easy on the eye. Tudor cast him against type in the role of a heartless *roué*, and in doing so has given him a great (if small-scale) role and brought out great qualities of interpretation and art.

And so this Tudor-refined Valmont, this smiling villain, this cheat and charmer, this pretty, elegant and tailored rake, conspires with a blue-clad Mme. de Merteuil (Jane Landon) who will not in this gentle ballet be punished with small-pox in the end; to a Straussian waltz he seduces his first victim (Alfreda Thorogood) then capers to exultant brass; to a Bellini-ish air he transforms his bashful second (Margaret Barbieri) into an impatient nymphomaniac and makes delicate flower-like gestures as she undresses him; he is chased through doors and windows; he sends his victims' husbands as replacements to his *rendezvous*, groping in the dark to their mild disillusion; and in the end, naked, disgraced, abandoned and perhaps faintly ashamed, he advances towards us to a minuet with a beautiful opening gesture of the hands which, because of Wall's utter sureness of touch in comedy, could be said to fall between apology, resignation, defiance and amusement. It was a wonderful performance of an extraordinary work.

2.2.69

Cranko

Antigone

If I were a choreographer or producer the only thing that would make me want to turn an existing play into a ballet would be a conviction that there were elements in it which I could bring out in dancing better than the author had expressed them in words; and the only thing that would make me adapt a 'classic' like *Antigone* would be that I was all burnt up with the knowledge that I could make it speak a direct message to a modern audience. By a 'classic' I mean a work which hardly anyone has read, though most people have an idea of what it is about.

Likewise, if I were a choreographer intent on creating a tragic ballet, the only thing that would make me want to adapt an old Greek play would be that I saw something modern in it which would move ordinary blokes and birds to pity and terror.

John Cranko's *Antigone*, which opened the Royal Ballet's season, is a puzzler. I think Cranko must have had the worthy intention of making a real tragic ballet: yet there is nothing to show he had any strong feelings about his subject-matter or studied to get to the heart of it. The only time the new ballet comes near to being moving in a tragic sense (it has several passages of choreography when it is *visually* moving) is at the end when Antigone goes to her death off-stage and Creon, shunned by his people, is left to bear the weight of a coveted crown alone: but much of the success of this ending is due to the simplicity of Beriosova, who can't put an arm wrong, and the majesty of Somes, who can freeze the back row of the gallery by raising a finger. Here, as elsewhere, the conducive score of Mikis Theodorakis, the best kind of functional ballet music, gives sinewy support.

But if Cranko was *not* trying to make a tragedy in terms of ballet we cannot condemn him for not succeeding. This fifty-minute work emerges as little more than a chronicle. Is that perhaps what he meant it to be?

Now, I can imagine making an abstract ballet on an epic theme, in which inset pictures of individual suffering or heroism stood out against a background of warring clans, mourning women and migrant peoples—something between Massine's *Présages* and Jooss's *Green Table*. I can imagine a less abstract 'historical novel' of a ballet, a *War and Peace* or *Chartreuse de Parme*, in which, against a similar grand skyline, clearly defined characters enacted their loves and sorrows. I can imagine a tragic ballet which *concentrated* on the predicament of its heroine, analyzing in movement the passions to which Sophocles and Racine gave words. What I cannot see is why a choreographer should want to tell a story without a plot about people whose characters are not distinct, and whose problems seem remote from ours today.

Cranko has given us a Bayeux tapestry. You can't tell one geezer from another, especially under their kinky crash-helmets or eye-shields; and without a bit of writing to give you the strength of it you'd never guess who's who or what they're carrying on about.

There is the stuff of several tragedies among Cranko's eleven episodes. The love of Antigone for her cousin, whom she sends to war; the despair of Jocasta, who kills herself to bring her rival sons to their senses; the strife between the brothers; Antigone's determination to honour the dead; Creon's Macbeth-like solitude. By piling so many events one upon the other—we even see the death of Oedipus—the choreographer makes it hard for us to become involved with the fate of his heroine.

Again, apart from scarcely being able to distinguish the brothers and their cousin (Gary Burne, David Blair and Donald MacLeary—all delightful dancers), we are curious to know just why the sons of Oedipus hated each other, and how this hatred developed. Did one of them snore or was he insufferably breezy at breakfast? I am not being funny. Since Freud, Ibsen, Proust and, yes, Martha Graham, we have a right to demand more than mere gesturing silhouettes. Nowadays, what's more, if we could be shown that Abel was really a lousy creep we should be ready to take the side of Cain.

It would be frightening to think that British choreographers were now too secure behind the mannerism of ballet to confront each new problem almost (but, of course, not quite) as if no ballets had ever been invented before. Professionalism has its dangers.

25.10.59

Brandenburg Nos. 2 and 4

The hope of giving Cranko a hearty welcome back after his pioneering endeavours in Germany, the satisfaction of having a work to music of Bach in the Royal Ballet's repertory, our first switching on to Dorothee Zippel's orange sky with the boys in orange tights, white singlets and single file, the marvellous cast of our most angelic young dancers—were we not bound to have—did we not, after the curtain calls and the choreographer's cosy, cajoling speech, convince ourselves that we had really had —a super good time?

What went wrong with *Brandenburg Nos. 2 and 4*? After all, Cranko is a choreographer of invention, able to analyze music, and with a sense of what *goes* on the stage. After a few seconds of the first allegro movement of No. 2, for boys only, it became clear that they were committed to keep their bouncing and jigging and semaphoring going in time with the music until it stopped; and the panic question loomed 'Will they drop dead before we go mad?'

The impression of busyness produced by this literal echoing of the rhythm in visual terms was profoundly unacceptable to the senses. Balanchine's interpretation of eighteenth-century music was never so unimaginative. Of course, when one of the solo instruments did its little piece, Christopher Gable or Anthony Dowell stepped out of line to make a charming flourish. Then the jigging was resumed. Why on earth couldn't they have walked some of it?

In the slow movement, when the girls join the boys, there is no longer a nervous obligation to jig, and Cranko follows the music more freely and in a different way. Yet as steps grow more elaborate—with girls lifted or opened out like scissors to be slid along the floor—we are conscious of a lack of clear pattern and of logic, and the repetitions are annoying. There may have been a pattern in Cranko's mind, but it was not of such a kind as to register on the stage, so we become confused and bored. In the third movement the jigging starts again.

The opening allegro movement of Concerto 4, with the two flutes, is given to the girls to jig in; they also tittup, that is, *bourrée*, and it is a relief when Sibley demonstrates prettily to the first interruption by the violin. I think it a theatrical—not necessarily a musical—mistake to have eight couples in the andante: it seems like lovers' lane or the visit to the clinic, especially as one of the movements taken up by couple after couple suggests artificial respiration. At the end, when the pairs line up with an odd man out, and Sibley is fitted in by the simple expedient of everyone-move-up-one, this is an ingenious way of illustrating the musical resolution.

The final fugue is Cranko's most complex invention and, alas, to me his most chaotic. With so many different things going on in different parts of the stage the eye cannot take in his intentions; for he has conceived a way of paralleling the weavings of the music which is too hard even for these splendid dancers to expound clearly. Merle Park has a subtly funny moment after the violin solo when she leads the company in to resume the fugue. But the thing doesn't work.

13.2.66

Card Game

Musical jests and japes have not been uncommon in history from Haydn to Saint-Saëns, but it is doubtful to what extent Stravinsky intended his *Card Game*, written as a ballet for Balanchine in 1937, to make us laugh. Charrat's version for the Ballets des Champs-Elysées was alternately romantic and sinister.

In John Cranko's *Card Game*, previously given in Stuttgart, and danced by the Royal Ballet at Covent Garden on Friday, he sets out to make us laugh. This, after all, is not very difficult, for we leave a lot of our sophistication behind when we go to the ballet; and a boy in *Les Patineurs* only has to fall on his backside, then shoot an outraged glance at the audience, to score an easy guffaw. The 'jokes' in Stravinsky's music are quotations from other composers and Cranko has taken these as his licence to go all out for farce.

Before saying anything is unfunny one should perhaps present one's credentials. I think I go for nuances, the things you nearly miss altogether. I also like the surrealist and unexpected. I laughed at the dress-rehearsal of Nevill Coghill's *Doctor Faustus* when two turbaned nudes did the Indian rope trick. The rope rose, one boy climbed up it and disappeared while the second played a tambourine. The rope fell down followed by a bleeding head, arms and legs, to be packed into a bag which the second boy had ready. (On the opening night the rope collapsed before the boy could climb it.) I was dazzled by the wonderfully orchestrated farce of the National Theatre's Feydeau and laughed, but less compulsively than most. What really sent me into fits was a silent character called Coffee Boy whom Zeffirelli inserted into *Much Ado*. The way this oafish waiter watched the goings-on of his betters, his interested features occasionally lit by a leer of semi-comprehension, puts me in a good mood whenever I think of it. OK, so I'm in a good mood.

Cranko's jokes are broad. Even a non-card-player can get the point in his version—which, by the way, I think extremely musical, much more so than the Bach—the point that the Joker being 'wild' can sway the fortunes of the game by turning himself into any card at will. Christopher Gable in pink, blue and white tights, carrot wig and clown's make-up is certainly *wild*—in the sense of camp parlare.

The first big joke is the one about woman being man's plaything—the Coppélia joke. That is always popular. Annette Page, who really is a very funny girl, goes limp, wobbles and is supported about on a tilt by several men. The second deal is a straight flush of hearts, all men. I particularly liked Keith Rosson's solo: there was something about the combination of his burly physique, his grace of movement and a sort of good-natured wit that made subtler sense than a lot of this comedy. The Joker interrupts, strutting with thumbs in imaginary waistcoat, cocks snooks, and finally, after some filling in (there was too much music for the humour), disperses the boys with Hunchback-of-Nôtre-Dame cursing gestures. In the third deal, two main jokes. A tousled Lynn Seymour getting in everyone's way, then parodying the bit in Balanchine's *Serenade* where the man's eyes are covered and Fate beats her wings; and Gable in a tutu doing supported arabesques to the quotation from Rossini.

I think Dorothee Zippel's set—the hands of a gambling giantess—a mistake. There is some clever choreography and some padding. The real joke is that I am beginning to think it funnier as I write about it than I did in the theatre. It's a bit provincial, but I don't want to spoil your fun. I feel about ballet audiences like my grandmother did about some cousins of ours. She said 'The Yorkes are very easily amused'. But then, she would have thought it common to call a Knave 'a Jack', as they do on this programme.

20.2.66

Poème de l'Extase

A new work by Cranko, a new role for Fonteyn, homage to Scriabin (born a hundred years ago) and, as it turned out, homage to Klimt—such were the exciting elements combined in *Poème de l'Extase*, which the Royal Ballet gave at Covent Garden on Tuesday. That the work had been created for Stuttgart, where Dame Margot danced it last year, made no difference to us.

It was the crest of the wave of *Art nouveau* which has been sweeping across the western world in recent years. Scriabin was the Russian Wagner and the Russian Debussy, yet this was probably the first time his music had been played in the Royal Opera House. Gustav Klimt, on whose work Jürgen Rose's glowing designs were based, was the Austrian Beardsley. It took the South African-born John Cranko to bring them together.

In an introductory scene with sofas and lampshades, Fonteyn, the

Diva, with a Japanese hairstyle, and wearing a filmy Primavera frock, is giving a party for ladies with huge hats when the Boy, Michael Coleman, declares his love for her. As the semi-realistic furniture disappears, and fantastically figured silk curtains tumble down before a night sky studded with ruby stars, the scene is changed to the inside of the Diva's head, and the rest of the action, a prolonged *pas de six*, depicts her thoughts, as she weighs the Boy's passion against the four great loves of her past life and decides to reject him.

Apart from some shivering undulant gestures by Fonteyn, in which she conveys the very essence of the *Art nouveau* style, the choreography is classical. The four lovers, David Drew, Desmond Kelly, Peter O'Brien and—in the most spectacular part—David Wall, clad in wreaths and leafy tights, come soaring through the peacock Byzantine draperies, which float back into position behind them like the wings of Loie Fuller; and as the music surges to its transcendental climax and swoons to death they leap higher and lift and swing Fonteyn more vertiginously around them, in a whirlpool of remembered love. Naturally enough the flesh-and-blood, awkward, fidgety Boy in his frilled pink King's Road shirt cannot compete with these rainbow dreams.

It was *un frisson nouveau*.

20.2.72

Helpmann

Elektra

The applause after Robert Helpmann's *Elektra* at Covent Garden on Tuesday seemed to last longer than the ballet. It was quite invigorating to hear such a demonstration—particularly as Helpmann took his calls with a smiling reticence which was the height of good style: and I wondered if the ovation was entirely due to the fact that people liked the ballet or to its being the first one Helpmann had staged since 1946, or to pleasure at seeing Nerina and Blair in a new work, or relief at not seeing Fonteyn and Nureyev, or to the house being full of Australians (I saw Coral Browne enthroned above).

Elektra is not only very short (it seemed like ten minutes) but also very sensational. It opens with drums and brass in a bursting boiling rage. Scarlet floorcloth and a flight of scarlet steps set off Arthur Boyd's huge images of love and death drawn in black and white. Nerina, made-up witchlike with streaming vermilion hair, gloating over her avenging axe, is Elektra. Blair, naked and redheaded, is Orestes.

There are eight male purple Erinyes or Spirits of Vengeance who fling Elektra through the air in a variety of breathtaking dives. Monica Mason and Derek Rencher as Clytemnestra and Aegisthus are the only other characters, and we see them having mad sex while the children gloat and suffer.

Later Clytemnestra becomes a loathsome thing and drags herself on by her hands, a long gold train worming behind her. This train reversed becomes a red blood-bath-mat. The Queen is axed and her husband runs to greet the weapon of retribution.

Aeschylus and Athene absolved Orestes. Helpmann doesn't. After the double-murder it takes the Erinyes just thirty seconds to crucify Orestes upstage, and we are left breathless.

Elektra is tremendously effective. It may be vulgar, but it isn't genteel. Helpmann has not lost his blazing sense of theatre; and his new work, though less profound, is the nearest thing to Martha Graham's *Phaedra* on this side of the drink.

Malcolm Arnold's railway music is clearly composed as film music would be—or, in fact, as Graham's scores are—as an atmospheric accompaniment to the drama. There are strange noises in it, including a weird whoohooing sound, which I'm told is the brass doing glissandos.

The sets of Arthur Boyd, Australia's Chagall, must be seen: they are a shot in the arm. And the ballet is the more welcome for revealing to us the volcanic passions hitherto concealed beneath Nadia Nerina's pretty placid countenance.

31.3.63

Tetley

Field Figures

The 'season' is in full swing. During a week of events the most remarkable was Glen Tetley's *Field Figures*, given by the Royal Ballet at Sadler's Wells. This is one of the most important creations of our time. 'Important'! How we dislike our conventional adjectives when dealing with something great. And 'great'! What is great? That which intensifies our being, so that we live centuries in a second.

To tackle Stockhausen's score, to find his way fearlessly in that subterranean labyrinth of electronically processed sound, was even more heroic, perhaps, than Jerome Robbins's attack on the *Goldberg Variations*, which is going on in New York about now. How could Tetley see the end of such a task and not doubt his powers? His genius had armed him for the ordeal. His victory was glorious. Not for a second in the course of the long work did his invention fail. Though he is still young, his pioneering predecessors—Isadora, Nijinsky, Graham—reach down to haul him into Valhalla.

The Royal Ballet dancers are no more used to this kind of work than their audiences. We could not believe our eyes to see how Deanne Bergsma, Desmond Kelly, Vergie Derman, Nicholas Johnson, Paul Clarke, Sandra Conley and Peter O'Brien rose to the occasion, mastered it and came through with streaming flags. Never again can we doubt that classically trained dancers can adapt to the idiosyncrasies of modern style. Proof was needed: they provided it. Balancing, rolling, catching, falling, knotting and carving nameless patterns with new variety of pulse, they achieved something none of their colleagues has so far had the honour to attempt. It was a walkover win.

30.5.71

Laborintus

I read that at the first performance of Berio's remarkable composition, *Laborintus II*, which Glen Tetley has staged as a ballet for Covent Garden, there were eight actor-mimes. I take it that this performance was in Italy,

as most of the text is in Italian—with a little Latin, English and French—
and the score was commissioned to celebrate the 700th anniversary of
Dante's birth. I imagine that these mimes spoke none of the words of
Sanguinetti's poem, which at Covent Garden are clearly enunciated by
Cathy Berberian from the pit, but embodied some of the spiritual confrontations arising from the crisis of a soul which the poem evokes.
Perhaps these mimes—doing the minimum, one guesses—may have
helped people to take in the words and music. Tetley's choreography for
eight dancers only distracts.

In an interview in *About the House*, the handsome and instructive
magazine of The Friends of Covent Garden, the choreographer explained:
'Most of the text is in Italian . . . I thought it best to use the original. . . .
The sound of the words is what matters most.' Does he suggest we might
profitably read Dante aloud before learning Italian?

Poetry is of course made up of sound and sense. When the young Yeats
writes 'With vapoury footsole among the water's drowsy blaze', the little
meaning there is barely survives those xylophonic vowels. But when
Dante writes *'Lasciate ogni speranza voi ch'entrate'*—words which I heard
rising from the pit, but find no equivalent for in the programme's English
translation—he means to impress us with the solitude and desolation of
hell. To say in this case that 'the sound matters most' is to equate the 'All
hope abandon' of hell's gate with the chiming of a surburban door-bell.

This surprisingly cynical attitude to the text is sustained throughout the
invention of the choreography. 'It isn't a message ballet. It's really about
these six wonderful bodies I have to work with.' So thanks a million, Mr.
Berio and Mr. Sanguinetti, for the trendy accompaniment, and if you
think anybody cares what you were on about you can lasciare ogni bloody
speranza forthwith.

The wordless shrieks of the singers, the gibbering, muttering and
rustling of the chorus and the influx of electronic music (while Nureyev
is doing something with *his* wonderful body) towards the end build up
an incredible labyrinth of sound, through which we can well imagine the
soul's perilous journey in the dark. I hope Ashley Lawrence may record
it. The composition is certainly dramatic and might conceivably be in-
carnated in film, as I have sometimes imagined Eliot's *Waste Land*. To
divide it up into solos and *pas de deux*, however lovely and inventive,
seems to me madness.

6.8.72

Petit

Paradise Lost

Slumped across a table in some murky night-joint in frenzied Montreal, I opened a gin-dulled eye to read in a fragment of English newspaper that Roland Petit had enjoyed a triumph in London; and as memories of my old life swept over me a bitter cry broke from my lips. Actually, I had thought in Paris last year that Petit had got into a swing of creativity and I was thrilled that others had also seen the flashing signs.

What I saw was Nureyev, born from a neon egg, exploring a new world of sense, trying out the possibilities of sight and touch and smell. This happened to the squeaks and whirrings of Marius Constant's electronic score, which were like a world cracking out of chaos. I saw Adam lie flat, and a red sun rise on Martial Raysse's basic landscape, and Fonteyn's Eve emerge from Adam's rib, and some extraordinary, imaginative and alarming choreography as they got to know each other while the music went ping, pop and click. I saw the patriarch of mankind have the first orgasm, standing marvellously on his head.

Then I saw the Tree of Knowledge, and the Serpent portrayed by five men who were cleverly not joined together so that they could assume a variety of shapes. I saw Eve in a new light as bitch and whore, and saw Adam seeing her thus. And a painted screen with eyes and lips came down and Adam, after circling the stage hugely, dived through the lips. Then I saw a crowd jiggling in unison to more urgent rhythms and Adam balancing strangely in front of them, then spinning and lifting Eve in another electric bit of *pas de deux*, and the *corps* again, then Adam dragging Eve while she clung to him and he repelled her.

Fonteyn's Eve had an amazing directness of drive and drama. Nureyev's Adam was ablaze with energy and life. Petit had given them impossible things to do and I saw that they were good.

At the end they didn't through Eden take their solitary way. Adam was struck dead by a thunderbolt of Martial Raysse; and I wondered whether, in the final tragic composition of Fonteyn nursing the legs of an upside-down Nureyev, Petit had leapt forward to Paradise Regained and that this was Mary with Jesus.

N

So Petit didn't follow Milton; but Milton didn't follow Genesis. He had no authority for making Satan become the Serpent.

Here is the true version of the initial encounter of our first forefathers, which Moses suppressed.

> *When he woke to find Eve lying near,*
> *Adam got a new kick—it was fear.*
> *So he gave her a shove*
> *And said 'Move over, love.*
> *Everyone knows that I'm queer.'*

12.3.67

Pelléas et Mélisande

There are times when I could willingly strangle Margot Fonteyn, the hundredth anniversary of whose first appearance on the stage is now being celebrated throughout Europe and Central America.

She has been so well brought up either by her Mum or by that potent pedagogue Dame Ninette de Valois that she has perfected the art of answering questions at length and saying absolutely nothing. She would never, even under torture, admit that pink was her favourite colour for fear of offending orange and mauve.

This quality of old-school decency is allied to another of her out-standing characteristics—her loyalty. She is disgustingly loyal. She is not just loyal to her friends, and the Royal Ballet and the Queen: she is loyal to everyone. If she had a flop in a new ballet by an old friend you could be sure that he would be asked to do her *next* ballet for her. It is maddening.

Roland Petit's ballet to Schönberg's *Pelléas et Mélisande*, which was given at the RAD Gala before the Queen on Wednesday and shown to the public on Thursday, has received a lot of publicity; and one of the funniest scenes for ages was the colour television programme of Petit, Fonteyn and Nureyev talking about it in a classroom.

Well, Petit talked and was very vital and volatile and French; and Margot talked because she was afraid Roland might be giving the impression of talking too much, but when Rudolf was asked a question she answered it for him with indecent haste.

There was a sense of rivalry in the air, and if Nureyev had brandished a red flag and dropped his pants he could not have stolen the scene more effectively than he did. With the simplicity of genius he had procured a book. While the others talked he slowly turned the pages, saying nothing, with an ineffable, pussycat semi-smile on his face. He won.

Roland Petit is a romantic and he specializes in ballets about famous lovers—Carmen and Don José, Quasimodo and Esmeralda, Adam and Eve. Also, being used to cater for the Parisian public, who are easily bored, he likes to astound with new gimmicks.

The gimmicks in the case of *Pelléas*—apart from some eccentric choreography—were provided by the designer Jacques Dupont and they were entirely acceptable. The pretty dappled gauze front-cloth was looped up backwards to become an umbrageous tent; and at one moment Mélisande's long hair was represented by an immense diaphanous cloak which covered the whole stage.

However, the three characters—even though energetically danced by Fonteyn, Nureyev and Keith Rosson—together with Petit's desperate inventiveness, failed to fill out the forty minutes of Schönberg's dreamy poem. The *corps de ballet* are used almost as a décor: they represent the forest dryads or woodland creatures, as it were the birds who will cover with leaves the bodies of the babes in the wood.

Mélisande has to love Golaud, then love his brother Pelléas better. Golaud has to stab Pelléas and he takes ages over this. Pelléas has to die and he takes aeons over this. Pelléas and Mélisande have a lot of music to fill in after they are dead, and this last dance represents eternity, and it seems like an eternity to us, too.

30.3.69

Revivals

Massine's *The Good-Humoured Ladies*

The Good-Humoured Ladies was reproduced by Massine for the Royal Ballet at Covent Garden on Wednesday, with Lydia Sokolova, who had danced Felicita at the Coliseum in 1918, in the role of the old Marchesa Silvestra. It is still an enchanting work, it was perfectly staged and danced, and triumphantly received.

The overture has scarcely begun when we realize that the special flowing unaccented quality of the music is the result of orchestrating harpsichord sonatas. An even river of sound carries us blissfully back to the eighteenth century.

The setting is a miracle of subtlety and daring, admirably painted and lit. Ruddy, purplish, the little square sleeps in the sunshine, with its far side in romantic shadow; and beyond, the white bell-tower rises above trees to a torrid sky.

Each one of the dozen or so bright coloured costumes is a superb creation: to see them in action together against the décor is to realize that Bakst was the supreme genius of stage design in our century, and to believe that yellow satin really is, as Oscar said, a consolation for all the miseries of life.

It would be fatuous to complain about the slightly confusing intrigue, for nobody ever bothered to follow the plot of a Goldoni play on stage or was the worse for neglecting it. The interweaving of flirtation, disguise and deception is part of the style. The jerky puppet movements invented by Massine show us the Guardi period through a distorting mirror and prevent our vision of Venice being too sweet, like a historical novel by a lady novelist.

I admired Anya Linden's melancholy arms as she languished in her crimson dress; Antoinette Sibley's twinkling merriment as the mischievous maid; the stylish dandy of David Drew; Ronald Hynd camping *en travesti*; Brian Shaw with flying yellow coat-tails; Stanley Holden doddering but courtly; and Alexander Grant, a capering, zany waiter.

Lydia Sokolova as the vain and pompous Marchesa was outstanding. Every look and gesture told. There was an extraordinary moment during the slow number. Constanza laments, a street musician plays a violin; then the Marchesa on the arms of Rinaldo and red-nosed Captain Faloppa crosses the stage. These three stare at Constanza, and as they go off Rinaldo throws a coin to the busker. Nothing and everything happened. Diaghilev lived again.

15.6.62

Nijinska's *Les Biches*

Few new ballets or revivals have been so enthusiastically received at Covent Garden in recent years as the production of Bronislava Nijinska's *Les Biches*, given for the first time by the Royal Ballet on Wednesday. Apart from enjoying the ballet—which the audience clearly did from first sight of Marie Laurencin's drop curtain onwards—everyone wanted to acclaim the famous choreographer, Nijinsky's sister, whose influence was strong on the young de Valois and Ashton, and who had come in her seventy-fifth year from America to stage her first work for our company.

Sunny Monte Carlo in carefree 1924! And what a new departure it must have seemed when Nijinska mixed classical steps and modern behaviour. Without *Les Biches* the early work of how many choreographers, not to mention Cochran's revues and their successors, would have been different.

That was the *original* thing about the ballet. The *special* thing about it is its ambiguity. The girls are not *really* in modern dress, because in 1924 women did *not* wear ostrich feathers on their heads, except at court. The scene is *not* a house party, *nor* is it a brothel. Have the three athletes who enter this whispering world of women just dropped in from the beach, or are they customers? Is the older woman with the Chanel pearls a hostess or a madam? Is the female dancer in the blue *gilet* with white gloves, who gets off with the leading man, meant to be a page-boy? Are the two blue-grey girls having an affair? When the two athletes slump on the sofa are they exhausted with sex or female nattering? In fact, is everybody making love or conversation? It is so delightful not to know.

The pink women walk on point, giving a stylized waggle to their hips, with hands turned up at the wrist, smiling and looking down: they tittup, stride delicately and occasionally prance. While some are dancing, others may be gossiping in groups. The muscle-men advance dubiously on to the empty stage, three Claras in a Kingdom of Unknown Sweets. They flex their biceps and do double turns to prove their virility; and the bassoon warns us they are thick in every sense. They show off to the girls, but seem indifferent to them. On comes Georgina Parkinson as the Page-boy, picking her way; she spins, struts and attracts David Blair. The blue sofa is brought into play by the pink girls; it is used as a vaulting horse, then as a screen from behind which to spy.

Svetlana Beriosova was unexpected but happy casting for the Hostess in beige lace with cigarette-holder—the role made famous by Nijinska and Sokolova. Alone and with her two men, she bounds—this is a very vertical dance, the Rag Mazurka—smokes and rattles her beads. In the Andantino, a twilight *pas de deux* for Parkinson and Blair, the couple suddenly interrupt their *arabesques* and classical *port de bras* to grasp hands and charge up and down in a ballroom tango. There follow Merle Park and Maryon Lane in the funny *Chanson dansée*; then a jolly leaping finale.

Francis Poulenc's celestial dance music is the greatest. I was once able to thank him for it by an anonymous 'miracle'. In 1955 someone rang up from the Diaghilev Exhibition (I was still in bed) and said they'd seen Poulenc at the box office. 'Put on *Les Biches*', I said. It had newly been recorded. That night, *chez moi*, Poulenc said: 'Today I had a marvellous experience. Climbing the steps to your exhibition I was suddenly greeted with a burst of my ballet music. I had never heard it so well played. I was thrilled.'

6.12.64

A chance conversation about *Les Biches* with Cecil Beaton set me wondering about revivals of old ballets. Is change desirable? Inevitable?

Last week I wrote that the special thing about *Les Biches* was its ambiguity. Only a clot could fail to see that a work with several layers of meaning is richer than a work with just one. This ambiguity enhances the choreography as metaphor and simile enrich poetry. Beaton said that in the Twenties *Les Biches* was even stranger. The girls' dresses were more contemporary; make-ups were chalkier, less human. There was a pervasive air of mystery; one even felt that this was a fantastic circus, and that the prancing plumed girls might be ponies.

I liked these ideas and asked Frederick Ashton about them. He said Diaghilev had been broke in 1924 and the dresses had been made of cheap materials. Make-ups were always more exaggerated then. He thought Beaton only remembered the atmosphere weirder because he had then been naïve.

Mme. Sokolova, who had not yet seen the revival, confirmed Mr. Beaton's memories. She said the mystery and sophistication of the work

banished all question of laughs. She thought that in 1924 Ashton would
have been naïver than Beaton.

13.12.64

Nijinska's *Les Noces*

It has taken forty years since the first performance of *Les Noces* in London
for this masterpiece of Diaghilev's final decade to reach our stage again.
In 1926 all the critics were hostile, jokes were made about mothers-in-law,
The Times recorded that two people left the stalls in the middle of the
ballet, and H. G. Wells wrote in defence of the new work.

During the Forties and Fifties Ninette de Valois, who scorned most of
Diaghilev's later ballets, often told me that *Les Noces* was the one great
work which should be revived. Perhaps some uncertainty as to whether
British dancers could give the Russian feeling held her back from putting
it on, or the difficulty of fetching Mme. Nijinska from America, or doubt
if she would remember her choreography if she did come, or simply the
cost of the singers. When there was a question of Jerome Robbins making
a new version for the Royal Ballet it was the problem of getting four
grand pianos in and out of the pit which is said to have defeated the
project.

Now Frederick Ashton has piously invited Nijinska to restage her
choreography at Covent Garden; this she has done—with the devoted
collaboration, I believe, of Michael Somes—and at last *Les Noces* is
triumphantly acclaimed.

Stravinsky's conception of *Les Noces* was extraordinary in 1915 when
he began to compose the music, became more extraordinary when he
scored it (between 1918 and 1923) and still seems extraordinary today.
There is nothing quite like it. The preparations for a peasant wedding and
its consummation are conveyed in snatches of song, now commonplace,
now poetic, with invocations to the saints, drunken exclamations and
certain conventional remarks by parents or guests which were so traditional as to constitute a kind of indispensable liturgy.

The spoken and sung words were originally to have a rich coloured orchestral accompaniment like *Le Sacre* or *Petrouchka*, but after a long process
of brooding and elimination the work became a cantata with four pianos and
percussion. The pianos combine with cymbals and a bell to toll thrillingly
at the end. Edwin Evans thought the idea of the bell sound and the whole percussive element in *Les Noces* might have come from a taxi-ride, one Sunday
in 1914, in the deserted City of London, when Stravinsky stopped the cab to

listen to the 'changes' being rung on the bells of St. Paul's, 'taking occasional notes on the back of an envelope'.

Les Noces did not seem like an unfamiliar work to me on Wednesday: from old photographs and from many drawings by Gontcharova of the piled-up wonderful groups of men and women which I had seen over the years, I knew what to expect. How original and yet how simple some of these groups are—such as the heap of interwoven girls on which the Bride leans her elbow, pondering on what lies in store for her! Sometimes the girls on tiptoe move as if on rails parallel to the audience. Perhaps Nijinska inherited some ideas from her brother's ballets. How powerful is the concerted celebration of men and women at the end, how solemn the parents' benedictions! What a grand realization of Stravinsky's score!

The *corps* have the most dancing to do: led by Parkinson and Dowell they were superb. Beriosova and Mead were remarkably touching in the elemental poses of the Bride and Bridegroom. Of the parents I particularly admired Romayne Grigorova as the Bridegroom's dumpy mother. Lanchbery launched the rockets of song, speech and percussion; while the pianos were played by Richard Rodney Bennett, John Gardner, Edmund Rubbra and Malcolm Williamson. It was a famous occasion.

27.3.66

Balanchine's *Ballet Imperial*

On Wednesday, 5 April, Balanchine's *Ballet Imperial*, a work set to the second piano concerto of Tchaikovsky and first given in a slightly different form by Kirstein's American Ballet Caravan ten years ago, was presented by Sadler's Wells at Covent Garden.

How can one find words that will not soil a masterpiece? The concerto seems like a familiar landscape seen now for the first time in the company of a lover. We can only say it was a great work heroically danced, and from among its innumerable beauties choose a few to comment on.

From the beginning we know we are at court: the *corps de ballet* salute each other like people who are conscious of their own worth, an unassailable hierarchy. Fonteyn appears as an Empress, with Somes her Consort, and Nerina and Clayden to marshal her aristocracy; Grey, Field and MacMillan disport themselves on the steps of the throne. How deftly the ballerina's *pirouettes* with their varied finishing poses are fitted to the descending arpeggios of the first piano cadenza: and how subtly the second becomes a *grand pas de deux* with variations and coda! In the romantic second movement, how mysteriously the ten women swing into

Bronislava Nijinska rehearsing André Eglevsky. Drawing by Mikhail Larionov

arrowheads with Somes as their apex, suggesting the aerial drill of birds! How wonderful when Fonteyn comes in hymeneal pomp to her kneeling cavalier, parting the branches of an avenue of girls! How nobly Somes takes his leave, the nocturnal rite concluded! And with what pounding heart we watch the whole company rise and flash in the air together in the final mazurka, like jewelled rockets shooting from an imperial crown!

Observer, 9.4.50

Balanchine's *Serenade*

Balanchine's *Serenade*, which was given at a Gala performance by the Royal Ballet at Covent Garden on Thursday, and which I saw on Friday, is thirty years old. It was the first ballet he invented in America. When we consider how long it has survived and how often it has been performed and what a favourite and a 'classic' it has become, it is odd to learn the way it was originally put together.

The story is told in a biography of Balanchine by Bernard Taper which Collins will shortly publish here. It was invented as a demonstration to his students of how the classroom steps they practised daily could be used as the raw material of a theatrical work of art. The first evening seventeen girls turned up, so he showed how seventeen could be employed in a *corps de ballet*. 'The next evening only nine girls were present, and the third evening six; at each session he simply choreographed to the music with whatever students he had. Male students began attending the classes, and he worked them in. At one point, where the girls were supposed to rush out, one fell down and began to cry. He choreographed the incident right into the ballet.'

When it was decided to mount the work on the stage some parts were cut and others elaborated. A Tchaikovskian story of ill-starred lovers began to emerge. Then, as Edwin Denby spotted, in creating *Serenade* Balanchine did something else. To compensate for any lack of temperament and bravura in his young dancers which might make them look or feel inferior to Russians, he put the emphasis on team-work and kept the ballet formal, in spite of its romantic music. In doing this, I should say, at the risk of over-simplifying, he created the American style of classical dancing.

It is a pleasure to see our dancers in the familiar simple blue costumes, in roles we associate with Tallchief or Hayden or Magallanes. Nerina leads the allegro in the first movement; Beriosova is the girl who joins the class late and she waltzes with MacLeary in the second movement; in Tchaikovsky's last movement, which is placed third, the long Russian melody with a background of plucked strings brings on Blair to be a focus for the weaving girls; and in the Elegy, placed at the end, it is Annette Page who is MacLeary's angel of fate and guides him on, blindfolded, to arouse Beriosova's hopes and longing before leaving her in despair to be lifted on high as a sacrifice to the unknown god.

10.5.64

A well-rehearsed performance of Balanchine's *Serenade* made a propitious beginning on Thursday to the Royal Ballet's new season.

> *The music of the moon*
> *Sleeps in the plain eggs of the nightingale.*

In the absolute prose of *Serenade*'s opening group, with its rows of girls standing in simple dresses, heads down and arms hanging, is implicit all the poetry of motion, pattern and feeling which is to follow. Few scenic sunbursts could make as much impression as this pale group of girls in grey-blue and white against a sky the colour of summer thunder, with a subtle greenish light brushing their neat bodices.

The melting of three patterns into one; Nerina's first darting entry; a static semi-circle turning into a wheeling circle; the reforming of the opening group, through which Beriosova threads, as if lost in a forest, to take her place; her low-flung turning waltz with MacLeary; the Russian tune bringing in what Tchaikovsky intended as the last movement; its slow enunciation with five girls in line, one arm raised, then its acceleration with Nerina steering into some choreography which seems the prototype of so many of Balanchine's last movements, with their confrontations of teams of girls; Beriosova alone on the floor to begin the slow movement, approached by Blair, with Page covering his eyes; the spinning of Fate's magic weathercock; the long sad theme bringing on girls to be lifted in transit one by one; the beating of Fate's wings, the leading off of the hero, the raising of the heroine aloft on her three-man chariot to be carried in procession to the sacrifice—these are some of the work's most memorable passages.

Only the beating of Fate's wings—Page's arms—before she leads Blair away from Beriosova, did not make the tragic impact it should, perhaps because of a lack of urgency or a mistiming, or because longer arms are needed.

11.10.64

Balanchine's *Apollo*

Mary Renault's evocations of classical Greece may have their tiresome
side—the trouble with historical novels is that you are always waiting for
the moment when Louis XIV will appear and say 'Après moi le déluge'—
but in her latest, *The Mask of Apollo*, she shows an extraordinary insight
into the minds of theatre people and imaginatively describes the performance of Greek tragedy in the language of today's theatre.

Her narrator, a tragic actor, sits quietly before an archaic mask of
Apollo before 'going on', much as we are told Nijinsky secluded himself
during the process of make-up so as to assume the character of the role he
was about to portray. On lucky days this actor is conscious that the god
takes over and speaks through him. I think this is a fine way of describing
'inspiration'—a word we are no longer allowed to use. It is clear to me
that the god is present on some nights in the theatre and not on others.

I fear he wasn't on Tuesday night at Covent Garden, when Donald
MacLeary danced Apollo, with Beriosova, Parkinson and Mason as his
Muses in John Taras's careful staging of Balanchine's first Stravinsky
ballet, *Apollon Musagète*. This was the opening night of the Royal Ballet's
season and the programme, which included *Serenade* and *Rite of Spring*,
sounded propitious enough: but well rehearsed and danced as it was, the
early masterpiece of the master-choreographer was rather less thrilling than
it ought to have been. Why?

Very difficult indeed to say. First, MacLeary, who is so good at being a
Prince, had not a god's implacable authority. (I recall, not quite irrelevant-
ly, Uchov's King in the Kirov *Sleeping Beauty*, who made one conscious of
how the Divine Right must have shown itself in the old days.) MacLeary
may in time come to acquire something of this.

Then, not having seen a ballet at Covent Garden for a week or two, I
was suddenly struck by the smallness of the proscenium opening: its
height seemed no more than four times that of a man. This is disastrous
in *Apollo* (as I should so much prefer to call it), which needs the empyrean;
and it cannot be denied that John Craxton's blue, white and grey rocks,
with their dark blue and gold markings and outlines, which look clean
and striking on first view but seem more Shop-window Primitive on
consideration, hedge the ballet in.

Beriosova, since the transformation of Fonteyn and Nerina into guest
artists, is now our one *ballerina assoluta*, and everything she does is done
with care, seriousness and art: but I should prefer her colder, harder, as

Terpsichore. Does it sound absurd to say the glorious girl was too expressive? Difficult for her not to be, with those melting eyes.

Parkinson and Mason are obviously well cast, but the latter got a laugh at the end of her solo by the way she put her hand to her mouth and shot Apollo an apprehensive look. Without going back to the wigs and make-up of 1928, the girls still appear to need some stylizing element to de-humanize them—as it were, a mask to speak through. The grace and polish of our English style have turned an archaic frieze into a Hellenistic one.

What a wonderful work it is—odd, simple, subtle! Was the contact of finger-tips at the end of Apollo's solo, which leads into the *pas de deux*, a reminiscence of Michelangelo's Jehovah and Adam? How the interweaving presages Balanchine's later choreography! Strange that the god is asleep, head on the Muses' hands, when the divine summons is heard in the score. The magic music starts while a spell is woven, and the Muses are symbolically harnessed to Apollo's chariot before he ascends Parnassus to fulfil his mission.

20.11.66

There have been other casts for *Apollo* at Covent Garden, and the big news is that Keith Rosson was tremendous as the god. I wouldn't have believed it of one so Herculean in frame. He really let himself go, which is a rare thing to see a Royal Ballet dancer do. His arms yearned upward in prayer, his eyes flashed holy fire. Of course he was possessed. As a result Balanchine's old ballet seemed the best thing that had happened in years. I was transfixed; and wondered if even Maris Liepa could do as well.

27.11.66

Balanchine's *Agon*

It is clear that *Agon* was given a Greek name so as to tie it up with *Apollo* and *Orpheus*, works with which it has nothing in common except a masterly Stravinsky score. (I recall a time when the myth of Amphion was mooted to complete the trilogy.) Stravinsky's sources were French renaissance court dances—*sarabande*, *bransle* and *gaillarde*—and there are hints of baroque attitudes in Balanchine's ballet, which is as extraordinary as Petipa at the Darktown Strutters' Ball.

'About pride,' said the poet O'Hara. 'Classic dancing shifted into a "character" style by a shift of accentuation,' wrote the poet Denby. 'More concentrated movement than in most nineteenth-century full-length ballets,' wrote the poet Kirstein.

It is Shakespearean, say I. Trumpets announce a tournament as in *Richard II*. The war of the sexes recalls *Love's Labours Lost*. Wendy Ellis's and Alfreda Thorogood's smiles are those of Kate and Beatrice. Michael Coleman's scornful look is that of Coriolanus for the plebeians.

The fretful reader guesses that I have aired my literary fancies in despair of describing Balanchine's inventions step by step, for which even if I had memory and words, there would not be space. A detailed account may be found in Denby's *Dancers, Buildings and People in the Streets*. I advise those too swift despairers of ballet's potentialities as an art to take a look at this witty work, which is the product of a mind creative strictly in terms of dance. One of the contests in *Agon*, incidentally, is that between composer and choreographer, who complement but never echo each other on the tight-rope of 20 minutes.

4.2.73

Robbins's *Dances at a Gathering*

It isn't every night you see a ballet by Ashton and one by Jerome Robbins on the same bill, and it isn't every night the Royal Ballet dances choreography by one of America's three genius inventors—in fact this is their first from Robbins—and it isn't every night you see Nureyev, Dowell, Wall and Coleman in the same piece—not to mention Sibley, Seymour, Mason and Jenner. Last Monday the Robbins (it was originally mounted for the New York City Ballet) was preceded by *Enigma Variations*, Ashton's poem about the sunset of Victorian England, which provided an interesting contrast.

There are ten people in the new work: the other two are Laura Connor and Jonathan Kelly. What happens? Against an inconspicuously changing sky, to eighteen piano pieces by Chopin played by Anthony Twiner and lasting an hour, the young people meet, dance, compete a little, reflect, tease, become involved, have fun and forebodings and settle down.

Let dancing = form, let expression = colour; then Robbins's ballet is a drawing gently tinted, but with the pencil everywhere visible. The touches of emotion he has brushed in transform it from a *divertissement* into a work of art.

The music conditions dance and mood; and the 'running order' of the numbers—the way Robbins builds up the atmosphere, then changes it, at the same time varying his dancers or gradually allowing them to accumulate—is magical in itself.

After a bemused Nureyev has established a gently mazurka-ish climate for the picnic, and Mason and Wall with shining eyes have waltzed, and Dowell has liltingly lifted Sibley to the slow op. 33, no. 3, Mason dances capriciously alone. As a fourth, fifth, sixth, and seventh mazurka are piled on, to Mason are added Dowell, then Nureyev—and the men dance back to back, and the five play at posing for photographs—then Wall, then Seymour. Mason and Coleman have a rapid mocking waltz, then Sibley, Seymour and Connor a pensive virginal trio. To an eighth mazurka Nureyev and Dowell compete briskly. To the Etude, op. 25, no. 4, Mason flaunts serenely as if before a mirror. Three girls are slid, lifted and caught to a childish waltz.

A fifth waltz, op. 70, no. 2, brings whimsical Seymour twirling and flirting round Kelly—in vain; she tries to charm Wall, who sends her up; Coleman, too, leaves her to be funny and Isadora on her own. A languorous grand duet for Sibley and Nureyev, and a Cyrano solo for him. Drama, despair and hope to the fateful Scherzo op. 20, no. 1. To the Nocturne, op. 15, no. 1, ten dancers watch the sky anxiously; Nureyev lays a hand on the world they have got landed with, as if swearing allegiance to a new soil; all bow, form a ring, take arms, Poles become Americans (as Robbins's own Russian-Jewish family had), circulate like New Englanders in a work by Graham or de Mille, and prepare to face a dull Sunday afternoon.

Well, ballet is an art after all. Seymour was such a miracle of Mozartian comedy in that waltz I was sure she had sprung it on them. I was right. Next day Robbins said: 'We didn't know she was going to do that.' She had surprised the most Mozartian of choreographers.

25.10.70

It was a real pleasure to go again this week to *Dances at a Gathering* and *The Rite of Spring*, to see them immaculately performed and rapturously received by a packed house. The difference between a full house and a packed one is that the gallery slips are crowded to the corners, the people standing at the back of the stalls circle impede our progress to the bar, and little girls kneel in the gangway beside me, bobbing up and down distractingly, or sit on my feet.

Everything about Robbins's Chopin ballet exudes genius—except the queasy colours of the shirts and dresses; and the dancers dance it so radiantly that one cannot doubt they delight in the wonders of its choreography and enjoy being shown off at their best.

Nureyev is thoughtful, then inspired, then exultant, then solemn at the end. Mason and Wall waltz in a gentle dream. Wall fits perfectly into this play of gently changing moods, switching easily from tender to funny to gay. Mason has the gift of shooting comic question-marks through her Greek mask of melancholy. In a second's syncopating pause she can become (as a friend suggested) Maggie Smith. In the Etude op. 25, no. 5, Sibley and Dowell, divinely matched, kneel, stand still as the music sweeps by, then join it in a big dance which is *'nuptiale, auguste et solenelle'*. Seymour has a way of being that type of modern heroine, Georgie Girl, funny girl, whom we love for being the odd girl out: she responds to Chopin like a lover. Coleman's deft somersaulting of Mason, his timing of a pause and double-take, prove him her match in comedy. All these, with pretty Ann Jenner, pert Lesley Collier and David Ashmole in more self-effacing roles, combined to make the poem live.

31.10.71

Jerome Robbins's *Dances at a Gathering* has now been two years in the repertory of the Royal Ballet.

To those who have been proud of the way our company performed this American masterpiece in the past it may come as a surprise to learn that members of the New York City Ballet to whom I spoke in New York were shocked by the British dancers' exaggerations and their expression of individual personality. 'They play it for laughs,' I was told. The Balanchine dancers were in no doubt that they did it better and in a way nearer to the choreographer's intentions. They would probably prefer the new cast without Nureyev, whose personality is so strong that his slightest gesture can appear portentous, and with Connor making her witty points less markedly than Mason. Seymour I do think is beginning to go too far. Coleman has the exact spirit of the ballet; and Sibley and Dowell are always magical together.

22.10.72

Robbins's *Afternoon of a Faun*

Jerome Robbins's *Afternoon of a Faun* is a miraculous re-thinking of Nijinsky's ballet to Debussy's music. Instead of a Greek hillside we have a ballet classroom during the lunch break—a fine simple set in white nylon with door, windows, skylight and *barre* by Jean Rosenthal, which somehow suggests New York in a heat-wave. All boys are fauns in the afternoon, and this one, reincarnated by Anthony Dowell, is dozing on the floor. The rising tide of music hoists him to practise some steps, gazing narcissistically in the imaginary mirror of the proscenium opening. When the girl comes pacing slowly in, it is Antoinette Sibley. They try out a few lifts, still observing themselves dispassionately, dancers not people. At last Debussy gives the cue—it is summer, after all—the boy kisses the girl's cheek. You might think such a thing had never happened to either of them before. Up goes her hand to the love-wound. Then, overcome, she leaves the scene of the crime.

Sibley's reaction to the kiss is quite different from that of Tanaquil LeClercq and other Americans I have seen in the role. *They* were startled and shocked: *she* was startled but pleased. Sibley and Dowell were beautiful together. *Faun* is a work which everybody must acclaim.

17.12.71

O

The Changing Scene
(1963–1965)

Gontcharova and Larionov

In 1934 I found in a bookshop in Norwich a glamorously illustrated pamphlet on the late glories of Diaghilev's Russian Ballet: this contained an essay on theatrical costume by Nathalie Gontcharova and reproductions of some of her designs, notably the third decor of *Coq d'or* in blazing colours. How this glossy fifteen-franc booklet reached Norwich I cannot imagine—it must have been rare even in Paris: I suppose an angel brought it. For several days I was splashing imitation Gontcharovas in poster paint on large sheets of cartridge paper.

Now Gontcharova has died in Paris, aged eighty-one. She was born within a fortnight of her husband Larionov, who survives her, and within a year of Picasso, of Epstein and of Fokine, for whose production of Rimsky-Korsakov's last opera she was to do her first and most famous stage designs.

Gontcharova was somebody who enhanced the life of her friends because of her wonder at the beauty of the world about her. She was the gentlest of women, but a fighter on the barricades of art.

28.10.62

Larionov had been an invalid since 1950 and used to receive one reclining on his bed in the crammed studio flat in rue Jacques Callot. But he was the most energetic reclining figure you could imagine. Gontcharova and Larionov were the same age, and their friends feared for the partner destined to survive the other: but Larionov was taken to hospital the day before Gontcharova suddenly died.

Our last meeting was a happy one. They had decided to make one of their rare excursions to a local Russian restaurant in order to give me a treat. I was in Paris to see some new ballet, but it was hopeless to explain this or to talk about time. They said my Diaghilev Exhibition had brought them luck; their early pictures and designs were increasingly in demand; and they wanted to celebrate.

Blinis, caviar, bortsch, zakouskis, *boeuf Stroganoff*, pastries, fruit, pints of cream, vodka and varied wines were urged upon me, while the two dears sat gloating; and of course most of the ballet programme was over by the time we parted with many kisses.

Larionov's was a searching, original and restless mind. I bet the angels' wings are getting a new look.

12.6.64

Truth

Martha Graham gave a little talk, grave and gay, before the class her company demonstrated to an audience of critics and dancers on Monday. She said her father, a doctor, had given her her first dancing lesson at the age of four, when he warned her never to lie to him because her body would give her away. The famous Graham technique, evolved in the solitude of her great mind, which was so gloriously shown us by the company that morning—'one equal temper of heroic hearts'—and which made possible the works of art we have witnessed this season, is a method of telling the truth.

15.9.63

Flamenco

The star of a crowded week turned out to be a short, fat, bald, lame man with a disproportionately large head, who got laughed at when he first walked on to the stage of the Piccadilly Theatre on Monday, but who dominated the audience so absolutely and with so little effort that he brought the curtain down at last to a storm of joyous acclamation.

This was Enrique El Cojo, the Sevillian teacher of Flamenco, who appears only at the very beginning and the very end of the programme called *Fiesta Flamenca*.

El Cojo's appearances are really incidental. The programme is built round Manuela Vargas, a long threatening spear of a woman, with striking looks, personality and technique; but it begins with El Cojo giving her a lesson, or pretending to.

El Cojo's glory is that he has only to place his arms, hold up his head, snap his fingers and sketch a pelvic undulation, barely moving at all, and instead of a short fat man we see whole processions of incandescent beauties with flowers in their hair moving through the centuries to 'the fatal music of guitars'. (The last phrase is Augustus John's.)

12.5.63

Theatre

The other day I was given a preview of Philip Johnson's New York State Theatre at Lincoln Center, which will be opened by New York City Ballet in April. It is the most handsome, the grandest and—for a 2,800-seater—the most intimate theatre I have seen.

Johnson, who with Mies van der Rohe designed the famous Seagram Building, worked on his plans with George Balanchine and Lincoln Kirstein. As might be expected from this combination there are ideal sight-lines, space, luxury, a respect for European tradition and a pioneering freedom in the use of new materials and techniques.

Diagonaling across a plaza with the Philharmonic Hall on your right and an unbuilt new Metropolitan Opera House in front of you, you penetrate the simple stone and glass façade of the building. The entrance hall is wide and low-ceilinged, the booking-offices in a wall of red marble ahead of you. The surprise comes later. As you climb one of the two marble staircases on the right or left end of this hall, holding the great curving hand-rail of neutral travertine, and as the staircase doubles backwards, you see one of two huge sculptured groups towering above you. At least you will, but when I was there they were swathed in sheets so I only got the scale. These, Lincoln Kirstein told me, were enlarged from small groups of acrobats by the late Elie Nadelmann, and carved in the quarries of Carrara.

The groups stand at either end of an immense room, its height and length suggesting St. Petersburg or the Doge's Palace. The floor red marble (*merlino rosso*), the ceiling very plain—gold-leaf. The inner wall is the outer convex curve of the auditorium, with a long bar below, and on the other three sides walkways run around, so that theatregoers emerging from their first, second, or third balconies can either take a walk to look out on the plaza or quiz their boozing brethren on the internal parade ground below. Light from the northern glass wall will be broken by a floor-to-ceiling waterfall of bronze, gilt and silvery metal beads. And the most original idea in this noble hall, fit for the reception of emperors, presidents or Beatles, is that it will be quite dimly lit—no chandeliers. Shafts of light on the Nadelman sculptures, and the golden ceiling glimmering in the gloom.

Johnson calls his theatre the last baroque opera house, and the auditorium is a red and gold horseshoe, only with rows of seats (and at the sides standing room) instead of boxes. On the top level 500 seats at two dollars, which is cheap for ballet in New York.

The most marvellous thing is to look down on the *flattened* curves of red stalls, which embrace the stage but with aristocratic restraint. This, the low placing of the stage, and the uptilting of the horseshoes away from it, make for good relations between performer and spectator. The fronts of the concave horseshoes are moulded into flattish convex bulges of dull gold, undecorated but for rosettes of plastic and metal holding lights. The proscenium arch, the size of Covent Garden's but capable of a higher scene, unmasked, is of expanded metal, a kind of openwork Jackson Pollock in a different gold.

The gold ceiling has a huge light-bag, which will descend in intermissions to reveal itself as a flashing globe. Around this innumerable spotlights are hidden in a pattern of spreading and overlapping arcs such as you would make if you dropped four pebbles in a pool very close together.

15.3.64

History

The Great Historical Event of 1964 was the arrival here in rapid succession (following Martha Graham's triumph in 1963) of the Americans, Merce Cunningham, Alvin Ailey and Paul Taylor with their troupes. These very different companies gave us a picture of the width, range and possibilities of the experimental dance and must pep up our ideas on dance in general. The last was presented by Robin Howard, who had made possible Martha Graham's visit in 1963. In addition, Mr. Howard has inaugurated a £20,000 fund (he doesn't own up to how much he himself has contributed) to further the study of Modern Dance techniques among British dancers: so he is the Bloke of the Year.

31.1.64

Red Army

With the help of a few drinks (but with no ice in them at the Albert Hall) it is easy to have a good old emotional wallow listening to singers of the Red Army rendering 'The Volga Boat Song', 'Tipperary', 'Annie Laurie' and 'Auld Lang Syne'. A stout gentleman in front of me burst into impassioned applause as the first notes of these old favourites rang out, and, in the last, when the chorus joined hands and began to sway it was too much for him altogether.

The mood of the programme was very hands-across-the-sea-ish, but I was less stirred by the direct approach of a song called 'Do Russian people want war?' Whatever Russian people want, it's quite clear that English people want Russian music, songs and dancers. This great thought occurs to me in a week which has seen not only the Red Army at the iceless Albert Hall, but MacMillan making a ballet to Shostakovich's *First Symphony* and Nureyev dancing with and without Fonteyn at Covent Garden.

But it was the Red Army dancers I had gone to see, and they were of course prodigious. Concentrating on a few difficult steps which become dazzling when performed at speed, they ring a number of variations on them. The squatting cobbler's step, for example, is performed straight, advancing towards the spectators, in a circle, as a sideways skim, with the dancer supporting himself backwards on his hands, or combining with lateral leaps or wheeling movements. The wheeling spins in a circle are done with the dancer throwing himself alarmingly into a position parallel with the floor. One man dared this while expanding his accordion. Virtuosity can go no farther: in fact, that has always been the trouble with virtuosity.

24.2.63

Greece

The Greek Art Theatre's production of *The Birds* at the Aldwych would not really be my business if Karolos Koun had not produced it as the all-out singing, dancing show Aristophanes probably intended; so that I feel justified in sticking my nose above stairs to make a few rustic points. But this is only a pretext to boost an old mate of mine who happens to be one of the most distinguished stage designers of today.

I suppose there *was* a time when flamenco dancing, as performed impromptu in Spanish caves or cafés, was unknown on the English stage: and I suppose there may come a time when the mysterious and hypnotic dances that Greek soldiers or fishermen sometimes get up and perform in cafés, solo, or in twos or threes or joined to each other by handkerchiefs, may regularly be compiled into spectacles and become a commonplace of the London theatre. Except to a few lucky tourists these Greek dances, which are believed to descend in an unbroken tradition from classical times, remain unknown here. But some of them, delightfully springing out of the play's action to sung accompaniments, were arranged by

Zouzou Nicoloudi for Karolos Koun's production. Documentation for the folk dances was provided by Dora Stratou, whose fame as an expert has indeed reached me here. These are not brilliant, they are even monotonous. Yet combined with the plangent melodies of Hadjidakis they thrilled me in a new and curious way. The combination of modern tunes and ancient steps abolishes time; the classical world shimmers in today's market-place, and while the same ships glide for ever between the islands, I am on my way to hear Socrates, smoking a cigarette.

And, of course, the classical element in modern life, and vice versa, is a dominant theme in the art of Iannis Tsarouchis, whose set and dresses for *The Birds* I admire so much.

In *The Birds* Tsarouchis did not try after big effects. It is not for any spectacular elements that his work so excites me, but for its modest fitness for the purposes of Aristophanes and Koun, its subtlety and the loving care with which it contrives diversity within unity.

The set is plain—a few timbers, platform and steps against blackness. The costumes for the Birds who adorn the stage throughout most of the action are sun-tan coloured tights with greyish non-realistic feathers sprouting oddly out of their shoulders or backsides or over their goggled eyes.

There is a certain amount of pale blue and white about. Jigging dancers sidle on to hang strings of triangular flags and bare lightbulbs. The comic masks of the indignant gods revealed to me the link between the masks of old Greek drama and our papier mâché fairground giant-heads.

24.5.64

Madam

My heart warmed to Ninette de Valois when she said she had to fly home from New York because Sol Hurok had insisted on seven *Sleeping Beauties* running and she couldn't face more than four. That woman has the makings of a first-rate ballet critic in her.

5.5.63

The *Tsamikos*. Drawing by Iannis Tsarouchis

India

'Krishna, come, come soon.' Krishna, being dark blue, has always been one of my favourite gods. When his mother ticked him off for eating mud he opened his mouth and she beheld the entire universe.

I cannot have been the only uninitiated Westerner who, confronted with a glimpse of the infinite complexities of Indian music and dancing at this Festival, felt like Krishna's mother. Lord Harewood fell for the sacred sub-continent years ago; then saw Balasarasvati, who had never been out of India before, dancing in Tokyo in 1951. His decision to have demonstrations and recitals, together with a thrilling exhibition of Music and Dance in Indian art, in Edinburgh, turns out to be one of the halcyon inspirations of this festival.

'Krishna, come, come soon, come soon and show me your face!' The same happy despair assailed me at the thought of Balasarasvati's limitless lore and repertoire as at the realization that I could not possibly follow the rhythms and counter-rhythms of the drummer Palghat Raghu in the introductory demonstration on Tuesday. For Balasarasvati, on whose family tree I can count twenty-two musicians or dancers deriving from an eighteenth-century ancestor at the court of Tanjore, has ninety-seven *padams* in her repertoire. The *padam* is a lyrical number in three parts which forms the fifth item of the necessary six or possible eight in a Bharatanatya recital. Of *padams* the dancer performs six in Edinburgh, announcing her nightly choice before the show. The story of Krishna and his mother quoted above forms part of one of them.

I had long known the fame of Balasarasvati (born 1918) and read about her in *The Other Mind*, the late Beryl de Zoete's record of her inspired wanderings. And suddenly here the legendary dancer was; the living embodiment of countless centuries of sculpture, painting, music, dance and song: for in India all these are part of one art designed by Shiva to lead us to a comprehension of the two infinities—inwards, inside us, and outwards, beyond the stars.

Above medium height, plump, attractive, in green and yellow, with bells on her ankles, flowers in her hair and a diamond in her nose, she stands looking preoccupied and rather cross, waiting for her music cue. (When not dancing she thinks she is invisible.) She renders the invocation and the early formal passages of the recital. We admire her strength, control and flexibility, but are not carried away.

In between dances she twitches her sari and looks anxiously at the dance master. Then comes the *varnam* (part four), a big scene in which a love-lorn lady's confidante appeals to her mistress's absent lord. Now we see the encyclopedic richness of the gesture language. The first of three *padams* is on a similar subject; in the second, a jealous wife is bitchy about her rival, and Balasarasvati might be Millamant or Célimène—'Gone are the days when she came by to borrow jewels and saris.' This is comedy almost as we understand it, with gestures replacing words. Last is the episode of Krishna eating mud, and I see Balasarasvati shining with awe, and I too am filled with awe and become Balasarasvati, and we are both Krishna's mother.

25.8.63

Juliet

When I was invited to plan the Diaghilev Exhibition in 1954, Lady Juliet Duff was my keenest collaborator, giving me introductions to a Proustian world of people in Paris who might have a Bakst in their bathroom, and sharing in my dejection when someone refused to lend. Then, in Edinburgh, during the final spurt, she would be up till all hours cutting out leaves to stick in spirals round Leonard Rosoman's vermilion columns.

Exhibitions, like the theatre, thrilled her; and last year she was at Stratford, hammering away like a Nibelung at midnight, breaking up chunks of plastic which were to give a jewelled sheen to the giant sculptures of Astrid Zydower. Shakespeare's First Folio had been dedicated to her ancestors; George Herbert was a relation and so was Philip Sidney (and she would have behaved exactly like him at Zutphen); Belloc loved her; and she knew and quoted her poets.

She was always delightful, and even in her eighties, always surprising. It suddenly struck me as she arrived to lunch in the country one day a year ago that she might think my leather trousers rather odd. Wrong! *'Just* what I want!' she exclaimed, meaning for the garden. Last September, motoring from Edinburgh, we stayed in Westmorland, where we both come from. 'I don't really like lakes', she confessed: but before the ruins of Lowther Castle, sprouting willow-herb, where in youth she had feasted with emperors, Juliet commented 'I think it looks better now'. Her favourite restaurant was Lyons Corner House.

Juliet's will said 'No flowers. No memorial service'; but the unwitherable bouquets have long since been ordered—by Diaghilev, by Bakst, by Nijinsky, by Cocteau, by Poulenc, by Tchelitchev; and it is too late to countermand them.

10.10.65

Albert Hall

If only the Albert Hall were a ruin we could rush in and perform opera in it, like they do in the Baths of Caracalla. We shall certainly miss it when it goes—but it is partly gone already. That is, the pretty festooned Wedgwood dome has been covered with a buff-coloured cubistic ceiling, which no doubt improves the acoustics.

But it still gives me a dreamy sensation, when the lights are dimmed, to look up past the rows of boxes, whose looped curtains frame as cosy a glow as ever beckoned from suburban villa, to that cold twilit Roman terrace beneath the arches, round which I imagine many a hungry youth ranging in search of someone to love him and Berlioz till the end of time.

5.1.64

Debussy

I do not at all approve of Peter Darrell's attempt to bring Debussy's *Jeux*
up to date. Like Nijinsky's version, it is about two girls and a boy finishing
a game of tennis and starting to flirt. Cooling drinks and garden furniture.
Suddenly one of the girls slips a gun out of her handbag and follows the
other off stage. A shot rings out. This is pretty unforgivable. But on
Monday the shot didn't ring out, because the gun didn't go off. Depart-
ment of utter confusion. Always keep a spare pistol in the wings for
Debussy ballets, Fokine used to say.

3.11.63

Cod Piece
or
What you will

Dramatic fragment given to the principal 'onlie begetter' of West Side Story *in the
year of Shakespeare's Quatercentenary*

CURIO: Will you go sup, my lord?
DUKE: What's cooking?
CURIO: My lord,
        A dish without a name—or rather, one
        Which young New Yorkers, gleaming in the pride
        Of sable leather prick't with steely stars
        And jeans new bleach't with codpiece prominent,
        Do hold most dear; but chiefly those, methinks,
        Incorporate in bands to rule the street,
        Who lads of alien colour spur to brawls,
        Dancers who from some seething tenement
        Do howl their mistress' name repeatedly
        To the west o' the island; and from Germania's pride,
        The ivied university of Hamburg,
        It takes its common workday cognisance
        And 'Hamburger' is hight.

DUKE: O faugh! It stinks
          Of old man's joy-stick, which our tarnish'd maids
          And minions too of baser appetite
          Do suck o' Sundays. Give me some pot, man, prithee,
          And let's to billiards.

                              Unpublished, Spring, 1964

CLASSICS

Fourteen ladies, to my knowledge, danced Giselle in England last year.
Sunday Times, 31.1.65

No one in England knows what *Coppélia* is all about.
Observer, 16.9.51

Everyone goes to sleep for a hundred years at some time during his existence, and which of us has not fallen captive to an impossible Swan?
Observer, 12.9.48

We are thinking of taking on a special *Swan Lake* critic.
Sunday Times, 22.10.67

KING AND QUEEN: What on *earth* are we doing, standing round here like a lot of *fools*?
LILAC FAIRY: My dear, but you must be *mad*! Don't you *realize*? *You* have been *asleep* for a hundred *years*!
KING AND QUEEN (*miming frantically*): Who, *us*?
LILAC FAIRY: Yes, *you*. Isn't it a *scream*? But *I* and *this* young man, who is a *prince*, my dear, have *come* for absolute *miles* in order that *he* should *kiss* . . . etc., etc.
Ballet, Vol. 5, No. 6, June 1948

Well, we are one more *Nutcracker* nearer death.
Sunday Times, 31.12.72

Giselle

Rambert's production; Gilmour and Gore

Although in 1946 I saw for the first time such admirable works as *Symphonic Variations*, *Les Forains*, *Les Amours de Jupiter*, *Dramma per Musica* and *Fancy Free*, and although in that year I beheld such dancers as Fonteyn, Chauviré, Alonso, Eglevsky and Babilée, what moved me most of all was Marie Rambert's revival of *Giselle*, with Sally Gilmour, Walter Gore and Joyce Graeme.

I saw this production several times at Sadler's Wells in July (on one of which occasions the Queen was present), but Gore was ill at the time; so, for that and other reasons, the production did not achieve its full ripeness until the Ballet Rambert's winter season at the King's Theatre, Hammersmith. It is of the afternoon performance on the last day of that season that I shall be writing.

Why was this *Giselle* so successful? Hugh Stevenson's designs were not outstanding. The small orchestra under Arthur Oldham did not play Adam's tinkling music at all well. Neither Gilmour nor Gore are preeminent as dancers. I think the secrets of Marie Rambert's triumph are feeling, thought and care. Instead of 'running up' a revival of the old ballet from what she remembered of previous productions, she would seem to have cleared her mind of preconceptions and, attacking *Giselle* with a fresh point of view, to have realized the qualities which originally made it so moving a work. Having felt the romance and the tragedy, she would naturally subordinate everything to the idea she—so to speak—shared with Gautier and Saint-Georges. The other reason for the success of this *Giselle* is the extraordinary appropriateness for their roles of the three principals and the extent to which they have been able to enter into them.

Walter Gore plays his part in the early episodes with a simple directness, which is the best way of making plausible the role of prince in peasant's guise. It was a good idea to restore the sprightly *pas de deux* for the young villagers (of which the music is probably not by Adam); Belinda Wright and John Gilpin dance this with zest. Marjorie Field as Berthe, the mother of Giselle, mimes in a natural manner, filling well and unobtrusively her place in the story.

The entry of the court is effected without the usual excess of ceremony. Sonia Arova is a gracious and credible Princess—neither a haughty dummy nor a glamorous showgirl. It is important for the sake of dramatic irony that she and Giselle should feel a mutual attraction before destroying each other's happiness. I like the hawks on the huntsmen's wrists. The dresses of courtiers and peasants blend agreeably together when they are simultaneously on the stage; and there are not too many people dressed alike, which always gives the effect of a revue chorus . . . .

Sally Gilmour's rendering of Giselle's madness is so real that it seems not to be the result of art at all; but I am told that when she is moving us to tears every movement has been carefully tried out and timed, and nothing left to chance. From the time when she first clasps the side of her head in realization of her lover's deceit we are gripped with pity and terror. Just as when Toscanini conducts some hackneyed piece—say 'The Ride of the Valkyrie'—we seem to be hearing it for the first time, so, at this moment, do all previous productions of *Giselle* evaporate from our memory, and we become personally involved in the present tragedy of a betrayed girl. It was here, too, that I realized how a minor score like Adam's can surpass greater music in making a perfect accompaniment to ballet. The commonplace tune was caught up and transfigured by the unfolding action—or rather, the music seemed to be produced by the tottering footsteps and wild looks of the heroine. . . .

The last few seconds of the act, after Giselle's death, which are usually made tedious by a wooden tableau and a conventionally sobbing Albrecht, are magnificently filled in this production by Gore and the *corps de ballet*. Nothing has been left to chance or forgotten. Gore's sudden outburst of wrath is as terrifying as real anger. Hilarion's fear can almost be shared; and one can feel physically the powerful efforts the Duke's friends make to disarm him. This struggle is immediately followed by Albrecht flinging himself on the dead girl, raising first her arm, then her head, as if in a desperate attempt to restore her to life. Then, all hope gone, he clasps her shudderingly to him and gazes like a lost soul into her face.

I have often thought how boring the second act of *Giselle* can be. Marie Rambert has brought it to life. In her production, far from being a dancing exercise of which the meaning has been forgotten, it is charged with drama. Whereas most Queens of the Wilis go through their movements in the accepted cold manner and are content with making the traditional imperious gestures, Joyce Graeme is a white flame of cruelty throughout.

Her eyes flash baleful fire, and every gesture of her hands and arms seems animated by inhuman force. As she moves alone in the blue light, consecrating the grove, we wonder what sinister rite is about to take place among the trees. The return of Giselle to the grave is staged with an unearthly effect which would have delighted Gautier and his Romantic friends. Giselle seems to lose her corporeal nature before our eyes. Slowly deprived of animation she glides away from her lover, arms extended in a last human gesture of longing. Just as she reaches her grave an invisible finger seems to beckon; she falls backward lifeless and disappears from sight. Albrecht is left alone.

This revival of *Giselle* is not quite perfect, but it is as good as Marie Rambert could make it with her present resources, which, as they include Gilmour, Gore and Graeme, are not inconsiderable. Those people who read this without having seen the production may protest 'The man is mad! Are not Fonteyn, Chauviré and Alonso much better dancers than this Miss Gilmour?' I am bound to say they are. It is in the purely dancing passages that Gore and Gilmour are least satisfactory. But their musical acting, or, shall I say, their dramatic dancing, is superb. And where can the line be drawn between mime and dancing in a ballet like *Giselle*? In a good interpretation they are inseparably fused. And Sally Gilmour *is* a better Giselle than the three ladies you mention.

Ballet, Vol. 5, No 1, January 1947.

Fonteyn

At the name of Fonteyn the critical octopus is wont to exude not ink but syrup. The fact remains, however, that the angelic Margot is better in some roles than others, besides being, like the humblest *corps de ballet* girl, at the mercy of her producers. Why is it that in the Sadler's Wells production of *Giselle*, newly revived at Covent Garden, she makes so little effect? Absurd to say that the role of Giselle does not suit her: few roles could be calculated to show off her varied gifts to better advantage. Fonteyn should be wonderful in it, but somehow she is not. I think the producer must be to blame.

Giselle is a beautifully constructed work, a minor theatrical masterpiece: that is why it has survived, almost alone of Romantic ballets. It is also a barnstorming melodrama and must not be treated in too genteel a way. Emotion is laid on thick in the story and music, and a producer should take every opportunity offered him to introduce touches of lurid exagger-

ation. At Covent Garden Robert Irving's approach to Adam's score is far
too faint-heated. Climaxes in the action, such as Giselle's finding the sword
and her confronting stare at Albrecht before falling dead, are slurred over
by the producer. In Fonteyn's mime there is too much pretty but fussy
detail: I should like more elimination, more stylization, and each gesture
given its full singing, poignant value.

I recommend the Covent Garden direction to study a film of *Giselle*
with Markova and Dolin now showing at the Rialto. Much of it they may
mock, and its doll's-house settings are not comparable with Bailey's.
Though the recording is brassy, Sir Malcolm Sargent rides the old war-
horse of a score as if he were proud of it. Neither of the stars is photogenic,
but they have the grand tragic manner. Markova dances divinely; her
rendering of this, her greatest role, has all the moments of telling emphasis I
should like to see in Fonteyn's.

Observer, 18.5.52

Markova

No one can dance *Giselle* like Markova, and no one should try to. Hers is a
personal and extraordinary interpretation which defies analysis and which
it would be fatal to copy. She breaks every rule and gives one of the great
performances of our day.

Alicia Markova has been dancing *Giselle* for over twenty years, so she
must be at least—twenty-five. She looked no more when she made her
welcome return as a guest artist with Sadler's Wells at Covent Garden on
Monday; in fact, her elf-like attraction has increased with the passage of
time. Her strength, no doubt, has diminished: but, in a curious way, the
less strongly, accurately and classically she performs the traditional steps
the more expressive she makes them. It is as if the Classical Style has
helped her find what movements and poses are best suited to her 'Markova
Style' of dancing, and she has discarded anything which is not useful to
her.

In *arabesque* she bends her raised leg; her back is not strong, and she
'gives' at the waist; her arms are seldom fully extended. Perhaps there are a
dozen girls on the stage with her who could dance *Giselle* better than
Markova: but could they make us look at them, or give us melancholy
autumn thoughts between pleasure and pain? Let them try!

Two other dancers gave perfect performances that evening: Brian Shaw
in the first act *pas de deux*, responding with delicious resilience to the

bouncing tune of the *coda*; and Alexander Grant as the Barber in *Mam'zelle Angot*, the very spirit and god of Fun. If one were a king one would go about impulsively knighting performers who gave one such pleasure. I liked Somes's romantic Prince in *Giselle*; also Lindsay's smooth *bourrée* and menacing gestures as Myrtha.

On Wednesday Fonteyn returned after six months' absence to the stage of Covent Garden—a stage carpeted with flowers and echoing with passionate acclamations.

Observer, 22.3.53

Carlotta Grisi and the young lady of Yarmouth; Fonteyn and Somes

A gentleman from Great Yarmouth writes to ask whether he should allow his little girl, now ten years old, to take up ballet as a career. 'From what I have heard', he continues, 'I would not let my daughter take up acting, for I believe there are some unprepossessing characters about. I do not imagine ballet is the same, but . . .'.

My thoughts kept reverting to the young lady of Yarmouth during the performance of *Giselle* by the Royal Ballet before the President of Peru. Would she inspire the love of unprepossessing poets and choreographers, as did Carlotta Grisi, who gave us *Giselle*? Would she, like Salome and Fonteyn, dance before the heads of State?

Carlotta was born in 1821 in a desolate village in the mountains of Upper Istria. Here there was a derelict palace in which the Emperor Francis II had once slept; and Carlotta was born in the Imperial bed. The place was so wild that mice ate fearlessly on the table, and bears wandered in the streets. At seven she danced at La Scala. Then Perrot, already a dancer of note, came, saw and was conquered by her: he 'groomed her for stardom', but they were never married. She danced at Her Majesty's before she appeared at the Paris Opéra and captured the heart and pen of Théophile Gautier. He invented the story of *Giselle* for her, and Perrot arranged her dances, though he was not given credit on the programme.

Carlotta triumphed, and for more than a decade reigned over Europe. At thirty-four she retired to a villa near Geneva, the gift of Prince Radziwill, who was her daughter's father. She died in 1899.

I should not have lost myself in dreams about the past of *Giselle* or the future of the Norfolk ballerina if the production at Covent Garden had been better: for despite the presence of Fonteyn and Somes, and although

Alicia Markova
in *Camille*.
Drawing by
Cecil Beaton

Peter Clegg bounced brilliantly in the first act *pas de deux*, it was pretty dreary.

To begin with, Emanuel Young conducted Adam's score in an utterly lifeless way. This is perfect ballet music, as well calculated as Gautier's scenario to sustain the admirable dances and sweep the romantic drama to its conclusion. There was no sustaining or sweeping on Thursday. The handling of the crowd is unimaginative. I could never believe in Leslie Edwards as a gamekeeper. Then, the young men in furred hats, who go hunting without boots, with nothing but silk tights to cover the expanse between ribs and ankle, look so *vulnerable* to the sneers of peasants and the tusks of the wild boar.

I began to wonder what agent Prince Albrecht had employed to get that cottage for him without any questions being asked in the neighbour-hood, and if Prince Radziwill had to disguise himself as a peasant to win Grisi's love, and whether it had been more fun when the Wilis all wore different national costumes, as they did in the first Paris production—when Giselle with her ultimate gesture reunited Albrecht with the under-standing Bathilde—and whether the young lady of Yarmouth would not, after all, prove well able to look after herself.

28.2.60

Seymour

A stylish performance must be recorded which has taken place recently: that of the Canadian Lynn Seymour in *Giselle*. I particularly recall her body's curve as she hung in the air, her arms *en couronne*, breeze-bent like the stalk of the flower she flings to Albrecht: for a second we breathed the dead fragrance of the Romantic ballet.

27.3.60

Nerina and Bruhn

It was interesting to see Erik Bruhn, whom we had known as the kilted hero of Bournonville's *La Sylphide*, portraying the character of Albrecht in that other poetical ballet of the Romantic period, *Giselle*. While *La Sylphide*, with its butterfly heroine, its witches and tartans, is more of a fairy tale, *Giselle* has a more tragic, more dramatic story, that of a betrayed girl driven to madness and death, whose love survives the grave and enables her to save the life of her repentant betrayer.

Bruhn, who was perfect as the sad, Scottish nympholept, is too reserved to give more than a hint of that romantic abandon and despair which are necessary in *Giselle*, though no one could perform better than he does the exacting dances invented by Perrot or Coralli for Albrecht.

Yet there are signs that abandon and despair are going out of fashion. The turning point of the drama is the Act I curtain, when the prince in peasant's clothing, watched by his noble fiancée, his would-be father-in-law, their court and a crowd of vintagers, raves over the dead body of his deluded mistress.

This is probably the most powerful emotional scene, the biggest tear-jerker in the ballet repertoire; and the poet Gautier, when he planned it for his successful rival in love, Perrot, to perform over the body of their adored Carlotta Grisi, took good care to ensure that the composer Adolphe Adam should lay on the agony good and thick in the storm of lamentation with which the first act hurtles to a close.

In the present (post-Nureyev) staging of the scene at Covent Garden, the Prince, unable to bear the sight of Giselle dead, hides his face in his squire's bosom way upstage. The raving is left to Giselle's mother, and even when she is played by so striking a mime as Gerd Larsen this is not nearly so effective.

So I wonder if the Kremlin or Dame Ninette have decided that too much passion is embarrassing in ballet (after all that tableau did sound pretty corny as I described it above) and to stick to the dancing. And I wonder if your ballet critic, who, after all, goes to plays, too, for pleasure, and who wept buckets twice this week over the inspired acting of young Peter McEnery in *Look Homeward Angel* at the Phoenix, should only compare one dancer with another and one arrangement of steps with another, without looking for life, drama, emotion, reality, meaning or truth in a ballet.

But Bruhn played his early scenes simply and naturally. In Act II he soared, though it was sometimes hard to see his black-clad figure in the dim lighting. Anya Linden is an admirable Myrtha. And as Giselle, Nadia Nerina has never danced better or played so well.

8.4.62

Chauvire and Nureyev

After all the excitements of the first act, the first part of the second act of *Giselle* can be quite a drag, but with Anya Linden steering the admirable *corps de ballet* of Wilis through their mystic gyrations in the current production at Covent Garden, tension mounts steadily. Watching this Myrtha consecrating the glade for her baleful rite and summoning the cohorts of zombie virgins, I tried to analyse what made her performance so effective. It was not only that she had eliminated all inessentials to arrive at a ringing simplicity, she had found a way of accenting certain looks and movements which gave them definition, and there was a suddenness about her gestures which conveyed an impression of evil power.

As Giselle, the attractive Chauviré had her moments, but she is not dynamic and her line is not always pure.

I imagine it is Nureyev's intention (or the intention of whoever taught him his version of the ballet) to take the ham and melodrama out of the role of Albrecht, to make it more realistic in detail and thus more acceptable to a cynical modern audience. If so, he does one thing which is quite out of keeping.

During his dance of exhaustion, just after executing some soaring back-cabrioles, he runs off-stage. To complete the pattern, his Giselle has to do the same. This is disastrous to the dramatic tension, because it is vital that we should see every stage of the hero's agony. When he runs off we cease to worry about the destruction of Albrecht and begin to wonder if Nureyev is sucking a lemon in the wings.

Apart from this lapse, Nureyev plays the part of a man dancing himself to a death of exhaustion more realistically than any other Albrecht I have seen. Eager, it seems, genuinely to wear himself out, he has inserted towards the end an additional series of *brisés*. He gets weaker and weaker, and seems to be really passing out when the dawn comes to save him.

It has always puzzled me how the limp Albrecht should have the strength to carry Giselle back to her grave. But she is weightless, incorporeal, you may say. In that case she doesn't need carrying. Better, I think, to have her drift and fade away, leaving him prostrate, yearning at the air. Chauviré descended, standing, into a trap.

Nureyev ends the ballet, kneeling, with a gesture which seems to ask for our pity. This is in keeping with his interesting portrayal of Albrecht as a mixed-up kid too young to be responsible for his actions, pathetic rather than tragic, a bit like Shakespeare's Romeo.

27.5.62

Fonteyn and Nureyev

He who plays the Prince, that is to say the chief male dancer in almost any old classical ballet, has the awkward problem of satisfying his conscience that his Albrecht, his Siegfried, his Florimund and his Sugar-puss are all distinctly differentiated characterizations.

About Albrecht in *Giselle* Cyril Beaumont wrote:

Is he, despite his pleasing exterior, merely an aristocratic libertine, who has assumed . . . appropriate peasant guise, in order to accomplish his evil design, or is he a man of honour who, having fallen in love with one of his tenants, and realising the immense distance which separates them on account of their difference in station, pretends to be one of her own class the better to gain her affection? I incline to the latter view.

But Mr. Beaumont, though going on to surmise that Albrecht's betrothal to Bathilde was 'merely the prelude to a marriage of convenience', does not tell us if he believes the prince intended to marry Giselle bigamously or to seduce her, then disappear.

One supposes that, like most young people, he did not think very far ahead. But I should like to see someone play him as a charming but utterly selfish villain, who only begins to suffer and grow up at the sight of Giselle going mad.

Nureyev's Albrecht, quite different from his melancholy passionate Siegfried in *Swan Lake*, is a little boy—Peter Pan. He is all out to have fun, but is very spoilt; doesn't like being held forth at by Giselle's mother, and waves naughtily over her head when she takes the girl into their cottage to rest. When Giselle goes mad and dies he cries on Wilfred's shoulder; then unable to face the sight of death runs off, leaving Berthe to do all the mourning.

The key to Nureyev's interpretation, as I have written before, seems to be his childish hand-to-mouth gesture. During the second act he grows up a bit and does some strenuous dancing before the final collapse, during which he crosses his feet, not forgetting to point his toes. There is something undramatic about this slight figure, who starts out to face life in a neat all-over beige outfit like a pantomime principal boy, and who is so very much the victim of circumstances.

Of Giselle Mr. Beaumont writes:

> Even her own mother regards her daughter as something of an enigma. Is she not always scolding Giselle because of her mad craze for dancing . . .?

In fact, she seems to me another very 'modern' type. Fonteyn flings herself impetuously into the role, and her charm clothes with credibility even the melodramatic passages—the hurling of the necklace, the clutching of the sword.

She and Nureyev have worked out a natural give-and-take of behaviour between them which makes the traditional mime of Larsen and Edwards as Berthe and Hilarion appear stilted. The sweet sadness of her clinging gestures as she slides into the tomb are moving, and she carries through to the last tremor of her disappearing fingertips.

3.3.63

Fonteyn and Nureyev

The best Hamlet and Ophelia in London are to be seen not at the Old Vic,* but at Covent Garden—that is to say, Rudolf Nureyev and Margot Fonteyn in *Giselle*.

Everyone knows Fonteyn is great: it is nice to be able to record that she is also improving. Her 'mad scene' is an amazing triumph of feeling and virtuosity.

* Reference to the opening production of the National Theatre company at the Old Vic.

What happens? The whole thing begins with Nureyev making rather silly explaining-away gestures to Pamela May, his royal fiancée, who has surprised him playing at peasants. On his kissing her hand, Fonteyn flings herself with sudden frenzy between them. May explains—very politely, under the circumstances—that Nureyev is her man. After her burst of violence Fonteyn is still as a frozen statue: and this is when we know her heart is broken.

When she begins to move again, we realize also that her wits have gone. Watching Fonteyn last Saturday, I thought at once of Ophelia. As she recalls past happiness (*'Nessun maggior dolor'*), takes a step or two, then kneels to pluck an imaginary fortune-telling flower, 'Thought and affliction, passion, hell itself she turns to favour and to prettiness.' (When that blustering Laertes spoke these words after Rosemary Harris's bawdy 'mad scene' at the Vic it was a right giggle.)

Then Nureyev, who has been gazing blackly ahead of him (clearly conveying that the first reaction of this spoilt and selfish prince is rage at being caught out), makes a gesture towards her.

Fonteyn stumbles on the sword, but Nureyev snatches it from her like lightning almost before she has lifted it. She kneels beside Pamela May observing the rich James Bailey velvet which had first fascinated her a short while ago. She is shaken by a little gust of laughter. She takes a run across the stage, but suddenly a cold chill strikes her—she doubles up, clasping her middle.

Next she is blown towards Nureyev, who is now standing transfixed with horror, his hand to his mouth. She begins to dance her number with the *ballottés*. The cold chill again. She looks at her hands, which are beginning to die, gazes desperately around, clutches at the air, then pleads, pleads with fate.

Her mother, Gerd Larsen, catches her. Nureyev runs to her. By a movement of Fonteyn's head we know she has heard death calling. She falls. Nureyev kneels and Larsen pushes him off. After his attack with the sword on Hilarion (Leslie Edwards) Nureyev rushes off to hide his head, but he is still on stage, arrested in profile on the slope at the back when the curtain falls. All this is very wonderful and overpowering.

Annette Page and Brian Shaw were perfect in the previous peasant *pas de deux*. In Act II Deanne Bergsma, with her steely *bourrée* and fine, long, sustained *jetés* was an impressive Queen of the Wilis.

Fonteyn is such a skilful artist, such a professional, that even if she had two broken legs and was too deaf to hear the orchestra she could still give the impression of an immaculate performance. One extraordinary gift she has is of, as it were, drawing her outline. Of course, this must be a way of *feeling* the body into a true pose; but when Fonteyn stands with folded arms and head sadly inclined I do have the feeling that Ingres has nipped out of heaven and drawn the back of her neck.

In between acting superbly Nureyev performs his virtuoso steps—including an endless series of soaring *entrechats*—with style and musical sense, which is more than you can say of Peter O'Toole's murderous delivery of the soliloquies in *Hamlet*.

10.11.63

Seymour and MacLeary

A few more thoughts on the staging of *Giselle*. Was it not extraordinarily skilful of the Marquis de Saint-Georges who planned the libretto (Beaumont thinks he did the first act without Gautier's help) to get over his exposition in such record time?

By the end of three minutes we have seen the vintages, we know Hilarion loves Giselle, we have seen him spy on the transformation of Count Albrecht into the peasant Loys, and the latter's coy courtship of Giselle has begun. As Beaumont points out, the scene of Hilarion spying on Albrecht is vital to the understanding of the subsequent action, and it is well put over in the Royal Ballet's production.

Later in Act I when Giselle shows Albrecht the gold chain and medallion the Princess has given her, he goes round asking the peasants what has been going on, and none of them seems to know. Of course I realize that if he was scared and took off there would be no *dénouement*, but at least they could mime that a grand lady had been dishing out jewellery and was now in Berthe's powder room.

As expected, Lynn Seymour brought a contemporary feeling to the role of Giselle. The pretty, romantic side of the character was counteracted by a sense of humour and a little peasant awkwardness. Her mouth hangs open in surprise when she hears the kisses blown. She is skittish and has a giggle during the *pas de deux;* she is petulant with Hilarion.

When the tell-tale sword is produced she touches Albrecht's chin with delicate surmise. Her grimace when the sword is snatched from her, her automatic curtsey to the Duke, her look of sadness to find no lover's arm crooked in hers when she begins to sketch the dance with the *ballonnés*, her silly blankness alternating with a more tragic expression, her shambling to and fro, and her final pointing at Albrecht with an aghast recognition before she falls dead—these are all arresting: and there were moments when her face rang out.

Georgina Parkinson was the Queen of the Wilis and her clear rhetorical style, her great leaps and imperious *port de bras* contrasted with the softer style of Lynn Seymour. The Canadian ballerina was lucky to have Donald MacLeary to partner her in what would be her début in *Giselle* if she had not, as I am told, danced it once at a matinée in 1960.

12.7.64

National Ballet of Canada; Heeley's designs; Kain and Nureyev; Tennant and Stefanschi

The National Ballet of Canada's production of *Giselle*, which they have presented at the Coliseum, is much the most intelligent I have seen; and I suspect that Desmond Heeley's sets are the best that anyone has seen, at least since the original Paris production of 1841. Perhaps Benois's first act of 1910 was as good.

Of course Peter Wright's staging is very like his Covent Garden one, but the collaboration with Heeley has given it an added lustre. The Toronto company have been lovingly rehearsed and they emanate a singular poetry.

Heeley's blue-grey and ochre first act is like one of those Romantic prints of exceptionally clean rustics being idyllic amid alpine scenery, in which the engraver's medium made it impossible to obtain very strong colours, so that everything was mellow. As Giselle's Mother, Victoria Bertram was perfect. I saw two good Hilarions, the bandit-like Hazaros Surmeyan and the frank, open Jacques Gorrissen. Charles Kirkby's countrified Prince of Courland—who gets angry with Albrecht at the end—and his pretty, well-bred daughter Bathilde, were ideal. The Peasant Dance had become a *pas de quatre*. Every group was picturesque.

The shaggy fir forest of Act II, with its dank pool, is marvellously mysterious, though too whitely lit. I admired the Wilis' costumes and their ruthless regimentation. I saw two baleful, potent Myrthas, Nadia Potts and Vanessa Harwood.

Karen Kain's tender Giselle wears her heart on her sleeve—and melts ours. Lovely jumps, dreamlike arms. The Giselle of Veronica Tennant is in the tradition of Alonso, Markova and, I suppose, Pavlova. She is a passionate little creature, with strong technique.

We are familiar with Nureyev's Albrecht. He has rather outgrown the

Thurloe Place

MW/62

Rudolf Nureyev, 1962.
Drawing by Michael Wishart

playful, pseudo-peasant boy of Act I and comes into his own when the time arrives for tragic posturing, not to mention the heroic jumps and *entrechats* of the dance of death. As for young Sergiu Stefanschi, I asked where he had learnt his acting—from Peter Wright? No, he thought Wright had never seen him. But this Romanian had studied in Russia. His charming face was transparent to the joys and troubles of the soul, which he seemed to feel so genuinely. It was extraordinary.

13.4.75

Coppélia

Historical note

First mounted at the Opéra in 1870 just before the disastrous war, *Coppélia* may be regarded as the last splendid flower of the Second Empire: it is in some ways the ballet equivalent of Offenbach's light operas. The catchy tunes of Delibes and an amusing libretto have kept it alive to this day, and in the last twenty years I have seen it danced in Paris, Rome, Copenhagen, New York and London. Several people have had a go at the choreography for *Coppélia*. The original version of Saint-Léon is still given (more or less) in Paris; in Copenhagen Harald Lander arranged an entirely 'character' ballet, with lots more *czardas* to interpolated music, and all the classical dancing omitted; in London we have Dame Ninette's edition of the choreography invented by Ivanov and Cecchetti in St. Petersburg in 1884, and handed on by Sergeyev.

Coppélia is a tricky ballet, and presents problems all round. The ballerina playing the soubrette part of Swanilda has to excel in *demi-caractère* as well as classical dancing: that is to say, she must dance a saucy role with a light touch, must carry off the impersonations of the second act, must have technique and style for the final *pas de deux* in the grand manner, and must lend her role conviction and unity by suggesting that her character is developing and she is growing up in the course of the ballet. Merle Park, lately entrusted with the role at Covent Garden, has very much the perky presence for Swanilda; she dances with a gay assurance which promises well.

For Franz, Swanilda's errant boy-friend, the problem is to bounce and look pleased with himself without losing our sympathy: and the brilliant, smiling Gary Burne manages this without apparent qualms.

Dr. Coppélius, the maker of clockwork dolls, who is obsessed with the ambition of imbuing them with life, has probably the hardest task of all. He has to be funny, for this is a comedy ballet; he has to be sinister, for his workshop where the second scene is set must seem a place of mystery and danger to the lovers who separately venture there. Yet he must be appealing too, for he is Pygmalion—a lonely man yearning for a child or

lover, an artist striving after a masterpiece, a thinker and weigher of souls.
After all, what nobler alchemy than to give life to a doll? But he must not
be too pathetic, or the balance of comedy is lost. I think Leslie Edwards'
quiet rendering is excellent, only lacking, if anything, in bite.

Did you know that Franz was first danced at the Opéra by a woman
(and it still is), and that this woman, Eugénie Fiocre, was painted by
Degas? Did you know that Giuseppina Bozzacchi was making her first
appearance in public when she created the role of Swanilda at sixteen;
that Napoleon III, who was to be deposed three months later, was there,
and that she was presented to him, and that it was his last visit to the
great Opéra he built; that among Giuseppina's 'rave notices' was one from
the poet Théophile Gautier, who had written the scenario of *Giselle* thirty
years before and who was a hack critic like me; that the little ballerina died
six months after her début, on her seventeenth birthday, during the siege
of Paris; and that Delibes played the organ at her funeral?

1.11.59

Peter Farmer's designs; Miklosy, Loggenburg and Hayworth in Carter's production

Peter Farmer's new décor for *Coppélia* looks incredibly old—it looks as if
it was made for the original production in 1870 and left gathering dust in
that storehouse of the Paris Opéra's (which one used to pass on the way
from Le Bourget airport) for seven thousand years: and this is just right.
For *Coppélia* is a ballet you can't easily monkey about with and make
smart and modern.

Last week I wrote that Delibes's other ballet, *Sylvia*, needed to be
modernized and perhaps turned into a comedy, implying that the story of
the nymph of Diana and her precious chastity was too silly to hold the
interest.

Coppélia is a different matter: (a) you have the Hoffmannesque
atmosphere, which is a special mixture of mystery, comedy and romance;
(b) you have some Hungarian dances; and (c) you have quite a decent
sort of story about a mysterious ordeal a boy has to go through before
getting his girl, in the course of which the girl proves her courage, wit and
initiative and shows you what a good wife she will make. If you smarten
up *Coppélia* Hoffmann goes out at the window.

Then, the character of Dr. Coppélius. Ever since Helpmann, and
perhaps before, there has been a tradition of playing this role for laughs. I

think it should be played dead straight. Instead of winking at the audience, the old boy should be preoccupied by his creative experiments and by the business of getting through the day's work. If he is a clown how can there be any mystery and how can we feel his triumph when he thinks he has succeeded in imparting life to a doll, or pity him when he is made a fool of?

Terry Hayworth, in the Festival Ballet's production at the refurbished Wimbledon Theatre, gives a brilliant comic performance, but I should dearly love to see just how seriously and realistically he could play the role. I think the laughs would still come, but they would be of a different kind.

The traditional choreography, which I believe to be largely Petipa's, has been somewhat changed by jolly Jack Carter, who can't leave anything alone. Margot Miklosy has the soubrettish quality plus the ballerina quality which are needed for the title role. As Franz, the handsome Dudley von Loggenburg, with his dazzling smile, *joie de vivre* and sense of fun, is ideal.

17.11.68

Bruhn's production for the National Ballet of Canada

Erik Bruhn's production of *Coppélia* is designed by Maurice Strike in a child's storybook way, in rainbow colours. Its transformation (not scene-change) from street to studio is accomplished with miraculous speed and ingenuity. It contains a little Petipa, a lot of Bournonville-Bruhn and many crafty ideas.

Gorrisen's unclownish Coppélius rightly shows an artist-craftsman's serious side; Tomas Schramek is a sophisticated Franz and Tennant a vixenish Swanilda; he as well as she joins in the *Variations sur un thème slave*; the Dolls and the staging of Scene II are novel and entertaining.

13.4.75

Nureyev and Bruhn

Nureyev danced his first ever Franz in *Coppélia* on the last night of the National Ballet of Canada's season at the Coliseum and made a lively occasion of it. Erik Bruhn's Dr. Coppélius was Shelley turned Franken-stein, the artist gone mad with dreams of power, Faust. This was one of the most moving pieces of acting I have seen on the ballet stage.

20.4.75

Park, Kelly and Jefferies; Genius of Erik Bruhn

Much as I adore the Royal Opera House, the Royal Ballet and everything to do with them—and I have been passionately in love with Merle Park for years—I must admit that after the colour and impetuosity of the Canadian *Coppélia*, Monday's performance of the Delibes masterpiece at Covent Garden seemed a tame, lack-lustre affair, and I thought Park might have learnt her miming on the telephone.

Although, as Franz, Desmond Kelly fought heroically to make the party go, it was as if one had looked in on a provincial panto which nobody took seriously any more. The workshop scene was dreary, the final festival perfunctory. Half the trouble lay with the music, so lifelessly played by that fine orchestra that instead of sweeping the dancers along on its tide it seemed to present a barrier through which they had to fight. Stephen Jefferies is feeling his way into the role of Dr. Coppélius, but until we have a new production there is no hope for him to become a miracle-worker like Erik Bruhn. I am still stunned by the beauty and expressiveness of Bruhn's gesture for the act of creation ('I made these dolls: I can create *life*'). He splayed the fingers of both hands out from his head like an aura, proud as the Moses of Michelangelo.

27.4.75

Swan Lake

The allegory; Nerina

Unless the common cold incites hallucinations, I saw an unusually moving passage of mime at the end of Act I in the performance of *Swan Lake* at Covent Garden on New Year's Day. The Swan theme first sounds, softly but urgently, while the peasants are taking leave: it is like a summons of fate, catching us unawares. Benno, the Prince's friend, is the first to see swans crossing the evening sky. Although his subsequent dialogue with the Prince is restricted to such commonplaces as 'Shall we go shooting?' 'Yes, get the crossbows.' 'What about old Wolfgang?' 'Oh, he won't want to come'—the message came over to me more momentously. This was, of course, due to the artistry of Leslie Edwards and Alexis Rassine, to the careful production by Ninette de Valois, and to the tragic prompting of the music. The two men, while 'talking', keep glancing anxiously up into the dusk and the music speaks for their unexpressed premonitions. 'Youth passes. Destiny beckons. Friends part. Love destroys. Who can tell what swift decision may change his life for ever?' It is for such moments as this that we go to the ballet.

We also go for the dancing; and Frederick Ashton's new 'Neapolitan Dance', performed on Thursday by Rosemary Lindsay and Alexander Grant, was the gayest event of the evening. It is the most giddy, impish and delightful number, as typical as the girl's solo in *Les Rendezvous* of Ashton's idiosyncratic genius. How pretty, too, is the Waltz of the Six Princesses, to which their feather fans lend a delicious irregularity! Rassine's qualities are not best suited to the martial simplicity of the third-act solo; but his mime is impressive throughout. It is hard to judge danceable *tempi*, but I feel the first act *pas de trois*, if played quicker, would give Lindsay, Clayden and Shaw a better chance. Anne Heaton makes much of the small role of chief peasant girl.

As for Nadia Nerina as Odette and Odile, she often gives pleasure by her dancing though she never moves by her interpretation: nor do I believe she ever will. I think it a mistake to cast any girl for a role in which she can never excel. Let Nerina dance *Coppélia* and *Casse-Noisette*. *Swan*

Lake is not for her. Pert features such as hers assume a kind of expression-less solemnity when crammed into a tragic mould. Yet her dancing is fine.

Every act of *Swan Lake* has an exciting climax. That of Act I, I mentioned above. The parting of the lovers concludes Act II: and here is a passage of music which becomes more tragic if played *accelerando*. In Act III the demons vanish in smoke, and Siegfried runs desperately forth. Only the suicide of the lovers in Act IV, as my friend Cyril Beaumont has pointed out, fails to come off in the new production. It is merely a running exit *en diagonale*. I suggest a Tosca-like leap from Rothbart's jagged rock.

Observer, 4.1.53

Nerina and Bruhn

We've had it. *Swan Lake* can never be danced again. At least, not this way. It isn't just me, coming from America, hopped up with Balanchine and Martha Graham—everybody else has suddenly realized that the Royal Ballet's production won't do any more. People sitting round you in the theatre realize it; Peter Williams, writing in *Dance and Dancers*, clearly realizes it; even the directors of the Royal Ballet realize it and mean to take steps.

Did it need the advent of Nureyev, whose Albrecht I could only watch with my mind's eye from Winnipeg, to shock us into this knowledge?

But before we consider what is wrong we must welcome Erik Bruhn to Covent Garden: we have waited a long time for him and I hope he stays. He was made up as Hamlet, pale as death, with dark eye-shadow; this was very effective. In the garden scene, as he watched the peasants dancing, a princely politeness tempered his congenital melancholy; then the passing flight of swans and the prospect of sport excited him to action.

In the lake scene he partnered Nerina with skill, style and self-effacement. His little gesture of alarm, fist to lips, when he thought Odette had flown away and left him, seemed to be one sign of the new wave of naturalism which is going to sweep away this production and change the face of ballet in Britain.

In the palace scene, at last, Bruhn danced; and although he was not on form, being convalescent from a leg injury, it was a joy to have a dancer of such quality in the company. Strong technique, control, good manners, and, on top of all this, that absolute simplicity which is one component of greatness. He has a high, easy jump and correct line: he brightened up the otherwise rather dull variation by performing, *en diagonale*, a series of double turns in the air ending in *arabesque fondue*, a spectacular step learnt in Russia.

Nadia Nerina is also a wonderful dancer. The strength of her fine feet and legs, her delirious extensions and her soaring jumps are the more admirable because of her perfect placing, her timing, her line and a gift she has for conveying rapture. She is now at the height of her powers and should be seen at least once a week.

So what are we to do with the Royal Ballet's *Swan Lake*? First, scrap the orchestra. A new young school of conductors must be educated, who will be kept in ignorance of Tchaikovsky till their thirtieth birthdays, and who may then be allowed to discover the magic secrets of his scores. In the meanwhile, gramophone records or silence.

Then, I see the whole story much more in terms of *La Dolce Vita*, with the hero as a modern man (a ballet critic?) in search of some impossible ideal. As nobody here can dance the czardas or mazurka, we'll have the twist. And there'll be a use in the party scene for that kind of male dancing (still to be found on our stages) which should only be done by consenting adults in private.

1.4.62

Arova and Nureyev

Certain evenings of ballet are special and peculiar—not necessarily first nights, and not necessarily those when everybody is in top form: Friday night at Covent Garden was one of them. Sonia Arova, Bulgarian-born but a British subject, was dancing her first *Swan Lake* with the Royal Ballet; Nureyev, marvellous and unaccountable as ever, was her partner; and the direction had suddenly—and without warning—allowed Nureyev to make several welcome changes in their production.

Startling, delightful changes! In Act I, which I urged the other day should be given a mood of autumnal melancholy, an additional short dance has been inserted for the Prince after the *pas de six*. He does mournful *pirouettes en attitude* while Benno plays the mandolin. The Princess-Mother no longer lectures her son on drink and the necessity of marriage. She gives him a crossbow, and he is delighted. Is this symbolic of saying 'Be a man! Grow up!'? It's O.K.

In the *pas de trois* Parkinson showed a thrilling way of thrusting her leg out in *arabesque*; Lane had timing and judgment; Usher ended on his knee neatly. They were acclaimed.

In Act II the passage of mime in which Odette explains her situation is no more. She flutters and swoops, suggesting fear. Can we still get over Benno's unsporting inclination to shoot sitting swans?

Benno is cut from the *adage*. Odette now has only the Prince to balance and swoon on. Nureyev lifted Arova high and landed her gently. She has a grand manner. Arova speeded up the spinning end to her solo; and this was one of several places in which Tchaikovsky's music, conducted by Lanchbery, took on a new drama and came to life. At the end of the act Nureyev saw no swans departing: he seemed to pray.

Derek Rencher had been the friendly Benno: he was also the Master of Ceremonies in Act III, and I liked his austere authoritative interpretation. Nureyev, refusing the prospective Brides, did not want to upset his mother, but said 'No, really!' The *tempi* of the Czardas, which worked up terrifically at the end, were much improved. Park and Usher, nimble Neapolitans, had an ovation.

In the bravura *pas de deux*, Arova, after being raised from the ground, pirouetted in *arabesque*, ducking under Nureyev's supporting arm. Nureyev gave his somewhat disjointed though brilliant solo an air of improvisation, and did double turns with his arms *en couronne* above his head. In the *coda* he executed some frenzied *pirouettes* and his long hair stuck up in a cockscomb. Arova's backward hops on point were sensational.

24.6.62

Fonteyn

Gautier wrote about the fabled swan-women of German legend:

> *De ces femmes il en est une*
> *Qui chez nous descend quelquefois*
> *Blanche comme le clair de lune*
> *Sur les glaciers dans les cieux froids.*

Some of us felt a little daunted to hear that the not unfamiliar second act of *Swan Lake* had been chosen to form the first half of the programme at this year's Gala in aid of the Royal Academy of Dancing; but watching Fonteyn going through the holy motions of the *pas de deux* I realized with a pang, once more and more than ever, that there was no higher manifestation of live art to be seen anywhere in the world today.

Supported by the self-effacing Michael Somes and Derek Rencher, and surrounded by the Royal *corps de ballet*, Fonteyn was accompanied by

Yehudi Menuhin, placed with his cellist in a stage box. The full-bodied,
vibrant tone of Menuhin's playing and the fact that he took certain
passages a shade slower than usual made us hear the music anew.

From her tremulous entrance to her tragic departure Fonteyn danced
with such sureness, such relaxed ease and such exactitude of musical
phrasing, that we knew this was her greatest performance. Coolly,
passionately and inevitably she unfolded her pearly diagrams. She danced
as simply as a stream flows. We were lost in a dream of 'implacable
whiteness'.

9.12.62

Fonteyn and Nureyev

So we have a new Nureyev, an 'English' Nureyev all of our own; a
beautifully behaved modest and controlled Nureyev, giving simply and
splendidly a well-thought-out, carefully rehearsed performance. Marlowe
wrote about 'Brave horses bred on the white Tartarean hills'. This noble
creature, it seems, has been tamed by Fonteyn.

For who could show temperament or be other than on their best behaviour in Fonteyn's presence? Watching her dance in *Swan Lake* for the
first time with Nureyev on Thursday, one was struck in turn by her
modesty, by her assurance, by her courage at taking on old or new feats
of skill, by her peculiar expressiveness, and above all by the carry-through
of style which bound action, dance, pauses—even curtain calls—into an
artistic unity.

Act I is much improved. After the opening *pas de six*, Prince Siegfried
obliges with a solo. Nureyev seems to be trying to recall a dance he knew
long ago; looks thoughtful, hand to mouth; and improvises light jumps
from side to side, then in a circle. This is delightful. The tune he does it to
is a cousin to that for the Vision of Aurora. The number has an autumnal,
elegiac quality exactly right for this scene. The teenage prince is in
mourning for lost youth.

Admirable, too, is the innovation of the Princess-Mother's gift of a
cross-bow. This seems like the challenge to manhood. Nureyev is en-
thralled with it, a child with a new toy. Later, as we know, the swan
theme will sound, a call of destiny. It would be something if this most
known of all Tchaikovsky's phrases could be played in such a way that we
felt we were hearing it for the first time.

In Act II the *pas de deux* with Nureyev perfectly supporting Fonteyn is one of the wonders of our ballet world. Fonteyn has a spiritual technique (as opposed to physical technique) which is, I suppose, a kind of theatrical knowhow. Nobody observes, or should, that her left leg, in *développé*, goes twice as high as her right. Watching her sad, pretty face, we seem to be experiencing an adventure of the soul.

As Odile in Act III Fonteyn had the most with-it methods of seduction I can remember, which included an irresistible, hypnotic close-up stare into her victim's eyes and an Oriental backwards grovel with flaying arms. Not being a complete square, like most Princes, Nureyev suspects there is something dodgy going on, but is powerless against her glamour.

Fonteyn, brave girl, undertook the thirty-two *fouettés* and did them almost on one spot, though she didn't manage a neat finish. Nor did Nureyev for that matter, to his whizzing series of *grandes pirouettes à la seconde*. But he had given us some huge jumps and perfect *pirouettes* in Act II; and when at the end of the coda he held her for ages in a diving pose high on his shoulder, we were pretty thrilled.

Let's have some more rethinking of the ballet, because in *Swan Lake* the Fonteyn-Nureyev team-up is really very much all right.

10.2.63

Thoughts on production; Nerina and Blair

Duck shooting finished on Monday, but the *Swan Lake* season opened the same night.

It would be tedious to recount the various metamorphoses of *Swan Lake* in recent decades. Suffice it that when the Helpmann-scripted production was staged in 1963 by the Covent Garden branch of the Royal Ballet—and I welcomed the new look, just for the sake of a little variety, my God!, whatever second thoughts anyone might have about it—it was apparently decided to keep the old Sergeyev-recorded version going in the Touring Company. Sensible idea.

One of the innovations in the Helpmann show was a Prologue showing how Odette, playing in the woods with her companions, attracted the attention of that old owl Von Rothbart and was turned into a swan. I guess Helpmann wanted to make the story clear to cretinous teenagers and to suppress the (recently unfashionable) passage of mime, in which Odette, when she meets the Prince, tells him what happened. Well, on Monday Nerina restored the trad mime with its pretty, meandering 'narrative' music, thus rendering the new Prologue redundant. It is even, as I suspected from the start, undesirable, since it brings the ballerina on almost as soon as the curtain rises, and thus detracts from her glamour.

I must have been thinking and writing about the ideal production of *Swan Lake* for thirty years now; because when still at Balliol I designed a Cubist setting (never used) for Dolin, the first dancer I ever met and tried to bend to my will. I therefore venture to submit the following points to the consideration of future producers.

1. Without getting carried away by the allegory business, consider that the ballet is a basic, classic myth about Man and Love. The youth attains manhood and puts aside childish pleasures and affections; he falls in love with a glorious, unattainable girl and she returns his love; he betrays her; she forgives him; but passionate love when satisfied cannot remain on the same high level, it either ceases or turns into the calmer companionship of marriage. (This last step of commitment and acceptance of adult responsibility is represented by the couple's taking the plunge into the lake.)

2. So the Terrace Scene, with the Prince's coming of age, is autumn because it is the end of youth. If you put a Prologue before this to describe Odette's transformation you destroy the unity, and the Prince is no longer the hero at the centre of the myth.

3. Remember that the first sound of the Swan theme—beating wings, beating heart, the Summons—is all-important. (Lanchbery brought this tune into his new Prologue.)

4. Don't *fundamentally* change the choreography of the two Lake Scenes (believed to be by Ivanov).

5. Interpolate your own brilliant dances in the Terrace Scene and Palace Scene parties.

So I find the new Prologue a liability and mourn the merging of the tipsy old tutor and the romantic friend Benno in a nebulous official. On consideration I definitely like Ashton's last act less than the old one. In the Terrace Scene I tremendously admire Ashton's *pas de quatre*.

This last dance was well done on Monday by Park, Sibley, Shaw and Usher, and Sibley's variation seemed particularly inventive and thrilling. Nadia Nerina, supported by Blair, made her first appearance since her accident, slightly bandaged but full of dash, gallantry and daring. The character dances went with a swing and the *corps* of swans was impeccable.

By next Sunday more Royal Birds will have winged across the Garden.

6.2.66

Carter's new production; Lane and Aldous with Gilpin

My old friend Anton Dolin, who sometimes sends me words of en-couragement from remote corners of the earth, wrote the other day, after I had laid down once and for all how to produce *Swan Lake*, 'I have cut out your piece to send to Lucia Chase'. Well, I can tell you, the wires were buzzing at Oxford on Tuesday night! 'Hold everything', I cabled, 'There may have been a terrible mistake.'

For London's Festival Ballet Jack Carter has redone *Swan Lake* from start to finish, basing his version on the original Tchaikovsky score of 1877 (published in Russia, 1957) which was very much juggled around with by Petipa and Drigo in 1894, and later by others. Any choreography (accepted by us hitherto as traditional) which would not fit in with the order of Tchaikovsky's numbers has been ruthlessly scrapped by his devoted collaborator. The result is sometimes as startling as if, in church, the parson went to the lectern to read the Epistle and instead sang 'God Save the Queen'.

It is thrilling to go back to school (or rather, Oxford, where I first saw the second act of *Swan Lake* with the glorious Markova and Dolin) and, at Jack Carter's knees, start again from scratch. He seems to think Tchai-kovsky wrote the libretto. Perhaps. Last year I found in a biography that the composer had heard the complete *Ring* at Bayreuth the year before *Swan Lake* was produced; and I suggested that the German theme, the lake and Siegfried's name might have a Wagnerian origin.

The biggest 'novelties', apart from Carter's dances and new music or old music used differently, are as follows: to the brief Prelude there is a Prologue in which we see Odette (without companions) turned by Rothbart into a swan; there is a sprightly coda after the sacred *pas de deux* in Act II; the five Fiancées in Act III are all from different countries and bring their local colour with them; Odile is danced by another ballerina than Odette, she wears white, competes with the other girls and is later confronted by Odette and a few swans; not only is there no Black Swan but there is no 'Black Swan *pas de deux*'—this was apparently an inter-polation. So, it seems, was Benno, the Prince's friend—invented in 1894 because the aged Guerdt could not hold up his ballerina. I could not be more shattered if you told me Oscar Wilde had written Horatio into *Hamlet* because Irving felt he had too many soliloquies.

I hope that Jack Carter intends in the coming months to stand back and look at his grand endeavour and consider whether Tchaikovsky really

knew better than Petipa, Ivanov and Co. what was theatrical. I shall be
thinking, too. After all, we are in this thing together. Oxford has got
Swan Lake for a week's run, and we can look forward to a time when all
ballet companies perform nothing but *Swan Lake* every night. We might
as well get it right.

About some of the big issues involved I intend to reserve judgment
(first sign of late middle age): more about the music later, too. So Lucia
Chase must just wait. Some of Carter's choreography is fine—I liked the
huge hemicycle of couchant swans within which Odette does her solo.
The bits of Ivanov and Petipa I spotted were pretty good too, and showed
distinct promise.

About the following points I am quite certain. The Prologue is unnecessary. The international competition for Fiancées is a very good idea
and makes much more sense of Act III. Of course Odile should wear
white—Cyril Beaumont always said so. (About the confrontation of
Odette and Odile I am not sure, as the subsequent curtain is at present an
anticlimax, with Odette left on the floor wondering what to do.)

The close of Act I must be improved. When the fatal swan theme
sounds, what happens? The Prince is saying goodbye to the peasants. The
Tutor is tottering off, sloshed. The Jester sees the swans and capers with
glee. The Prince looks cheerfully at the Jester, but never once at the sky.
The Queen Mum comes on, fussing about something. The Prince says
'I'm off shooting' and goes. As the curtain falls the Queen is going out
again and the Jester is left hunched quizzically on the steps. I miss Benno.

John Gilpin was a breezy, boyish Prince, whizzing away *à la 2de*;
Maryon Lane of the lovely gentle extensions was Odette and dazzling
Lucette Aldous Odile. The whole company danced with tremendous zest
as if they loved every minute. It was an enthralling evening.

13.3.66

Fonteyn and Nureyev

To see Margot Fonteyn as Odette in *Swan Lake* after many months'
absence is a moving experience, especially when one has at the back of one's
mind the thought that any performance she gives of this great role may
be her last. The extraordinary quality of her portrayal of the Swan
Princess is in no way diminished.

What exactly does this special quality of hers consist of? First of all,
what is she *not*? She is no dazzling beauty, she is not a strong dancer for

speed and jumps, she has not got the steel bow of a Russian back, she has no big extension in *développé*, others have more perfect legs and firmer feet. It is necessary to say this in order to salute the masterpiece that art, thought, work and will-power have made of her.

She has thought herself into beauty, modelling her mask from inside; and nothing could be lovelier than the pale, sad face worn by her Odette. Starting from her miraculously small waist, she has drawn in space perfect patterns for her arms and legs, giving to the traditional geometry of the classic positions that subtle innuendo we call 'line'.

In particular she has concentrated on *port de bras*, and she has a way of not so much *placing* her arms in a position as of letting them be wafted into it and stopping by chance just at the right moment. I have often noticed that there is conspiracy between her eyes, neck and arms.

Finally, she lets the music give her phrasing as we let the air give us breath, so that her speeding-up and slowing-down and finishing seem exact, inevitable and effortless.

Nureyev supported Fonteyn on Monday with devotion. It was very pretty to see how in the *pas de deux* her *pirouettes*, starting fast, slowed down to a halt. At the end of the act she perched a foot on his bent knee and he held her waist with one hand as she leant beautifully forward, back arm raised, front arm hanging: this pose, symbolic no doubt of the swan's taking flight, was elegiac and noble.

18.2.68

National Ballet of Canada; Kain and Surmeyan

Leonardo wrote in his Notebook that it is the extremities which lend grace to the body; and invented the early English school of ballet. Michelangelo, who had seen the newly unearthed Belvedere Torso, went one better, twisted the whole body into a shape more expressive of the soul; and invented the Russian school.

It is hard for a layman to divine the secret skill of turning bodies into works of art, and choreography into moving sculpture. It may have something to do with movement starting from the small of the back, or following through, or the crossing of limbs, or the relation of the head to arms and legs. Balanchine, in creating a new kind of athletic classicism for America, has sometimes seemed to be throwing *épaulement* overboard.

Karen Kain, who was the Swan Queen in the National Ballet of Canada's *Swan Lake* at the Coliseum on Tuesday, is graceful and sweet in an English way but as streamlined as a Balanchine dancer. She danced Erik Bruhn's choreography—with which Ivanov seems to have taken liberties—with easy style. Her Prince, Hazaros Surmeyan, is a fine, strong classical dancer, but the grace of his upper extremities, i.e. hands, is over-florid and he danced the melancholy solo in the first scene with no expression other than a dancer's 'on parade' smile. A pretty Black Queen in lieu of Rothbart was an innovation: she seemed to be the madam of the lake. Celia Franca's Queen Mother was unusual (for ballet) in looking delighted with everything. The *presto* ending the Act I duet was odd. A very grand Czardas and Mazurka. Some lovely groups at the end.

28.2.72

Gielgud and Breuer

Ruskin was always saying this or that picture was 'the greatest in the world'. At the risk of being thought 'old and foolish' like Ruskin or King Lear I would suggest that Maina Gielgud is the most impressive Odette-Odile, in *Swan Lake*, to be seen in the Western World.

I use the word 'impressive' deliberately. She is not everybody's Odette, even if she is undeniably potent as Odile; for she is a big girl as ballerinas go, and she has an unusual, striking face, which you could not call pretty even if you found it extremely attractive. So had Markova. Making one of her rare appearances with Festival Ballet at the Coliseum on Monday, Gielgud flung herself, physically and mentally, into the tragic role of Odette, and her tremendous *arabesques* as well as her passionate emotion evoked a tremendous and passionate response in the audience. When a big girl 'flings herself' into something it can be a bit much, but Gielgud curbs her impetuosity with aristocratic restraint—and anyway the splendid Peter Breuer was there to catch her. Knowing just where to stop—that is what art is.

What prodigies of technique we saw in the ballroom scene, too. Her balances, her unsupported *pirouettes* on point! His leaps *en attitude*, his *grandes pirouettes*, his catches and lifts! Breuer is an heroic dancer. His dramatic interpretation of Siegfried is much improved too, even though in Act I he is incredibly ungrateful for the peasants' presents. One *must* be nice to peasants or they start carving rude words on trees.

4.5.75

The Sleeping Beauty

The Sadler's Wells Ballet prepares for America

Perhaps *The Sleeping Beauty* is the most wonderful ballet in the world: it is certainly one of the best productions by Sadler's Wells. To set off on an evening's abandoned enjoyment of Tchaikovsky's score under the direction of Constant Lambert is like being driven at great speed through a rich, varied and beautiful landscape in fine weather. No ballet contains more lovely dances and none gives Sadler's Wells a better chance to show their mettle.

It is because of this, and because we hope it will knock New York for six, that we old *abonnés* are hopeful that a few details can still be improved. The King, Queen and Countess have not the grand manner of mime. The King is too stiff and ungracious, the Queen too ingratiating, the Countess too flouncy. Helpmann could teach them. As Prince Charming he never makes a meaningless gesture and never moves without seeming a Prince. As the Lilac Fairy, Beryl Grey smiles too much and her hands are too fulsome. Grant should always do the principal Ivan. Could not Shaw dance Bluebird? Elvin is exciting as the Blue Princess, but as Fairy Crystal Fountain her open *attitude* (Moscow style, I am told) stands out oddly among those of the other five fairies. No good regretting that the Forest Scene is not conceived in more subdued colours, that Carabosse (English style) is a comic rather than sinister character, and that the best cast cannot dance every night.

America cannot fail to be impressed by Messel's production—the décor of Baroque architecture seen through wistful, latter-day eyes, and the gay, glittering costumes in a mixture of styles only possible in fairyland. To Margot Fonteyn, Aurora of England, the superlatives of newspaper hacks must seem as tedious as trumpet-music in Heaven. She dances the choreography of Petipa and we see flashing and fading before our eyes works of great art.

Observer, 14.8.49

R

Bruhn with the Royal Ballet; Nerina

Last week Erik Bruhn continued his stately progress through the Royal Ballet's classical repertoire, and we were thoughtfully invited back from the country on Bank Holiday to watch him in *The Sleeping Beauty*.

Gerd Larsen was a friendly and glamorous Queen with a smile for everybody, but Derek Rencher as the King never seemed quite sure of his throne. Franklin White had a more naturalistic and believable interpretation of the Master of Ceremonies than his hallowed predecessor.

Of the fairies in the Prologue I liked Lynn Seymour and Antoinette Sibley; Monica Mason was miscast as Woodland Glades; and Georgina Parkinson had quite the right idea of style for the Lilac Fairy.

In the *pas de six* of cavaliers Bryan Lawrence was outstanding, which perhaps he shouldn't have been. I felt sorry as usual for the page who had to shake his fists in the air to give warning of the arrival of Carabosse at the Christening. Is that the way the butler would announce Lord Beaverbrook at Buckingham Palace? Ray Powell, as ever, projects a potent spine-chill as the witch.

In Act I we still have those tiresome *tricoteuses* with forbidden socks for their Communist children. Nerina as Aurora bounded on like a hound of spring, and looked suitably embarrassed on being told she had grown up to be quite a pretty girl by her fool of a father. She is such a sure technician that she can calculate all her brilliant effects to a T: she drew some divine diagrams in the Rose *adage*, and if the pauses when she balanced while changing hands from partner to partner were slightly prolonged, as if she were awaiting a roll of drums, her final pose and gesture of triumphantly extended arms was given an easy throw-away flourish.

Aurora's eight Friends were well rehearsed in their trite routines. Nerina was as thrilling as ever in her swooping *manège*, and, pricked by the spindle, she fell like a shot bird. Her *danse de vertige* was pretty and touching.

In Act II, the Hunting Scene, they have at last softened down the Countess's snub to the Tutor. Stanley Holden had a nice new line, comic but subdued, on the boozy Gallison. Bruhn made his appearance wrapt in the stylish melancholy which is *de rigueur* for ballet Princes. His grand manner and good manners are so intense that one feels unshaven.

When that boat appears wobbling on roller-skates it's always a near thing that the moon-intent Prince doesn't see it before he should. Maybe that is why they've turned off the moon. As the vision of Aurora Nerina took her thrilling spiralling dance at speed; her footwork was impeccable; she swung in bold *arabesques*.

In Act III, kissing Aurora awake, Bruhn shadowed her face. In the Florestan *pas de trois* Merle Park was neat and gay, Seymour witty and chic. In the Blue Bird *pas de deux*, Lawrence, deputising for Usher, made a slip in his partnering and got nervous, but then festooned through the air with the greatest of ease; Sibley was swift, sudden and enchanting.

Bruhn left off his smart brown wig for the ball—a mistake. The cool assurance with which he waited for Nerina to dive into his arms and their perfect judging of distance and timing were impressive. The *pas de deux* was fine; the variations less so. His was fussy, with elaborations put in to make it more difficult. He sometimes hunched his shoulders and his *jabot* flew in his face. Her variation is a trite one, but she danced it correctly and ended well.

29.4.62

Chauviré and Nureyev

A pop dancer—that's what we've got—a pop dancer, at last. What the telly did for art, what Billy Graham did for religion, Nureyev has done for ballet.

Admittedly, ballet had a public before, but it was a public of mad old maids in moth-eaten musquash who never went to any other form of entertainment except the Chelsea Flower Show. Now Nureyev is dragging in quite a hep crowd, and as these kids have never seen any ballet before they simply scream their heads off as soon as he leaves the floor.

Pop dancers, like pop singers, have got to have a gimmick or some special thing about them, like tears or a wiggle or a half-starved little-boy look; and I think Nureyev's thing is that even when he is behaving in a withdrawn and gentlemanly way you feel that he may suddenly snarl and bite you in the neck. Hints to other prospective pop dancers: play hard to get, treat your partner like a bad smell, and wear your own hair in costume roles.

As the Prince in *The Sleeping Beauty* Nureyev behaved with such a weary reticence of royal distinction, as if his smile would confer earldoms, and all the time I felt the lurking menace. I remembered Great Catherine's mad husband whom she so rightly murdered, who used to hang dogs up by the hind legs and flog them to death, and that neurotic Scandinavian monarch who liked torturing or being tortured by his footmen. Nureyev was

Baudelaire's *'roi d'un pays pluvieux'*. All this means that he has personality and gave an interesting interpretation.

Newcomers to *The Sleeping Beauty* were no doubt surprised that they had to sit through the first 116 years without the Prince appearing at all; and even then he only joins in some old-time dancing in riding boots. They have to wait till near the end of the very last act before he takes off the boots and takes off.

Nureyev has the most beautiful legs and a high jump, so he looked good in white tights, and the beginning of his variation, as he leapt diagonally downstage, was breathtaking: but it is a dull variation, he mistimed the start of his *manège* of spinning jumps and his shoe came off, so it ended in anti-climax. I must say he picked up his shoe superbly.

I never saw Yvette Chauviré dance Aurora before, but she no longer seems to have the speed or strength for the role. Her movements appear tentative and she seldom follows through, as if afraid not to be there in time for the next one. Her final variation was done with style, but the Rose *adage* had been too openly an ordeal.

Graham Usher dances the Blue Bird well, but he should start his difficult *diagonale* of *brisés volés* more gently and build up his jumps to a climax instead of running out of breath and elevation. Antoinette Sibley as his mate conveys a sense of rapture, which is what ballet is all about.

20.5.62

Stevenson's and MacDowell's new production for Festival; Pontois and Gilpin

The lights dim at the Festival Hall; the open drawers of the boxes (presumably crammed with Lord Mayors and their molls) recede into shadow; on Norman MacDowell's baroque proscenium arch a single gleam of light bounces from the central trophy, like that which struck the 'boss of the shield of Sir Leoline tall' in *Christabel*; and we prepare to be swept away by the first new production of Tchaikovsky's *Sleeping Beauty* to be seen in this sceptred isle for seven thousand years.

The Lilac Fairy stands, wand extended, outside the palace gates. She is presenting us with the fairy tale. Good. Gates open. Our eyes light on a Henrietta Maria costume—good! Van Dyck's was the prettiest period for clothes. The architectural palace set in beige-gold monochrome (arches between columns a bit weak), skilfully conceals the shallowness of the stage—though it cannot conceal the dwarfishness of the pros opening—

contrives two staircases at the back and seems to have as many entrances
as the Teatro Olimpico. Courtiers goldish with Garter-blue accents.

The Fairies, renamed Charm, Generosity, Beauty, Gaiety, Temperament,
set me wondering what *are* the ideal characteristics in a woman. Perhaps
the Lilac Fairy stands for Cooking. Helen Starr is an ideal one. The line-up
of spun ballerinas ends brilliantly.

Surprise, surprise! Carabosse is Circe and a woman, Seraphina Lans-
down, red-haired and leaping—a beauty, a woman scorned, baleful,
venomous. She makes the big scene and the act ends as well as a Beatles
record. Applause, applause.

Act II. Restful Italian garden, with peacocks on a *tempietto*. We have got
rid of those black and mid-knit-wear hags and instead the Chamberlain
calls to order the garland-weaving peasants for using *florist's wire*. The
Princess's suitors, obviously extremely kinky foreign art students, arrive
in time to beg the King not to have them hanged for this, and when he
relents it is a big moment for all devotees of flower arrangement. In the
Waltz the girls have baskets of flowers, the men have garlands and the
tiny tots (yes) have festoons—and jolly pretty ones too. Hurrah! And here
we first become conscious of Ben Stevenson's additions to Petipa's
choreography, and applaud their discretion and decency.

Our unknown Aurora is Noelle Pontois from Paris, short, sweet,
modest; legs a bit long for her top half; lots of brio, nerve and balance;
more expressive at the extremities than sound in the middle. (Try putting
that into French.) The balances of the Rose Adage go well. Pontois does a
fine solo, but some basic geometry is missing in the torso.

One hundred years pass and MacDowell shows us a dripping forest pool
—he's not quite at home with landscape. New ideas: the Prince's Tutor is
a foppish Abbé and the dirty drunken peasants with the picnic-baskets
send him up—Splendid! Clearly Revolution is on the way. Gilpin is the
Prince. The hunting habits are in autumn colours as they should be. The
nobility flirt and fuss convincingly. After the *farandole* we hear a new tune
and Gilpin does a spectacular solo, ending with *pirouettes* and a drop on
the knee, which seems a bit too springlike for this dank autumn weather.
The vision of Aurora is first seen in the pond. Pontois and her attendants
all wear high-waisted green drifting *Empire* dresses. What heavenly music
this is! The Panorama moves.

The last act architecture has gods in niches, seems subtly made up of old
prints, but is spoilt by a big gold Thing in the middle between the staircases which I think must be hiding something (the organ?). Negroes hold
candelabra. In the *pas de quatre* Stevenson has lifts and near splits which

look too modern and there is an unfamiliar tune and new choreography for the two men, delightful Dubreuil and Heubi.

The Blue Bird's blue stands out from the subdued colour-scheme like a bad deed in a courtly world. He is André Prokovsky, who sacrifices too much in order to beat high from the ground—hunched shoulders, strain. His Princess is Galina Samtsova of the glorious back and grand manner.

Gilpin has a soaring new solo to a thrilling new tune and scores easily. Pontois ends her evening of victory with a fishdive and dazzling solo. It occurs to me that what Pontois lacks in comparison with Samtsova is mainly *épaulement*. *Épaulement*, the subtle angling of the body, is to ballet what the twisted torso was to Michelangelo. It is the greatest part of ballet and greatly neglected in this country.

And do you welcome Festival Ballet's big show, Mr. Buckle, though it was obviously put on in a mad rush? I do, I do.

27.8.67

Unpacking Diaghilev's Bakst production; MacMillan and Kay in Berlin; Seymour and Holz

Three weeks ago I had the extraordinary experience of unpacking, in a warehouse in the outskirts of Paris, baskets of costumes of the Diaghilev Ballet, including a number of Bakst's incredibly gorgeous silk and velvet dresses, embroidered in gold and silver thread, for *The Sleeping Beauty*.

Then ten days ago, I saw in the Theatre Museum in Leningrad some of Vsevolojsky's pretty little sketches for the original 1890 production. Last Sunday, I saw Kenneth MacMillan's new production of *The Sleeping Beauty*, called in German *Dornroschen*, at the Deutsche Oper in Berlin.

MacMillan has been in Berlin about a year. I am told that he found a few good soloists there but had to create a *corps de ballet* from scratch. His achievement has been remarkable. He has no outstanding dancers (one of the fairies' cavaliers had wonderful *ballon*) and Lynn Seymour, who has been suffering from wretched bad health, is not ideally cast as Aurora, though what she gave, under the circumstances, was honourable: but the company put up a fine show and there was a permeating style throughout.

The music under Ashley Lawrence sounds much the same as at Covent Garden (the Berlin brass is superb), but there are two new numbers in the *divertissement*. Carabosse, a tall baleful man in drag, arrives without transport down a big staircase attended only by two minute dwarfs in tall powdered wigs. The Hunting Scene takes place in winter and while the

Panorama music plays the stage revolves and the Good Fairy leads the Prince up and down ingenious staircases. The Florestan *pas de trois* is given back to the Jewel Fairies.

What I particularly admired was the eighteenth-century dignity and grandeur with which everybody behaved. Inspired by Cyril Beaumont's descriptions of Diaghilev's production, I have been saying for years that the fairies should be inhuman and aloof, and not too damned obliging. MacMillan's fairies have this superhuman quality.

When Rudolf Holz, the Prince, first sees the vision of Aurora, he goes down on one knee and inclines his neck so slowly and nobly that we realize what it meant to be bred at Versailles. It is wonderfully touching that the couple should be actually married at the end by a priest hung with ikons, who holds crowns over their heads in Russian style. Why has no one thought of this before?

Yes, Russian style. Barry Kay has had the million-dollar idea of dressing his court like the court of Catherine the Great, but placing them not in Leningrad but in Moscow. Everything is gold: where there is colour it barely emerges from the gold.

Against barbaric Kremlin arches, brick overlaid with gold, parade the stupendous hooped, padded and glittering dresses. The Hunting scene, viewed through snowy undergrowth, is a silvery idyll, with only the Prince and the Countess standing out in tawny apricot, fur-trimmed. A hundred years later, of course, it is the court of Alexander III in 1880. The fringed skirts are caught up at the back, the bustle has just disappeared: fantastic uniforms, top boots. The Jewel Fairies are Fabergé Easter eggs.

No praise could be too high for Barry Kay's ideas or for the thoroughness with which they have been carried out.

15.10.67

Wright's and Bardon's new production for the Royal Ballet; Sibley and Dowell

On Friday the Royal Ballet gave us their first new production of *The Sleeping Beauty* since they reopened the Royal Opera House with that masterpiece of Tchaikovsky and Petipa in February 1946. If the validity of classical ballet is to be judged once and for all, let it be judged by this production of this ballet. If this is really no good then traditional ballet is no good.

Isadora pitied the poor dancers of the Maryinsky and ridiculed their art, and Kenneth Tynan is always on about the death of ballet today. Al-

though I am utterly under the influence this week of darling Isadora—
having seen a preview of the movie about her with divine Vanessa
Redgrave—I think if she came back now she would be certain to acclaim
the wonders of classical ballet in Peter Wright's glorious production.

He has placed the action in the late medieval period. Henry Bardon's
settings verge on monochrome: they are very meticulous, these russet
tents, brown rocks and caves, silver woods, beige 'towers and battlements
. . . Bosom'd high in tufted trees.' The dresses of Lila de Nobili and Rosti-
slav Doboujinsky are miraculously rich and subtle, but tend to the pallor
of metal with only occasional hints of a lurking rainbow.

The Queen, Pamela May, is still *accouchée* to receive the guests at the
christening. The King, Leslie Edwards, a masterful, genial, armoured
Edward III, is very proud of his coroneted baby. There is a fine fire
burning in the monumental hearth.

The Fairies are wonderful. At last they conduct themselves—even the
darting happy ones—with a degree of otherworldly majesty and aloofness.
Ria Peri, slow and stately. Christine Beckley, with a kind of Oriental pride.
Jennifer Penney, serene, gracious and unfolding. Georgina Parkinson, to
some inserted music, is a dragon-fly. Lesley Collier, a flickering humming-
bird, her music taken very quick. Monica Mason, agile but imperial, with a
superb change of expression on the last pose. Yes, we have gained a fairy,
and the supreme, sweet madonna of a Lilac Fairy, Deanne Bergsma, is not
in the line-up of supported *attitudes*.

Julia Farron's Carabosse is a baleful tornado, orchestrating her court
of monsters. It is touching that the Lilac Fairy, on departing, spares a
special blessing for the old, humiliated Master of Ceremonies, Stanley
Holden, who has made a muddle of the invitations.

At the coming-of-age the white-clad princes from the four corners of the
earth make their entries through the arches of the garland dancers. Then
comes Antoinette Sibley. She is shy though radiant, a solemn and dedicated Princess who takes her ceremonial feats of equilibrium with an
almost holy air in that most breathtaking of dances, the Rose Adage. Her
leaping, turning coda is divine. It is a good idea that the King and Queen
are not present when Aurora pricks her finger: they have to be fetched.
We see Aurora laid to rest in a turret of the castle which has become
transparent.

In the Hunting Scene, the dark-clad Dowell is carried in on a litter. He
is alarmingly royal, sad and beautiful. He has a new and yearning solo
with tragic gestures, hand to neck, two hands to the heart. Sibley as the
vision is liquid, elegiac, arms curving round her face. The journey by

boat, steered by a gnome-like Charon, is admirably contrived. 'The woods decay, the woods decay and fall.' Carabosse asleep in her lair, 'quiet as a stone', is awoken to hamper the course of love and virtue.

Rightly the end of the Quest is beset with peril and horror. 'Bats with baby faces in the violet light whistle and beat their wings.' But 'Childe Roland to the dark tower came' and having scattered his final foes climbs up the walls like Romeo to wake his Beauty on her brackeny bed.

Then, to our surprise, Prince Charming leads Aurora down the steps to dance a new magic Ashton duet. The castle sinks beneath them and they are on top of the world. The tune has a long lyrical line and Dowell bears Sibley aloft in big sailing movements; each has a superb solo; then as the stage darkens he sweeps her up and off into the light. This is thrilling.

At the wedding we are mercifully spared the Red Riding Hood dance; and Michael Coleman and Jennifer Penney are splendid Blue Birds. There are heroic fishdives in the *Grand pas de deux*; Dowell leaps with incredible soaring nobility; Sibley trips ecstatically and the evening is crowned by her triumphant smiles. The orchestra under John Lanchbery is alive.

22.12.68

Park and Nureyev

I had never seen Nureyev expressing fear on stage before. It was the moment when the Prince, nearing the castle of the Sleeping Beauty, is attacked by the repulsive monsters of Carabosse. He covered his ears with his hands, bent double and became like a little boy.

It was a very good idea to show the Prince afraid, just before he vanquishes his enemies, because, as we know, totally fearless people are seldom as nice and certainly less brave than those who feel fear and overcome it. I told Nureyev how genuinely frightened he had looked. He said 'I was terrified'.

The whole journey, zig-zag through the woods in the little boat, is beautifully arranged, with the Lilac Fairy going on ahead to light the way and indicate a change of direction. Nureyev was marvellous here, too. It is usual for Princes in boats to make expansive Excelsior gestures, as if to say 'Onward, Christian soldiers': but Nureyev's small, tentative movements of the hands, combined with the awed look on his face, were expressive of doubt and wonder.

The final conflict, the climb up the ivy and the awakening are contrived by Peter Wright with absolute understanding of what is magical and dramatic; and it is obviously the right thing to follow the kiss of life, which Aurora has been waiting a century for, by a loving *pas de deux*—instead of everybody rushing off to ask what the latest fashions are in time for the Wedding. ('My dear, those hipster belts we wore in the reign of Richard II are *out!*')

The *pas de deux*, to some interlude music for violin and orchestra which I think was cut after the first dress rehearsal in 1890 following a rude remark by the Emperor Alexander III, and during which Henry Bardon's solid-looking castle cleverly disappears, leaving the lovers on a mountain peak—or rather a tableland—of ecstasy, is the most typical Ashtonian dreamy-ethereal duet, with the ballerina carried in aery parabolas and with a soaring swinging solo for her cavalier. Nureyev, who had earlier danced most poetically the new melancholy yearning solo of the Prince's loneliness, supported Merle Park and performed this solo so gloriously—so light, impetuous, elegant and passionate. I thought he had never been in better form.

Most ballet critics—have I said this before?—are either Fairies or Witches or both, and I'm a Jester. I am also a critic who longs to praise. Last week I wasn't going to spoil my appreciation of Peter Wright's original, intelligent and exciting production by pointing out a single defect. There were, though, one or two points I wasn't entirely happy about, including the woolly wigs for the Fairies' blue-faced cavaliers at the christening. Why the long *tutus* which conceal the girls' thighs, it may be asked? Well, Diaghilev never allowed the short *tutus*, but lately we have got used to seeing a lot of leg. Perhaps it is time for the fashion to change.

Why a tent for the wedding? After all, as a friend pointed out, it wasn't as if they hadn't got plenty of room in that castle. A tent is bound to be rather formless, but it does make a change from boring old architecture; and, in fact, why the hell not?

And so, crowned with flowers, laughing and triumphing, we run hand in hand into the year '69, which will be the year of Isadora.

29.12.68

Fonteyn and Nureyev; Sibley and Dowell; Jenner and Wall; Park and MacLeary

When Peter Wright put on his new production of *The Sleeping Beauty* in 1968 most of the critics didn't like it, but I did. Now that it has been re-furbished I want to suggest how it might be better still.

The Prologue as planned by Petipa is a masterpiece of stagecraft. In the instructions he gave Tchaikovsky for building up the Easter parade of fairies he didn't put a foot wrong, nor did the composer fail to deliver the goods. Every tune, every bar told. The choreography was a complete academy of classicism. I've never seen the six fairies' variations better danced or more clearly differentiated than in the present production at Covent Garden. To see Seymour with her Cleopatra arms in the first, Collier shining in the second, Vere in the third mostly backwards one, Parkinson with her sudden changes of direction and elegant wrists in Ashton's inserted fourth, Jenner in the fluttering fifth and Mason in the pointing sixth, is to see stars. For the Lilac Fairy's big swooping movements we had Bergsma, then Derman. The drama of Carabosse, after all the dancing, ends the act perfectly. Even Grant's know-how did not eclipse the powerful impression made by Ronald Emblen as the witch.

Henry Bardon's subtly angled Gothic palace and Lila de Nobili's gleaming bees-wing dresses combine in a golden dream of the Middle Ages.

Act I on the sunny castle terrace has its wonderful musical and choreographic architecture too; garland dance, glorious Rose Adage, dramatic spindle episode and spell. Wright plunges us straight into the garland dance, cutting preliminaries. Our Auroras this fortnight have been ebullient Sibley, Fonteyn substituting style and pussycat-sweet demureness for technique, charming tremulous Jenner and patrician Park.

Bardon's set for Act II is more or less James Ward's 'Gordale Scar' at the Tate. O.K., but this act also has its equipoise of Petipa architecture and atmosphere, autumnal nostalgia of minuet and farandole interrupting the Royal Hunt, then the heavenly geometry of the Vision. De Nobili's gentry seem to have risen straight from table tombs, rigid in stone grey, heavy with heraldry. To sacrifice all the melancholy gaiety of this scene to some grim whim for monochrome is the biggest single mistake in the show. The Prince's entry in a litter is a bit medical too.

Well, we had Byronic Dowell and Pushkin Nureyev, and Wall, tender as Keats, and Tennysonian MacLeary. And Tchaikovsky's sweetest tunes are those that tell of saddest thought. The journey in the boat on the rain-stung water of the Panorama music, through a grotto with a romantic chimney-view of sky, into dense forest, passes thrillingly. After the awakening there's Ashton's ecstatic *pas de deux* to what sounds like a viola concerto, but isn't, with the Prince turning, turning ever slower to the cadenza.

Bardon's third and best shot at a tent for the Wedding is still a let down, the court empewed as for the trial of Cranmer. We need Colonnades. There is a lack of *épaulement* in the *pas de trois*, particularly in the first girl's variation which seems to hark back to the bad old days of British ballet. But Wayne Sleep looks like becoming the best Blue Bird in the business. And Nureyev worked up a frenzy and Fonteyn flowered; and Sibley with Dowell, Jenner with Wall, Park with MacLeary are all set to live happily for at least a decade hereafter.

26.3.72

Farmer's designs for the Royal Ballet's new production

A new *Sleeping Beauty*! I remember once walking at dawn uptown from Greenwich Village and seeing the summit of the Chrysler building transformed, by the sun coming through the mist, into a nacreous Tarnhelm of Tiffany glass. I immediately conceived a new *Sleeping Beauty* in which the Prince, a rustic Huckleberry Finn character who saw his Vision of Aurora on television, would come to wake her at dusk in the garden of her Park Avenue penthouse, to light up with his kiss the darkened windows of New York, and set the spell-bound traffic speeding down the avenues. I make a present of this idea to Balanchine in return for the generosity of the American Friends of Covent Garden, who have paid for the Royal Ballet's new *Sleeping Beauty*.

Peter Farmer's designs are a complete disaster. The Petipa-Tchaikovsky ballet is as grand a challenge to a designer as Wagner's *Ring*. How to create a whole mythical world? Bakst did it in one way, Oliver Messel in another: both looked back to the Bibienas for their architecture. The first act at least of Henry Bardon's recent production, a golden renaissance dream, with Lila de Nobili's iridescent costumes, was beautiful.

I suspect Farmer's uncertainty about colour made him restrict himself to a range of blues for the Christening, greens for the Spell and reds for the Wedding. Even with these self-imposed limitations he puts every foot wrong. The bluey-greeny, turquoise and lime group round the pricked pink-clad Aurora is a sickly sight. The dozen men in the last-act Polonaise have plain silvery-white Louis XIV coats and a wealth of orange ostrich feathers in their hats. It is obvious to me that the feathers should have been in three tones, so as not to make a solid bar of colour.

The periods are all mixed up: Henri III and Watteau at the beginning, Louis XIV and Marie-Antoinette at the end. The architecture is Bibiena or, rather, Messel with all the zest gone out of it. The black background of the first scene is depressing, the red decor of the last, claustrophobic. The one excellent idea is the breeze-blown muslin curtains of Aurora's bedroom.

18.3.73

Analysis; Desiderata

There is such a lot of dancing in *The Sleeping Beauty* that without a judicious admixture of suspense, variety, mystery and surprise the work, with three long intervals, can become wearisome. Let us consider the Royal Ballet's new production act by act.

The Prologue was perfectly planned by Petipa. After the exposition—baby, nurses, royal parents—comes the display of gift-bearing fairies, then the introduction of conflict with the threats of Carabosse. It would be hard to improve on the recent Peter Wright-Henry Bardon Prologue, with the Queen in bed, the Fairies coming down a shaft of sunlight and Carabosse vanishing up the chimney; and MacMillan has not done so.

Now the Fairies run down a black ramp behind the dull blue columns, like the shades in *La Bayadère*; and Carabosse comes in beneath her funereal canopy from the other side, attended by hairy monsters and a mobile of bobbing ravens. I do not object to the canopy or Alexander Grant's portrayal of the witch. The Fairies' six variations are still danced with style and cometing Lesley Collier scores heavily in the 'finger' dance. Deanne Bergsma is an ideal Lilac Fairy; Ria Peri rather too smarmy. Their dance is attributed to Feodor Lopoukhov.

Act I, Aurora's coming of age, must have a feeling of spring or early summer. In theory Peter Farmer's perspective of nostalgic trees is O.K., but he is clearly not interested in trees as such. Few stage designers are. MacMillan's new Garland dance is fussy and looks cramped. (Seldom has the stage appeared so small as in this production.) The Rose Adage is always a marvel, and it has been stylishly danced by Antoinette Sibley—flamboyant; Alfreda Thorogood—waiflike; and Merle Park—wellbred. Again a superbly planned scene by Petipa with exposition of knitting needles, dance of display, pricking, mounting drama of *danse de vertige* and concluding Spell. The closing of gauze curtains to represent the growing forest is unambitious for Covent Garden.

One reason for setting Act II in mid-eighteenth century, as Messel did and Farmer does, is to make it look like an Oudry tapestry or a hunting picnic by de Troy in the Wallace Collection: but it doesn't. It may be autumn or, as in MacMillan's and Barry Kay's beautiful Berlin production, winter. A thrilling contrast to the previous scenes, Act II can be a woodland dream. Now, with a characterless landscape, an absurd gibbering fop in lieu of the old tutor, the Prince as a Napoleonic hussar with a litter instead of a horse, nearly everything is pointless. Ashton's melancholy solo, interpreted by Dowell, Wall or MacLeary, catches the mood; but I think it a pity (though justifiable) that the vision of Aurora should be in pink. An unfolding panorama is welcome, but this is a dull one. The antics of Carabosse, stage centre, distract from Aurora's awakening.

A filigree of Jewel Fairies by Petipa, MacMillan, Ashton opens Act III. An oddly ineffective Hop o' my Thumb dance inserted for Wayne Sleep is new. Both Collier and Thorogood have been fine partners for Michael Coleman's soaring Blue Bird. Supporting his wife, Wall seems bursting with pride and has picked up some flashy finishing gestures, but Thorogood's quaint charm is not regal. I like Park's Aurora best, though Sibley's projects more. Only Ashley Lawrence does justice to Tchaikovsky's score.

Only think what one could put into *The Sleeping Beauty*! Tennysonian splendour falling on castle walls; epic landscapes like Rubens's 'Château de Steen'; the varied foliage of trees, as in Domenico Tiepolo's frescoes at Villa Valmarana; the magic of things seen through a dark arch like Thomas Sandby's watercolour of the Covent Garden Arcade in the Mellon Collection!

1.4.73

Makarova and Nureyev

On Friday 8 June Natalia Makarova and Rudolf Nureyev danced together for the first time in *The Sleeping Beauty* at Covent Garden. This must have been quite an ordeal, as the scenery arrived back from South America only at the very last moment, and they had no time to rehearse on the set.

They rose bravely to the occasion, but both showed signs of strain, she by a tendency to fall outwards in her supported *pirouettes*, he by fiendish grimaces in the preparations for his unsupported ones. I liked her best in the vision scene, when she restrained her smiles, for when she smiles she shows too much teeth. Why smile anyway? It never used to be considered the thing in classical roles. If you can make your eyes shine, which I remember hearing Martha Graham advising her dancers to do when there were Press photographers around, you've done quite enough for humanity.

Makarova is a wonderful creature, made of Venetian glass. Long, fine-wrought arms and legs extend from an arched imperial torso. And how light she is, and what extensions and jumps! Is there to be another famous partnership? You'd have thought that Nureyev, after dancing in his own production of *The Sleeping Beauty* with the National Ballet of Canada twice nightly in every town in the United States, might get a bit muddled in adapting to our version. The engine was running to form, and on time, and the passengers clearly enjoyed their trip as much as ever.

17.6.73

Evdokimova and Breuer

Of several Auroras in Festival's rough and ready *Sleeping Beauty* I saw Eva Evdokimova, that tall girl with a sensitive face, who may well have been dancing the role for the first time. She was so nervous in her Rose Adage that we longed for her to succeed, and she was best in the dream and drift of the Vision scene. What a torture for even the most experienced Aurora to make her first running entrance down steps! If she looks down, which Evdokimova did, she is not a real Princess. Breuer does not seem to like these old princely roles (nor did Nijinsky): he wore the expression of a bemused window-dresser.

16.9.73

Nureyev's and Georgiadis's new production for Festival; Evdokimova and Nureyev

'And fleet the time carelessly, as they did in the Golden World', was the pretty phrase Shakespeare gave to Charles, the Duke's wrestler; and I have often thought what kind of golden world I should evoke if entrusted with a production of that greatest of ballets, *The Sleeping Beauty*. Now Nureyev and Georgiadis have done it for me at the London Coliseum, a theatre already echoing with glorious names, from Diaghilev to Harewood; Festival Ballet's new production of the Petipa-Tchaikovsky masterpiece (which Nureyev and Georgiadis have previously staged for La Scala and the National Ballet of Canada) is very much As I Like It.

With so much to say about the thrilling drama, dancing and design, I must plunge in somewhere: so I begin with King Florestan. Donald Barclay is every inch a Bourbon—that proud nose, that immense golden mantle loaded with ermine, that majesty! His tall, gentle queen, Linda

Donald Barclay
in Nureyev's
Sleeping Beauty.
Drawing by
Sam Abercrombie

Darrell, is regal too. When in Act III the curtain rises in silence on a ruddy tableau of the court poised for a *ballet de cour*, we see for the first time what those spectacles must have been like, when *le roi soleil*, dressed by Gissey or Berain, led his peerage, with their manes of feathers, in a formal dance. In this beautiful Sarabande it was the minimal movements of the royal couple, done with such authority, which gave an insight into the nature of absolute monarchy and the power of rulers who raised Chambord, Versailles, the Arc de Triomphe and the Paris Opéra upon the fertile soil of France.

Since we have begun with Act III let us continue with it. The white-clad Polacca was wonderful, for Nureyev has imparted a fresh quality of style to the company. At the beginning of Patricia Ruanne's variation, in the charming *Pas de cinq* for Adam Luders and four ladies, I suddenly heard the glitter of diamonds coming from Terry Kern's timpanist. Paul DeMasson was Bluebird to Dagmar Kessler's radiant Florine: they had the most exquisite costumes with back-swept feathered headdresses. The funny Pussycats were presented as a sort of surprise item by the Catalabutte of Terry Hayworth, an arthritic old boy bent double after a lifetime of waiting in draughty ante-chambers.

Eva Evdokimova came into her own in the *Grand pas de deux* and displayed her strange delicacy. She had been rather tentative in Act I, but gathered strength and confidence. That Nureyev should support her so loyally, then dance his daring variation, after all his remembering, inventing, devising, staging and rehearsing, seemed the most refined and princely labour of this Hercules.

Although the ballet begins and ends in the time of Louis XIV, the Hunting Scene, when Nureyev in Nattier-blue first bounds on to beat the Dukes at target practice, is populated by ladies in fantastic hats *à la* Marie Antoinette: no more elegant creations ever came out of the Avenue Montaigne. Surely the white coach should have dirty wheels? The Intermezzo, a kind of Maiden's-Prayer music to which Nureyev has arranged a long solo, is not something, I think, that Petipa would have thought suitable for dancing.

The Vision Scene, the shifting Panorama, the journey in the magic boat, the death of Winter-Carabosse, the discovery of the hibernating court and the awakening of Proserpina-Aurora is a tale of mystery and imagination.

There are seven Fairies in the Prologue, besides Carabosse and the Lilac Fairy—who are both lovely women in long court dresses, respectively Alexandra Pickford and Valerie Aitken—because Nureyev has two girls dance the second variation. Their dances are almost pure Petipa as we know

S

it, though Nureyev says the swooping sixth may be by Feodor Lopoukhov, brother of Lopoukhova. (Nijinska told me the stabbing fingers in the fifth were her addition.) I loved the way the Fairies were carried in, as if too precious to set foot on floor before their time to dance.

The Lilac Fairy only appears *after* Carabosse; her late arrival, as in Perrault's *conte*, enabling her to make her saving gift. Dramatic episodes are the Witches teaching peasant women the black art of knitting, the confining of these *tricoteuses* in the stocks, their reprieve from execution, Carabosse setting the four handsome rival Princes, Dudley von Loggenburg, Paul Clarke, Kerrison Cooke and David Long, against each other, and their deaths by the sword.

20.4.75

The Nutcracker

Benois in Victoria; Aldous and Kelly

I was fascinated. Arrived early to see Festival Ballet's production of *The Nutcracker*, and seated in the steep circle of the New Victoria Cinema, Wilton Road, I began to study the architecture. The walls were divided up by pilasters made of six Chinese ice-cream cones one inside the other (two with concealed lights), getting bigger as they went higher, as if they were going to turn into fan-vaulting, which they didn't. Between these were tall chinoiserie-Gothic recesses, supported by slender Ionic columns. The colours: mushroom pink and warm dark beige. The lighting: subdued. The effect: magical.

It might have been designed by Alexandre Benois, as this *Nutcracker* was—though he would have insisted on more interesting textures; and I suddenly realized that the Metro-Goldwyn style must have derived via José-Maria Sert from the Russian Ballet of Diaghilev—that is from Bakst and Benois, with a few cubist kinks from Picasso and fan shapes from Larionov and Gontcharova; and all were ultimately related to the Brighton Pavilion. No wonder I instinctively decided in 1954 to hang Benois' designs for *Le Rossignol*, borrowed from the Ashmolean, on a yellow and silver paper designed by Nash for The Prince Regent's Pavilion. And here was a super-spectacular setting for that super Christmas spectacular, Tchaikovsky's, E. T. A. Hoffmann's, Alexandre Benois' Winter-Garden, Palm-Court, Biedermeier, Drosselmeyer, Rumpelmeyer *Casse-noisette*! And on the Brighton line, too, though 'the line is immaterial'.

And when the curtain went up, the drawing-room for the Christmas party, which might have been in the Biedermeier style, *was* in the Chinese style. What a pity that the proscenium opening should be on the low side, and the stage a bit too shallow so that it was difficult to achieve subtle lighting effects. Also, in the Land of Snow, a white floorcloth is essential.

The children, as ever, were much better actors than the grown-ups, who seemed to have had no one to tell them when they were looking ridiculous. But Vassilie Trunoff was an excellent Dr. Drosselmeyer, with the right blend of *bonhomie* and mysteriousness. The *corps de ballet* of snowflakes were well drilled. There was some good clean fun in the Kingdom of Sweets. The girls of the Valse des Fleurs had the prettiest dresses.

Desmond Kelly as the Prince looked and behaved very like Gilpin. His *entrechats* and turns were neat, his manner was easy. Lucette Aldous made an ideal Sugar Plum Fairy: her balance, precision, impetus and smile all combined to convey the sparkle and glamour of that most seductive of sugar-pussies.

If Festival Ballet and the Rank Organization would like their production and their theatre turned into authentic marzipan by next Christmas, I have one or two ideas up my embroidered sleeve, and I offer my services. (This is a paid advertisement.)

10.1.65

Nureyev's production for the Royal Ballet

Intelligence, an enquiring mind, quickness of perception and a sense of humour do not necessarily turn a good dancer into a good choreographer. But, because he possessed these, as well as such an evidently accurate memory and sure eye for restaging ballets learnt in Leningrad, I always had a hunch that Nureyev would turn out to be a real choreographer.

He has staged his own versions of *Swan Lake* and *Sleeping Beauty* in Vienna and Milan, but we had to await this new production of *Nutcracker* for the Royal Ballet to see original work by him in England.

Coming out of Covent Garden on Saturday 2nd March, I thought that the big Act II *pas de deux* was in itself proof that Nureyev had it in him.

But a choreographer, besides inventing groups and dances, has to be a producer; he has to tell a story and hold the interest of the audience—this last being the prime necessity in all the theatrical arts. In *Nutcracker* the dramatist-producer side of Nureyev does not show up too well.

We see the outside of the house with (projected) snow falling, and guests arriving for the party. We go inside, see a troupe of children (Royal Ballet School) and realize that the grown-up ballerina—Antoinette Sibley in this case—is pretending to be one of them. Her god-father, Drosselmeyer, with the black patch, who is a magician and presents puppets and life-size dancing dolls, is Anthony Dowell, and he will later be transformed into her fairy cavalier.

Now, theatrically, this party does not go with a swing. Particularly annoying are the comic grandparents, doddering through their minuet.

(How much more original if, rheumatic as they are, they really danced it with old-world grace, like the Countess singing Grétry in *The Queen of Spades!*)

Clara, the heroine, falls asleep in an arm-chair before the guests leave. Dim-out. The rats invade and Clara has to buy them off with all her dolls in turn, but protecting the precious Nutcracker her godfather has just given her. This bit is taken from Hoffmann's story, and while we're on that subject I rather wish that Nureyev, instead of making Drosselmeyer become the cavalier—for which there seems to be not even a Freudian justification—could have restored Drosselmeyer's talked-of nephew, who is studying in another town, whom Clara associates with the Nutcracker and who arrives in the end (for the story covered several weeks) to become her fiancé.

The toy soldiers fight the rats and the Nutcracker incarnate is, rather confusingly, Wayne Sleep. Dowell, young and handsome, vaguely denominated 'the Prince', appears to do a fine *pas de deux* with Clara and conduct her to the land of Snow. (This scene is mysteriously omitted from the programme note.)

The original Petersburg Snowflakes had white pom-poms on sticks: Nureyev's have fluttering hands. Their *ballabile* is not attended by Clara, which puts them, so to speak, in brackets, and they exit with some difficulty up a ramp adorned with baroque angels like the Ponte Sant' Angelo.

After the interval Clara and the Prince travel in a golden boat to a grotto, where she is attacked by bats which turn out to be her relations, distorted by her dream. The scene changes to Clara's toy theatre, but she *does not watch* the Balanchinean charges in diagonal of the Valse des Fleurs or the rather dull *divertissement* of Spanish, Arab, Chinese, Russian and Dresden china (a *pas de trois* to the Mirliton music) dances.

In the (Sugar Plum) *pas de deux* Nureyev retains bits of Ivanov, such as the thrilling dives, but he glorifies Ivanov in this passionate classical dance. Watching Sibley and Dowell in their splendour, moving to this supreme Tchaikovsky dance music, I thought Nureyev had perhaps consciously made this a stylization of the love act, whose climax is followed by languor.

I must admit the dance seemed less remarkable on Wednesday because Doreen Wells did not *project* like Sibley, and David Wall was off form ('flu?). Wells, however, so small and young, was more acceptable than Sibley at the children's party.

The man's solo is Vainonen's. Nureyev's arrangement for the girl's solo (with celesta) is an improvement, with pretty *battements*, but he has tacked a gentle *manège* to unfamiliar music on to the end and we are caught out clapping before we should.

We are back to the squeaky mouse-music in darkness to accompany a noisy scene change; then the lullaby going-to-bed music. Clara is asleep in her chair at the party, but wakes up just to run to the front door—which necessitates another noisy scene change—before taking her nutcracker to bed.

The designer Nicholas Georgiadis, being Greek born, has a healthy Parisian fear of the obvious and the *déjà-vu*. In this production his preoccupation with style and manner are somewhat damaging to the ballet's mood.

10.3.68

Benois' production; Ruanne and Cooke

Nutcracker is a charming but awkward ballet, the two scenes of the Snowflakes and the Kingdom of the Sweets being merely 'tacked on' to the Party scene and the nocturnal Battle with the Mice. The expression 'tacked on' is Alexandre Benois'. Of the first production of Tchaikovsky's ballet in 1892 he wrote: 'It was impossible to imagine anything more cheerless than the décors of the first act: the ballroom in President Stahlbaum's house reminded one rather of a *Bierstube* decorated in German Renaissance style instead of one of the cosy and poetical interiors of the eighteenth century that one so often meets in old-fashioned provincial towns in Germany.'

Benois embodied his own ideas in productions of *Nutcracker* for La Scala in 1938 and for Festival Ballet in 1957. His *mise-en-scène* for the latter should be a precious survival, for we have only a seldom-seen *Petrushka* at Covent Garden to remember him by: unfortunately the rebuilt and repainted sets which have been on display at the Festival Hall since Christmas are a travesty of Benois' pretty designs. Did the old boy stipulate that his sketches should remain his property? Am I right in thinking they recently came up in a Sotheby sale? It looks as if the scenic artists have had to improvise.

The ballroom walls are the colour familiar from underground lavatories in boys' schools. The gilded *boiseries* are painted in a hard metallic way, very unlike the old boy's impressionistic touches. The snowscene is as soulless as a two-pence coloured print. The Candyland has so much glitter-dust on its pink and green architecture that it has become Disneyland. The atmosphere which Benois carefully and lovingly planned has evaporated.

On paper the series of seven ladies dancing the Sugar Plum Fairy for Festival looked impressive. I missed Maina Gielgud because she danced only on the day after Boxing Day before vanishing into Central Europe. I wanted to see the Italian star Elisabetta Terabust, whom I had heard praised, but she hurt herself. I saw Patricia Ruanne, but although she is an able dancer she has not got all that it takes, and I doubt if some of the other Sugar Plums had either.

In this famous and thrilling dance (even with its altered choreography) the ballerina must have a superb figure, polished style *and* glamour. A neck too long or too short, imperfect knees, sticklike arms, a comic smirk, just won't do. It is also necessary that the dancer should have rehearsed persistently with her partner. Ruanne and Kerrison Cooke were a bit rough. If they couldn't get those difficult dives just right it would have been better not to have attempted them.

Interesting what Benois wrote about the magical music of the Sugar Plum Fairy's *pas de deux*. It is, according to him, 'not ordinary ballet music. It was composed a year before Tchaikovsky wrote the sixth symphony—the Pathétique—which is permeated with a sense of approaching death, alternating with moments full of a passionate thirst for life. The music of the *pas de deux* has many similar features. Why did Tchaikovsky impart a tragic character to the dances of the Fée Dragée? . . . Is not this *pas de deux* rather an attempt to restore a "Hoffmann atmosphere" to the ballet?'

13.1.74

La Sylphide

Les Ballets des Champs-Elysées at the Prince's

The old fairy-tale ballets hold just as much comment on life as any mimo-drama of the modern psychological school. Everyone goes to sleep for a hundred years at some time during his existence, and which of us has not fallen captive to an impossible swan? *La Sylphide*, the ballet in which Taglioni made her name in 1832, has now been revived by Boris Kochno for his Ballets des Champs-Elysées at the Prince's. It is the story of a young Scotsman, who, on the eve of marriage, abandons his flesh-and-blood love to follow some hallucinatory Sylph into the forest. He has apparently attained his Ideal, but in trying to bind her to him he breaks off her wings and she dies.

Schneizhöffer's music is pretty; the settings of Serebriakoff and the dresses of Bérard could not be bettered as an essay in romantic *pastiche*; and Gsovsky has guessed sensitively at the old choreography. Skorik as the Sylph, Philippart as the forsaken bride, and Algaroff as James, dance admirably.

Observer, 12.9.48

Ballet Rambert at Sadler's Wells

A bit of history. We begin with Walter Scott. Because the Waverley Novels had made Scotland the Mecca of the Romantic imagination, Charles Nodier travelled there from Paris and was inspired to write *Trilby ou le Lutin d'Argaïl* (The Elf of Argyll) about a male fairy who loved a ferry-woman. This was a best-seller, and ten years later the singer Nourrit, who had met Taglioni as a dead nun in *Robert le Diable*, devised the libretto of *La Sylphide* for her, reversing the story, so that a mortal man could pursue an aërial ballerina. With the first night of this work at the Paris Opéra on 12th March, 1832, the Romantic Ballet was born, Lami's filmy white skirts started a ballet fashion which is still alive, and Taglioni made her name.

Covent Garden saw *La Sylphide* on 14th July of the same year, and

Taglioni, who had been married to Comte Alfred Gilbert de Voisins at Old St. Pancras Church twelve days before, repeated her former triumph, partnered by her brother Paul.

The Danish choreographer Bournonville saw *La Sylphide* in Paris and determined to reproduce it in Copenhagen. Because he could not obtain the original music of Schneizhöffer, he commissioned the Dane Lövenskjold to fit a new score to the libretto of Nourrit, and himself adapted the choreography of Taglioni's father. Long after Scott and Nodier were dead, and Nourrit had committed suicide and Paul Taglioni had died in 1884, leaving princely Windisch-Graetz descendants, and Marie Taglioni had died in the same year, leaving princely Troubetskoi descendants, the old ballet continued to be performed in its pristine integrity at the Royal Theatre, Copenhagen.

In June, 1951, a party of English critics were invited to Denmark to give opinions of the Royal Ballet and its repertoire. They were astounded by the untouched nineteenth-century perfections of the Bournonville classics *La Sylphide* and *Napoli*, by the vitality and gift for miming of the Danish dancers, by the brilliant technique and noble manner of the men. The modest Danes had allowed themselves to be 'discovered'; a whole issue of *Ballet* was devoted to the revelation; and it became inevitable that the company should appear in Great Britain and the United States.

In 1953 the Royal Danes danced for the first time in London, and *La Sylphide* was seen at Covent Garden once more.

In 1955 they (opening with *La Sylphide*) were acclaimed at the Edinburgh Festival: the kilted James Reuben and his winged enchantress had come via Paris and Copenhagen, back to Scotland.

Now Elsa-Marianne von Rosen, a Swedish dancer from the Royal Danish Ballet, has produced *La Sylphide* for the Ballet Rambert, and the pretty old work has at last entered the English repertory. To avoid confusion with *Les Sylphides*, Mme. Rambert tells me she will call it in future 'The Sylph of the Glen'.

7.8.60

To anyone familiar with the old print after Lepaulle's painting it must be a moving moment when the curtain rises on the Ballet Rambert's production of *La Sylphide*, or *The Sylph of the Glen*, to reveal the kilted Highlander sleeping in his armchair by the fireside with the winged fairy hovering tenderly beside him, in a variation of the group made famous by Marie Taglioni and her brother Paul.

The Sylph, although it is a slightly reduced reproduction by Elsa-Marianne von Rosen of Bournonville's ballet as given in Copenhagen, is probably Mme. Rambert's biggest splash to date. No one could fail to enjoy the revival of this pretty old ballet with its admirable and cautionary story, its witch, its Scottish dances, its fairies, its magic effects and its childish music.

Only one question teases me. Faced with two existing scores for the ballet, the original Paris one of 1832 by Schneizhöffer and the Copenhagen one of 1836 by Lövenskjold, would I, just because there is an extant Danish choreographic version to the latter music, have elected to take this over, lock, stock and barrel, as Mme. Rambert has done, or would I, in view of the fact that Schneizhöffer's music is greatly superior, have had a shot at faking up some new-old choreography for the Paris score, borrowing what I needed from Bournonville, but trying to excel him?

After all, Bournonville was a good choreographer, but his works are not sacrosanct. The virtue of his ballet which the Royal Danes have kept alive is that it is a perfect period piece, with all the bloom of the 1830s on it. Should one have a shot at the impossible or settle for a lesser good? This is a huge question, and, incidentally, it is what *La Sylphide* is all about.

James is engaged to Effie, but a fairy appears, whose unearthly beauty beckons him to the hope of a transcendent superhuman love. A fortune-telling witch who prophesies that Effie will wed Gurn—another rustic suitor—rather than James, is rudely expelled by the latter: nevertheless James, during his very wedding party, rushes out into the forest in pursuit of the Sylph.

A Sylph, though, like perfect love, is ungraspable. The vengeful witch gives James a magic scarf which will bind his fairy to him, but when he enfolds her with it her wings drop off and she dies.

They might quote Blake on the programme:

> *He who bends to himself a Joy*
> *Doth the winged life destroy.*

Flemming Flindt is quite splendid as James. He looks and dances much like the young Eglevsky, only he has finer extremities. His leaps and beats are exhilarating; his bearing is proud, his features expressive; he gives a candid definition to his movements which is exceptional; and, watching him, one wonders why dancing should ever have been considered an unsuitable calling for men.

As his unattainable ideal, Elsa-Marianne von Rosen seems ideally cast. The Sylph is not a woman, but a butterfly. She is a flighty, carefree, soulless thing who can love only with her antennae. Witness the little clapping gestures she makes in mid-air. Von Rosen, with her elfin northern pallor and spun glass limbs, is a fairy we can believe in.

Rambert's own Lucette Aldous, a charming dancer with a nice flow of movement and many other good characteristics, is much more an attractive mortal. I cannot tell if she might grow more into the part.

Shirley Dixon is touching as Effie; Gillian Martlew is a vigorous and utterly convincing witch; and the *corps* have gusto. The Ironsides' farmhouse set is all right, their lakeside landscape less so. People are still pretty vague about Scotland.

31.7.60

Don Quixote

Ballet Rambert's at Sadler's Wells

Whether regarded as a curiosity, as an entertainment or as a vehicle for
Lucette Aldous, the old four-act ballet *Don Quixote*, which Ballet Rambert
gave at Sadler's Wells on Thursday, is tremendously worthwhile.

It *is* of great historical interest to see how Petipa in the eighteen-sixties
improbably adapted themes from the romance of Cervantes to the require-
ments of Russian court ballet; how his steady collaborator Minkus turned
out the necessary music; and how in 1902 the then revolutionary choreographer Gorsky, discarding most of Petipa's dances, performed a sort of
Jerome Robbins operation and pulled the ballet into a more dramatic,
realistic and exciting whole. (I have no doubt that Gorksy's version,
reproduced for Rambert by Witold Borkowski of Warsaw, was the *West
Side Story* of its day.)

As entertainment, *Don Quixote* pours forth such a varied flow of jolly
dances, only slightly interspersed with comic mime, that one is kept in
high spirits throughout the evening. I believe you could put it on for a
run in the West End, but the dancers would be dead in a week if you did.
When, for heaven's sake, have we been given a mad *divertissement* in the
first act of a ballet? It's like getting drunk immediately after breakfast.

As Kitri, the innkeeper's dancing daughter, Lucette Aldous bursts like
a new comet into the select heaven of brightest stars, just as Jeanmaire did
overnight in *Carmen*. She was clearly born to excel in the swift, the witty,
the mischievous and the exhilarating: in fact, this brilliant *demi-caractère* role
could have been made for her, and I don't mind betting that on the
strength of her performance alone Sol Hurok will have Ballet Rambert on
Broadway in no time.

The story—of Don Quixote's adventures and humiliations—is only a
pretext, and most of the time the Don sits watching *divertissements*; but
John Chesworth, admirably schooled and made up, gives him so exactly
the right blend of authority, inspiration and absurdity that we care deeply.
John O'Brien does the waddling Sancho very well too.

The music is full of what a colleague wittily described as 'worn-out clichés' but it is just as well-tailored to its carefree purpose as Coward's for *Sail Away*. A bigger band would help to give it more punch. The sets and dresses are first-rate.

Voytek, the designer, drawing in his Spanish backgrounds with sweeping charcoal strokes, hints that the whole thing is only a dream—for instance, Don Q's lance is a recurring motif, and holds up a curtain in the inn. There are many and striking sets, and there is some delightful machinery. I thought the yellow drop for the Dryads could be made more interesting, though. The costumes, reminiscent of Clavé and Picasso—how not?—combine into happy colour schemes. Voytek is with it.

The company by their utter abandon made up for any lack of individual virtuosity. In the only familiar *pas de deux*, which comes in the final *divertissement*, Kenneth Bannerman supported Aldous triumphantly—as he had throughout—and his lifting her high overhead and suddenly dropping her into the deepest fish-dive was the climax of a giddy fantasia.

29.7.62

The Australian Ballet at the Coliseum

As if by some perverse and decadent whim the Australian Ballet chose to open their short season at the Coliseum with *Don Quixote*. One might have thought that the only reason to mount this endless three-acter at all would be to show our convict cousins the kind of rubbish that used to amuse the snobby old Pommy bastards who transported them for sheep-stealing a century ago.

Admittedly, this pseudo-Spanish Russian ballet provides a miming role for Sir Robert Helpmann, who is to Australia what the Statue of Liberty is to America, and a series of coruscating dances to show the paces of Lucette Aldous and Rudolf Nureyev: yet how absurdly constructed it is! The poor old knight spends most of the evening standing at one side of the stage trying not to distract attention from the dancing. The choreography—by Nureyev after Petipa—is a mere display of technical skill. The score of Minkus, even when edited by the incomparable John Lanchbery, is as mechanical as a music box—and, by God, it makes you realize what a fountain of marvellous melody Tchaikovsky was.

Having said which, I must admit that the opening night of this ebullient troupe was a triumph. Not for years have we seen a mime so solemn, grand and obsessive as Sir Robert, keeping a miraculous balance between the heroic and the absurd. Lucette Aldous, so pert, light, neat and pretty, makes it exactly clear what justified this old-fashioned kind of ballet in the first place. Rudolf Nureyev, looking about twelve, clowning like a tipsy monkey, dancing like a suicide, brings down the house.

There is so much dancing in *Don Quixote* that one emerges slightly dazed; and I look forward to seeing Sir Robert's and Dame Peggy van Praagh's company in something more recumbent this week.

7.10.73

Raymonda

The Australian Ballet at the New Victoria

'O, swallow, flying from the golden woods . . .' Oh yes, I do see the point
of reviving *Raymonda*. This full-length ballet with music by Glazounov
and choreography by Petipa was first given in Russia in 1898, but Benois
wrote in his memoirs that the plot was too complicated and that the ballet
lasted three hours.

The point is that it is a big thrill when suddenly a whole new classical
ballet sunbursts upon you, with a whole new dazzling score full of eighteen-
carat tunes (some of which, naturally, are familiar), and a series of dances,
classical and character, which bear the stamp of sterling Petipa. Obviously
Rudolf Nureyev has done some drastic editing—the story is reduced to
a party, a dream which turns into nightmare, a party with chivalrous
combats and a party with Hungarian dances. Some of the vestiges of the
original story—an abduction (now part of the dream), tilting, archery,
duelling—seem perfunctory, but when you look up the original scenario
in Mr. Beaumont's 'Complete Book' you feel glad to have lost the White
Lady and King Andrew II of Hungary, and to be left with more time for
drinking. The present work is really very simple indeed.

And the score is so marvellous, and it isn't Tchaikovsky. Glazounov
has the same variety of invention, but into certain tunes he injects an
extra vein of Straussian voluptuousness, a sick, decadent, Tennysonian
over-sweetness, glittering in its autumn golds, which is irresistible just
for a change. 'The splendour fall on castle walls . . .' 'Now sleeps the
crimson petal, now the white . . . Now winks the gold fin in the porphyry
font; The firefly wakens; waken thou with me.' Of course, there are open
tinkly tunes, and dragging gypsyish ones, and mournful Slav ones, too.

Then it was bold as brass and good as gold of Nureyev and the
Australian Ballet (for it was for them the revival, now showing at the New
Victoria, was mounted) to commission not a pretty chocolate-box sort
of designer for this Mum-delighting sugar-plum of a ballet, but the stark,
ruthless and imaginative Ralph Koltai, who laid on his slabs of polystyrene in the superb *Jew of Malta*, and in this case lays on his strata of

metal foil—as if he were building a monument for Nicolas de Staël. The subtle costumes are by Koltai's usual partner, Nadine Baylis. I don't think the sets are quite worked out enough—the heraldic banners should either be carried much further, then 'broken down', or not attempted—but that doesn't diminish the credit due to Nureyev for choosing Koltai.

A clever set is the one for the dream. The tapestry portrait of Jean de Brienne flies up, the chair Raymonda was sleeping in glides off. Trees come down, and for their duet with the golden syrup tune (whose line is like an Art Nouveau tendril) the lovers are in a wood. Then I saw that Koltai had heard what I heard in the music. His trees are Tiffany glasses—blobs on tapering stems, iridescent with the greeny-bluey-pinky-goldy-silveriness of ancient Roman glass, long buried.

The orchestra under Robert Rosen gave us a good idea of golden Glazounov; the Australian Ballet gave us a goodish glimpse through parted curtains of the diamonds Petipa has to offer. Heather Macrae and Karl Welander glowed and blazed, leading the Czardas. Fonteyn, *bourrée-ing* gently backwards, clapping to her Oriental tune, or with hand provocative behind head, was a pearly vision. Nureyev rocketed. Together in the dream duet, to which Ashton would have added a sheen of poetry, they shimmered in the gloom. 'Now lies the Earth all Danäe to the stars.'

19.2.65

The Changing Scene
(1966–1968)

Edinburgh

The Scots are Scotcher than ever. A most informative and beautifully laid
out exhibition in Edinburgh's Waverley Market celebrates the bicentenary
of the New Town, one of the glories of Britain. Recommending me to visit
this exhibition, which is called '200 summers in a city', the Lord Provost
remarked, rather tactlessly I thought, 'There's never been an exhibition
like it': and indeed it is delightful. There are the usual letters in *The Scotsman*
about creaking seats in the Usher Hall, and Sir Nicholas Sekers feels
obliged to point out that 'It is in the interests of commerce' that the
Festival should be more generously backed. Professor Trevor-Roper
lectures on 'Scottish enlightenment'; and throughout the city the words
'No Popery' are chalked on the blackened walls.

Everything seemed unfavourable for the visit of New York City Ballet
to this year's Festival. They could only bring twenty-five dancers. The
Empire theatre, borrowed for a week from Bingo, is what it always was.
A month or two ago I heard that the booking was nil and tried to give
the company a boost. We all know that the ballet-starved Scots only want
to see *Giselle* and *Swan Lake*: but Balanchine was to bring some of his
most advanced works, with no scenery and the most difficult scores.
Jacques d'Amboise got sick at the last minute and couldn't come. Robert
Irving has had to travel to Glasgow daily to rehearse the B.B.C. Scottish
Symphony Orchestra. Balanchine couldn't rehearse his second programme
because the theatre returned to Bingo on Tuesday afternoon.

But the whole thing has been a great success. Houses have been full and
appreciative. Two things stand out. Balanchine's endlessly varied inventions, and the wonderful talent of Suzanne Farrell.

3.9.67

Striptease

Jane and I arrived at Raymond's Revuebar in time for the 10.50 show,
with the place quickly filling up and Jane losing her original fears that
there would be few other women there. In fact about a quarter of the
customers were women. Men were mostly middle-aged: a few foreigners,
a few Yanks, a few Scots, mostly North Country. Some smoked pipes.

Canned music. When the pink spangled curtain parted there was a

'Welcome to the International Festival of Striptease '67' number, with girls in pink feathers and helmets, two out of eight of whom had bare breasts, though all walked quickly around waving their arms. It became clear that the proscenium opening, which a tall girl could reach with her hands, was too low to allow of subtle lighting effects . . . our first solo stripper, Tanya Rombova ('From Russia' the programme said, though it seemed unlikely), started off in a long brown dress, but soon shed it to the music of *Hello Dolly*.

The pace increased. Lady Flam went mad on a bed. Adele Warren stripped off on horseback and, lying back voluptuously, spread the horse's tail over her face and murmured again and again 'Niiice . . . Ummm . . . Vairy niiice'.

The performance of Tami Sabra 'from Israel' was rather subtle because she never appeared conscious of the audience. Dressed in a scrap of leopard skin, she was tied up inside quite a small cage. 'Un homme . . . un homme . . . je ne pense qu'à un homme . . .'. She wanted a man. I wondered what sort of bloke had caged her and whether he might not come back.

I couldn't make out what the next lady's gimmick was unless to reveal with her final gesture that she was not a natural blonde. She was followed by a provocative redhead with a diamond-studded revolver who showed a lot of bottom and, seated astride a bentwood chair with her back to us, drew a feather boa slowly between her legs.

The star of the show, Carole Ryva from Paris, was rather different from all her predecessors—short, blonde, with a sharp, witty little face. She chatted up the front rows in a bird-like baby-voice—'Voulez-vous, vous et moi?'—before climbing on to her befeathered bed. Then she behaved as a girl really might who wanted a diamond bracelet. She bounced, made baby noises, stuck her behind in the air, pretended to get cross when the electrician projected a polka-dot pattern all over her, nibbled the erect end of her feather boa and smacked it. In fact she paid us a lot of attention and was pretty cute.

At the end the audience stampeded for the exit, and I thought how much more natural the whole thing would be if they were allowed to storm the stage and carry off the girls. 'Did you enjoy it?' asked Jane. 'No, I could hardly wait for the end.' 'Oh, I loved it,' she said. 'But then I suppose men see girls behaving like that all the time, and it's all new to me.' 'I forgot to ask where they stabled the horse,' I said.

21.1.68

Israel

A very few years ago when Bethsabée de Rothschild was planning the formation of her Batsheva Dance Company for Israel, I remember responding rather apathetically to her questions about possible choreographers.

I was thinking that simply because she had supported Martha Graham so heroically in the past she couldn't just rush off to Israel and push a few handsome Israelis into a class-room and make them dance and then ring up all the cleverest choreographers and commission ballets from them and create a company with a style. Well, I was wrong. She has.

The programmes I saw at the Bath Festival had ballets by Graham, Morrice, Tetley and Pearl Lang. All interesting, all well danced. The dancers look good and work well together. Ten of them were born in Israel.

7.7.68

Saratoga

Driving south from Montreal through the dancing mountains of Vermont, a land flowing with milk and maple syrup, I came to Saratoga Springs.

This is the most extraordinary place, a mixture of Newmarket, Bournemouth and Marienbad, whose infinite flat grassy acres are planted with sedate groves and aimless avenues. Here among the race tracks, the golf courses, and the thermal springs—to whose healing waters Sir William Johnson was borne by Mohawk braves in 1767—in a hollow by a waterfall stands the Saratoga Performing Arts Center, which, thanks to the imagination of Governor Rockefeller, Lincoln Kirstein and others, has become the summer home of the Philadelphia Orchestra and the New York City Ballet.

The delightful theatre, now in its second season, is covered, but the sides are open, so that, in addition to the 2,500 seated inside, many more can watch from the grass slopes without. Sight lines and acoustics are fine, and to watch a ballet here on a summer night is a delightful experience.

It seemed quite natural at Saratoga to find oneself at 9 a.m. watching the caracoling and curvetting of Lippizaner horses in the company of a few experts on bloodstock, plus, Balanchine with Suzanne Farrell in full make-up, white tutu and diamonds. I was about to quote Oscar Wilde, and say,

'You can't have *got* up; you must have *sat* up!' when I realized we were being photographed for *Life* magazine and began to elbow my way into the foreground.

23.7.67

Death of Ballet

Kenneth Tynan wrote the other day that ballet was a dying art, and when I asked Sir Frederick Ashton whether he had read this he said 'Yes, and it's having a very grand funeral.' I don't know whether an art can be dying and excessively popular, but I can only say that if all the applause in all the London theatres where drama is being performed was played end to end it would not add up to half of what greets Fonteyn and Nureyev after one of their evenings at the Garden.

On Friday Margot Fonteyn and Rudolf Nureyev did their big silent movie act in *Marguerite and Armand*.

In *M and A* you really get your moneysworth of ecstasy and heartbreak from M and R, the world's sweethearts. It must be rather fun to do, because there don't seem to be any fixed rules and there are no holds barred. I always think I spot some tremendous new bit of business. After R flings in scorn that bundle of the earliest paper money ever printed at M, he has worked the veering emotions of the following passage into the equivalent of a Shakespeare soliloquy. No mean achievement. Then M totters off on breaking, heartbroken toes.

Oh divine creatures, since ballet is a dying art, mount your golden bed like Sardanapalus and let me be slaughtered by ruthless janissaries at your feet!

8.4.68

Grigoriev

Grigoriev, Diaghilev's *régisseur*, who died a few days ago, remained a faithful steward even after the death of his master. This year, since I started work on my life of Nijinsky, I have been sending him long question-naires, going into almost frivolous detail—'How many of Diaghilev's committee smoked?' 'What colour was the striped wallpaper?'

All these he answered minutely—with a few exceptions. I had asked a number of questions about Mavrine, who was Diaghilev's friend before

and even after he met Nijinsky. Grigoriev bracketed these questions together and wrote—or rather his wife wrote for him—'I cannot answer
questions 38–45 as I never took any interest in the private life of members
of the company.'

I was slightly abashed and felt with an onrush of unusual modesty that
a biographer's was perhaps a less honourable trade than that of *régisseur*
to Diaghilev.

15.9.68

Denby

'Daily life is wonderfully full of things to see. Not only people's movements, but the objects around them, the shape of the rooms they live in,
the ornaments architects make around windows and doors, the peculiar
ways buildings end in the air, the water tanks, the fantastic differences in
their street façades on the first floor.'

Like certain movies help you to see famous paintings or sculptures more
thrillingly than your young, efficient but innocent eyes could do without
their aid; like it is wise to read Ruskin on Venice or Mary McCarthy on
Florence and get all interested before you go there (and then disagree
passionately); like some critics can show you the point of some poems:
so Edwin Denby is the one to study and think about before you next look
at dancers, buildings or people in the streets.

His latest book of collected pieces is called *Dancers, Buildings and
People in the Streets.*

For instance, if you were going to Italy, to Rome, Denby would help
you to appreciate the special grace of young Italians strolling down the
street. If you were going to New York he would remind you to notice
'what a forty- or sixty-storey building looks like from straight below . . .
and . . . how it comes up from the sidewalk as if it intended to go up no
more than five storeys.'

He analyses the three kinds of rhythm people dance to in dance halls:
behind the beat, across the beat and on top of the beat, so if you were going
to watch those Victor Sylvester dream sequences on T.V., you might give
a thought to how the dancers step across the beat 'with a swooping flow
that corresponds over several measures to a phrase of the music. They
look gracefully sentimental, or as our children say, like creeps.'

Above all, if you were a ballet critic groping for words to describe what
happened in Balanchine's ballet to Stravinsky's *Agon* and why it was so

wonderful, you would find an ideal crib or key in Denby's essay *Three Sides of Agon*, armed with which, plus the record, you could knock all the other critics for six, get a raise of salary, win friends, influence people.

It is interesting to have an American dancer-musician-poet's view on some of our standard works. '*Antigone* . . . looked like first-rate material for a farce: all it needed was some tourists wandering about.' But on the whole Denby is very kind, having spent much of his life listening to the opinions of young people, like Socrates.

16.1.66

Sokolova

Walking down dear old Charlotte Street on Wednesday evening and seeing the crowds outside the Scala Theatre, I suddenly realized that Sotheby's sale of Diaghilev's scenery and costumes was going to be a festive occasion. Besides the familiar faces there were a number of dazzling young people in the latest beads; it was a packed house; and Mr. Peter Wilson's hospitable manner on the podium, together with laughter and shouting caused by the initial failure of the microphone, made the party go.

Three-quarters of the way through the sale the stage was cleared, there was a pause, then to music of Tchaikovsky's solemn polonaise dancers of the Royal Ballet School came on in procession wearing the costumes Bakst designed for *The Sleeping Princess*.

This production at the Alhambra in 1921, which nearly ruined Diaghilev, was the most gorgeous ever presented on a stage, and here were one baroque backcloth and several dozen costumes which had survived from it. I happened to know that this polonaise for thirty dancers had been arranged by Mme. Sokolova in four hours without a piano.

Even if I hadn't, I should have been moved by this marching and counter-marching, and by the princely demeanour of these young people, the heirs of the Sun King, who founded the first Royal Academy of Dancing. I knew these dancers wouldn't have been there at all if Lydia Sokolova, Ninette de Valois, Ursula Moreton, Anton Dolin and Alicia Markova hadn't joined the Diaghilev Ballet. Mme. Sokolova was the first: she joined in 1913. Thilo von Watzdorf (who had organized the sale) and Peter Wilson brought her on to take a call, so it was a great occasion as well as a festive one.

21.7.68

Requiem

A month's mourning having been decreed, the flags here were still at half-mast; and New York City Ballet gave a single performance of a work to honour Dr. Martin Luther King. This was Stravinsky's *Requiem Canticles*, with choreography by Balanchine, costumes by Rouben Ter-Arutunian, lighting by Ronald Bates and with the chorus and orchestra conducted by Robert Irving.

The composer writes in our programme: 'I am honoured that my music is to be played in memory of a man of God, a man of the poor, a man of peace.' The idea of the ritual was more noble in conception than impressive in execution. It did not quite come off. Still, the gesture was made, and it was glorious to hear in Stravinsky's elliptical score the note of doom, the hope of life eternal.

In the Prelude a body of angels in transparent white gowns are seen in twilight. In the Exaudi they light their candelabra one by one. In the Dies Irae they surge about, potential Lucifers. In Tuba Mirum the hero appears —and this is Arthur Mitchell, a Negro—robed in purple and gold. During the orchestral meditation called 'Interlude' the angels move the lights like chessmen on the floor and, stooping, illumine the hero's path to heaven.

In Rex Tremendae he is led through diagonal avenues. In Lacrimosa, arches are formed and a weeping girl, Suzanne Farrell, passes beneath them. In Libera Me the angels move in circles. Then, on the first chord of the Postlude, Mitchell is raised aloft, and Farrell, like a timid soul in purgatory, threads her way through a Stonehenge of blessed beings.

26.5.68

Tahiti

Who has not, at sometime in his life, got hooked on the idea of South Sea islands, following in imagination the travels of Cook, Stevenson, Gauguin, Rupert Brooke and Maugham, thrilling at the sound of such words as 'atoll' and 'hibiscus', poring over a map to gloat on the magic remoteness of Tahiti, and dreaming of orgies in the scented darkness beneath friendlier stars, to the steady rhythm of breakers on the reef across the lagoon?

And suddenly, presumably for the first time in history, here is a company of Tahitian dancers and singers in London, and at the Saville, and everyone seems to take it absolutely for granted. How spoilt we are! They are called *Iaora Tahiti*, which means Hello, Tahiti, as we learn from the useful glossary in our programme.

The most wonderful things about the Tahitians, apart from their apparent good humour, are the colour of their skins, a pinkish gold, and its texture, silky: there is nothing else like it. The girls have small breasts, which makes a change, and small waists from which the thighs are seen broadening delightfully, with the skirt supported at their widest point. One of the men, the second from the left in the final line-up, had the most beautiful torso I have ever seen. When he stood, stooping slightly forward and to one side, it was pure Praxiteles, if I may say so.

So *Maeva* (welcome), Tahitians, and *maruru* (thank you) for coming all this way across the *moana* (sea); I enjoyed your *paoa* (dance) and *himene* (song), and I will now draw to a close with the useful cry of *Aue* (exclamation to express all sentiments)!

22.1.67

WESTERN EUROPE

Roland Petit is a romantic and he specialises in ballets about famous lovers, Carmen and Don José, Quasimodo and Esmeralda, Adam and Eve.

Sunday Times, 30.3.69

Béjart is the oddest hit-or-miss creature.

Sunday Times, 28.4.74

It is bewildering to see how these Danes have got miming in them. To keep an unbroken tradition means the continuous following of good examples.

Ballet, Vol. 11, No. 7, August 1951

When Antonio's audience is a success and spurs him on to Dionysian frenzies of improvisation, then the clock strikes thirteen and the theatre catches fire.

Observer, 30.12.51

France

Petit's Ballets de Paris at the Marigny, Paris

The Théâtre Marigny stands amid chestnut trees in the gardens at the foot of the Avenue des Champs-Elysées where the young Marcel played with Gilberte and where in a later volume his grandmother had her final attack and took refuge in the ladies' cloakroom before going home in her carriage to die. Within this little theatre hung with red damask and lit by crystal chandeliers, Roland Petit's new venture had its beginning.

Les Demoiselles de la Nuit is a ballet in three scenes on a theme by Jean Anouilh, with a specially composed score by Jean Françaix and scenery and dresses by Léonor Fini. The story is a new version of the cat-into-woman, lady-into-fox fable. The curtain rises on a dilapidated *salon* in the lonely villa of the cat-Baron de Grotius. Several cats, dressed in the utmost elegance of 1880, are grouped around on sofas, ladders and chairs. The dark red walls have been repapered in newspaper, which is already peeling off. At the back, half hidden by the ragged curtains of the door opening on the park, stands a young man in a frock-coat, holding his hat. He is afraid to come in out of the moonlight. At last the mystery of the house draws him in, and the cats flirt and play with him. Among them is one, Agathe, with super-feline aspirations; she has read all the books in the attic and aspires to humanity. She and the young man are in sympathy: they dance together. But every month the Cat-Baron weds one of his courtiers and tonight it is the turn of Agathe. The tawny tyrant appears and commands the young man, who is a musician, to play on his violin and accompany the nuptials. The power of music combined with the love of Agathe for the music-maker are strong enough to work a miracle. Agathe becomes a woman and flees with her human lover, followed by the angry cats.

Arriving in his bare garret the musician welcomes his mistress to a new life, and they celebrate their love. Agathe is distracted first by birds in a cage and then by the wailing of her former companions on the tiles above. Leaving her lover asleep she goes out on to the roof. The deserted youth awakes to find himself alone.

Agathe and the other cats dance a farandole among the chimneys by moonlight. The musician climbs out of a window and entreats his beloved to return. Following her over the roofs he falls to his death. Agathe's love revives when she sees he is lost to her forever, and with the gestures of a devoted wife she lies down beside him to die.

This work has many merits but it is badly constructed. The first scene is fantasy, the second romance, the third drama. All the settings are good, but the first with its bizarre and elaborate detail has nothing in common with the severe architecture of the second and third. The climaxes of the dancing are the courtship *pas de deux* in the first scene and the lovemaking *pas de deux* in the second: whereas the climax of action is in the third tableau when the young man falls and dies. No dancing to speak of is possible in the last scene because of the sloping roof and three chimneys which fill the stage: the suspense of the audience has to be broken while a solid roofscape is built up for the hero to roll down. The ballet has not digested the story.

The dresses are pretty and the cat masks inoffensive. The music of Françaix, coloured by feline wailings, is functional and sustains the action admirably. Petit's choreography is in places full of invention, and in others, such as the violin-playing dance, seems to echo his earlier ballets. There are some original dances for Gordon Hamilton as Baron de Grotius and for the many-coloured cats. For Margot Fonteyn in the role of Agathe, Petit has created movements full of character and charm, exposing new possibilities in her art. Her dances are a mixture of classicism and catlike *minauderies*, and she performs them with a mocking sweetness which has captivated her new audience.

Les Demoiselles de la Nuit is a nocturne during which, once or twice, the moon in all her white, ironic beauty, shines clearly through the clouds. *Allegro*, a *pas de cinq* by Janine Charrat on the Introduction and Allegro for Strings of Ravel, formerly used in Howard's *Mermaid*, has dresses by the dressmaker Jacques Fath. It is the height of 1938 elegance. Black curtains are framed by a proscenium of red and white striped silk. To the left and right two real negroes in white loin cloths and turbans, diamond bracelets and necklaces, bear crystal candelabra; these, and three black-draped women at the back who veil one bare breast with a black lace fan, form the décor and remain motionless throughout. Charrat, Marchand, Dalba, Skouratoff and Perrault, clad in black and white tights and diamonds, make a series of entries, dance, form groups and execute an exaggerated Lifaresque choreography. The impression left by the ballet is agreeable but slight, like lust in a dress-shop.

On Monday, 31st May, I saw the first performance of the equivocally titled '*adame Miroir*. Jean Genet, the author of the theme, whose books can only be smuggled into England with the greatest difficulty, tells us on the programme that the meaning of his ballet escapes him and that we must try to find it out for ourselves. Very well. The curtain rises on a gallery of mirrors—a sumptuous brothel or amusement arcade. A faceless figure in purple draperies—Death maybe (Skouratoff)—wields a black fan and disappears. A French sailor in white (Petit) comes in. He looks in the mirrors and his reflections (the *corps de ballet*) look back at him. Then one of the reflections (Perrault) rebels and attacks him; in the scuffle they grow amorous; one sailor gives his double a rose. Death—if it is Death—interrupts their affectionate exchanges, and seems determined to take one of them. There is a long and complicated chase. After a rough-and-tumble, Death himself reveals a glimpse of sailor's trousers under his draperies, and I will not swear that he and the sailor's reflection do not change clothes. At any rate the original sailor is pushed into a mirror and a purple-clad figure once more stands alone. Now the mirrors reflect only him as he stalks down a long perspective and passes through the glass at the end.

The idea of the ballet is excellent: it is an original conception and one well suited to treatment in dancing. The work was clearly under-rehearsed and prepared in a hurry; it may improve considerably: but at its first peformance it seemed too long and confused. The score of Darius Milhaud enhanced the atmosphere of strangeness. The setting by the Belgian Paul Delvaux, with its wine-coloured walls and gilded mirrors in false perspective, was wholly admirable. I should say that Janine Charrat had not fully appreciated the implications of the theme and had therefore not succeeded in stripping her choreography of its inessentials. There was too much restless movement which meant nothing.

Ballet, Vol. 5, No. 6, June 1948

Petit's *Tristan* at the Prince's

It one wandered (out of absentmindedness or curiosity, or chasing a runaway Pekinese) into a darkened theatre on a spring morning, and found an orchestra rehearsing the Prelude and Liebestod of *Tristan*; and if by chance the curtain were raised, and some dancers were at the same time rehearsing an unknown erotic ballet on a bare stage and against a background of whitewashed theatre walls, clothes-baskets and costumes hung

Renée Jeanmaire and Roland Petit
in *Carmen*. Drawing by Clavé

on rails—then it is probable that the strangeness of the situation and the occasional rhyming of sense and phrasing in the music and the ballet rehearsal would seem to one miraculously exciting, as one stood there silent and unsuspected in the stalls: but if, a few days later, one were invited (as a critic for the *Observer* maybe) to see a new ballet at the same theatre, the Prince's, say, and it turned out to be a *pas d'action* by Roland Petit to the music of *Tristan*, performed in practice costume against the whitewashed theatre walls, one might be tempted to keep secret one's earlier exciting experience and turn out some conventional phrases about 'The blasphemy of using Wagner's music without an adequate orchestra; the cynicism of M. Petit, who, despite moments of genuine originality . . . the trooper spirit of Mlle. Jeanmaire, who replaced Mlle. Vyroubova at short notice . . .' in fact the usual stuff.

But having telephoned that through to one's paper, one would probably rush back so as not to miss a moment of Petit's version of Bizet's *Carmen*.

Observer, 13.3.49

Les Ballets des Champs-Elysées at the Prince's

La Rencontre, presented by the Ballets des Champs-Elysées at the Prince's, is about Oedipus and the Sphynx, and it is very exciting. Sauguet's unpretentious music creates a magic atmosphere and provides an ideal dramatic accompaniment to the action; Bérard's set, though not seen to advantage on a small stage, is a marvel of simplicity; Lichine's acrobatic choreography is rightly violent and bizarre; and Kochno, who planned the ballet and produced it, has been perfectly successful in what he set out to do—which is as rare as the creation of a masterpiece. Lichine working with Kochno is a very different choreographer from Lichine without.

This Sphynx, danced by the very young and beautiful Leslie Caron, is three things: a woman fascinating a man, an acrobat performing his strange function, and a legendary monster thirsty for hot blood. In a desert place she awaits the flirtation-performance-encounter, and is massaged by three attendants. Oedipus (Babilée), with cloak and tall staff, comes to her. She mounts to her aerial acrobat's platform and asks her riddles. Oedipus answers them. They fight. Despite her long claws the Sphynx is mortally wounded, and, climbing again her rope ladder, she falls backwards and dies. Oedipus looks in her face and returns to the city, leaving her hanging by the feet. I can imagine no dancers but Caron and Babilée in these two roles.

U

Babilée's own first ballet, *L'Amour et son Amour*, is an attempt, very successful at moments, to interpret the mysterious, sensual and religious music of Franck's *Psyché*: that is to say, it is about a god making love to a mortal. Jean Cocteau's first set is a map, representing earth; his second, which I prefer, a chart of stars. Nathalie Philippart, as Psyché, white as Libyan sand, in her dress of ultramarine striped like Mediterranean shallows with turquoise, weaves her way, borne by zephyrs, to Cupid's cloudy bed; she finds ecstasy in the embraces of the winged god (Babilée), and is dismissed again to earth, leaving her lover involved in the incomprehensible business of deity.

Observer, 25.9.49

Petit's *Nôtre-Dame de Paris* at the Opéra, Paris

Very few people know, I believe, that Victor Hugo tried his hand at ballet criticism—that esoteric craft which has been brought to such a pitch of refinement in our day. Yet I found recently at the end of his review of some play, written for *La Muse Française* in the 1820s, these words: 'The dances of M. Gardel were well arranged.' One imagines that the baldness of this statement evoked few expressions of admiration in the poet's circle, for he soon abandoned the rigours of Terpsichorean analysis for less exacting literary forms—the novel, the epic, the drama.

How passionately Hugo strove for success in the theatre! Yet the very violence of his imagination defeated itself—he could not resist going too far—and in spite of the battles fought on his behalf true success on the stage eluded him. How bitter that *Rigoletto*, based on his *Le Roi s'amuse*, should prove one of the world's most popular operas—though rather nice for the money it brought him in *droits d'auteur*. His *Hernani* and *Lucrezia Borgia* were also operated. And in 1844 Perrot made the ballet *Esmeralda*, based on Hugo's novel *Nôtre-Dame de Paris*, which remained long in the St. Petersburg repertory. Now Roland Petit has tried to give the feeling (apart from just telling the story—which of course he simplifies) of that huge Gothic novel, on the stage of the Paris Opéra.

What a super-ballet there might have been if, in 1830, Hugo, Berlioz and Delacroix had got together—what a *Scheherazade*! Yet it might not have worked. The success of a ballet depends on so strange an alchemy that the blending of inferior elements often produces a finer work of art. The score of Maurice Jarre for Petit's *Nôtre-Dame de Paris* is quite vulgar; the sets of René Allio, though sensational in scale and manoeuvrability, are not the work of a great painter—yet the total effect is tremendous.

Impossible to imagine anything more Hugoesque—or, as the French say, *hugolien*. All the contrasts of light and dark, of tenderness and horror, of the grotesque and the sublime are here in Petit's ballet. And of course from the management's point of view it has got 'everything'. Love, murder, the brothel, the scaffold; mass movements of mobs dressed in the bright colours of Yves Saint-Laurent's 'abstract'—i.e. non-period—costumes alternate with voluptuous or lyric *pas de deux*; an intolerable din of drumming is succeeded by a sweet *cantabile* tune; the twin towers of the golden cathedral rise and sink, and inside the scaffolding of the belfry the hunchback swings on his bell.

This is essentially a popular spectacle; and it works; and it is a pleasure to see the gorgeous Palais Garnier crammed with the applauding people of Paris. Victor Hugo, who loved the man in the street, who wrote for the common reader and chose to be buried in a pauper's grave, has once more touched the hearts of the crowd and scored a popular success. (I noticed that *Rigoletto* was on next week.)

What is most masterly is how Petit has seized on the essential episodes of the story and how he has used his *corps*. With the minimum of trappings or props, the latter become in turn jesters, worshippers in church, beggars, soldiers, tarts and nightmares. Their rhythmical movements hammer home the ballet's veering moods.

As Esmeralda, Claire Motte is a strong dancer whose presence fills the stage. Jean-Pierre Bonnefous is her lustrous Phoebus; the obsessed and potent Cyril Atanassoff makes a haunting impression as the evil deacon Frollo; and as Quasimodo, Roland Petit has marvellously devised a means of being a hunchback without wearing a hump, and of being the partner in a classical *pas de deux* without seeming out of character.

10.4.66

Belgium

Ballet of the Twentieth Century at the Coliseum

Having been to the ballet every night for six weeks I am becoming something of an expert; and I can definitely assert that 1971 is a kind of *annus mirabilis*. I mean it's rather extraordinary that Rambert's Morrice should come up with *That is the Show*, that Tetley should give us his *Field Figures*, that Béjart should be such a revelation, that we should have Drew's *St. Thomas's Wake* and then Cauley's *Ante Room*.

Before I became an expert on ballet this month I had been slightly suspicious of Béjart—I mean all those clever ideas and the Ninth Symphony on ice and the ballet of popular protest—it was all hearsay anyway. Well, when the Ballet of the Twentieth Century opened at the Coliseum on Wednesday I was simply bowled over. Béjart's ideas *are* clever; his choreography is individual; his company is great.

In *Les Fleurs du Mal*, Baudelaire poems set by Debussy in a nacreous arabeardsleyesque setting by Joëlle Rouston and Roger Bernard, it is as if the six richest, sexiest and most beautiful people in the world formed an exclusive Sodom in the highest penthouse in Manhattan and, in an atmosphere of *ne plus ultra luxe, calme et volupté*, tried each other out for love. Man with woman, woman with woman, man with man. Nothing quite works out, of course, or for long; and you can't buy love with silver or gold. Dyane Gray-Cullert, a magical black girl who hovers among them, is somehow the symbol of the impossibility of love. She is the ' 'Tis-distance-lends-enchantment-to-the-view' girl, or Death or something. The tendrilly tangles of the lovely unlovers are superb Béjartistry.

As I never read programmes until afterwards, being too blind anyway, I was totally taken aback by Béjart's *Firebird*, wondering why the Princesses hadn't come on, etc., when I suddenly realized that he had scrapped the Russian fairy-tale altogether and, to one of Stravinsky's short suites, arranged a ballet about the spirit of revolution enflaming the workers. Musically, this was bound to involve a bit of cheating, but theatrically and politically it was a knock-out, and with Bortoluzzi as the Bird of Freedom we were uplifted and swam delirious in outer space.

13.6.71

At the Coliseum Béjart has continued to astonish and delight. He is one of the most interesting creators in the world of ballet today. He has put his stamp—his *griffe*—on the Ballet of the Twentieth Century. When a choreographer with a mind and original ideas of movement is able to make of his company one instrument—one weapon—perfectly suited to his purpose, then there is nothing left to ask.

I do not like everything Béjart does. But choreographers who are the artistic directors of their own companies have to make concessions, take chances, stick their necks out, play for safety, find an outlet for the odd man out.

So Béjart, who, like Dr. Johnson, loves the man in the street, the Common Reader, and aims to enhance his life—which is perhaps the noblest aspiration of the greatest artists, Shakespeare, Victor Hugo, Bach or Berlioz—I had better not drag in Andy Warhol, pop as he is—cannot resist the showy *Bolero*, which comes so oddly from the fastidious pen of Ravel. Stunningly as Béjart presents it, with his girl writhing and stamping on her huge vermilion table, surrounded by nine million panting men, I cannot surrender.

Bach Sonata (no. 5 for violin and harpsichord) must, I guess, have been invented as a vehicle for Suzanne Farrell, and it does not quite work. For one thing, though Farrell may have the most fantastic extension (90 degrees) she is a pussy-cat and she does not fit into Béjart's company. That strong and beautiful battalion are committed creatures: they expect to bleed and sweat and give birth and die. But pussy-cats are never committed. They may be as beautiful as Nefertiti, with the stamina of Nell Gwynn, but they only follow armies to have their heads scratched or for cream. Lovely Farrell's Balanchinean beatitudes contrasting with the eccentric movements of her partner Jorge Donn, seem un-Béjartistic.

But oh! the splendour of Béjart's other Bach ballet, *Actus Tragicus*! I watched the first part, Cantata 106, standing at the back of the Upper Circle, then, thinking it was over, got lumbered with standing at the back of the stalls until flung out, bleeding and naked, to *listen* to the rest from the bar. But I saw enough to recognize an epic told in bare classical style, printed in black and white, sung to reach the ears of angels.

The Jerk, to raucous modern music, was vivid. *Bhakti* was an extraordinary essay in which Bortoluzzi, Jorge Donn, Tania Bari, Daniel Lommel and marvellous Maina Gielgud led the explorers into strange territory.

20.6.71

Béjart's *Nijinsky, Clown of God* at the Coliseum

It is just as well that I am not the critic of a daily paper, because if I had had to write a piece immediately after the curtain fell on Béjart's *Nijinsky, Clown of God* at the Coliseum on Wednesday I am sure I should have used cruel words to revenge myself for the boredom and horror I had endured.

Now I have had time to recover my temper and to remember that I admire Maurice Béjart and—though I have only met him once—even feel a kind of love for him because of what he tries to do and because of the fire he obviously lights in his company. He sticks his neck out so far in the effort to make ballet a living thing rather than a genteel faded art-form for eunuchs of all sexes that naturally he runs the risk of sometimes having his head hacked off. Luckily the brave cat has at least nine lives. But this time it is chop-chop.

Nijinsky: rather a good subject for a play, film or ballet. The trouble starts when you begin to introduce the necessary conflict—Diaghilev *versus* Romola: then vulgarity looms. Homo or hetero, art or a baby? Mme. Romola, whose spirit, energy and charm I much applaud, began it herself in 1933. You'd be surprised how many people write to say how much nicer and nobler she appeared in my recent book than in her own. This was because she over-dramatized—as Béjart does. And of course the other obvious pitfall is to present Nijinsky—as perhaps he himself did in his 'Diary'—as the martyred Christ. This Béjart does.

There is not just one crucifixion, there are two and a half. Everything has to be padded out. The admirable, inexhaustible Jorge Donn is only one of—how many?—incarnations of Nijinsky. Each is attended by a clownish Doppelgänger. There are even two Diaghilevs, one a *papier-mâché* giant. Diaghilev is God and the Ballets Russes are the Garden of Eden, from which Nijinsky is expelled for getting married. I am not sure who the serpent is. Suzanne Farrell with her fabulous extension is the oddly Edwardian 'Girl in Pink'.

'I am both Man and God ... Nature is God ... I am nature' booms the voice. Intolerable. Pierre Henry's music is ping-pong-crash-woof-woof: this is intolerable, and the snatches of Tchaikovsky come as a relief. Some of the choreography may be fine, but it is swamped. To see the superb Paolo Bortoluzzi posing as a strip-cartoon version of the Spectre de la Rose and other dancers as the Golden Slave, the Faun and Petrushka is intolerable. Imagine a Pavlova-Sylphide poised daintily at the foot of the Cross. Can we ever watch *Les Sylphides* again? Béjart has even managed to bring Christianity into disrepute.

7.5.72

Béjart's *Golestan* at the Coliseum

If your idea of Heaven is to be surrounded by beautiful half-naked undulating boys as far as the eye can reach you missed your big chance if you did not see Maurice Béjart's *Golestan*, presented by his Ballet of the Twentieth Century at the Coliseum last week. In fact, his male *corps*, captained by the splendid and indefatigable Jorge Donn, was only 32, but where he recruited so many and such varied beauties, all with stunning bodies, I cannot guess.

I was amused that the critics of three daily papers I happened to read genteelly overlooked this side of the super-showman's super cabaret number lasting 90 minutes: because all the pseudo-philosophical palaver about old Iranian legends and the mystic heart of the Rose was clearly eyewash—though the Iranian band made attractive noises. I wondered how Béjart got away with it when he gave the work in Persepolis last year: but no doubt he knew his Persia.

The minor female element in this series of visions which tantalise a traveller in the desert (I felt sorry for the poor ragged posturing pretext of a hero, for nobody marked him) was represented by ladies in green tights with rose-pink headdresses, mask-like faces and stabbing points—the equivalent of the sadistic whipping girls of popular magazines with their ten-inch stiletto heels, and heirs of Balanchine's Siren in *The Prodigal Son*. These were led by impassive red-clad Suzanne Farrell as *the* Rose of Shiraz, who shimmied and stabbed with the rest of them, but kicked higher. As choreography—a free kind of classical—*Golestan* was not remarkable: as after-dinner entertainment it was first-rate. And Béjart, with all the wisdom of the Orient and of the Folies Bergère, had realized that the *Scheherazade de nos jours* must have a black-and-white setting.

14.4.74

Denmark

The Royal Danish Ballet at the Royal Theatre, Copenhagen

From the moment we steamed out of Liverpool Street the weather improved with dramatic—with balletic—suddenness: it was as if our departure from London had lifted a curse from the land. Invited by the Royal Danish Theatre, transported by the Danish Tourist Association, the seven of us are off to Copenhagen to see the famous and ancient ballet there.

Whether we are shown the best ballet first or not, our initial impressions of the company in Bournonville's *La Sylphide* are excellent. The chief difference between this version and the Gsovsky-Petit revival are: that the music is not by Schneizhöffer but by a Danish composer, Lövenskjold; that Gurn, the rival, is a comic character; that there is no big *pas de trois* to end the first act; and that here it is made clearer that the plot is motivated by James being rude to the witch. The music bears a family resemblance to the Paris score: there are the quotations from Scottish tunes and moments when one remembers *Giselle*. But whereas the French revival was a patched-up curiosity, this is an integrated and beautiful ballet, dramatically most moving. A first glimpse of Bournonville convinces one that he was a wonderful choreographer and makes one amazed that other countries have not borrowed his works. The first décor of the farmhouse interior is very like Serebriakoff's; the second of the forest is one of the prettiest I have ever seen. Modern designers have lost the art of inventing romantic woodland scenes: few of them having ever been out of doors, they produce a pastiche of a pastiche. This set is the real thing, and marvellously lit. In two ways the company proves superior to any I have seen. First, they have built up in two hundred years a tradition of expressive mime which is something new in my experience; and secondly, one senses a loving care for the minutest details of production which is seldom to be found even on the most illustrious stages in the world. We have no dancer in England or America who can act with he conviction of Poul Gnatt as the tormented James. The economy, placing and timing of his gestures are a delight to watch; and in lyrical passages there is a virile sweetness in his expression which I have not seen even in good French male dancers. Clearly, he is only one of a number of Danish dancers saturated in this grand tradition. As for Gerda Karstens as Madge, the witch, she is one of the most wonderful actresses I have ever seen. I recommend every dancer in the world to come to Denmark and learn from her performance. Margrethe Schanne is a charming Sylphide; I like Birthe Scharf's bewildered Effie and Larsen's foolish Gurn; and the *corps de ballet* dance with spirit. There are three clever effects. When the Sylphide runs into the fireplace she is instantaneously whisked up the chimney. When she is hidden by James's plaid on the armchair, the back of the chair comes away, allowing her to disappear most convincingly. At the end, her body floats marvellously up into the sky, cradled by two baby sylphs. This is lovely. I wish Cyril Beaumont could see it. . . .

It is fun to be faced with a ballet you have never seen before, and to have no programme to tell you what it is. In a formal garden with a temple on one side stands a small girl dressed as Cupid in a rose pink *tutu*. She is attended, fantastically, by priests in turbans and flowing robes. From the wings she beckons on in turn nine couples who execute dances in diverse styles. There are ancient Greeks, comic Quakers, Norwegian folk dancers, grotesque blackamoors, rickety Louis XVI aristocrats and others. I find this *divertissement* quite charming with its mixture of classical, character and folk dances. Gerda Karstens is very funny as the gawky old Quakeress. Finally Cupid has them all blindfolded and pairs them off with the wrong partners. There is a mild scrimmage at the end, with portly negresses clasping blond young demi-gods and half the party in full flight from the other half. I guess this uproarious charade to be a modern concoction; then I find on the programme that it is *Les Caprices du Cupidon et du Maître de Ballet* by Vincenzo Galeotti, who was director of the Royal Ballet in the eighteenth century. I have seen the oldest ballet in the European repertoire.

Harald Lander's *Qarrtsiluni* might be called the Scandinavian *Sacre du Printemps*. A community of Greenlanders crouch around on rocks waiting for the sun to rise after the long winter. One man executes a ritual dance, beating a drum, which continues at increasing speed throughout the ballet. At the end the sun rises and the whole crowd dances in exultation. With the exciting music of Knudåge Riisager, Lander's skilfully arranged mass movements and the remarkable marathon performance of Niels Björn Larsen, *Qarrtsiluni* is a moving experience.

It is bewildering to see how these Danes have got miming in them. Now I begin to realize what it means to keep an unbroken tradition: it means the continuous following of good examples. Margot Fonteyn, great dancer as she is, has never *seen* the way miming can be done in a part like Swanilda, so she cannot be expected to realize all its potentialities. I enjoy watching Inge Sand so much that I am wondering if I can possibly stay another week and see her dance *Coppélia* again. Some people here say that after seeing Margot Lander, Inge Sand seems a poor substitute. Maybe: but the important thing is that Sand saw Lander and has inherited the traditional business, to make of it what she can. It is the duty of every English dancer who contemplates the role of Swanilda to come here and see this eighteen-year-old girl and drink at the fountainhead of tradition. The water is purer here than in Paris, I think. Sand is criticized here for exaggerating the pathetic side of the first act, Swanilda's disappointment with Franz. Margot Lander was apparently gayer throughout. I do not find that anything Sand does oversteps the bounds of comedy. Her portrayal of the veering moods of love—jealousy, coquetry, tenderness and joy— is as touching in its inner truth as exhilarating in technical skill. Physically, she is minute, as light as a feather, with legs and feet as brittle as Venetian glass. She flies through the air as open as a pair of scissors and as swift as a boomerang. She has a pretty face and makes a perfect *soubrette*. This is her first big role.

Björnsson as Franz too has the audience hanging on every gesture. He has a charming personality, and could do well, I should think, in films. Rendered by him, the character becomes three-dimensional as never before: we see his charm, his good points and his weakness in such a way that we can clearly foresee the course his married life will follow with Swanilda. She will have her worries but be happy on the whole. Niels Björn Larsen's Coppélius in a wonderful make-up and drab old coat (beside which the appearance of our Covent Garden toymaker is as a Laura Knight to a Goya), is sinister as well as absurd; at times, like Malvolio, slightly pathetic. It is when one sees miming such as his that one realizes what a delicate piece of machinery comedy can be, incorporating elements which are not comic and reducing them to its own terms, uniting all by style. The small part of the Burgomaster is excellently played by Poul Vessel. In England there is a vacuum behind such beards: Vessel lives the part of the benign, friendly but slightly self-important farmer set in authority.

The second scene is somewhat different from what we see in England, the third almost entirely different. When Coppélius works his magic on the false Coppélia, he does not here impart to her successively the attributes of motion, sight and human feeling. These are more mixed up, and I miss the moving moment when her soul is born to singing violins. There is a fine climax to this scene, though, with Coppélius lying in despair and all the clockwork dolls working around him. These dolls are a fantastic lot, ingeniously devised. In the third scene we lose the futile Dance of the Hours, Prayer etc. and have nothing but Hungarian character dances, a *pas de deux* and a solo for Swanilda. The company do their stylized folk dances with a peasant vigour which is inconceivable in England. The dresses are very pretty, but the set, though absolutely in keeping, could be more distinguished. Delibes' adorable music is conducted with great gusto by Johan Hye-Knudsen. This is really what a ballet should be. I do not know when I have enjoyed anything so much.

Tonight there are fireworks let off in Tivoli gardens by little boy sailors. Some of the rockets and revolving machine-guns of flame are so noisy and dazzling that the crowd of beautiful blonds of every sex flee in terror. An apocalyptic sight—the destruction of Sodom.

Now, at last, *Napoli*, most famous of Bournonville's ballets! The great man had the idea in the stage-coach crossing France on his return from Italy, and sketched out the scenario on the Channel packet. As the ballet had to be finished in a few weeks he entrusted the composition of the music to four separate composers, one of whom was the *chef d'orchestre* and the others equally connected with the theatre. The ballet is in three acts: the action takes place in Naples at the beginning of the last century. On the quay of Santa Lucia, with the Castell dell'Uovo jutting into the sea in the middle distance and Vesuvius lying behind, Teresina, a peasant girl, is courted by two unattractive but eligible suitors, Giacomo, a macaroni merchant, and Peppo, who sells lemonade. Her mother encourages these prosperous candidates, but Teresina prefers the poor fisherman Gennaro, whose boat comes in with a haul of fish. Before these go to market, an offering is made to the Madonna through the monk Fra Ambrosio. After dark, Teresina evades her mother and goes rowing with Gennaro on the gulf. The gaieties of Neapolitan night-life are interrupted by a thunderstorm, which empties the street. Presently Gennaro's boat drifts ashore, occupied solely by its unconscious owner. When he revives he explains that his beloved has lost her life in the storm. He is reviled by the townspeople and cursed by Veronica, the mother of Teresina. Only Fra Ambrosio takes pity on him, as he finds him alone at prayer, and, giving him a miraculous picture of the Madonna, sends him out to sea once more to find Teresina. The second act shows the interior of the Blue Grotto at Capri. Naiads disport themselves around their master Golfo, the sea sprite. Teresina's body is brought in and she is transformed into a Naiad. Gennaro rows his boat into the cave and overcomes the magic of Golfo by his sacred picture. Human once more, Teresina is restored to him with a dowry of jewels, and they row home. The last act is devoted to merry-making and dancing the tarantella at Monte Vergine; and the lovers are happily betrothed.

Napoli is a splendid example of those long ballets of the Romantic period, rich in characterization and local colour, crammed with spectacular and picturesque effects. Would that we saw more of them! The scenario gives scope for every kind of dancing—for classical *pas de deux*, for character numbers and big *ensembles*. There are several small parts which demand skill in mime. The décors are varied and delightful: the dresses charming in their detail and historical accuracy. I like Börge Ralov much better in the role of the fisherman than as the Prince in *Giselle*. It is a part he has danced many times with the great Margot Lander. Kirsten Ralov is a lively and attractive Teresina. The comic suitors are played with rich gusto by Svend Karlog and Niels Björn Larsen: one can almost smell them. Aage Eibye mimes the singing of a fruity street-tenor most amusingly, accompanied by a solo trumpet. As Veronica, the mother, Gerda Karstens is a shrewd, masterful middle-aged peasant-woman, most realistic in her alternating moods of good humour and intransigence. When dusk falls in the first scene a thin plume of fire can be seen rising from the crater of Vesuvius, just as I remember it. There is little dancing in the grotto scene, but I would not have missed it for the world. The receding arches of blue rock are in the lost style of romantic scene-painting, and the little glimpse of sea and sky through the aperture at the back is enchanting. Gennaro's boat is steered through the cave-mouth and forward almost to the footlights in the most remarkable way; and the metamorphosis of Teresina happens with a speed which is uncanny. The last act, of course, is the finest part of the ballet. The *pas de six* and various tarantellas work up to a frenzied finale, when the lovers and Mamma are drawn on in a gaily painted cart to acknowledge the cheers of the crowd.

We are shown round the Danish Theatre Museum, which is in the little Court Theatre at the Christiansborg Palace.

It is strange today, when we have just read of the award of a C.B.E. to Margot Fonteyn, to be shown the first decoration ever bestowed on a member of the once despised theatrical profession. Neither Garrick nor Talma was given official recognition; and it fell to a Danish king to be the first to honour an actor, namely H. C. Knudsen who received the cross of Dannebrog in 1809. He worked as a ferryman during the summer and during the winter played in the Royal Theatre. His award was a result of patriotic demonstrations during the war against England! Mr. Neiiendam, the Curator and author of a book on the museum, tells us this and much more besides.

Believe it or not. There is living in Denmark today the ninety-year-old Hans Beck, who, more than anyone else, has been responsible for keeping alive the old ballets of Bournonville. Beck made his début as a dancer at the Royal Theatre on 30th November, 1879, two days before his teacher Bournonville died: and Bournonville was the pupil of Vestris!

Beck was apparently a splendid dancer, handsome and virile. There are many photographs of him in this museum, in *Napoli* and other works. Bournonville said of him: 'For his sake I could almost go back and work in the theatre again: his abilities are so remarkable.' Beck is a living text-book of Bournonville choreography. He remembers by heart solos he danced and taught half a century ago. In his memoirs, published in 1944, he wrote: 'It is with me as with old cavalry horses. As soon as they hear the bugle they know what to do. When I hear the music in a ballet class my feet want to perform the old well-known steps.'

Ballet, Vol. 11, No. 2, July 1951 (extracts from a much longer *Diary*)

The Royal Danish Ballet at Covent Garden

At last, after two centuries, the Royal Danish Ballet have sallied forth from Scandinavia and advanced as conquerors on London. I am delighted to see them enjoying the triumph I prophesied on first sight of them in Copenhagen two springs ago.

For what is this famous and ancient company particularly notable? For the wonderful ballets of August Bournonville, unknown outside Denmark; for splendid male dancers; for vital and expressive mime; for character dancing; and for the vigour and devotion of a well-disciplined *corps de ballet*. These treasures were all revealed to an English audience when Bournonville's *La Sylphide* was given in the opening programme. *La Sylphide*, copied from Taglioni's Paris version of 1832, but with new music by Lövenskjold and new choreography, has remained unchanged since its first production in 1836; and it is a gem of the Romantic period. There is an allegorical beauty in the story of a Scotsman who forsakes his bride for a wood-spirit, and, when she proves intangible, seeks to bind her to him with a magic scarf woven by an unfriendly witch, only to succeed in breaking off her wings and destroying her.

Margrethe Schanne is a light, delicate and whimsical sylph: no tragic heroine, but, more appropriately, a pathetic, capricious, devoted creature, loving as a butterfly might. As James, the kilted hero, Erik Bruhn gives a most moving performance, besides proving himself one of the very finest male dancers in the world. His elevation and aristocratic ease in the curious backward leaping movements of his solo are quite enchanting. Ever since I first saw Gerda Karstens as the Witch I have thought her a superb and thrilling actress: her cringing before physical threats, her possession by evil powers, her guile and her gloating exultation over the ruined James are conveyed with absolute mastery. How effective is the Scottish *ensemble* of Act I, in which children join! How poetic an atmosphere the two old sets create! A perfect ballet.

The first programme was completed with Galeotti's *Whims of Cupid and the Ballet Master* (1786), an amusing romp, the oldest extant ballet, and *Qarrtsiluni*, by Harald Lander (1942), which shows Greenlanders awaiting the sunrise after their long winter.

Coppélia was the chief feature of the second programme—but a changed *Coppélia*, a character *Coppélia*, a *Coppélia* such as London has never seen before. All the classical dancing is left out, and Swanilda is the only one in ballet shoes. Certainly I miss the dance of six girls in the first act, and to a lesser extent the final *divertissement*. We gain in compensation a feast of exciting character dances, joyfully performed. These are as gay and natural as improvizations, while the demeanour of the seated peasants, who watch them, is itself a happy sight. Inge Sand, as Swanilda, shows herself a subtle comedy actress, ranging through pathos, tenderness, coquetry and rapture; while Fredbjörn Björnsson is more charming, more vivid and more real a Franz than any we have seen. Niels Björn Larsen, who plays Coppélius, is another of the company's extraordinarily gifted mimes: his portrait is mysterious as well as absurd. Poul Vessel's Burgomaster is also a sketch from the life; and indeed every dancer on the stage seems to contribute to the vitality of the production.

Observer, 16.8.53

The Royal Danish Ballet at Covent Garden

Seventeen years ago the directors of the Royal Theatre, Copenhagen, invited seven English critics to see their ballet, which until then had been a well-kept national secret, and to report their reactions to it. We were all bowled over as much by the treasures of Bournonville choreography surviving from the Romantic period as by the extraordinary vitality of the company.

I devoted a whole number of the magazine *Ballet* to the Royal Danes, and wrote 'The Danish *corps de ballet* is equal to the best I have seen and their productions are more carefully staged than anywhere in the world; but what has pleased me most is to find that the ancient art of mime, which I had thought dead, is alive and kicking at the Royal Theatre.' We were particularly amazed at the brilliance of the male dancers.

Now that they are back at Covent Garden, it is clear that all the above comments still apply. Bournonville is still remarkable and still lovingly staged; details of production are incomparably perfect; the mime is marvellous and integral; the men are splendid. In addition to this we can now say that the Danes are extending their frontiers in choreography and technique, and that the girls are better than ever before.

Bournonville's *La Sylphide* is the Dane's nostalgic version of the Italian Filippo Taglioni's Paris production of a ballet based on the Frenchman Charles Nodier's romantic dream of Gothic elf-haunted Scotland. Watching it we breathe the dank mists and endure the hopeless loves of the eighteen-thirties and forties. Even Lövenskjold's commonplace music, occasionally enlivened by a reminiscence of Schneizhöffer's Paris score, by a snatch of (it sounds like) 'Coming thru' the rye' or by a genuine strathspey, *takes us back.*

The action is admirably worked out. There is local colour from Walter Scott, and the mixture of comedy with drama illustrates the Romantics' veneration for Shakespeare. Realism and fantasy are subtly mingled and alternated, just as conventional 'sign language' mime is combined with 'acting' mime and both flow naturally into passages of dancing.

Henning Kronstam is quite extraordinary as James, the Highlander torn between a mortal and a fairy love. He is noble, virile and real—a credible young laird, whose youthful vigour is not untinged by Puritanical rigidity, and whom an impossible love takes by surprise. He also dances superbly. As Effie, his bride-to-be, Arlette Weinreich too is a living, attractive personality, and when she is abandoned for the sylph and gives herself impulsively to the despised Gurn, she makes us accept the improbability. Flemming Halby's Gurn is a delightful creation, jealous and funny without ever being grotesque.

Anna Laerkesen as the Sylphide, with her light leaps and arrested, coquettish poses, embodies our ideas of Marie Taglioni and seems to have flitted off an old music title-page by Brandard or Chalon. As the Witch, whose rejection by James and whose weaving of the magic scarf brings about the tragedy, Niels Björn Larsen is—but I have run out of adjectives. His miming is so plausible and yet potent and terrifying, that I can only say as I said seventeen years ago about Gerda Karstens in the same role, that we have nothing like it in England. The Danish tradition of mime is passed on: it lives.

Flemming Flindt, the company's director and choreographer, seems to have a Romantic line of his own—the macabre. We remember *The Lesson* (after Ionesco). Now he gives us his version of Bartok's *Miraculous Mandarin*. For Vivi Gelker as the Girl who lures men to be beaten up and robbed he has invented some strange acrobatics: the gang of three men mould her into sinister passive contortions as if she were some tool of their whim. Flindt's own entry as the Mandarin is marked by a series of sudden alarming drops on one knee. The ballet contains striking images.

The last act of Bournonville's *Napoli*, a ballet which was the fruit of a year's exile in Italy, has for a background a bridge of Roman brickwork, from the top of which chidlren look down, and under which we see Vesuvius across the blue bay. This is a festival, with tambourines and tarantellas, with laughter, rivalry and fabulous feats of dancing; and if we sometimes think perhaps there are one or two tarantellas too many and begin to envy the spectators of the *divertissement* their bottles of wine, it is nevertheless very exhilarating and dazzlingly led by Solveig Ostergaard and Niels Kehlet.

The latter's smile and jumps won an ovation. And there was Aage Poulsen who danced very much as I imagine the young Nijinsky. But they were all delightful, and it was an evening to remember.

5.5.68

The Royal Danish Ballet at the Royal Theatre, Copenhagen

I had not been back to Denmark since I attended the very first spring festival of the Royal Danish Ballet in 1951. Copenhagen was again blooming with lilac and laburnum, and ships came and went to the quayside; but now it was a Queen with two children who sat in the Royal box, and girls in the parks exposed their bosoms insouciantly to the sun.

In 1951 Harald Lander ruled. It was he who showed our party of critics (who felt like Arctic explorers) the unguessed riches of the Bournonville repertory, the excellence of Danish male dancers, the company's care for detail and their skilful mime. I beckoned the Danes out to Edinburgh and London. They triumphed here and in New York. Danish dancers—such as Peter Martins and Peter Schaufuss (who appeared this season in Lander's *Etudes*)—are in demand throughout the world. With Beaumont, John Martin and Edwin Denby retired from regular journalism, *Berlingske Tidende*'s Svend Kragh-Jacobsen is *doyen* of the world's ballet critics.

Erik Bruhn was the star in 1951. He made an international reputation and has now turned to acting. His successor, Henning Kronstam, now excels in character roles. *His* successor, Flemming Flindt, now directs the company, and only danced once while I was there. His wife, Vivi Flindt, a dancer of wide range and forceful personality, is the ballerina. The girls are better than before; the men are as good as ever, and I guess that the little, whizzing, Puckish Niels Kehlet is the most popular dancer.

Vera Volkova has been teaching for 20 years in the school, but the problem of how to mix the Russian style and the Bournonville tradition can never be entirely solved; and to dance Bournonville's ballets in a Russian way would be like painting Longhis with the brush of Rubens.

10.6.73

The Royal Danish Ballet at the Coliseum

I am an old enough friend of the Royal Danish Ballet, who have just completed a week's season at the Coliseum, not to have to be polite. Whoever decided on their first programme ought to have his head seen to. To give us *La Sylphide*, the Bournonville ballet we know best—not only from the Danes' previous seasons in this country, but from performances by other companies—followed by Lander's *Etudes*, which Festival Ballet has rammed down our throat over the years, is playing safe to the point of pusillanimity.

Apart from anything else, the juxtaposition of these two ballets adds up to an evening of lousy music. When perfectly cast and produced, with the famous Danish eye for detail, *La Sylphide* can still seem like a delightful flashback to the Romantic 1830s, a proof of how Walter Scott plunged the whole of Europe into a Celtic dream.

This week three of the four principal characters were miscast. Anna Laerkesen is not sylphlike, particularly in her lower limbs, and she lands heavily. I have seen such simple, noble Jameses over twenty years, Poul Gnatt, Erik Bruhn, Henning Kronstam and the company's present artistic director, Flemming Flindt. Flemming Ryberg was clearly cast as the kilted Scottish hero because of his nimble feet and dazzling *batterie* (almost too rapid for the human eye in dim lighting): but he is short and has no presence. Pretty Eva Kloborg is only miscast in the sense of being too tall

W

for him. Lizzie Rode's Witch is potent and wonderful. When a cast of *La Sylphide* does not impose itself all the pretty *ballabili*, so neatly rehearsed, go for nothing; the magical effects and the proliferation of varied tribesmen and tartans under one roof appear comic.

Whatever I wrote in 1951 about *Etudes*, my present feelings were perfectly expressed by the nine-year-old son of a Coliseum official, who said 'Mummy, what are they doing?' He was answered 'The music is piano exercises and they are doing ballet exercises to them.' 'Yes, but Mummy, why are they doing them *now*?'

Of the two soloists who compete in brilliant steps around the stylish ballerina, Mette Honningen, the irresistibly smiling Niels Kehlet had a bad foot, so that at every whizzing series of turns and every daring leap, I flinched. His soaring competitor, Peter Schaufuss, was thus able to score slightly over him, despite an habitual Agony-in-the-Garden expression.

A number of recent ballets have made clear to us what the end of the world is going to be like. There will be plague, we are going to have difficulty in breathing, and to St. John's 'stars fall from heaven, men hide in holes', we can confidently add 'newspapers blow over the face of the earth'. Flemming Flindt's *Triumph of Death*, subsidized by Royal danegeld, is far the most elaborate apocalypse to date—towers of scaffolding, showers of stars, decibels of sound, tumbrils of plague victims, cages of prisoners, whole editions of the *Berlingske Tidende*.

A tremendous effort, whose most memorable scenes are the prisoners turned monkeys to scare their fascist jailer, the slow death of a beautifully tragic old couple, Kjeld Noack and Lillian Jensen, an orgy of naked greyhound girls in a dress shop, and the choreographer himself, stripped nude to be sprayed with pink disinfectant, Flemming the Divine, a candidate well endowed for streaking.

7·4·74

West Germany

Stuttgart State Theatre Ballet at Covent Garden

On the afternoon of 23rd May, last year, I came out from watching a rehearsal at New York State Theater into a downpour of rain. I got a taxi on Broadway, and had hardly banged the door shut when I saw John Cranko sheltering in a doorway; so I gave him a lift to his hotel on Central Park West. His Stuttgart Ballet were appearing at the Met. and I would have given anything to have been able to tell him I liked his *Onegin*, which I had seen the night before, but I couldn't.

It was with *Onegin* that the Stuttgart Ballet opened their first London season at a gala at Covent Garden on Wednesday and received acclaim. I then found it a really very successful achievement, admirably danced by the splendid company Cranko had created: but it was too late to tell him so, for, as everyone knows, the dear man died on his way back to Germany a month after I last saw him.

Admittedly, I do not like three-act story ballets, and admittedly there is something absurd about piecing together a patchwork of Tchaikovsky compositions to make a ballet on a Pushkin narrative poem the composer had already turned into an opera. Admittedly I did not see Marcia Haydée dance Tatiana in New York, and admittedly the company were dancing all out on Wednesday to prove how good they were and what a great man their beloved Cranko was. Well, they succeeded.

Cranko had a remarkable fluency of invention in the classical style, he was very clever at telling a story in dancing, and he had a marvellous sense of theatre. *Onegin* sweeps one along. And Haydée, who is an actress with Fonteyn's pathos and power, turns the whole thing into a masterpiece. By the time we arrive at Tatiana's rejection of Onegin to the *Francesca da Rimini* music we feel we have seen a romantic drama as thrilling as *La Dame aux Camélias* or *La Traviata*. I think Heinz Clauss is a bit stiff and unByronic as Onegin, but Egon Madsen's Lensky is a delight, the small parts are beautifully done and the company really surge into action to Kurt-Heinz Stolze's clever arrangement of Tchaikovsky.

On Friday a triple bill. In *Brouillards* to Debussy on solo piano, Cranko shows many sides of his talent: I liked best the whimsical Feuilles Mortes with Jean Allenby and Jan Stripling, and the grotesque Cake Walk. *Traces,* to the Adagio of Mahler's 10th Symphony, is a dramatic work about a girl haunted by her memories of life in a concentration camp: Haydée's performance and the staging by Jurgen Rose both made a strong impression.

I think *Initials R.B.M.E.* is the best ballet of Cranko's I have ever seen. This celebration of his friendship with Richard (Cragun), Birgit (Keil), Marcia (Haydée) and Egon (Madsen), danced by them to Brahms's Piano Concerto op. 83, with the backing of the whole dynamic company, is like a paean. Cragun's glorious *pirouettes* alone would have been worth travelling to Stuttgart to see, which, alas!, I never did in John's lifetime.

4.8.74

Stuttgart State Theatre Ballet at Covent Garden

How thrilled Poulenc would have been—he was such a nice man, though greedy and terrified of birds—with *Voluntaries,* the ballet Glen Tetley has made to his Concerto for Organ, Strings and Percussion, which the Stuttgart Ballet gave at Covent Garden on Thursday! And what an extraordinary stroke of luck for Stuttgart to have got Tetley as a successor to Cranko! Luck? I suppose what actually happened was that Marcia Haydée fell on her knees, with streaming eyes and hair, before a conclave of ruthless Town Councillors, while Richard Cragun strode up and down outside the Rathaus, cracking a whip.

Tetley's strenuous style of choreography, a blend of classical and modern, will be a complete contrast to Cranko's easier manner, and I can think of no one more likely to fortify this German company, which is already among the world's best. One of many incredible moments in his mainly classical ballet to Poulenc's very strange composition was when Haydée, poised *en attitude* in a silence when the organ stopped, leapt backwards into Cragun's arms and was lifted in the same position precisely as the strings burst in.

Cranko's Mozart *Concerto for Flute and Harp* was a very pretty white ballet, with some musical felicities; and in his Stravinsky *Jeu de Cartes,* wittily danced by all, Egon Madsen's Joker made me realize what Nijinsky must have been like in *Till Eulenspiegel.*

Stolze failed in his score for Cranko's *Taming of the Shrew* to do with Scarlatti what he had done with Tchaikovsky in *Onegin.* Even so, this does not justify the critic of *The Times*'s describing the divine Neapolitan's harpsichord music as 'trivial tinklings'. When I read this phrase I thought there must be some mistake. Nor was Cranko happy in his choice of designer for the two-act version of Shakespeare's play, for Elisabeth Dalton's architecture and colour schemes are dismal indeed. Yet his comic invention and the talents of his two stars rose above all setbacks, and on the Monday *The Shrew* brought down the house. Who—except perhaps Jerome Robbins—could have created so funny and effective a solo as that of Petruchio, and who else could have devised a way of making Shakespeare's farcical plot human and acceptable? Well, I will swim the Rhine to see Haydée and Cragun knocking each other about any day.

4.8.74

Holland

Nederlands Dans Theater at Sadler's Wells

Ballet first turned me on at Liverpool Street Station when I was sixteen. I had never heard of it before and here on Smith's stall was this book-jacket of a man dressed absurdly in rose-petals, standing on one leg with curly hands. Cut.

Spring, 1968, a little house on the edge of a cliff in California. And Mme. Bronislava Nijinska is saying: 'I was shocked when I saw how commonplace the *pas de deux* was that Fokine was arranging. It was my brother who made it into something.' By deforming the classical *port de bras*, by turning his arms into coiled *art nouveau* tendrils of convolvulus and his hands into snails and by emitting—if you'll pardon my English—a kind of perfumed gaze, Nijinsky created this magical sexless creature of unknown species to drift round dreaming Karsavina.

The point is that if the book-jacket had shown a bloke doing straightforward classical *port de bras* I might never have been hooked and the world would be a better place.

Port de bras is what I am on about, that part of the geometry of classical ballet which seems most mannered and artificial and which most distinguishes it from other forms of dance. Watching the *port de bras* of the Dutch dancers in *Recital for cello* (Bach) at Sadler's Wells on Friday I thought that if ballet dancers cannot make their conventional arm movements *mean* something by adding to them the expression of their eyes, they had much better drop the whole artificial business and hop about with hanging hands, winking.

Sorry to start on a sour note when writing about Nederlands Dans Theater, a company whom my simple-minded painter friend assumes to be permanently on tour, just because he saw them getting into a coach once on television. They are certainly hard workers.

Their opening programme was badly planned: we had to wait a long time for anything to happen. Van Manen's *Metaphors* is rather a nothing.

Solo for Voice 1 is a much more interesting van Manen duet, danced by Susan Kennif and Hans Knill to the accompaniment of an alarming black-velvet-clad soprano Death-lady with a mike, who sings and mutters non-sense by John Cage in several languages (but I spotted a line of Goethe—boast!) and drives the coiling white-clad lovers to death. Fine!

Tetley's *Mythical Hunters* was the first of two ballets with which he stole the season. Its title for once describes it exactly. Gleaming visions of the chase.

The most stunning piece was Tetley's all-male *Arena* to a thrilling electronic score by Morton Subotnik. All the world's a stage, or an arena —or a steam-bath in Greenwich village. The drinking fountain which bubbles coolly on the right gives that away. In between having beautiful sex the naked boys sit on tubular steel chairs, looking tiredly, boredly, interestedly or expectantly around. All life is here, as they say in the Sunday papers. *Plus vrai que le vrai,* as Cocteau said. Don't miss it.

20.4.69

Nouvelles Aventures was the first ballet we have seen by the company's leading dancer, possessed, prognathous Jaap Flier, and a lot of people tittered and jeered at it, and I nearly lost my temper and hit them. It *was* new and it *was* an adventure, and György Ligeti's score for three singers and seven instruments was full of wonderful twangs and whispers and jibbering and cracked trumpetings and crashes and silence.

The dancers stared at us and slept and crawled about and evoked pity and terror, which is what tragedy is supposed to be about, and even if sacks came down from the sky at the end and the kids got into them, which may or may not have been the equivalent of Charlie Bubbles's escapist balloon, this work was no laughing matter, and I was thrilled and purged.

The Anatomy Lesson, which we saw two years ago, is yet another splendid creation of Glen Tetley's, to add to his season's score—*Mythical Hunters, Circles, Sargarsso, Arena,* all stunning.

This too is a tragedy, with the brief joys of childhood, mother's love, wife's love and love of the beautiful world contrasted with the silence of the mortuary slab. Jaap Flier, as the corpse whose moments of earlier happiness are conjured up, gave a performance whose power it would be impossible not to applaud.

The Dutch have been a shot in the arm. Alas that the Royal Ballet's bigger company, now in New York, could not be here to steal some ideas from them.

4.5.69

Nederlands Dans Theater at the Lyceum, Edinburgh

One reason that Nederlands Dans Theater are a good company to invite
to the Edinburgh Festival is that they have an adventurous taste in music.
In their first programme, seen at the Lyceum on Thursday, all four works
had unpredictable scores which were worthily performed by the Nether-
lands Ballet Orchestra under Jan Stulen and by various soloists.

The paradox is that in Edinburgh dance companies attract a large local
audience, and the ladies hungry for a feast of dying swan and sugar plum
who arrived with their bairns breathless from Morningside must get a
shock when they behold the stark antics of the Dutch, danced to this far-
from-mindless music on the barest of stages. Not a swan in sight, not a
waltz within hearing.

I must say they took it manfully and the house was almost full. There
were a few titters at the spasmodic squawks and growls of the baritone
and two sopranos in Ligeti's exciting *Nouvelles Aventures*, but not from
the four-year-old girl next to me, who sat enraptured by Jaap Flier's ballet
to this music and clapped joyfully when everyone got into sacks and was
hoisted aloft at the end.

In this programme the choreography was not up to the music. There
was a certain aimlessness and straining for effect. When characterization
is abolished and costume reduced to the abstract uniform of all-over tights,
a ballet can only be about young people being young people, gaily or
grimly, probably erotically; and however prettily they tangle or tumble or
drag each other about, the work will depend utterly on the choreographer's
invention—on whether he can spin something beautiful in a new way.
Neither Flier in *Nouvelles Aventures* nor Hans van Manen in *Squares* to a
melancholy piano piece by Szilassy, with its frame of neon light by Bonies,
quite passed the test.

Even the great Glen Tetley showed signs of strain in his *Imaginary Film*
to Schoenberg's music of that name and to his Five Pieces for Orchestra.
Here there was a suggestion of drama, and pistols, and a benevolent ape-
man and a line-up of high-kicking Rockettes and a lady on skates who I
think was Death. But it looked to me as if this work had set out to be a
parody and then sprouted pretensions.

6.9.70

HOLLAND 329

Nederlands Dans Theater at Sadler's Wells

I hope Glen Tetley, the co-author of *Mutations*, with which Nederlands Dans Theater opened their three-weeks season at Sadler's Wells on Monday, is not going to get into a rut of Martian as opposed to human choreography. He is very good as it, but I note a tendency to make ballets about people fighting for breath and survival in kinky armour to the music of the spheres.

The *human* choreography of *Mutations* is mostly confined to three interludes by Hans van Manen and it is on colour film and partly in slow motion. First a man alone, Gérard Lemaitre, then him in a duet with Anja Licher, then a trio of Lemaitre with Marian Sarstädt and Eric Hampton. These short films alternate with the Martian goings-on below, and at the end are shown simultaneously on three screens, while live dancers perform the same dances; and the movement in them is often beautiful.

Then, the dancers on film, who appear on stage in the finale, are naked. To those of us who have never seen a naked body before the difference between men and women is at once apparent. Women's pubic hair grows in a more implacable way. Apart from this, there is one feature which men have and women are without: in sculpture and painting it can be stylized, but in ballet apparently not. This is a pity for, after all, a dancer's training stylizes his body and renders it godlike; so if nothing can be done about that feature I think naked male dancers should wear artificial ones of ideal proportion.

The old theatre had never looked so handsome. Long white canvas banners trailed on the gleaming white stage and there was a forestage built out over the obsolescent orchestra pit, to which dancers advanced on a white ramp rising from the back of the stalls. At first, when to the factory clangour of Stockhausen Johan Meyer came slowly forward in articulated white armour, I had the sense of a mysterious quest into the unknown— a sort of Siegfried's Journey to the Ruhr—but successive waves of dancers in kinkissimo costumes, attached to life-lines, on high clogs, with breast-revealing windows in their all-over tights, bearing handfuls of blood with which to bedaub each other, confused the issue.

8.11.70

In response to overwhelming public demand an additional performance of *Mutations* and *Twice* will be given on Thursday, 19 November, at

2.30 p.m. The Nederlands Dans Theater are packing them in at Sadler's Wells. They are full of spirit and determined not to be dull. The danger I foresee for them is in their panicky almost Madison-Avenue search for gimmicks.

Last week we had nudity, film on multiple screens, strobe and neon lights. This week three out of the four ballets shown on Tuesday were gimmicky. In van Manen's *Situation* we have a windowless graph-papered cell with nothing but a digital clock which tells the real time and a door through which the dancers come and go, banging it maddeningly. The sound is bursts of gunfire, taps running, baths filling and emptying, rain, walking on gravel, etc. It's fun recognizing them. There are two tense confrontations of a man and a woman and a man and a man. What hell are we in? Does it mean anything? No. Because it ends unexpectedly with a man trying out on a staring girl four different kinds of funny walk. We laugh. So what were we worrying about?

15.11.70

Dutch National Ballet at Sadler's Wells

Monday was an extraordinary evening for at least three reasons. That Nureyev was appearing for the first time at Sadler's Wells (where I saw my first ballet before he was born); that he was dancing Balanchine's *Apollo* for the first time in England; and that he was dancing with a wonderful company, the Dutch National Ballet, which I had never seen before.

I have seen a lot of Apollos, from Eglevsky to Villella and Keith Rosson, but Nureyev beats the lot. Nobody has ever put so much into the role. To select one detail, an example of how he rethinks and revives the noble choreography: when he gathers the heads of the three Muses, one by one, on to his shoulder, his right hand is like a tremulous tentacle. He is so touchingly childlike at the beginning, as he gropes his way in an unfamiliar world; then, when he is possessed by the godhead and does that odd semaphore gesture, his soul 'like a star, Beacons from the abode where the eternal are.'

The Dutch Muses showed us, as the company had already done in Balanchine's *Four Temperaments* and would again on Tuesday in Balanchine's *Concerto Barocco*, that they were first-rate classical dancers from the aristocratic Balanchinean stable. But the Dutch National Ballet is not one of those big companies which aims to give an anthology of past masterpieces. It exists for the best possible reason, namely to be the instrument of a creative choreographer. In 1909 Diaghilev could not have had a ballet without Fokine: the Dutch have Rudi van Dantzig. And he has a spark of genius.

It was clear after two or three evenings that van Dantzig, like Webster, 'was much possessed by death, and saw the skull beneath the skin.' In his passionate, tragic *Monument for a Dead Boy*, which Nureyev also danced with Frans Gelderblom, Yvonne Vendrig, Ellen Brusse and Benjamin Feliksdal, and in the grim *Epitaph*, he has developed a style of movement which can appeal emotionally as well as give visual satisfaction. Even more than in these I thought van Dantzig showed the power of his choreographic imagination in *Moments*, which has no story. This is danced to Webern's *6 Bagatelles* and *5 Pieces* for string quartet. In turn single dancers follow the isolated curlicues of sound and freeze into astral shapes. Among its six superb dancers is its designer, the tall, intense Toer van Schayk, who alternated with Nureyev in *Monument*.

The Dutch are lavish, using sometimes electronic music, sometimes a small string orchestra: but for their various *pas de deux*, of which Jack Carter's charming Romantic one showed off the brilliance of Sylvester Campbell best, they fill the pit with musicians.

7.12.69

Dutch National Ballet at Sadler's Wells

As the Dutch National Ballet had gone to the trouble and expense of bringing their own orchestra for their fortnight's season at Sadler's Wells it seemed a shame that they had to begin without it, their drums and double basses being held up at Harwich. Nevertheless, it was a triumphant opening.

Balanchine's *Episodes*, danced to three compositions of Webern and to his orchestration of a Bach Fugue, is one of the master's finest works; and the Dutch did justice to it. They are a more classically minded company than the Nederlands Dans Theater and we saw at once that they had soloists of style and personality.

Next came a new ballet by one of the troupe's two resident choreographers, Hans van Manen, and I thought it the best thing of his I had ever seen. *Adagio Hammerklavier* was danced to a recording by Christoph Eschenbach of the slow movement of Beethoven's Sonata op. 106. Although there was no décor but a black void and the three couples wore the simplest white costumes, and although van Manen mixed no eccentric movements with his noble classical choreography, he contrived to impart to his dancers a dreamlike strangeness, as if they were ghosts in a garden where time did not exist. Alexandra Radius and Han Ebbelaar, Monique Sand and Henny Jurriëns, Sonja Marchiolli and Francis Sinceretti were the happy ghosts.

The evening closed with Toer van Schayk's *Before, during and after the Party*, which was an expression of the choreographer's very sensible belief that 'our life on earth is a party on a sinking ship'. While waiting for the hostess, who turns out at last to be Cocteau's lady in white (and on stilts), Death, the guests desperately perform little formal dances, some of which are based on the ballet class. These are accompanied by commonplace old tunes on an on-stage piano, but jarring squawks on invisible strings are heard increasingly and finally the orchestra of doom takes over. This clever arrangement—or composition—was devised by Gilius van Bergeyk. The choreographer had designed the splendid set: a black room with a long picture window opening on a ridge of pink sculptured mountains lit from the side, reminiscent of Hockney's California.

24.3.74

At last a sixteen-minute *Daphnis and Chloë*! In his new version, presented by the Dutch National Ballet at Sadler's Wells, Hans van Manen has succeeded in doing what I bet Diaghilev would have loved to do. He has scrapped the long Fokine scenario with its pirates, its passage of time and its supernatural interventions and made a storyless ballet of the Second Suite. The original score was a symphonic poem from which Ravel would not let Diaghilev cut a bar: but the Suite, vividly played by the Dutch National Orchestra under André Presser, comprises all the lovely music of the third act and makes a perfect ballet on its own.

Van Manen has interpreted the dawn music as a rite of spring, with eight couples in ecstasy. The mime of Pan and Syrinx (which Ashton also turned into solos for the principals) is lighthearted competitive dances for Daphnis and Chloë (Han Ebbelaar and Alexandra Radius), with the hero carried aloft in mock triumph by his companions—as Lifar used to be in dead seriousness in all his ballets (never having got over *La Chatte*). The final Bacchanale, with its echoes of *Scheherezade*, ends in communal copulation. It is an inspired response to Ravel's finest passages of music. I also liked Jean-Paul Vroom's basic (almost pop) brown mountain outlined in rope, and the girls' rainbow mini-dresses.

Another celebrated score reinterpreted was Stravinsky's *Orpheus* by Rudi van Dantzig. Van Dantzig does not 'tell the story' as Stravinsky and

Balanchine plotted it, but gives us, so to speak, visions of the Artist and his Unattainable Ideal. A thrilling movement (never seen before) was Orpheus's throwing of the extended Eurydice backwards over his shoulders into the wings, which gave the impression that she was being snatched from him. Maria Aradi and Zoltan Peter were remarkable.

Toer van Schayk's *Pyrrhic Dances* to a percussive score by Geoffrey Grey has something of the ancient, heroic quality of Robbins's *Moves*. Van Schayk's portrayal of the Boy in van Dantzig's *Monument for a Dead Boy*, with his haunted face and tragic arms, was a matured marvel and one of the high-spots of this grand season.

31.3.74

Spain

Antonio and Rosario at the Cambridge

Only once or twice in a lifetime does one expect to see a dancer of the quality of Antonio, who, with his enchanting partner, Rosario, opened a season of Spanish dancing at the Cambridge Theatre on Thursday. That their first appearance in London has received so little attention from the Press seems, therefore, an excessive example of British reticence. It would be a pity if London theatregoers missed the chance of boasting to their grandchildren that they had seen the greatest male dancer of the day.

Some will find most pleasure in such impressionistic dances as *Triana*, to music of Albeniz, or Rosario's *Leyenda*, in which traditional steps and gestures are used in an original composition to evoke a mood of languorous and expectant yearning; others will respond immediately to the buoyant gaiety of the *Jota*; most will be astonished at the style and rococo perfection of the eighteenth-century *Bailes Boleros*, which incorporate so happily the *batterie* of classical ballet; all must be intoxicated by the controlled ecstasy with which the two dancers confront each other in *Seguidillas Gitanas*, seeming at moments the very martyrs of passion, together yet apart.

With what voluptuous hoarseness Rosario sings her little verses in the *Baile Flamenco*! With what grandeur she holds her body and controls her trailing skirt!

It has become a commonplace to say that Antonio's *Zapateado* is the greatest technical feat ever performed by a Spanish dancer. Watch the proud carriage of his neck and the concentrated fire of his eyes; mark the erect torso which seems to scorn the agitation of his lower limbs; then listen to the changing song of his feet—and marvel at the possibilities inherent in the human form.

Observer, 17.6.51

Ballet Espagnol of Pilar López at the Stoll

The severe and lambent classicism of Flamenco dancing, like that of the *adage* and *pas de deux* in ballet, renders the character of its exponents terribly transparent. Just as television reveals which politician is phoney and which isn't—if we didn't know already—so do these forms of dancing make it impossible for dancers to conceal their calibre, and to a certain extent their inner nature.

Watching the dancers of Pilar López at the Stoll, one gets to differentiate them. The handsome Mexican, Roberto Ximénez, is an effective and brilliant performer, with a tendency to be pleased with himself. Manolo Vargas, the other Mexican, far more sensitive, less emphatic, responding impulsively to gaiety and melancholy, has a thoughtful quality which diminishes his virility in Flamenco dancing. It was fascinating to see the other two men together in *Zapateado*. Alberto Lorca, half-Spanish, half-Dutch, was showy, with rolling hips, and eyes which sought to charm and hypnotize the audience. The Argentine Paco de Ronda had a simplicity and force which were more truly admirable.

Flamenco dancing is a ritual courtship: the man must be all man and the woman the quintessence of woman. Elvira Real is a lovely creature, provocative, proud and tender. Pilar López attains the *ne plus ultra* of style, so grandly stalking, so nobly leaning, curving and turning, so passionate, so restrained. What a man her partner must be, one feels, that this wise goddess should surrender to him!

Observer, 18.10.53

Luisillo's Spanish Dance Theatre at Golders Green

My introduction to Spanish dancing was in 1938 when Argentinita appeared for a few moments in a gala matinée at the Cambridge Theatre—on that same stage where in 1951 Peter Daubeny and I were able to persuade Antonio to make his London début. Was it a flamenco or a Goya number that Argentinita danced? She was no longer young, nor to my eyes beautiful, and by English standards she was well-covered, but she had only to incline her neck and flick her fan for me to see, with a shiver, a new world of ancient art opening before me. Spain!

Since the last war Elsa Brunelleschi, the chief teacher of Spanish dancing in this country, has taught many of us here to appreciate the dances of

Spain. In 1946 I asked her to write an article on 'Spanish Dancers in London'. After Diaghilev's *Cuadro flamenco* in 1921 and the appearance of Argentina and Argentinita in the thirties, all she could find to write about was a girl called Ana Nevada who played the castanets in an attractive ballet by Roland Petit called *Los Caprichos* for which Clavé did his first décor.

The position has changed now. We are familiar with the companies of Carmen Amaya, of Pilar López, of Antonio: we have seen troupes of folk-dancers, of flamenco dancers and of 'classical' Spanish dancers, and we have come to distinguish between them.

But something else has been happening. While we have been learning to enjoy the Spanish dance, some of the most intelligent Spanish dancers and choreographers have been growing dissatisfied with the limitations of their art and wanting to enlarge its boundaries.

The other day I went up to Golders Green to see Luisillo and his

Antonio in *Bulerias*. Drawings by Milein Cosman

Spanish Dance Theatre, who are doing a British tour and who were rapturously acclaimed. Afterwards I had a chance to talk to Luisillo about his problems and what he is trying to do.

Luisillo's company, with its score of dancers, its singers, guitarists and small orchestra, perform seven numbers. These are a 'symphonic' Sevillian piece to Turiña, a village scene leading up to Andalusian dancing, a Cordoba dance to Nin, a Galician village scene with softshoe dancing to bagpipes, a 1900 comedy number based on the street cries of Madrid, a tragedy called *La Espera* (Expectation) about a man condemned to death, and a flamenco café scene.

It is *La Espera* which seems the least predictable of these works, as well as the most significant of the way Luisillo's mind is working. Pilar López and Antonio have done Spanish 'ballets' before: Luisillo wants to give his drama a universal appeal. Like Peter Darrell with his *Prisoners*, like Béjart or Charrat or Robbins, he longs to deal with a contemporary subject— and to hell with local colour.

His problem is fundamental—and similar to that of Ram Gopal today, or even of Fokine in 1900.

22.5.60

Of all foreign dances that have come to England the Spanish are the most popular, and of all Spanish dance styles flamenco is the most elaborate, besides being the only one which offers the possibility of expressing emotion. But this possibility is limited. Our admiration for Antonio's steel spine and demonic footbeats, for the frenzy of Carmen Amaya in *bulerias*, for the swooping turns of Luisillo or for the magnificent curves of Pilar López's upraised arms cannot blind us to the fact that their art is not capable of expansion if it insists on remaining correct. To be a good *bailaor* is to excel others in technique, personality and style, but in the same old dances. Flamenco dancing is largely a business of rivalry and showing off: at best it may seem a splendid courtship of peacocks.

It is understandable today, therefore, when artists long to express their emotions and to express them in a new way, that Luisillo and other Spanish dancers (he is Mexican, actually) should yearn to break away from the old forms and *create* something.

What worries him, he was explaining to me the other evening, is whether, when he has discarded the more sensational and distinctive features of flamenco (and other regional dancing), there is anything left of a language of the Spanish dance to speak in. At the climax of a happy ballet is he obliged to execute a *jota*, such as that with which Massine rounded off *Le Tricorne*; and must all deep emotion be registered by fierce flamenco stamping? And will the public want to see him if he leaves this out?

Luisillo's dilemma, it seems to me, does not differ essentially from that of Fokine at the beginning of this century. It is the likeness of Luisillo's problem to Fokine's that gives me a clue to its solution.

Fokine rebelled against the artificialities of the old ballet, whose *entrechats* and *fouettés* no doubt seemed to him a dead end. He had to throw out all this baroque geometry before he could make *Les Sylphides*, *Scheherazade* and *Petrushka*.

This was a 'return to nature' like that of the Impressionist painters or that of Wordsworth and Coleridge, who discarded the personifications, nymphs, shepherds, gods and other trappings of the classical or baroque Olympus. Then Fokine started off from scratch and tried to tell a story (or project a mood) in the simplest, directest possible way.

It is true that Fokine and his dancers had the basic language of classical ballet to start from, even if they rejected many of its ornaments and conventions; but of Luisillo and most of his colleagues the same can be said. They have some classical and some 'free' dance training. They can jump, run, turn and raise an arm without falling down or getting out of breath. They have something to go on.

A 'return to nature' never did anyone any harm. I believe that if Luisillo or one of his compatriots tries to tell a story in a straightforward way, forgetting *zapateado* and all the ornate cadenzas of flamenco, he will manage very well. The glamorous feats of *bailaor* and *bailaora* will continue to crackle and explode in cave and *caffé*. When they can be of service to a broader art form they will be used again, like the *pirouettes* in Fokine's *Prince Igor*, and take their place quite naturally.

29.5.60

Antonio's Spanish Dance Company at the Royalty

The Royalty Theatre must be setting out to specialize in shows that only get going at about ten o'clock. Our evening with Zizi Jeanmaire began half an hour before the curtain fell: our evening with Antonio and his Spanish Ballet Company begins *after* the curtain has fallen, when a series of funny and exciting 'encores', which are skilfully planned improvizations, atone for all the pretentious nonsense that has gone before.

It is too late to regret the days when Antonio and Rosario danced alone on a stage all evening and held us under a spell. Antonio wanted a Spanish Ballet Company and he made one. 'Spanish Ballet was born', as he modestly states in an embarrassing programme note, deplorably translated.

Two drawbacks to having a Spanish Ballet Company are that you are going to ruin a lot of nice piano music by Granados and Albeniz by having it orchestrated for your indispensable orchestra, and that you will have to renounce to a large extent the solos and duets which are so characteristic of Spanish dancing in order to deploy your company in more spectacular formations. At the Royalty, Rosita Segovia is hardly allowed on stage at all without six fatalistic undertakers of extreme beauty and elegance following her up and down.

Antonio has some good dancers, but his *Variations on a Spanish Rapsody* [sic] to Albeniz is no more than what it sounds; while his *Jugando el Toro* a ballet about bullfighting which occupies the middle of the programme, is entirely ludicrous. Antonio as a youthful aspirant has to battle with a number of abstractions such as Vanity, Fortune, Fame and Fear, all dressed in very expensive mad carnival costumes with horns and feathers by Bernard Daydé, before arriving in the bull-ring. Then the stages of the *corrida* are enacted, and the victorious Antonio is borne in triumph, awarded an ear and acclaimed by the crowds.

There is something distasteful about this mummery, because, after all, bullfighting is a serious business, whether you like it or not. Cristobal Halffter's music is commonplace and Antonio's choreography rudimentary.

At last we get to the Flamenco, done in a set with hanging wheels crudely coped from Clavé's noble design for *Carmen*. Is Antonio as good as ever? The technique is still dazzling, but he seems to take the strain on his face, and in a serious dance like *Seguiriyas* scowls like a petulant martyr. Yet by the grotesque *Bulerias* we are quite won over. For Antonio is a clown of genius; and when he drags the members of his company—even the guitarists and the fat singer—into the middle of the stage and puts them through their paces one by one, we have such fun that we forgive him everything.

4.12.60

Antonio and Rosario at the Cambridge

The Cambridge Theatre at Seven Dials was full of memories when I went to see Antonio and Rosario on Monday night. It was fifteen years since the already famous 'Kids from Seville' made their English début there, with their singer and guitarists, presented by Peter Daubeny. And it was I who had *guaranteed* Peter that Antonio, with his flashing personality, his exuberant humour and his coruscating technique would be a sell-out. How worried we were when there were no notices in the (to us all-important) *Mail* and *Express* next day!

Time marches on. Spanish dancing became more and more popular in this country. Antonio became ANTONIO, then ANTONIO. Rosario left him, he enlarged his company, his repertory, his personality. We heard about his wealth, his estates in Spain. But on the stage, I thought, everything had got too inflated: beyond the big orchestra, beneath the bright sets, among the whirling girls, I looked in vain for the blooming of that mysterious flower. Then, when I wrote a bad notice about a new Antonio ballet I received a sharp rebuke, couched in the third person, on writing paper embossed with the insignia of the Order of Isabella the Catholic.

Was it a sign that Antonio knew something had gone wrong when he brought back for his last season at Drury Lane, and this season at the Cambridge, his old partner Rosario? And how extraordinary it was to see that *she*, though maturer, had remained the same—had perhaps improved —while Antonio's excess of personality, charm, glamour, star quality, sacred-monsterism and seeming self-fascination had eaten him up. Rosario's was the old, baffling, beckoning art of Spain, brought from the East, we are told, by gypsies. She was wonderful. But it was too late. Audiences were dropping off. The English were getting tired of Spanish dancing, of Flamenco. The Cambridge Theatre on Monday was not full.

In justice, Antonio's encores are still very good and funny. When he goes mad and clowns he is irresistible. His famous *Zapateado* with that feckless little circussy tune on the orchestra is still an amazing display of technique, and the stamping is pleasantly varied by a bit of striding around. It is in the 'big' solo numbers, *Baile por Mirabra* and *Martinete*, that the exaggerated yearning and grimacing become a strain. It may seem odd that at the orgasmic breaking points of the Flamenco dance, so much an art of excess (like Baroque painting and sculpture), we should demand an element of reserve, but I believe we have that right. Luckily in *Martinete* there was the face of a Caravaggesque angel, a basket-weaving boy seated at the side of the stage, impassive as the godlike punkah-wallah at the trial in Mr. Forster's *A Passage to India*, for the eye to rest on.

Rosario's *Caña*, placed after the show's opening number, i.e. danced cold, was nevertheless superb. Here was the ancient enigma, the everyday slang vibrant with heavenly messages, the priestess of the Love-Death, the glimpse down the well at noon.

20.3.66

Fiesta Gitana at Sadler's Wells

Just as we thought we never wanted to see—or hear—any flamenco dancing again, there arrives at Sadler's Wells a troupe which reminds us what the whole thing is all about. Their name, Fiesta Gitana, is slightly off-putting—there is something about the word Fiesta which suggests enforced heartiness as at an old-school get-together or jamboree—and we hasten rather slowly up from the country to see what they have to offer. And they are very good.

The first thing that strikes us about them is a sort of family feeling, as if they were used to working and entertaining together. This goes far to

Spanish dancers. Drawings by Ronald Wilson

abolish the gap between stage and audience—the inevitable chasm, both physical and psychological, of the orchestra pit. As we know, flamenco is an art of cabaret, and we should really all be sitting round the dancers, boozing and smoking. Only one of the dancers, Antonio el Camborio, seems not quite to belong; singing and dancing as he does with flamboyant energy, he nevertheless introduces a pop element—it is as if a poster had been hung among etchings. Then we find in our programmes that he is a guest artist.

The principal male singer, Naranjito de Triana, is remarkable, carrying off his marvellous shakes with a dignified reserve which earns our respect. The lady singer, Patro Soto, looks and sings charmingly too. Pedrito Sevilla is the chief of three guitarists, and I hope El Poeta is the one with long hair which curls up at the back.

In the dancing, *zapateado* is not spot-lighted as it is by Antonio at the Festival Hall: it takes its place along with the arm movements, the carriage of the head, the curve of the body, the *pitos* or finger-clicking, the turns and other flourishes as part of the flamenco dance. Curro Velez, the star dancer, is an exciting performer, virile, dramatic and self-assertive without ever being vulgar. His peculiarity is to arch his spine so much that his body is like a bow and his (flat) belly almost too prominent. Carmen Casarrubios is handsome and holds herself nobly; her arms are a joy to watch. Dolores Amaya, with the tumbling auburn hair, has the fine features of a princely race, and indeed she is the sister of the late and glorious Carmen Amaya and has the same kind of sacred fire.

Just to watch the ladies sitting round in the Cuadro Flamenco, holding themselves so upright, hand on hip or on thigh, smiling happily, comfortably, self-containedly or clapping the subtle rhythms, is to feel a glow of awe and gratitude towards these priestesses of the ancient art.

24.8.69

The Changing Scene
(1969–1971)

Superman

When Serge Lifar, whose autobiography *Ma Vie* has just been published in English (translated by James Holman Mason), danced *L'Oiseau bleu* before the sacred dancers of Bali they thought he was a demon and tried to kill him. This is one of several attempts at assassination in a name-crammed and eminently publishable adventure story. Oh for the pen of Arthur Marshall to do justice to it!

Trained in Kiev by Bronislava Nijinska, loved by Diaghilev ('Lifar, thank you. You are a great artist, a real artist, and I have nothing more to teach you'), appointed to command the Paris Opéra by Rouché, accompanied at the piano by Toscanini, seen off at airports by Picasso, cajoled by Pavlova, confided in by Mermoz ('You know this will be my last flight'), received before the war by Mussolini, invited in 1942 by Hitler to plan the victory festivities in Moscow ('I am an architect myself'), tried for collaboration, thanked by de Gaulle, blessed by the Pope! Our hero was also turned out of Buckingham Palace by King George V for making too much noise ('We then . . . went over to the Prince of Wales's apartments in St. James's Palace'), urged by the friends of Barbara Hutton to marry her ('I told them I was already wedded to the Dance'), and nearly killed in Warsaw by a sword hidden in some flowers which he noticed as he was making his exit-leap in *Le Spectre de la Rose* ('I avoided the blade').

Nearly half the book concerns the occupation of France by the Germans, and is of extreme interest. Those of us who have never lived in occupied territory can ask ourselves whether we should have struggled to keep our beloved ballet company going even at the risk of having to show Goebbels round the Opéra. He sounds rather charming. He remembered seeing Lifar from the gallery in Berlin in *Apollo* and *Le Fils prodigue* during Diaghilev's last season.

About one thing Lifar is modest. Although 'sought after by both sexes . . . I have always been a poor lover, like one who is a stranger to the sensual pleasure of the couch.'

There are several misunderstandings on the part of the translator, who was clearly dazzled by the prowess of Superman Serge. The 'gigantic bound of some eighteen feet' on page 111 was not 'high' but 'deep', i.e. from a rock into the arms of stagehands waiting below. When Lifar justifiably refers to his big role in *Giselle* as 'Albert-Hamlet' there was no need for a footnote saying 'Albrecht/Loys in the British versions'.

22.3.70

Gagaku

Gagaku, which has gone on for 1,000 years, is the most wonderful thing Japan has sent us since *Genji*.

It was exquisitely staged and lit within its square of scarlet rails. The bamboo organ, bamboo flutes, the harps and drums play an extraordinarily pungent music composed by Peter Maxwell Davies shortly after the Norman Conquest. The robes of the dancers—all men—are gorgeous but subtle, with their square hanging sleeves and long trains. These trains, trailing unruffled on the ground, impart to their wearers—as, for instance, at a moment when seven men advance, halt and advance with infinite slowness onto the stage—an air of such modest majesty that I thought I had never seen a really well-brought-up person before.

31.5.70

Nudity

Nudity will soon become a commonplace on the stage. Well, the female nude has been readily accessible for some years. The male nude, understandably less so.

At the Little Theatre, Garrick Yard, St. Martin's Lane, is showing until next Sunday (Monday excepted) a short play called *Narcolepsy* by a dead Japanese girl called Momoko Hosokawa. Plays are not my business, but this is a mime play with a choreographic element which is original. Two characters, a mother and her sleeping son: the text being a monologue by the mother—on tape.

The mother, mimed by Mara Lewellyn, gloats over her son's beautiful body. He is a male prostitute, but suffers from the inability to keep awake— a severe drawback, one would think, in such an overcrowded profession. She conjures him to renounce women—he once dragged home a girl— and to love no woman but herself: he can have as many men as he likes.

As she hovers around his recumbent figure, a witchlike Diana over her Endymion, he writhes in restless sleep, expressing first torment, then desire. The writhing, devised by Adam Darius, is the choreography: and it is varied, strange and wonderful to watch.

This is the first dance I have seen during which a dancer never stands upright for twenty minutes. Nathaniel Norwood as the boy looked fine and moved well, though the stripping off of his bedclothes, which took place halfway through, was rather an anti-climax.

21.6.69

Farewell

We cannot say goodbye to Sir Fred Ashton, whose retirement was marked by a fantastic Tribute Gala Performance on Friday, for as Sir Bobbie, the compère, pointed out, he is in full creative swing, and—I believe—his greatest work lies ahead. Never was there seen, and never again can be, such a selection from the complete works, with Dame Margot and Count Rudolf together in *Apparitions* and *M and A*, apart in *The Wise Virgins*, *Nocturne* and *Les Rendezvous*, and The Princesses Antoinette and Merle with Duke Dowell in numbers impossible to list and the whole Royal Ballet turned into a non-stop revue. Nothing gave more pleasure than the quick change of General Somes from the stern father in *M and A* into Daphnis for the finale. Try playing the game of choosing your favourite Ashton. Nothing harder, for Sir Fred ranges from tragedy to farce; he is a man for all dancers, a man for all moods, a man for all seasons.

26.7.70

Gilgamesh

Henryk Tomaszewski of the Polish Pantomime Theatre appears to owe nothing to anybody and to have started his theatre out of the blue. It has nothing to do with classical ballet or Martha Graham or Marcel Marceau or any known form of sign language. *Gilgamesh*, which is about mythical heroes, with no local colour, has a style all its own.

On a hunting expedition Gilgamesh the King meets a shepherd-boy, Enkidu, and after a fight they become friends and sleep together, but Enkidu has nightmares. They kill a Minotaur and Gilgamesh is bathed in milk, then ritually raped by Ishtar the priestess; but he loves Enkidu best and the lady looks none too pleased. Another nightmare ends in the shepherd's death: the King goes on a journey, dreams he is in a well, celebrates harvest and dies.

It's a good story, but it is rather drawn out and accompanied by taped music which doesn't help at all. What makes it gripping is the appearance of the two chief characters and their movements. As Gilgamesh Pawel

Rouba is a Slav Achilles: tall, dark, high-cheek-boned, with heroic muscles, he exudes power and magnetism. As Enkidu, the shorter, golden-haired Stefan Niedzialkowski is equally naked—he wears a sheepskin jock-strap—and equally muscled, but he has the face of an angel. The contrasted looks of these two men were in themselves sufficient reason for the show.

19.10.69

Participation

A gigantic Danish whore once told me in Paris that she had just passed the night with a man who was so small that she simply couldn't find him in the bed in the morning—she looked everywhere. And it occurs to me now that he must have been Baudelaire because of those lines in *La Géante*. '*Dormir nonchalamment à l'ombre de ses seins Comme un hameau paisible au pied d'une montagne.*'

Change of scale, new sensations, not to have to see shows in a theatre, ballet not just in the round but all around us, Wagner on a mountain-top in the pouring rain, that's what we're after.

Peter Dockley is the slightly cannibalistic-looking young man who makes those geometrical constructions in tubular steel for dancers or acrobats to move around in. When at the Mermaid last year I saw a yellow skeleton pyramid of his with a white man inside measuring up its possibilities I thought it was so beautiful I got the *Sunday Times* to send a photographer. But Dockley is dead against doing this sort of thing on the stage and thought me crazy because I liked the look of his act in a picture frame. He wants lots of these goings-on to go on in a big space all at the same time and for you and me to move in and out interrupting the performers and then for another crowd to charge in and race round and round us like on a race-track. And then he would love to herd his paying audience ruthlessly into a corner and watch enormous elephant turds fall on them from a great height while a mysterious gas disintegrated their skirts and trousers.

Heavily armed, veiled and padlocked in the right places, I went to the Round House, where—for last week only—Dockley had been given a free hand; and it was well worth a visit. It was like an *auto da fé* and a snake-pit and a public execution. When they burned Christians in the Colosseum I'm sure that jugglers and bingo and a pop group were carrying on in other parts of the amphitheatre: it was like that.

The Round House was murky. Imagine the Albert Hall lit only by one candle. A cruciform construction, with a tower at one extremity, occupied the central space. All around, underneath the arches, there were crowds of young people sitting or lying on the floor. One girl was feeding her baby. It was a sort of camp-fire feeling.

First one, then another, then a third acrobat came swinging, somersaulting and hand-standing along the bars. The sound kept reiterating certain statements as birds do and I felt sure that someone was trying to get a message through and rushed to the bar to borrow a pencil. (When I was a child I was told pigeons said: 'Take *two* cows, Taffy', but now I know they say: 'It's *your* house, Dicky'.) Uniacke Karamba, Uniacke Karamba, Uniacke Karamba many times repeated. Then I missed one while I was promising to return the pencil. Tell at the log at ye, Tell at the log at ye. Yake in Hew'n, Yake in Hew'n.

I gave up annotating and started mingling. Smoke was rising and a man in a suit of lights was standing ominously on top of the tower, casting glints about the dark walls. At another extremity of the cross there was a sitar player. At another acrobats in striking red and green costumes encrusted with cubes of foam rubber were walking on their hands. At another two men in fencing helmets were ceremoniously performing *kendo*, which is Japanese for hitting each other on the head with poles and uttering harsh cries. Suddenly the whole crowd gathered round the *kendo*.

I moved to the middle where spacemen in suits pocked with octopus eyes or mouths of foam rubber were invading with coils of silver flex, from which they proceeded to weave a web to envelop the whole structure. They then appeared to be preparing to stage an execution. Eventually they were all rolling helplessly, caught in their own coils, on the floor, silently begging to be beaten or given milk. Moved to pity, a woman in the crowd, which had by now followed me, held out her hand.

After I had mingled a bit I lurked. It was a thrilling Miltonic sight. It seemed to me that Peter Dockley's inventions were capable of infinite variations. We had some Mortadella and a very good salad and red wine and I returned the pencil.

28.9.69

Czech protest

One of the main drawbacks, I suppose, of being a people in whom Russia takes a fatherly interest is that you must submit to regular performances of

Swan Lake by visiting Soviet companies. Pavel Smok's *Ballet Prague* is in general an impassioned resistance movement against the old traditional ballet, and the first work he showed us, *Black Collage*, made a particular point about the difficulties rising from Czechoslovakia's geographical situation.

Now, if you or I go moping about the world complaining to our friends, say, that our wife has left us or that we only have ten more years to live, people soon get fed up: if on the other hand we make a joke of it we get more sympathy. Smok in *Black Collage* made some alarming jokes and put over vividly a feeling of insecurity. Smok's own sound-track incorporates snatches of *Lili Marlene*, a Hitler speech, a Bach fugue and, of course, *Swan Lake*; and the moments of tragedy, appeal and protest are made more telling by the skits on Petipa, on folk-dance troupes and on military troops, by the kicking around of a helmet and the pouring of bucketfuls of blood. At the end the dancers back away, staring at us in silence.

The company have tremendous life and fire and spirit, and I think Smok has done a great job. He will be glad to hear that when the Bolshoi Ballet come here in two months time they are to open with *Swan Lake*.

18.5.69

The Opéra

The Brighton Pavilion
Is a joke to the million,
But to friends of mine
It's a kind of shrine.

And a shrine, a holy of holies, is what the Paris Opéra is to a number of people including Ivor Guest, the historian of nineteenth-century ballet. Yet this superb institution, this supreme monument to the Second Empire (though in fact only opened after 1870), has always filled me with a kind of exasperation. What should be a machine for producing works of art has so often been merely a machine for eating money.

Compared with poor old Covent Garden the Opéra enjoys an immense subsidy; the grant we get for our ballet would barely pay for the electric light bulbs in the endless gilded foyers and galleries of the Palais Garnier. Yet as one talented *maître-de-ballet* succeeds another we wait in vain for some redeeming masterpiece. Juggernaut defeats them. The system cannot have been devised solely to provide jobs for the second cousins once removed of senators' mistresses, and yet. . . .

John Taras has now been ballet master at the Opéra for six months; and it is inconceivable that at any previous period of the ballet company's history they should have given so respectable a rendering of Balanchine's wonderful *Serenade* and *Symphony in C* as they did on Monday. In old days Opéra dancers were always eager to establish their individuality: Taras has schooled his troupe to give a modest and faithful rendering of these two impersonal masterpieces.

It was the best programme and the best danced that I have seen at the Opéra in thirty-five years. It really looked as if Taras was winning the battle.

But you needn't think he's going to be allowed to get away with it. Not on your Byzantine life. The government has changed since Taras was appointed and he is to be replaced by Roland Petit.* Now Petit is an old and dear friend of mine, just as Taras is, so I am bound to wish him the best luck in the world. He'll need it.

29.3.70

Dagestan

Lezginka, the Dance Company from Dagestan in the Caucasus, opened at the Albert Hall on Saturday last.

Dagestan men do not have legs. Instead they have black leather tentacles, on the bent-over tips of which they stand. These tentacles enable these creatures from another planet to propel themselves high in the air and to scud across the ground on what earth-dwellers would call their knees.

Dagestan ladies do not have legs. Instead they have wheels. Or perhaps it is ball-bearings—one can only guess, because we are never permitted a glimpse of their lower limbs, which are concealed throughout by long and lovely Oriental garments. It is their smooth progression, a gliding motion more serene by far than the most perfect *pas de bourrée*, that makes us realize they are legless.

One of the more marvellous numbers was the Dance of Drummers. About ten men hold a conversation on drums carried under the left arm, each tuned differently. The drumming is breathtaking, then suddenly these Martians begin to execute the most incredible jumps and turns, still holding their drums under their arms. There is a warrior's dance with sparks flying from clashing swords; and there is a tightrope walker who takes a

* Petit did not in fact take up the appointment.

chair on to the wire with him as well as a stepladder, which he climbs.

When Dagestan became an autonomous republic of the U.S.S.R. in 1921, our programme tells us, 97 per cent of the people were illiterate, and women had no rights of any kind, being disposable like chattels and saleable, too. Now Dagestan has a women President, Rose Eldarova, and of 178 deputies 75 are women.

Still, these emancipated ladies, who have presumably been encouraged to throw off the Muslim faith along with their veils, retain in their pretty dances the traditional attitude of sweet submissiveness to their mustachioed and booted masters. Only occasionally in a comic flirtation number does one or the other make a show of girlish independence in order to teach a village Casanova a trick or two.

23.3.69

NEW TRENDS
IN BRITAIN

Western Theatre Ballet's ballets are frequently about homosexuality, ritual murder, escaped prisoners and other West Country matters, but by far the most are about Lesbians.

Sunday Times, 13.5.60

Marie Rambert has been the muse of British choreographers.

Observer, 21.10.51

Who are the Four Horsemen of the Apocalypse? Well, Anna Sokolow and Robert Cohan are two of them.

Sunday Times, 3.4.73

. . . some gymnasium of the mind.

Sunday Times, 19.3.74

Note

The new thing about *Western Theatre Ballet*, founded by *Elizabeth West in 1957*, was to take ballet on a small scale to places where it had never penetrated before. She was also determined to use contemporary music and contemporary themes. This policy was continued by *Peter Darrell* after her death. *Darrell's* love of new music was equalled by his passion for the dramatic and the bizarre: yet he was a classical choreographer. In *1969* the troupe became *Scottish Theatre Ballet*.

Ballet Rambert, famed for its pioneering in the *1930s*, grew more grandiose after the war; then in *1966 Mme. Rambert* dismissed her corps de ballet and reduced her company to a small group of soloists hell-bent on experiment. The group was directed first by *Norman Morrice*, then by *John Chesworth*—later with the aid of *Christopher Bruce*.

Inspired by *Martha Graham*, *Robin Howard* founded the *School of Contemporary Dance in London*, established it at the *Place in 1969* and, with *Robert Cohan*, inaugurated the *London Contemporary Dance Theatre*. This has been the spearhead of London's avant garde *ever since*.

Although *Ballet Rambert* is senior to *Scottish (Western) Theatre Ballet* I have placed them second to associate them more closely with *London Contemporary Dance Theatre*, for they train their dancers by the *Graham*, as well as the classical, method.

Western Theatre Ballet

In Somerset

Western Theatre Ballet was founded three years ago to take ballet where angels fear to tread. The folly of its founder, Elizabeth West, has met with a measure of reward, for her troup now receives £3,000 a year from the Arts Council. But shoes alone cost £1,300 a year. The twelve dancers are paid £12 a week each, roughly £7 10s. of which they spend on bed, breakfast and beastly suppers. They use a piano when they demonstrate a class, but the music for their ballets is canned.

Twelve delightful dancers, including a calm ballet master, Erling Sunde; a stylish repertory; some pretty costumes and a jolly wardrobe mistress; a stage manager to fix the lights and sound, and sprinkle rosin on polished platforms; a bus; some friendly sponsors in Bristol; and an overdraft.

Returning from a tour of Holland, where even small towns have fine theatres, they set off last Monday, aided by a cheque from the Gulbenkian Foundation, for a three-week tour of the West Country, and I went with them.

Monday, 7th November. Things start inauspiciously in Chippenham, Wilts, because apart from one girl having a bad foot and one boy a bad mouth, British Railways have ingeniously sent the scenery to Birmingham. Miss West talks, playing for time, and a *barre* is demonstrated: then, as no van comes through the fog, another date is fixed and those who cannot make it are offered their money back. Winter begins suddenly.

Tuesday, 8th. Off on bus at 9.30. Sunny, but feet frozen. Sylvia doing purple knitting, Clover deep in Duff Cooper's *Talleyrand*, boys mostly staring into space. Suzanne reads horoscopes aloud. We all cheer up between Bath and Wells, Dennis stretches stockinged foot to catch sun. Skips for evening performance unloaded at Bridgwater. We push on to Taunton.

Before afternoon lecture-recital in big North Town School, eat lunch in girls' dining room. Dancers indignant at having to pay Somerset County two shillings for this. Headmistress ropes in needlework class to iron costumes.

Intrigued to see reactions of 500 seething girls between eleven and fifteen, mostly witnessing live ballet for the first time. They watch dancers doing their *pliés, tendus, ronds de jambe* at the *barre* with interest. When it comes to centre practice I catch some of their excitement myself. Having seen steps worked at separately, the kids find the performance of a brief *enchaînement* quite miraculous. The men's *doubles tours en l'air* take their breath away; they are longing to shout and clap; and little Max Natiez, who turns brilliantly, gets a huge roar of applause. I haven't had such fun for years. . . .

And so we board the bus for Bridgwater, wondering if there will be time for tea before tonight's show.

13.11.60

Western Theatre Ballet ask a guarantee of £60 for a performance and £40 for a lecture-recital. At Bridgwater (where the pubs announce 'No Gypsies') they were sponsored by the Arts Centre, which hides in a street of handsome Queen Anne houses, boasts a decent little theatre seating 200, and is guarded by a high-principled cat.

'And did those feet in ancient time . . .?' wondered Blake, bemused by the legend that Jesus came as a boy to Glastonbury. This would have seemed to me less improbable during the war when I was stationed in Somerset and first went on pilgrimage to Avalon, lured as much by its strange conical hill as by its holy history, than that I should one day see ballet there.

With Sedgemoor flooded, Glastonbury was almost an island again. No time for the dancers to climb the Tor in the rain as I did, or to visit King Arthur's grave in the Abbey ruins. They had rehearsals and a class, before dancing for the Street Society of Arts, in the gymnasium of St. Dunstan's School—named after the West-countryman who was abbot here exactly a thousand years ago.

Western Theatre Ballet are doing a remarkable job: they deserve not only every penny and as much publicity as can be afforded them, but beautiful new miniature ballets by Ashton, Petit, Robbins and Balanchine.

20.11.60

As a footnote to the pieces on Western Theatre Ballet in which I tried to give a glimpse of the splendours and miseries of a touring troupe, I quote from a letter of Elizabeth West:

Dorchester Ballet Club, who saw us at Weymouth, want to sponsor a new ballet and ask how much it would cost. At Sherborne 300 boys and 300 girls saw us, and were wonderful. The posh girls' school in the evening were wonderful too—Suzy swore most of them were wearing eight-guinea shoes. Cirencester a very good audience. Laverne lost half a front tooth. . . . Max tore a tendon and danced a whole ballet on one foot—he's off. Brenda fractured her wrist and will be in plaster for six weeks. Buddy, the driver, doesn't get lost so often.

27.11.60

At the Edinburgh Festival

On the programme of 'Triple Bill', the three ballets with singing given by Western Theatre Ballet with the Scottish National Orchestra at the Empire, Edinburgh, last week, 'the help of Richard Buckle' is acknowledged 'throughout the presentation'. What actually happened was that Lord Harewood invited Elizabeth West to consider this project in Edinburgh. When Kurt Weill's *Seven Deadly Sins* and Stravinsky's *Renard* had been decided on, I urged the organizers to open with a French work, and M. Tony Mayer of the French Embassy and Felix Aprahamian suggested Milhaud's *Salade*.

I think it was I who proposed that the small company should deliberately take up as little space as possible on the wide Empire stage, using sets or backcloths which would stand out against the surrounding gloom like a lit booth on a dark night.

And, having failed to secure Chagall for *Renard*, I enlisted the Australian painter Arthur Boyd, who has a similar genius for populating his haunted landscapes with images of a personal folk-lore. (Incidentally, the designers for all three ballets are Australian.)

After that I became involved in other work and attended not a single rehearsal. If anyone thinks it odd that I should criticize productions I had a hand in I can assure him it isn't the first time, and these notes are written in the same spirit as I might offer verbal advice, with the view to getting the show right for Sadler's Wells and Leeds.

Salade (like other old Massine ballets) has an exasperatingly complicated *commedia dell'arte* story, which it would be easier to scrap if it were not wedded to sung words of comment. Of course, it is done 'modern' in a piled-up Neapolitan waterfront set and inspired dresses by Barry Kay. The only way for choreographer Peter Darrell to overcome the effect of confusion left by the non-stop flicker of action is to school his dancers to absolute precision. The best number is a comic tango.

Renard, well played and sung (conductor: Alexander Gibson), is a marvellous piece. I think choreographer Rodrigues should give his Cock, Dennis Griffiths, more varied attitudes to perform on his perch; and Suzanne Musitz's Fox should have one more expression. The collapsible set is fine, though you would not guess Boyd's stature as a painter from it.

The Seven Deadly Sins of Weill and Brecht is another small masterpiece. This new interpretation by Kenneth MacMillan, *without* Lotte Lenya, and supposed to be heretical, is still enormously effective; and I shall long remember the warmth, assurance and timing of singer Cleo Laine, Anya Linden's 1920-ish waif-like elegance, the strange inventions of designer Ian Spurling, and the unexpected 'Prodigal Son' gesture with which one of the Family (the singers) welcomes back the daughter whose sinning in the cities has paid for their house.

A programme which, though under-rehearsed, was worthy in its novelty of Harewood's first triumphant festival in Edinburgh.

10.9.61

Off Leicester Square

Those who were distressed that Christmas Day went by without the Beatles sending any message to their subjects, and who have not got seats for the Astoria, Finsbury Park, can console themselves with a visit to the Prince Charles Theatre, where Western Theatre Ballet are performing a short numero by Peter Darrell, *Mods and Rockers*, with music by John Lennon, Paul McCartney and George Harrison. I wouldn't exactly call this a ballet, but it is good value. My mother liked it, anyway.

In an open-work set representing a café, adorned only with the portraits of you-know-who on a record sleeve, two Beatle- (or Cardin-) jacketed males and three female mods are shaking. A wa-wa-ing on the mike from one of the combo in the pit is the signal for a gang of rockers in black leather to take over the floor. They rock and the mods cast up their eyes.

A *pas de deux* is accompanied by a voice wailing *This Boy* (by George Harrison); there is a fight, and Simon Mottram, the chief rocker, in form-fitting leather-look pants, gives Sylvia Welman, the chief mod girl, the come-on and they beat it up the old M1, leaving both sides raving.

To one who has been long in Covent Garden pent, watching *Swan Lake* nightly for over forty years, it makes a change. The kids put it over with terrific zing. John Lennon, Paul McCartney and George Harrison are the greatest composers since Beethoven, with Paul McCartney way out in front. I'm told I have to go all the way to Whitechapel to get a pair of those pants.

29.12.63

At Oxford

If I had been told when I was at Oxford thirty years ago that I should see the day when two ballet companies played concurrently in that city you could have knocked me down with Sweet's Anglo-Saxon primer. But so it turned out this week, with the Ballet Rambert at the New Theatre and Western Ballet at the Playhouse.

Finding myself in the neighbourhood, I had to choose between them and as I knew the former would be at Sadler's Wells in July, decided on the latter.

Peter Darrell really has chic in his choice of themes and music, in his determination to be contemporary, and in his throw-away humour. On Wednesday the four ballets had music by Milhaud, Debussy, Bartok and the Beatles (what other ballet company could offer such delightful variety?) and not a note of Tchaikovsky was heard all evening. Unfortunately the music has to be canned and the results were not as good as they might have been. I sympathized because we had been having technical problems with sound at the Shakespeare Exhibition.

A Wedding Present, though not new, was unfamiliar. Mrs. Bellamy's son has got married and there is a party at her boarding house. Among the guests is a boy who had an affair with the son, and who is still in love with him. The boy writes a compromising inscription in a book the pair are taking away on their honeymoon. Very good so far—the movement and the emotional bits were sensitively staged and there were no false notes. Gale Law had got the boy just right and Robert Verbrugge was touching as a third boy who loves the deserted one and tries to console him.

The honeymoon *pas de deux* in a seaside bedroom develops into drama when the discovery of the book leads to the husband's confession and the wife's despair. This scene was admirably played by Suzanne Hywel and Laverne Meyer. The ballet was still all right, except that one might think the bride a big goose not to accept the fact that most men have something of that sort in their nature.

But 'the marriage is wrecked', the programme tells us, and this is where Darrell's with-it choice of music lands him in trouble and the story collapses—at least in my view. Because Bartok wrote some dance tunes into the last movement of his third piano concerto we have to have another party with dancing back at the boarding house. And, if I read it right, the wrecked marriage is represented by the wife rushing in looking like La Goulue with an inordinate amount of rouge on her cheeks, being the life and soul of the party. This was a big let-down after the fine and subtle beginning.

21.6.64

At Sadler's Wells

It's not an easy thing to make even a bad ballet—I couldn't do it, smart as I am—and there are fewer human beings on this planet who can make a good ballet than can do almost anything else. To make a full-length, three-act ballet—and on a modern theme—building up story, music and choreography from scratch, as Peter Darrell has done for Western Theatre Ballet (who now have a base at Sadler's Wells), and to bring it off even 50 per cent is marvellous. Darrell brings it off 70 per cent. Perhaps more.

Well, he does if you judge the show as a whole. None of the individual elements of *Sun into Darkness* is going to win gold medals. But I think my favourite critic on pink paper, who knows much more about music than I do, is a bit hard on Malcolm Williamson's score. You can't have Britten or Stravinsky or Henze all the time, and 'Waltzing Matilda' played on a mouth-organ would be good—even perfect—ballet music if it helped the dancing and action of a given ballet to make their utmost effect. Williamson's music sustains Darrell's ballet faithfully and rises to all its occasions: besides which, I should say, it has tunes, tang, texture and variety.

The story is by David Rudkin, author of that strange play, *Afore Night Come*, and it sets out in the same way to show the survival of primitive needs or rituals in the modern world, and achieves the same brooding atmosphere. A Cornish village celebrating a carnival appoints a stranger, whose motor-bike has broken down, Lord of Misrule. The sinister clergyman and the garage proprietor who is also mayor make the Stranger drunk, and the orgy reaches a climax when the Stranger has sex with the mayor's wife at the end of Act II. The third act is a little confusing. Both the mayor's daughter and his son—a simple creature who is the butt of the village—are in love with the Stranger. Yet when the clergyman produces a sort of wild beast costume out of his bag of tricks and the Stranger is degraded, then incited to attack the boy, the boy kills him with a spanner.

Darrell is not an inventor of new movement so much as a story-teller in movement. His choreography is a conventional mixture of the classical and the conversational. But he has a powerful sense of theatre, he is a first-rate director and he knows just what he can get away with before a sophisticated audience and what he can't. He is not a genius but he is a very clever boy.

His company are terrific. Not John Dexter casting and directing Wesker's *Kitchen*, not Jerome Robbins cooking up *West Side Story* got together more admirable a group of young people or drilled them to give performances of such conviction in such harmony with each other. David Jones was the mayor; Elaine McDonald was his wife who becomes the priestess of the ritual; Laverne Meyer was the pathetic son; Donna Day Washington was the pretty daughter; Harry Haythorne was the clergyman; Gary Sherwood was the glamorous Stranger, hero and victim; and Peter Cazalet and Robert Verbrugge were two Carriers who did a violent and fantastic number, dressed as apes, and partnered Robin Haig and Suzanne Hywel, who were prostitutes. They were all very good indeed and very credible—even in incredible roles, such as the clergyman's.

Harry Waistnage's set, made up of regroupable units—garage, dump of petrol drums, house built into cliff—became more exciting as the lighting grew lurider, i.e. After Night Come.

15.9.66

Western Theatre Ballet's ballets are frequently about homosexuality, ritual murder, escaped prisoners and other West Country matters, but by far the most are about Lesbians, and in my innocent way I took for granted that Peter Darrell's latest work *Francesca*, given at Sadler's Wells on Thursday, was about Lesbians too—only to be told in the bar afterwards that it was about vampires. How *could* I have been so thick—with all that winding of red scarves round necks?

Vampires! You have to hand it to Darrell, he's always on the ball. It is high time someone spoke out about vampires, that scourge of week-end house-parties, and *Francesca* is a fearless exposure to Roussel's *Petite Suite pour l'orchestre*. The atmosphere is dolce-vitaish; the women at this smart gathering wear towering hair-dos like Roman Empresses and Peter Cazalet's set has a giant Mantuan caryatid for candelabrum. Only Francesca lies on her Pauline Borghese sofa, in white, yearning—for blood, of course. Robin Haig was very good at this. Her first victim is a village girl, her second the hostess, Suzanne Hywel. Come to think of it, the ballet was partly about Lesbianism after all, for the hostess was clearly mad about Francesca: she just thought Francesca wanted something different. Everything Darrell does has a sense of style and originality, and his marvellous small company are perfectly drilled to fulfil his intentions, but I am afraid *Francesca* is not entirely successful. Was it the old trouble—too much story for the music?

But it really is pretty remarkable how Darrell avoids the clichés of ballet subject-matter. And it is staunch of him to persist in giving us serious music. The programme opened with MacMillan's *Las Hermanas* in its Georgiadis set with Frank Martin's Concerto for Harpsichord; then followed Cranko's *Beauty and the Beast* to Ravel's *La Mère Oie*; and the final work was Darrell's *The Brothers* to Bartok's Music for Celesta, percussion and strings, with a clever new set (slightly over-elaborate) by Barry Kay and fine performances by Elaine McDonald, Laverne Meyer and Peter Cazalet. The Sadler's Wells orchestra was conducted by Kenneth Alwyn.

5.2.67

The first night of Western Theatre Ballet's tenth anniversary season at Sadler's Wells on Tuesday was not only a triumph, but a vindication of the policies of the late Elizabeth West, now continued by Peter Darrell. In 1957 West took her tiny troupe, in a bus, dancing to Bartok on tape to any school or village hall which would pay a few pounds for a performance. Here and now we see a slightly larger company of eighteen, well disciplined by their recently appointed ballet master, Alexander Bennett, and dancing, to a small orchestra under their new musical director Kenneth Alwyn, four new (or unfamiliar) ballets by four different choreographers, before a packed and appreciative house. Put out more flags, fling down the ticker-tape, sound the ships' sirens, tap your bows on the music stands for the glorious achievement of Elizabeth West.

Overture, danced to Stravinsky's Suite for Small Orchestra, no. 2, is a classical improvization for six dancers by Laverne Meyer, the company's Associate Artistic Director, and it is probably the best thing he has done. The brio and unexpectedness of the choreography match the wit and sting of the score; and because Donna Day Washington had sprained a ligament, Brenda Last, one of the founder members of the troupe, returned from the Royal Ballet to do the springy leading role, borne aloft by the exuberant Simon Mottram. This was delightful.

Prefaced by Alan Rawsthorne's Concerto for Ten Instruments and accompanied by two exposed fiddlers playing his Theme and Variations for Two Violins, Jack Carter's *Cage of God* seems not only a remarkably happy wedding of music, programme and movement, but also one of its choreographer's most successful creations. Most ballets are about Adam and Eve these days, but, after all, Scarlatti played variations on the same theme nightly for years to his spellbound King and Queen of Spain, and why go beyond basic myths—Romeo and Juliet, Frankie and Johnny, Oedipus?

Carter's *Cage* focuses on Cain and Abel (Robert Verbrugge and Sean Cunningham), although Peter Cazalet's Adam, Robin Haig's Eve and Valerie Sanders's Serpent all have clear and telling points to make. Then there comes a Mourning Woman (Suzanne Hywel) who hymns the guilt-ridden fate of man. The way Carter illustrates this Family, lumbered with a corpse who persistently clings to his brother's leg, all hanging together in a tragic, dragging tangle, reminds me of Géricault's *Raft of the Medusa*. Patrick Procktor's set interprets God's cage, man's arena, as a grey ruined bath-house which becomes transparent for a few seconds after the murder of Abel to reveal a scarlet place of skulls. The unobtrusive costumes seem just right.

Flemming Flindt from Denmark danced in his own horrific ballet *The Lesson*, which has a soundtrack by Georges Delerue and is based on Ionesco's play, with the mad professor become a ballet master in an elaborate, realistic studio by Bernard Daydé, with piano, mirrors, curtained windows, chairs. The alarming Wardress-Pianist, who moves like an automaton, sets the scene for the arrival of the insouciant pupil-victim. Then appears the Ballet Master bowing shyly, to invent for her little *enchaînements* at the *barre*. At last he makes her put on the fatal shoes and the dance of death begins. After his consummation the man cringes in shame before the Pianist, who shows a momentary impulse of motherly pity towards him before resuming her mechanical routine in preparation for the next pupil. Elaine McDonald and Arlette van Boven are excellent as Pianist and Pupil. Flindt, having imagined the ballet obsessively, tears through it tremendously.

Chairs are in—the common wooden chair, that is. (No dancer would be seen dead on a throne, nowadays.) A chair had been the Serpent's Tree of Knowledge in *Cage*; more chairs had played their ritual part in *The Lesson*. In Walter Gore's amusing *Light Fantastic*, to music of Chabrier (orch. Alwyn), they are used as instruments of flirtation—sort of male fans, as it were. Peter Cazalet, mooning timidly after Janet Kinson, was the wistful Pierrot-hero of this work, with Simon Mottram exuding forceful male hormones as his Harlequin-rival.

25.6.67

Scottish Theatre Ballet

At Sadler's Wells

What a tremendous undertaking it is to make a ballet lasting two hours. Peter Darrell has now produced his second full-length work. His first, *Sun into Darkness*, had a modern Cornish setting, even if it dealt with ancient rites. His new work, with which Scottish Theatre Ballet opened their two-week season at Sadler's Wells on Wednesday, is a fairy-tale, *Beauty and the Beast*.

The older we get the readier we become to abandon our theories and shed our principles. A few years ago I should have deplored a fairy-tale ballet (and so would Darrell, I believe). Today I think you can tell your own kind of truth, do your own thing, in a fairy-tale form just as well as in any other way. Or course, it has to do with yourself—the way ideas present themselves to you—and a bit to do with fashion and what you have got tired of and reacted against.

So if I risk a generalization today I may well say the opposite in five years time. Here goes! I think we needed Darrell's new work to show us that to make two-hour ballets is no longer on. The whole tendency of art today—we are only concerned, however, with music and dance—is to become terser and more concentrated. Since Webern, Boulez and Stravinsky's *Agon* composers use fewer notes. Since Martha Graham who, following the trail (I will not say in the steps) of Isadora and Nijinsky, has abolished virtuosity and ornament, fewer movements have been made to mean more. Hence a long ballet seems against the spirit of the times.

Beauty and the Beast is a perfectly good myth, as myths go. Pasiphaë lusted physically for her bull: Rosaline, the Beauty, had to overcome physical repugnance for her monster and learn to love him out of pity. Perhaps Mme. de Villeneuve's story was about marrying an old husband. And the story could have been treated in the concentrated way in which Graham treated the myths of Medea, Circe, Judith and Agamemnon. In which case, probably, Darrell would only have needed, say, six dancers and thirty minutes.

But I am talking about what Darrell might have done instead of criticizing what he did. He told in a lively imaginative way, to commissioned music of superior quality interspersed with electronic nerve-storms, a tale of a debt-ridden merchant, his two disagreeable elder daughters, their suitors, the youngest daughter Rosaline who is loved by the Beast, an enchanted Prince who is rescued by her love: and there are interesting episodes of statues coming to life, the moon and its reflection, the sun's apotheosis.

In fact, Darrell and his small troupe have entered into direct competition with Ashton and Covent Garden—and on *their* ground he cannot compete. Although Peter Minshull's glittering sets and costumes are original and effective, you cannot (unless you are Graham) make an apotheosis on a half-empty stage. Where the excitement should be greatest, in the solos and *pas de deux* of Donna Day Washington and Tatsuo Sakai, the choreography is most conventional. And it is clear that Thea Musgrave would have been happier not to have to pad her score.

23.11.69

Ballet Rambert

The Company Reconstituted; Jeannetta Cochrane

To me, fair friend, you never can be old, for the mere sight of your name in print, Marie Rambert, evokes images of youthful passion, enthusiasm and invention; and now I can indeed say that as you were when first your eye I eyed, such seems your beauty still, because the Ballet Rambert, which went for twenty years through a period of competing with larger, more conventional companies, is now back in its original form as a small experimental group.

The first programme at the Jeannetta Cochrane Theatre was entirely propitious. *Numeros* is a ballet by Pierre Lacotte without any music but the percussion provided by the dancers' hands and track shoes. It had clever lighting and was cleanly danced by Peter Curtis, Hazel Merry and three others.

Time Base is the first ballet of John Chesworth. When have we seen so successful a first ballet by any choreographer? It is about time—you misunderstand me—it (the ballet) is about (has as its subject) Time (see the Oxford Dictionary, whose definition, read aloud by a male voice, with some double-tracking, forms part of the sound accompaniment of Chesworth's ballet). Time. When in the chronicle of wasted time. Time enough and not enough time, Lilian you wait in vain. Extraordinary groups; wonderful projections by Nadine Baylis; words; taped music by Lutoslawski; a solo by Jonathan Taylor in front of an optical perspective, which is a startling effective image of man's mind boggling at the idea of infinity; at last the awaited blood-bath. It does occur to me that Chesworth may be the man to show us how Graham's technique can be married to the classical.

Intermède, by Pierre Lacotte to music of Vivaldi, is a gentle comedy in terms of classical dancing, with Patricia Rianne, Terence James and eight others unfolding some inventive choreography but showing just a shade too much that they see the joke. In the early MacMillan *Laiderette*, Kenneth Rowell's pale, sad, mysterious set gave the stage an unexpected width, and the guest artists Maryon Lane and Christopher Gable impersonated the faceless girl and her heartless host.

20.11.66

Tetley's *Ziggurat* at the Jeannetta Cochrane

Let me grope my way towards a description of Glen Tetley's thrilling new work, *Ziggurat*, which was given by Ballet Rambert at the Cochrane on Monday. Music by Stockhausen. Décor by Nadine Baylis. Tetley's barefoot choreography owes more to Graham than to classical ballet.

The atmosphere is that of science fiction—or rather of William Burroughs, in whose novels the reader mounts on a heroin rainbow to a silent world booming with childish memories amid the recurrent orgasms of outer space.

Against an empty sky (with the sides of the stage and the lights exposed), within a simple skeletal building, sits enthroned a gold-helmeted god or robot, arms stiffly outstretched, either blind or in a catalepsy.

Between him and us a team of men are striving. They have a pathetic hand-to-mouth gesture. Are they hungry? Can't they breathe? Do they want to say something? Are they praying? A change of lighting or a blast of mechanical sound sets them capering apart in panic. I recall Fritzy Lang's film *Metropolis* which showed a nightmare picture of regimented proles pouring incessantly into the hell-mouths of a city's underground workshops, sacrificed in their mindless millions to keep the engines running.

But a Ziggurat, the programme tells us, besides being an Assyrian temple built in diminishing terraces, 'was worshipped as the earth-soul'. Well, the Hanging Gardens of Babylon and/or the Tower of Babel was a way of aspiring to God in Heaven, which was noble or cheeky according to which way you look at it. So presumably these men in unprecedented openwork net tights, which give the effect of scales, are striving to sustain an ideal of God, king or country or the gold standard.

The god-robot topples sideways; the men rush into his temple, pull him out, and lying side by side, with him on top of them, vibrate to revive him. I recall the story of the young nobleman on the retreat from Moscow whose company used to huddle around him to keep him warm, the outside soldiers continually dropping dead. But God lies on the floor and they back terrified into the temple.

Now into the music, stereophonically from right to left, come bursts of childish song (prettily truncated so that hardly a word is left whole).

Screens swing down to form ceiling and backcloth, and a series of projections is launched with some huge staring eyes.

To the accompaniment of joyous treble squawks plus *musique concrète*, electronics, piano and percussion, there follow several numbers. Girls in white introducing a springlike note; the God carrying one man between his legs; a *pas de deux* in red lights on a rolled-on path of plastic, which the girl subsequently gathers into crackling bunches and bundles off (does it symbolize what Burroughs calls 'jissom'?); finally a big group with *attitudes* and lifted girls. This has been the main and longest part of the ballet, though I have abbreviated it; and it contained ingenious choreography. As far as meaning was concerned, I assumed that God was letting his subjects have a bit of fun on Sunday as a reward for working so hard the rest of the week.

The screens slide away; girls roll off; men form up in profile, and as they bend double the erect god-robot is seen to be standing like a charioteer in their midst. Noble image.

The above, based on notes made in the dark, was written on the morning after the first performance. Tuesday night I went again and could see hardly anything I had described.

The group of men in the first part were *not* striving, so that cancelled my *Metropolis* idea. They were *travelling*, buffeted about in a space-ship, struggling to exist in an unfamiliar element, fearful of losing shape and breath, locked like Francis Bacon's victims in a glass cage. I think the god toppled because their fear and disillusion had made them lose faith in him: but faith of a kind was restored to them after they had frolicked with a few girls and acclaimed the beauty of the universe.

'Of course it's about regeneration' said C. I tried out a few theories on Glen Tetley, who expressed polite interest. My girl friend J. got a bit more out of him. 'Of all the animals we are the only ones who know their past and their future,' he said. 'What is the meaning of that gesture, hand to mouth?' 'We all carry our Ziggurats around with us,' Tetley replied. J. thought he had said 'cigarettes' and crosspurposes set in. 'Don't worry!' cried Marie Rambert. But I do worry, because however handsome a work may be to look at, if there are ideas in it they should be within grasp. I suspect a certain woolliness of thought.

26.11.67

At the Jeannetta Cochrane

The use of non-dance music for dancing, which Isadora began around the turn of the century, was bound to be followed by choreography which was more loosely related—or related in a more subtle way—to its music: and Nijinsky with his *Faune* was a bolder pioneer than ever Fokine had been.

And, of course, it was bound to be followed by new kinds of movement expressing—or trying to express—a wider range of emotions. In this, too, Nijinsky, abetted by Diaghilev, paved the way for Graham, Cunningham, Taylor, Tetley and Morrice.

Ballet Rambert's ten-day season at the Jeannetta Cochrane opened on Wednesday, and the first ballet was Glen Tetley's *Freefall* to Max Schubel's piece for harpsichord, piano, double-bass, clarinet and cello. Equally admirable were Tetley's inventive pounces and tumbles and the impetus and control of the dancers who performed them.

Morrice's *1-2-3* was made for the Batsheva Dance Company in Israel earlier this year, and now receives its first performance by Ballet Rambert. I think it is Morrice's best ballet. The music for violin, viola and cello is by the Israeli Ben-Zion Orgad.

What I see is a flapping, undulant river of glittering plastic (held and agitated by invisible hands in either wing) in which Chrisopher Bruce disports himself in naked gaiety and abandon—more wonderful Tetleyan tumbles. He is joined by Peter Curtis, and then I see, in the words of Hopkins,

> *how the boys*
> *with dare and with down-dolphinry and bellbright bodies huddling out,*
> *are earthworld, airworld, waterworld thorough hurled, all by turn and turn about.*

Next comes a girl, Mary Willis, to introduce a note of competition into this pagan picnic. And she goes out and comes on again in one of those mystery Graham-garments, which at first appears to be a cloak then is seen to fan out from her secret centre, and to which she attaches both boys so that at the end we are left wondering.

Them and Us, a brand-new work by Morrice, has taped music by Iannis Xenakis 'whose elements are clouds of sound—like clouds of smoke—made up of an indefinite number of particles' and who 'to control his clouds of sound . . . applies the theory of probabilities, the only theory capable of dealing with great numbers' (Jan Maguire). I saw his *Metastasis* in New York, which 'was composed with Maxwell Boltzmann's theory of gas', and thought Balanchine's choreography had lost its way in it.

With the aid of a number of witty masks by Nadine Baylis, Morrice does a satirical piece about people conforming to types, in the middle of which (incongruously) two dancers with lions on elastic leads get tangled up embarrassingly. I thought for a moment the idea was to send up a computerized score by making a ballet about mass-produced people, but I think I must be wrong and will look again.

In the pub in the interval a young man told us he was working on a ballet without dancers in it.

2.6.68

Moore's *Remembered Motion* at the Jeannetta Cochrane

It seems to be a sign of Ballet Rambert's self-confidence that they should not have given such successful works as Morrice's *Hazard* and Tetley's *Pierrot Lunaire* during their latest London season. Indeed, they have built up a strong and varied repertory of new ballets in a remarkably short time.

The newest presentation was produced in the workshop and briefly mentioned in this column a few months ago. *Remembered Motion* is devised by Geoff Moore, who is twenty-three and has never been a dancer.

His sound-track is self-sufficient, being a sort of spoken dramatic monologue with only little occasional bursts of twangling instrumental music by Malcolm Fox, who is twenty-one—yet monologue is not really the word for it because although only one girl's voice was used it has been turned into a palimpsest of overlaid sounds.

She is being analyzed and she is in bed with her lover, or perhaps she is just pouring out her unhappy memories to him between bouts of ecstatic love-making. Sometimes the words are spoken straight, sometimes speeded up or truncated, and there are mechanically contrived *glissandi* and *glou-glous* which, perhaps, represent the journey through time or into the depths of the subconscious. The result, recorded and with sound treatment by David Vorhaus, is a wonderful piece of work.

The girl's character is divided between two dancers, Gayrie MacSween and Nicoline Nystrom, so that we see her simultaneously as active and passive, as spectator, lover and patient; Peter Curtis being the man, lover and analyst. Most of the ballet is a *pas de deux*, but there are beautiful glimpses of four conjoined girls who are revealed now and then by a change of lighting inside a tall orange chimney or canister to the left of the stage, a quadruple caryatid of goddesses or fates. Geoff Moore's sound-track comes over more important than his choreography, but he's a smart guy.

A programme which includes with this Ben-Zion Orgad's Trio for Strings, accompanying Morrice's *1-2-3*, and Stockhausen's Kontakte and amazing Gesang der Jünglinge which accompany Tetley's *Ziggurat*, is aurally rich. A bit of Kurt Weill on the piano in between, being the score for Tudor's *Judgment of Paris*, sounded almost sentimental and old-fashioned. Tudor's comedy, in which Julia Blaikie, Patricia Rianne and Gayrie MacSween were the world-weary prostitutes, was greeted by loud laughter.

The Waiter was played by Paul Taras, a newcomer to the company, who was subtle and funny and who had been as subtle as was humanly possible in Chesworth's bawdy *Tic-Tack* to that tune of Kreisler's the week before.

9.6.68

Chesworth's *H* at the Phoenix

The stage of the Phoenix is an ideal size for Ballet Rambert and on the opening night of their short season (which runs another week) all the ballets given looked good on it.

John Chesworth's new work *H* was postponed until he could obtain permission to use the music of Krzyszof Penderecki, and I don't doubt that for Chesworth it seemed the *only* music possible as an accompaniment to his work: others might think an alternative could have been found.

The interesting noises and silences lull us into a sense of unpreparedness for the booming chord of D major which concludes *H* and which should send us reeling out to obstruct the Charing Cross Road until war has been abolished from the earth.

For *H* is not a ballet but a blow—beneath the belt, naturally—like *US** or the Oxfam ads. Two white-coated lady scientists in the universal lab dispassionately record the madness and suffering of self-destructive mankind.

The idea is striking to say the least and Chesworth has found images of molten radioactive flesh which do him credit. I nearly caught myself writing that we had *had* the ballet of protest, that the *H* has gone out of horror—then I remembered that I was the sworn foe of gypsies, fairies and jesters in ballet, the champion of the contemporary, and stopped in time.

* A 'protest piece', partly improvized, directed by Peter Brook for the Royal Shakespeare Company.

But I will say that in the end the public get wise to the most shocking shock tactics—that staring-out-the-audience lark, for instance; that you either have to keep moving pretty fast nowadays not to get out of date, or else stand dead still; and that it might be possible next week to bring off even more piercingly than this creepy-crawly shocker a danced ballet about a child mourning over a broken doll.

Meaning in ballet!—Oh well, Tetley's *Ziggurat*, which got us all guessing a month or two ago, still seems wonderful to look at, full of powerful images and flashing messages; and Stockhausen's score is a joy—'*Et O ces voix d'enfants, chantant dans la coupole.*'

But as for meaning I now merely see an idyllic interlude between two nightmare battles or journeys, during which a god topples, is revived, takes an interest in men and leads them forward to the conquest of new worlds.

It is now generally accepted back in the buildings that Morrice's exciting *Hazard*, with its Salzedo score, is about Christopher Bruce and Jonathan Taylor as two stags in the rutting season—and jolly marvellous they are. Tuesday was altogether a good evening.

11.2.68

Morrice's *That is the Show* at the Jeannetta Cochrane

I suddenly realize as I sit down to write this that I have no idea what Norman Morrice's new ballet is called as I haven't even looked at the programme—the second one, because I lost the first one in the bar and the excitement. Well, I have looked now; and it is called *That is the Show*.

The music of Luciano Berio is like what happens when you are dying and all experience past, present and future is whizzing by at such a speed, and a life-time of childish doubts about time and space, life, death, before and after is utterly dissolved and resolved, and remembrance of things past is too feeble a phrase for it because all the world's a stage for ever and pleasure is no different from pain. I do not know if it is good music, with its palimpsest of voices in several languages, but it took us to the moon and back and filled the theatre with angels.

So I suppose Norman Morrice had been waiting and watching, learning, absorbing and practising, and taking a bit from Graham here or Tetley there—as Ben Nicholson took bits from Picasso and Alfred Wallis and Mondrian and became absolutely his marvellous self—when suddenly he heard this music and knew what to do and how to do it.

Nadine Baylis is a very clever, ingenious designer, but I think she knew cleverness was not called for, and what she did was white and simple. The wonderful company, you could tell, knew what they had got landed with and were proud and showed it in the modesty of their dancing; Sandra Craig and Christopher Bruce being the principals who live and love and die and are reborn.

It was pelting with rain when we came out, but we walked slowly home through it, because we knew nothing really matters except masterpieces. Then we dried our hair and drank champagne, which doesn't happen every day. I suddenly recalled Delacroix's description of how, when he was first shown *The Raft of the Medusa* by Géricault, he was so excited he ran all the way home. And you don't see somebody doing *that* every day in the streets of Paris either, not even in the Romantic Period.

9.5.71

At the Young Vic

'A what?' called Marie Rambert across the dark arena of the Young Vic. 'A jig-saw', replied John Chesworth, continuing his instructions to the group of dancers who were going to improvize *Ad hoc* to the fitful accompaniment of Anthony Hymas, cued by lighting signals from, presumably, Chesworth himself.

It was all rather fun, for in *Dance for New Dimensions*, i.e. in a horse-shoe, which the buoyant advance guard of British ballet began trying out in the Cut on Thursday and which continues for another twelve per-formances, anything goes; and the experiments of seven choreographers (so far) have flowered or withered in an atmosphere of total intimacy. It was the nearest thing to being in bed with the Ballet Rambert.

Intimacy is what we gain in exchange for relinquishing the stage picture, intimacy enhanced by the friendly audience and by the dancers' utter naturalness. *They* seemed to be thinking and behaving rather than dancing: *we* seemed to be at a party rather than a show. And what character and variety their faces have—the eager Graham Jones, the intense Ptolemaic Marilyn Williams, Medicean Joseph Scoglio, frank Peter Curtis, faunlike Christopher Bruce! And once, when a blue Lautrec light fell on the tilted nose of Sandra Craig, she was an ageless sphinx of desert and night-club.

Bruce's '*for these who die as cattle*', the most successful work shown, began in a mood of epic adventure, then, as four men lay dead or dying, and Craig and Burge Lucy mourned without expression to the sound of no music, and Bruce ran fingers through his victims' hair, realizing the waste of war, Wilfred Owen's message came across.

Jonathan Taylor had arranged a long number for Bruce to Prokofiev's Violin solo (Op. 115), a *tour de force* taxing to all parties. We had Bartok and jazz. Much the funniest turn was a deadpan duet created by Pietje Law for Scoglio and Julia Blaikie to Jack Buchanan's *Good-night Vienna*.

One word of admiration for the fine white floor by Marley, vinyl stretched over wood and felt, on which coloured patterns were projected before or during numbers: a super-idea, no doubt, of Nadine Baylis.

12.3.72

Taylor's *Listen to the Music* at the Jeannetta Cochrane

I can tell from the start that this is going to be one of those articles in which I drag in my private life and bolster up my fleeting whimsies with the opinions of others. Dear God, where will it all end?

Looking at the way I was dressed the other night, Marie Rambert commented 'Sometimes you are so with-it, and at other times you are—without it.' The same might be said of the programme of Ballet Rambert, now roistering at the Cochrane Theatre. For some reason there was much more life in Wednesday's than there had been in the first night's the week before. To the latter I had taken a country neighbour, and thought he might enjoy the Tudor merrie-making of Jonathan Taylor's *'Tis Goodly Sport*: but he found its heartiness only relieved by the yearning solo of Joseph Scoglio, who in Christopher Bruce's bearded absence suddenly shone out as the bright particular star of the company.

I badly missed Paul Taras in the drag role, wondered if he had left, and was still languishing for him on Wednesday when he leapt on to the stage during Tetley's *Ziggurat* and lit up the scene with his vitality. This early (1967) work of the American choreographer, with its panting spider-men galvanized into fearful activity around their blind god, its heart-piercing Stockhausen score and its perhaps unnecessary projections by over-brimming Baylis, still thrills me with its mystery and terror; but I think it gets lost in the lyrical middle section, and the pampered beauty who was with me said she thought it was only *pretending* to mean something, which annoyed her.

Jonathan Taylor, deviser of the notorious *Bertram Batell's Side Show*, is a man of ideas; his latest joke is called *Listen to the Music* and it is inspired by a kind of radio programme in which a woman instructs children how to move to music. To bits of *Casse-Noisette* and *Francesca da Rimini*, Bizet, Auber and Gershwin, six dancers are told to get up, sit down, close their eyes, find something, get hold of it. 'Is it big?' What Lucy Burge gets hold of is part of Gideon Avrahami, and the question 'Is it hard?' brings down the house. One boy falls out wounded and bleeding, the two just mentioned begin making love, a girl collapses in a box, and finally Scoglio is left alone to dance a frantic solo to Debussy. The odd thing is that this becomes quite serious, even though, at the end, our hero is attached to wires and ascends gracefully to heaven.

8.10.72

At Sadler's Wells; Falco and Bruce; the designs of Baylis

So Norman Morrice is back from his six-month sabbatical and Ballet Rambert are back at Sadler's Wells after fifty years in outer space in the round at the Young Vic, and Nadine Baylis, their designer-in-chief, who specialises in the sexy and terrifying, is complaining that there is less room, except heightwise, than at the Jeannetta Cochrane.

And after all these years of studying the Rambert dancers' faces in the round in the flesh on the spot, suddenly to see them in a frame in perspective in a row reveals to us the fact that they are a rum lot—one man bald, one hairy as Esau, one fashionably black and nine foot tall (therefore only suited to leading roles) and one girl with a weight problem. All they lack is a few pregnant Chinese.

Two new works, both interesting. *tutti-frutti* by American Louis Falco was a kind of exercise in being all shook up. The dancers, led by Christopher Bruce and Marilyn Williams, had learnt Falco's language of dislocation and the thing worked. The taped score by Burt Alcantara was apocalyptic pop, i.e. the swelling, repetitive, vaguely Oriental, Hammond organ kind. It seemed clear to me that we were on a trip, seeing our bodies and other people's in an odd way, having crazy sensations together and apart. The Neapolitan ice-cream coloured costumes (whence the title) and the iridescent suspended chimney-pots of William Katz reinforced my impression that these were Patrick Procktor's 1968 flower children dreaming in the penthouses of Manhattan, and Procktor, who happened to be with me, arrived at the same conclusion separately. A fine surge of sound: a pretty, funny vision.

Christopher Bruce's *Duets* I thought was an original experiment in everybody being slightly out of sync., i.e. doing the same movement not quite together. I'm told, though, that *occasionally* they were meant to be more together. Movement mostly classical: three couples: a peaceful idyllic mood, enhanced by the delicate chiming music of Brian Hodgson, electronic with a bit of concrete, which I took to be cow-bells but was told was glasses (drinking). Nadine Baylis's simple set was (for her) downright pastoral.

She is really the company's star. Her silver set for Morrice's horrific *Blind-sight*, her pendant tatters for Tetley's *Rag-dances*, her white gymnasium for Morrice's *That is the Show* are all marvels. But, for the season's opening ballet, Morrice's *The Empty Suit*, the company rebelled and wore squalid practice clothes, determined to look their worst.

23.9.73

London Contemporary Dance Theatre

Opening of The Place

And so Lord Goodman opened The Place with a flourish on Tuesday and the London Contemporary Dance Company began its first season in its fine new home. Martha Graham, who had inspired in Robin Howard the amazing labours which are producing such shining results, was not present in the flesh, as six of her dancers were, but then, as Browning said, Never the time and The Place and the loved one all together.

The central work of the first programme was an early Graham piece, which we have always heard about and never seen, and it was of prime interest. *El Penitente*, danced to music of Louis Horst and with props by Noguchi, is for two men and a girl and is inspired by Mexican religious observances.

Robert Cohan as the Penitent scourges himself and prays; Noemi Lapzeson appears to him as Mary Magdalen, as Virgin and Mother; and William Louther, in primitive mask and crown of thorns, is the Christ who gives him his cross to bear. These are three intense and passionate artists, and a religious mood shone through the childish trappings.

Cohan's *Side Scene*, which preceded this, had props suggesting a playground, and five dancers played charmingly at games of skill, including love. The music was sixteenth-century. Cohan's *Sky* we have admired before. This time Noemi Lapzeson and Robert Powell were here from New York to perform the poetic rituals of the Sky People and the Rainbow People.

In the second programme Cohan's *Shanta Quintet* to music for string quartet and sitar by John Mayer put the company through their paces and showed us how well trained and rehearsed they are; there were Grahamish costumes and some grand stylized copulation. *Hermit Songs*, a solo by Alvin Ailey to songs by Samuel Barber, was about St. Francis in ecstasy and it was marvellously danced by Louther.

Barry Moreland is a new name. In *Cortège*, a piece to Bach on the harpsichord for seven girls, he makes an auspicious début. There is a coffin and they are mourning, but at the end they rejoice, and this seems quite acceptable.

Cohan's *Eclipse*, which like *Sky* is to music by Eugene Lester, gave an opportunity for the superb Lapzeson and Cohan, with Dawn Suzuki and Dinah Goodes, to expound some slow mysterious acrobatics. We see more new works next week.

7.9.69

Cohan's *Cell*

Everything about Robert Cohan's latest work, *Cell*, given by the London Contemporary Dance Company at The Place on Thursday, is novel and impressive.

First we see a wonderful decor of Mycenean simplicity by Norberto Chiesa—a white polystyrene ramp, between white walls, which swerves mysteriously round a corner at the back, leaving us to imagine the worst. For this is a ballet of nightmare, terror and break-down. The taped sounds of Ronald Lloyd keep us guessing—liquid rustlings, havoc on piano strings, strange whimpers and glutinous whirrs.

The appearance of the six dancers is interesting too, because they are so contrasted: Noemi Lapzeson with her pale, exotic beauty; blonde Clare Duncan; Micheline McKnight who looks Indian; Norman Murray a handsome Negro; Robert Dodson, tall and romantic and the chief character; Robert Powell, small, pale, vulnerable, with frightened eyes and a mop of brown hair. They wear less clothes in each of the three 'movements': first, Kings Road gear in grey and murky pink, then violent-coloured all-over tights, then almost nothing. This no doubt symbolizes their gradual removal from everyday life, increasing isolation, or the stripping down of personality to essentials.

I have often thought that if I were buried alive with my girl friend like those people in *Aida* the last thing I should sing about was love. However the three couples flung into this cell begin to console themselves by love, and it doesn't work for long.

Falling, embracing, sliding, hiding in corners, groping round walls, clutching, crawling, photographing Powell, a scarlet starfish on the floor. There are some striking poses. At the end when the five others have run out to be shot by whoever lurks round that corner—God the jailor—Powell is left to panic alone. Panels in the two side walls become transparent to reveal the silhouettes of the two other men—crucified. A strobe light flickers. Madness has come. Powell's legs bicycle mindlessly in the air. A shower of white bricks begins to fall. Powell, frantic, begins building, building. Is he walling himself in?

Clover Roope's *Solo and Trio for Two* to music by Alexander Goehr is a distinguished piece of choreography, beautifully danced by Clare Duncan, Linda Gibbs and Derek Linton. Barry Moreland's *Hosannas* is a rather Gothic dance for three to Scarlatti against stained-glass windows. Cohan's *Hunter of Angels* is Jacob wrestling with the Angel—Cohan with Powell—who turns out to be Esau, and it happens in and out of a double aluminium ladder and is quite gripping.

It is a cheering thought that, thanks to Robin Howard, who has sold hotels to pay for it, we have a modern dance company in this country into which Martha Graham's fine dancers can fit without destroying its balance; and although we cannot expect to keep the Graham dancers for ever, thanks to Howard's London School of Contemporary Dance, also housed at The Place, there will be a constant stream of young people following in their train.

The London Contemporary Dance Company have made the most propitious début in their new home and I hope they will live there happily ever after.

14.9.69

Louther's *Vesalii Icones*

You wouldn't think the Queen Elizabeth Hall was suited to dancing, but the dancing of William Louther to Peter Maxwell Davies's *Vesalii Icones* suited itself to the Queen Elizabeth Hall in such a way that Tuesday was one of the most exciting evenings for years. The fact that the stage was not a stage actually helped. The band were sunk a bit down in front, but the solo cellist was on the same level as the dancer—except that *he* didn't stay on the same level, but clambered up steps and in front of or behind her, and at one moment played the piano. This all established a sense of intimacy which made me think of Isadora. Art became part of life.

And Louther's choreography, woven around the Vesalius anatomical engravings, which Davies had made into Stations of the Cross, was wonderful. Louther, as everyone knows, is a Negro and a Graham dancer. His naked figure conveyed in tragic poses the glory and horror of man's destiny as animal, hero, son of God, work of art, feast for worms and finally skeleton.

I was reminded in a way of Petrushka with his dual nature of man and puppet. And the marvellous newness of the sound, as well as the Shakespearean richness produced by mixing in and transmuting other men's music, sacred or profane, reminded me of Stravinsky's ballet too. Peter Maxwell Davies seems capable of tricks as divine as that by which Stravinsky made his orchestra simulate panting accordions—to suggest, inexplicably, the enormity of the Russian winter.

14.12.69

Cohan's *Stages*

Robert Cohan's *Stages*, which the London Contemporary Dance Theatre are performing daily including Sundays, but excluding Mondays and Tuesdays, at The Place, until 9 May, is about myths and heroes. WHAM!

Do you know Thurber's story about the obscure youth who flew solo round the world in a rickety do-it-yourself plane, and how people only realized what was going on when he was half way round, and how America had to manufacture an image for him (it was a sort of joke about Lindbergh), and how when he landed in triumph, with the President waiting, he turned out to be awful? If I remember right he was a rat-like type, rude and mean: he didn't talk, he snarled. And he wasn't modest: he was boastful.

Heroes are ordinary men, but they do something extraordinary. Like writers. And in this century, success, publicity and the over-excitement these engender, can have an alarming effect on their nervous sytems. They start hitting reporters and smashing cameras, or they take too many sleeping pills, like Marilyn. Being a writer, that is, having a strong imagination, I do not need to experience this to know what it is like.

This experience is what Cohan's amazing ballet is about, more or less. You have to see it. It must have been boiling up inside him for some time; and I guess he had labour pains. OUCH!

To begin with, Cohan turned The Place back to front: where you usually sit, they perform: and vice-versa. This is, for some reason, marvellous. Part One is dark ancient myth, the first man earning his spurs (his soul, his passport from bestiality to humanity) in confrontation with the Minotaur. That monster, which has to be faced, is not just the terror that crawls out from under a stone or lies in wait round the blind corner, but the you at the down-down-down-bottom of you. Cohan uses film— close-ups of William Louther tasting, touching, feeling. And Robert

North and others in veined tights are other selves and experiences. The whammy costumes are by Peter Farmer. WOW! The lighting is by John B. Read and the film sequences are by Anthony McCall, whom I herewith dub Ritter (that's German for Knight) Read and Marquess McCall. ZOOM! The first part has electro-music by Arne Nordheim.

The second part has 'open music' by Bob Downes, and oh boy! William Louther, the modern hero, struts in his stadium and the kid-gymnasts gawp. The back of his peterfarmer T-shirt is cute. Left alone, the hero displays his ordinariness and Louther his gift for comedy. Then he has to meet the modern monster, as the Beatles did, and Marilyn did, and Mohammed Ali did and George Best did. The Temple of Fame has luminous steps. In it are revealed the silver-faced sirens. Silver columns rise, the lighting is psychedelic. The flashing ballyhoo of pandemonium.

But on the top step of the high altar-pyramid of sacrifice, like Samson rebellious, Samson Agonistes, Cohan's hero-victim turns. He pulls down the pillars and the roof, and amid the smoke he shoots—shoots *us*. AARGH! Then he resolutely walks through a door whose sign lights up: EXIT.

2.5.71

Robert Powell's last performance

Sometimes something unexpected comes across. I was at The Place on Wednesday to see the first performance in England of Anna Sokolow's *Scenes from the Music of Charles Ives*. Charles Ives was that Sunday composer who never heard any of his own music played (can that be true or did I dream it?) and who I think was posthumously 'discovered' by Balanchine. The great choreographer arranged several of Ives's pieces as a ballet, and I well remember the extraordinary sensation of seeing and hearing *Ivesiana* for the first time at old City Center.

Out of the four pieces used by Anna Sokolow, two—the second and the fourth—namely, 'Central Park in the Dark' and 'Unanswered Question,' were part of the Balanchine ballet, and therefore familiar. Mysterious magical music! The third piece is called 'The Pond/The Cage/The Pond' and it was danced as a solo by Robert Powell.

We foundation members of the Old England Martha Graham Fan Club recall our first sight of Powell when he was one of Graham's extraordinary principal dancers. No Graham soloist was ever like another. They did not come out of a mould. Think of Bertram Ross, think of Helen McGehee, think of Ethel Winter, think of Noemi Lapzeson who is now the star of Dance Theatre, think of Robert Cohan, who is its boss.

Robert Powell's solo at The Place was sad, strange and over-powering. Here was this youngish man (thirty?—I never know people's ages) with long hair and a lot of ribs, rolling on the ground and curling up. What I saw was Grünewald's crucified Christ in the big altar-piece at Colmar. In the interval, as I stood slightly stunned near the bar, a friend came up and said 'Powell has decided to fly back to America tomorrow. He wants this to be his last performance. He is going to do some other kind of work.' This was all news to me—I think it was news to my informant, Bob Cohan.

Nobody who danced as Robert Powell did on Wednesday could be said to have danced in vain.*

30.1.72

At The Place

Here are some of the things they do to avoid actual dancing at The Place. In Stephen Barker's *Fugue* Robert North in a tail-coat unwraps a number of small musical instruments and wraps them up again while two girls stand about and two blind tramps grope across the stage, briefly recovering their sight to perform infantry drill movements. In Xenia Hribar's *Treeo*, Paula Lansley, as a sexy Eve, scoots around on a mobile Tree of Knowledge, learning the facts of life from Stephen Barker's smooth Tempter, and when the latter takes time off to teach Namron's brutish Adam the use of spade and pneumatic drill, shouts plaintively 'You fancy him!' *Out-side-in* by Anthony van Laast and Micha Bergese starts during the interval with the dusting of a motor-bike and incorporates shadow-play. In Noemi Lapzeson's *Conundrum* girls do quite ingenious and sculptural things with knotted mushrooms, calling out 'Anthony' or 'Harold' when they need lifting. In her *Cantabile* (not new), there is of course a ballad-singing Miss Havisham on a bicycle. In Richard Alston's *Tiger Balm* four nightgowned ladies mourn a very active naked North to the accompaniment of a death-rattle.

Robert Cohan's *People—Alone*, with its handsome painted screens by Norberto Chiesa, which are turned into platforms by angelic scene-shifters, is, I think, about lonely people who either go mad or *are* mad, like the simpering old maid of Clare Duncan, pathetic in 1930s flowered

* Robert Powell committed suicide in 1977.

D2

chiffon. Bob Downes's commissioned score is an exciting composite of tapes, voices and such delicate instruments as the Chinese bamboo flute.

3.9.72

At the Shaw

London Contemporary Dance Theatre must be in the money, what with all their colour film sequences and expensive-looking sets and costumes: they also seem to be bursting with ideas.

Of new works shown at the Shaw Theatre during the Camden Festival I have briefly mentioned Robert North's *Still Life*, which is perhaps a fragment of autobiography in dance and film. North is seen escaping from bestial family life in a gloomy back street to fall in love with Linda Gibbs as she gets borne away on a tube train, then catching up with her later in the Lasson Gallery, where the two of them lose themselves in a peculiar landscape something between the Barbizon school and Monticelli. Full of ingenuities, though one has to admit that when film and dance unfold together, film always wins.

The point of myths is that they have a universal application, but when that storm-tossed intellectual, Robert Cohan, gets hold of one—as he did in *Stages* and has now done in *Myth*—he tends to envelop it in such veils of transcendental mystification that its meaning ends up a dark secret between God and himself. His *No-man's Land*, with handsome costumes and a gleaming metal Hades by Peter Farmer, is self-confessedly about Orpheus, but when I asked a company official if *Myth* was about Theseus I got a rather snappish 'Don't know'. Heroic attitudes by Micha Bergese, Siobhan Davies and the company ; a booming score by Burt Alcantara.

Bergese's own *Hinterland* shows three grey spinster sisters dreaming of the man they might have married, who, in each case, is Micha Bergese. Very cleverly worked out, and the old popular tunes are a pleasure in themselves. Miss Davies's *The Calm*, to an original score by Geoffrey Burgon, combining a live counter tenor, Kevin Smith, with taped trumpet, violin and harp, has some very fine dancing.

Cathy Lewis's *Extinction* is an effective surrealist treatment of the end-of-the-world theme, with white-tie-and-tailed courtiers ensuring that their pretty prince, Bergese, survives longest. North's all-male *Troy-Game*, to the irresistible rhythms and rattles of Batucada music, is a funny joke about Greek athletes—and incidentally a smash hit.

2.3.75

The Changing Scene
(1972—1975)

Muse

Always on the move, standing on her head and doing cartwheels, she was called 'Quicksilver' by her nurse, and *Quicksilver* is the name of Dame Marie Rambert's autobiography. But just as Falstaff was not only witty in himself but the cause of wit in other men, so this perpetual mobiliser has electrified all those who came within her orbit, some of whom have been the most luminous inventors of movement in our country. Without her to launch them, the new stars of Ashton, Tudor, Howard, Gore and Morrice might never have swum into our ken.

No one who has grown as familiar with the classics of European literature as Marie Rambert has could fail to express herself with easy elegance. Her book is three things: the extraordinary story of how a Warsaw girl of Jewish descent became the wife of an English playwright and a founder of ballet in England; a series of impressions of great dancers, Isadora, Pavlova, Karsavina, as well as a description of working with Nijinsky; and a history of Ballet Rambert from the 1930s. The first will enthral those who delight in the diversity of human experience, the second will thrill lovers of art, the third will instruct students of ballet history.

We read how this rebellious subject of Nicholas II, joining a march of protest in 1905, was nearly cut down by Cossack sabres; how, after it was reported in a newspaper that she had burst into Isadora's dressing-room with tears and kisses, she 'dared to cry out' that she intended to dance; how she sat in the stalls with Diaghilev watching Nijinsky in *Narcisse* and heard the great man murmur under his breath 'What beauty!' then ask her 'Isn't he at his most perfect in this?' Rambert writes: 'I had been put very quickly *au courant* of Diaghilev's relations with Nijinsky, and could not but share their admiration for each other.' How witty, how tender!

Most readers will be amazed, I think, that this youthful pioneer of eighty-four, who has presided over the creation of Ashton's *Façade* to Walton's music, the invention of Tudor's *Dark Elegies* to Mahler's songs, and the construction of Morrice's *That is the Show* to Berio's uncanny Sinfonia, looks forward to a time when a divorce from music will give choreography a wider range.

23.7.72

Fonteyn

Friday was Fonteyn night; and, what's more, the rumour was abroad that this was to be the divine creature's last appearance at the Royal Opera House.

Fonteyn and Nureyev gave their famous interpretations of *Marguerite and Armand*, a melodrama which now creaks like a haunted house and which is perhaps to be allowed to subside in the quicksands of oblivion. But we were there—and Margot's mother and Dame Ninette were certainly there too—for the curtain calls. Dame Margot gave her old partner, Michael Somes, a flower and kissed him. She gave Leslie Edwards, her old friend, a flower and kissed him. She gave the rest of the bunch to Rudolf Nureyev, who bowed most exquisitely over her hand. Flowers fell; tears, too.

23.12.73

A tallman

Tall men have always been irresistibly drawn to sit in front of me in the theatre. One of these was Pavlova's manager and perhaps husband, Victor Dandré, who often had the stall in front of mine when I began to get free seats in 1939. Apart from being a first-rate view-blocker and the architect of Pavlova's career, he was the most uninformative biographer who ever lived.

30.9.73

India

Kama Dev, who has hitherto given only solo recitals of Indian dancing in London, brought to the Commonwealth Institute on Wednesday a small company with whom he has been touring in Persia, France and Italy.

We expect colour and glitter in the costumes of Indian dancers, but the materials and ornaments worn by this company have a special subtlety. One is constantly surprised and thrilled by an imaginative combination of colours.

Kama Dev was the first dancer to show us the exquisite style of Kuchipudi. He continues to seek out the lesser-known forms of Indian dance. It took several journeys to the State of Orissa in North India before

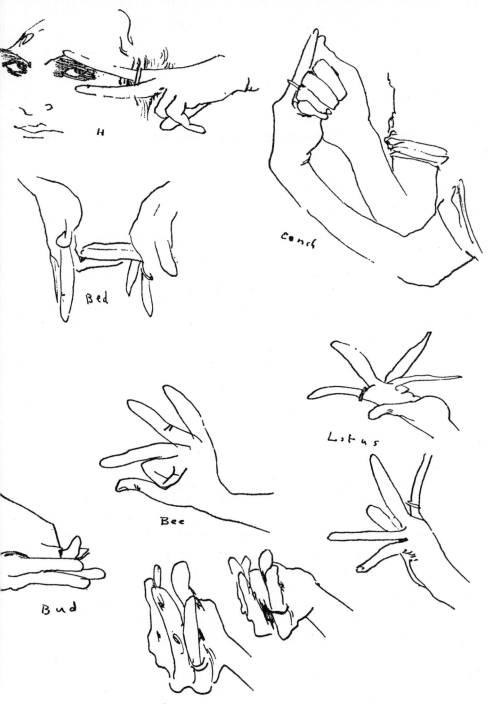

H

Conch

Bed

Lotus

Bee

Bud

Kama Dev performing *mudras*.
Drawings by Patrick Procktor

he was able to beg the secrets of Chhau dancing from the court of the local rajah. His two Chhau dances were the novelties of this programme. They are simple compared to the ornate classical numbers, but wonderfully expressive. It is odd that to represent a wounded deer or a peacock, the dancer should wear a doll-like human mask, yet it turns out just right; and the rather clumsy costumes with their commonplace colour-schemes seem a pledge of authenticity.

The miming of the peacock was extraordinary—I wished Sir Frederick Ashton could have seen it. It happens that I have often watched the pecking strut of peacocks, and Kama Dev conveyed it perfectly. The combination of refined artistic skill and naïve local flavour constitutes the charm of Chhau dancing, and I understood why Kama Dev had taken the trouble to study these out-of-the-way numbers.

We are familiar with Kama Dev's agility and potency in classical Indian dance. I prefer him in an abstract dance like *Thillana*, with its intricate rhythms, to such story-telling numbers as *Tarangam*, when the features can become almost too sweetly expressive. But, to tell the truth, I am getting fed up with the cocksure Krishna's flirtations with milkmaids. One of these centuries a girl is going to give him a good slap and wipe the smirk off that handsome face.

22.10.73

Massine

The noise was terrifying. There were only eight people in the top-floor studio at the Dance Centre in Floral Street, but the stamping, the shouting and the echoes made me think I was back in the army. Leonide Massine and I are old friends, but I had never watched him rehearse before. He looked around for another chair, but there was none, and I crouched hurriedly on the floor, leaning against the mirror wall. The rehearsal of *The Three-cornered Hat* continued.

Juan Sanchez of Festival Ballet was the Miller, and he was just being arrested. So off he went, and it was the turn of Noleen Nicoll as the Miller's Wife to dance her lamentation. The shouting began again. I really wondered the poor girl could take in anything, what with the echoes.

'Your steps are inexpressive because they are undecided. It's after 4! Tiri-tiri-*da*! *Eee*—one, two, *three*. In Spain you don't laugh about things like that. When you are arrested, you are arrested for good. All supplication! "*Don't* take him away".'

Massine (77 next August) got up to demonstrate her pleading—1, 2, 3, 4, with the gesture on the fourth beat. 'Be Spanish woman, not butterfly. Oh, NO!' He stamped furiously. The girl knelt, then rising, twirled her skirt. 'Express it choreographically, not emotionally. Now mood changes. Now she gets angry again.' Aside: 'Juan, *stop* that *zapateado*!'

'It's in rhythm, in movement of skirt, not in face, not smile, not grimaces. He's gone—then, "Ah! I show them all". Posture must have resolution. I'm only here twenty-four hours. I lost my voice teaching you.' (It was true: he was hoarse.) 'In Flamenco arms are turning either inwards or outwards.' He demonstrated, his arms becoming Ss. 'Three bars that's good.' Massine got up and was a prowling beast, then *shake*! 'Too much legato.' Aside to the pianist: 'Why you play so slow, by the way?'

He showed the girl again, languid then brisker. 'You can do the part, but you are slow to hear what I say. I have to torture you. This alone will make you an artist if you do it right. Now, the entrance of each part of the body. Audience only impressed by clear vision. Don't mix them up, it makes a salad. Go!'

In the music the cuckoo mocked the Miller's Wife. Cuckoo! Cuckoo! 'It's a nasty gap. Keep through the same face.' Then came a marvellous pose which I remembered. She lent forward, bending her advanced knee, fluttering her hands behind her. Was she being a bird? ('Yes, a wounded bird,' Massine confirmed later.) It was like a poet's simile in physical terms, simple and great. 'That would be almost good, only you have jerky movements. Dancing should be like singing.' Then, emphasizing the significance of a tiny movement of the wrist, 'Every little part of body counts. Flute is just as important in orchestra as clarinet and *hautbois*.' Then he murmured something about 'big sorrow' and 'Gardens of Generalife.'

Now the Miller's Wife knelt mourning upstage centre. Enter the Corregidor, the lustful old governor of the province, who had arrested her husband. He was a boy with a witty Latin face, and as he hobbled comically forward (shadowed by Terry Hayworth, who was also learning the role) I thought he would be good. Massine was harder to satisfy. Aside to me he said 'Woizikovsky was twenty when he played this man of fifty.' I hoped he meant seventy.

With his back to us, the Corregidor spotted the Miller's Wife. His delight and anticipation were expressed in two or three jumps with bent knees. This too seemed to me some kind of animal simile. 'No, my dear. You think "Where is that beautiful girl I see this afternoon. I must find her. I must have her." *Go!*' The Corregidor pounced, and the Miller's

Wife pushed him in the river. Massine clapped to stop the music. He demonstrated the rhythm of the girl's triumphant tattoo. '1-2-3; 1-2-3-4-5. Control your movement up to your nails!'

4.3.73

Death in Venice

It was only right that Frederick Ashton, that eminent Suffolk choreographer, should collaborate on Britten's latest seaside opera, *Death in Venice*. Very soon after his first appearance young Robert Huguenin as Tadzio takes the pose of Giovanni da Bologna's statue, in ballet called *attitude*, to show us he is the Hermes who will conduct Aschenbach's soul to the underworld. As his mother, Deanne Bergsma has much of the aristocratic beauty and 1911 elegance of Silvana Mangano in Visconti's film, which, even if Britten never saw, I bet Ashton did.

Arranging sporting events on the beach was an unusual assignment for Ashton, and the long-jump and discus-throwing are handled rather literally. The dream-sequence, with a *corps* of mad monks holding Tadzio aloft like a sublime incubus over the feverish author, was easy—remember *Apparitions*. The real challenge to the choreographer, and the one which his poetic imagination soared to seize, was in the last few bars of the opera. Would Tadzio raise his arm, as in the film, beckoning the soul of Aschenbach out to sea? No. Striding with bent knees slowly upstage to the chiming music, in a diagonal from the dying man's deckchair, he writhes his arms and twists his head contrapuntally, a Laocoon without snakes. Even thus, I knew, would Michelangelo, had he been a ballet master, convey the swimming of a godlike messenger through space.

24.6.73

Lindsay Kemp

I usually grind to a halt half-way through the novels of Jean Genet because there are so many words I do not know, but I get the message clearly enough to recognize that Lindsay Kemp's *Flowers*, which I went belatedly to see last week—and went two nights running, actually paying the second time—mirrors truthfully Genet's individual fusion of sex, masochism, religion, blasphemy, beauty and squalor.

Kemp devised this dragodrama, running now at the Regent (Poly)

Theatre; he directed it; and he performs in it with a talented company. The devising is brilliant, the direction is masterly, the performance is overpowering. Productionwise it is the most stunning show in London.

I kick myself for having been kept away from *Flowers* for so long by a summer surfeit of ballet and a distaste for the pallid pathos of mimes like Marceau, whom I presumed Kemp would resemble. Well, they have something in common, and Kemp's silent slow-motion arias are so long-drawn-out that they could be thought embarrassing. Yet I find them as necessary to the whole as, say, the appearance of Martha Graham with her company when she was over seventy.

Andrew Wilson's electronic score, with a collage of popular and classical music, sacred and profane, contributes enormously to the savage spectacle. The set, with its upper gallery, is mysterious. The ragged costumes could not be bettered. The make-ups are the most original and poetic since Kathakali.

Unforgettable scenes are the frigid reception of Kemp on his first slow entry into the dive, dressed as a raddled old bride, then the arrival of a Byronic groom, Neil Caplan, and the waltz that converts the pimps and whores into romantic dreamers; the mocking of the Crucified, which shocked me till I realized it was the modern equivalent of Breughel and Bosch, designed to arouse pity and terror; the Cavafy-like falling in love of the two angel boys, Caplan and Tony Myers, staring into each other's eyes at the café table, impervious to the strip-teasing whores (from Tudor's *Judgment of Paris*); the final unmasking in a welter of blood.

I have never seen strobe lights used to greater effect than in the last scene. It really was as if the Veil of the Temple were rent in twain. We could use a producer of Lindsay Kemp's genius at Covent Garden, at the Coliseum and at the National.

14.7.74

Gala

Any excuse for spending more money on concerts and exhibitions is welcome, and our entry into the European Economic Community provides a grander pretext than most: but of course it is only a pretext, for the Channel has seldom been a cultural moat. As Dame Alicia Markova said to me at the Gala on Wednesday, she had never felt other than European since her days of touring with Diaghilev. If classical architecture and Renaissance painting came from the Mediterranean, as well as opera and the sonnet form, Romanticism was a northern export: Shakespeare, Scott and Byron inflamed the imaginations of all Europe, Goethe's *Werther* broke the barrier between Germany and France, and Napoleon traversed Europe with the Italian translation of Macpherson's Ossian in his carriage. Incidentally, Victor Hugo left his manuscripts to the Bibliothèque Nationale of Paris, 'which will one day be,' he wrote, 'the Library of the United States of Europe.'

And so to Covent Garden and the *Celebration in speech and song* which opened the *Fanfare* at the Royal Opera House on Wednesday. There was a demo outside. A few hundred hooligans—not apparently there for anti-Common Market reasons—had assembled with placards demanding 'In Enoch: Out Heath', and however absurd their opinions I found it touching that these people who were there to boo the Prime Minister and did so noisily, should be left unmolested by the stoutest phalanx of police I have ever seen in this neighbourhood, and, at that, on the pavement outside Bow Street Police Station.

Received by Lord Drogheda in his new Garter, amid a crowd of towering Coldstreamers and several dishy servicemen from the Nine Countries in interesting uniforms, the Queen and the Duke of Edinburgh appeared a few minutes later in the centrally contrived Royal Box, with Mr. Heath, to be greeted by a very odd version of the National Anthem arranged by Carl Davis. Nearest to the Royal party on its left was the Archbishop of Canterbury in magenta, and on the right were the organisers, Lords Goodman and Mancroft.

The house was festooned prettily with pink artificial roses. The Duchess of Bedford had the biggest tiara. I saw three Directors, past or present, of the Edinburgh International Festival. Unable to compete with all the orders and medals around me, I wished I had followed the example of Prince Felix Yusupov on another gaudy night, and come wearing nothing but my Rembrandt, removed from its frame and stretcher, secured neatly on one shoulder with a safety-pin.

7.1.73

Gala

On stage at the Gala in his honour, King Solomon Hurok was not only given a medal by Mayor Lindsay for making the United States conscious of music, but invested with the order of Isabella the Catholic by the brother of the Spanish pretender and his wife, Franco's grand-daughter.

In view of American protests over Russia's behaviour to Jews, the appearance of lovely Besmertnova at Sol's gala was a miracle too.

Highspots of the Gala, which Agnes de Mille and Helpmann compèred, were Fonteyn's *Swan Lake pas de deux* with Desmond Kelly, and Isaac Stern playing the violin solo; Haydée and Richard Cragun in a new Cranko *pas de deux* with dizzy lifts; Van Cliburn tintinabulating in a Liszt rhapsody; and the divine Natalia Besmertnova with Mikhail Lavrovksy in *Giselle* and *Spartacus*. Her *soubresauts* were breathtaking, her arms a fantasy of delicate mannerism. She had luckily brought a varied wardrobe, and to console us for the indisposition of Nureyev she threw in *The Dying Swan*. Nureyev was hoping to get better in time for London on Thursday. Whether the Soviet artistes would have appeared in the same programme as him I don't know.

Another miraculous recovery was that of NYCB's Edward Villella, who could not dance at the gala, but was on again the next night. Hurok never took much interest in Balanchine's company, though years ago he gave them the old Chagall sets for *Firebird*, possibly to save storage.

27.5.73

Gala

There was a lot about death in the middle part of Tuesday's Gala programme at Covent Garden, which made a change. In Ashton's *Walk to the Paradise Garden*, to Delius, Merle Park and David Wall clung beautifully together, but Derek Rencher got them in the end. In Béjart's *Chant du compagnon errant*, to Mahler's songs, cold reticent Anthony Dowell came to fetch the impulsive life-loving Rudolf Nureyev and led him into the shadows. 'It's a sort of miniature *Song of the Earth*', I said to Kenneth MacMillan. 'Well not *quite*,' he said ambiguously.

John Neumeier's *Don Juan* so-called *pas de deux*, which accommodated a funeral procession of at least twenty chanting monks, is set to Gluck and to part of Victoria's Requiem. In this, not the Commendatore but the ethereal ghost of divine Donna Margot came to fetch Don Rudolf away— and serve him right with his proud Velasquez strut and naughty irresistible mannerism of flicking back an unruly lock of hair. Fonteyn's ovation continued for fifteen minutes, during all of which time it rained daffodils. 'I've never seen such flowers!' I exclaimed. '*I have*,' said Erik Bruhn.

9.3.75

China

How long, I wonder, does it take to learn to balance an egg on a stick of bamboo on the bridge of your nose? A few years of practice, several hours a day? To learn to balance a second egg on top of that must surely be the work of a lifetime. Perhaps many generations of egg-balancers must be born and die, inheriting and passing on their traditional skill, before a third egg can be added. This feat, part of a juggling act called the Jolly Cooks, is one of countless miracles performed by The Chinese Acrobatic Theatre from Shanghai, now at the Coliseum.

Another marvel of juggling, striking in its simplicity, is that of the Porcelain Jars. The artist makes a vase roll up his right arm, over his head and down his left arm. Then, swinging a larger jar—a *cache-pot* big enough to hold a good clump of hydrangeas—between his legs he catches it on his head, balanced at an angle on the edge of its base. Swinging it and catching it again on his head, this time on its side, mouth towards the audience, the juggler begins to rotate in a series of imperceptible little turns, and completes a revolution while the jar remains facing us full on.

The cyclist has established his circuit of the stage and maintains a non-stop *manège*, travelling backwards, seated on the handle-bars, pedalling with one foot, the other foot extended before him. A colleague following on a monocycle feeds him, at each circuit, a tin soup-plate which he catches on his toe and kicks deftly on to his head. When ten or twelve plates have piled up they are joined by a large tea-cup, transferred in the same way; and finally a tea-spoon lands tinkling in the cup. Throughout this enchanting operation the backward circling has never ceased.

8.7.73

Patronage

I want to kiss the Midland Bank not only on behalf of hundreds of young Promenaders seated on the floor of the stalls at Covent Garden for 50p, like a tribe of attentive Africans, but also on my own. The applause was like a football crowd's, and the rapture of youth after *Les Noces* and after Merle Park's *Romeo and Juliet* was reflected in the dancers' eyes.

14.4.74

Pastoral

I could not help wondering at the Festival Hall on Tuesday what thoughts the Polish song and dance company called *Mazowsze* inspired in the gleeful audience. Did these ingratiating smiles, these lilting tunes and these rainbow costumes beget in the majority of spectators a utopian nostalgia for a lost world of cosy peasant prettiness and pastoral peace?

They didn't in me. I thought what a smell there must have been in the barn after an hour of waltzing and cartwheeling. And how did they manage to keep 'fresh' those heavy embroidered costumes in a world without dry-cleaners? I also thought what hell village life must have been for a bookish lad like myself. Just as one was settling down, after a hard day on the farm, to a quiet browse through the complete works of Misckiewicz by the light of a tallow candle, there would come the dreaded knock on the door at six in the evening.

'On with your boots and feathered hat, Riczard! We're going to knock up the girls for a Chodzony (or a Crakoviak or humorous songs and dances from Podegrodzie, as the case might be).' And there the grinning louts would stand uttering harsh cries and throwing their caps in the air until I had pulled on the hated costume.

And knock! knock! at every door in the village, till the girls came wheeling out, with their false smiles and raucous voices. Then I should have had to go through the whole routine of cracking whips, cabrioling, cobbler's step, tumbling (Look, no hands), crashing at the girls' feet and walking on the elbows. What would particularly have terrified me, was doing flic-flac while attached to another man, head to toe.

The picture of Polish life presented by this large and (oh, well) colourful company seems over-sweet, just as the traditional tunes seem smoothed out by their orchestral arrangement, and the programme captions—'a popular, lively and dynamic dance ... beautiful, traditional wedding dances ... gay and carefree dance ... lively, wild and spirited' seem too bland to be informative.

Was there no rebel spirit—as it might have been me—to invent 'a harsh, awkward dance for embittered old maids,' 'a dance in which the local show-off is humiliated' or 'a community dance for baiting the village queer'?

13.8.72

Canada

In Toronto I thought of two dead friends, both great men in their ways. Pierre Dupuy, diplomat, hoped that Expo 67, which he ran, would bring the antagonistic provinces of Canada together. Peter Dwyer, who was at Oxford with me, devoted his life to fostering the arts in Canada. He was with the Canada Council when it began in 1957 and was head of it when he died last winter. That the Montreal company, Les Grands Ballets Canadiens, were doing a week in Toronto's huge O'Keefe Centre and being warmly applauded I took as a sign.

Toronto's National Ballet of Canada had just finished a 23-week North American tour with Nureyev in *The Sleeping Beauty*, presented by Hurok. In London a fortnight ago, Arnold Spohr, director of the Royal Winnipeg Ballet, told me that his troupe could now give several long seasons a year in their own city—unthinkable when I visited them ten years ago. The sixty-strong National receive $600,000 a year from the Canada Council, the forty-five-strong Grands Ballets Canadiens and the twenty-five-strong Royal Winnipeg $300,000 each. This about covers salaries. Production costs are raised locally.

Dancers are now employed forty-seven weeks of the year, a miracle in empty Canada. This is largely Dwyer's doing.

27.5.73

Teacher

The slow movement of Mozart's Piano Concerto in C major was playing when the news of Vera Volkova's death reached a flat in Covent Garden, and tears were shed for this beloved and beneficent woman who was for long at the very heart of the ballet world of London—though she was never offered the position of authority she deserved in the Royal Ballet School—who has exercised since 1952 a powerful influence for good in Copenhagen, and who was a teacher of Margot Fonteyn.

She was also mine, for in 1949 she consented to give me private ballet lessons in West Street. After a dozen of these she said I could join a class, but, being over thirty, I was too shy to expose myself. Vera had a gift for vivid phrase. To achieve a correctly drooping hand she recommended: 'Imagine your fingers are heavy.' For a nicely rounded forward position of the arms we were to pretend we were 'holding a huge snowball made of cotton wool.'

I have lived in Covent Garden opposite where Turner was born for nearly twenty years now, and the more I walk these streets between St. Martin's Lane, where Chippendale made the furniture for Lord Harewood's Yorkshire home, and Drury Lane, where an ancestress of mine sold oranges, the more sacred they seem. I think of the hours spent here working with Sokolova on her autobiography—shortly after I moved in she brought Woizikovsky, who also died recently, to lunch. I think of Mme. Karsavina rehearsing at the boys' club on the corner of Broad Court, and Massine in Floral Street. Then I think of Vera Volkova coming round for an intimate talk at midnight because it was the only time she could fit in during a lightning visit from Denmark. She used to send me comments on my articles, and liked, I believe, to retain some mild control over me. Well, because of her and the others, I will try to do better.

1.5.75

Index

Page numbers in *italic* refer to the illustrations